Traditional A
from the Ann

Traditional American   784.4973
folk songs   T675
                              c.1

Do not weed
Indexed in
Song Index of the EPFL

Popular Song Index 3rd suppl

ADULT DEPARTMENT

1. Fine Schedule
   1–5 days overdue . . . . grace period, no fine
   6-10 days overdue . . . . 25¢ per item
   11-19 days overdue . . . . 75¢ per item
   20th day overdue . . . . $2.00 per item
2. Injury to books beyond reasonable wear and all losses shall be paid for.
3. Each borrower is held responsible for all books drawn on his card and for all fines accruing on the same.

FOND DU LAC PUBLIC LIBRARY
FOND DU LAC, WISCONSIN

Buna and Roby Hicks at their home at Beech Creek, 1951.

TRADITIONAL AMERICAN FOLK SONGS

from the
Anne & Frank Warner Collection

ANNE WARNER

Jeff Warner, Associate Editor
Dr. Jerome S. Epstein, Music Editor
Foreword by ALAN LOMAX

SYRACUSE UNIVERSITY PRESS   1984

First Edition
   Second paperback printing 1985

Research for and publication of this book
were supported by grants from the
National Endowment for the Humanities,
an independent federal agency.

Library of Congress Cataloging in Publication Data
Main entry under title:

Traditional American folk songs from the Anne & Frank
    Warner collection.

   Discography: p.
   Bibliography: p.
   Includes indexes.
   1. Folk-songs, English—Atlantic States. I. Warner,
Frank. II. Warner, Anne. III. Title: Anne & Frank
Warner collection. IV. Title: Anne and Frank Warner
collection.
M1629.6.A7T7 1984   84-95
ISBN 0-8156-2313-5
ISBN 0-8156-0185-9 (pbk.)

Manufactured in the United States of America

Contents

BEGINNING IN 1938, shortly after their marriage, the Warners began to spend their month-long vacations every year collecting traditional songs in rural places along the eastern seaboard, north and south—in the Southern Appalachians, in the Adirondacks, in the White Mountains, on the North Carolina Outer Banks, in tidewater Virginia, even on Long Island. Those who gave them their songs usually were people with strong links to our country's pioneer beginnings. Traditional songs and the people who sang them became an all-absorbing family interest.

Frank Warner grew up in North Carolina and received a degree from Duke University. Though active in another profession, he traveled across this country and in Britain, speaking on and singing American traditional music. He appeared numerous times on radio and television and recorded seven albums of songs collected by the Warners. Frank Warner was president of the New York Folklore Society, program director of the Pinewoods folk music camp, and vice-president of the Country Dance and Song Society. He also was vice-president of the Nassau County Historical Society and a trustee of the National Folk Arts Council. He was the author of *Folk Songs of the Eastern Seaboard: From a Collector's Notebook.*

Anne Warner attended Northwestern University. With her husband, Frank, she has published articles in the *Appalachian Journal,* the *North Carolina Folklore Quarterly,* the *New York Folklore Quarterly,* and *SING OUT!* She herself has written articles for *Family Heritage,* the *Christian Science Monitor,* the *New York Folklore Quarterly, Folklore and Folklife in Virginia,* and the *Long Island Forum.* She contributed an article ("How Many Are on Our Side?) to the Pantheon book, *A Celebration of American Family Folklore.* She has written the notes for her husband's record albums. She has served as a trustee of the National Folk Arts Council, and, while on the administrative staff of Hofstra University, was advisor to the Folk Song Club and helped to produce two folk festivals on that campus.

Together the Warners were presented with the 1981 Annual Award at the Eisteddfod—Traditional Arts Festival—at Southeastern Massachusetts University, where they were noted as "relentless collectors with lives dedicated to the perpetuation of the oral tradition."

Foreword

THIS BOOK is a moving and magic testimony to the American folk process. Our country has grown so fast that if it hadn't been for stubborn old codgers like those the Warners found, and for song-hunters like the Warners themselves, we would certainly have lost the best of our past—the tales and tunes and lore that made life worth living back yonder, and which still touch our workaday history with color. These ballad rememberers have been, truly, our most discriminating antiquarians.

The Warners were among the first to perceive what a treasure lay hidden in these traditional vocal arts and to take steps to preserve them. They began using portable electronic recording gear long before most scholars had ever heard of field recordings. Here they were both scientific and cultural innovators. The field recording recaptures the whole of the performance—the nuance of the melody, its style, and the shape of the performing group. It may be played again and again and, so, fully analyzed. It is a document that can stand for all time as a communication about a particular culture, and thus supersedes the written manuscript as a scholarly tool. Moreover, when returned to its source community, it can revive arts that may have been forgotten and so function as a means of cultural feedback. Far better than any written document, the field recording can, when devotedly studied, reproduce the richness of a musical heritage. In consequence, books like the present one based entirely on field recordings are far more accurate and full of the true colors of folklore than those derived from the collector's notebook, no matter how faithfully kept.

For Frank Warner the field recordings offered another opportunity—a way for him to learn the vocal arts of his ancestors. Most citified singers of folk songs have been content simply to repeat the text and the tune of a traditional song, imposing their own dialect on the text and their own inherited singing style on the melody. They scorn to "imitate" the rustic artists, not realizing that the vocal styles they disregard are legitimate artistic traditions handed on from the past and essential to the impact of the songs they ornament. Apparently from the beginning Warner devoted himself to singing like the master ballad singers he met. He was a natural actor and he had a remarkable ear and great vocal equipment, and therefore he was able to memorize and reproduce a vocal masterpiece just as recorded, from beginning to end—the tensions between the flow of the text and the inexorable demands of the music, the shading of the vowels and the thwack and stir of the consonants, the timing of the whole song and all its parts—so that his ballads were like slabs of New England curly maple or Southern white pine boards, pungent with knotholes.

One evening at a singsong we chanced to learn what lay behind Warner's magic performances. Jean Ritchie, Pete Seeger, and others were singing, and Nick Ray filmed them all in slow motion. When we played back the reel we saw something extraordinary. While the rest of us held to one basic facial expression all the way through a song, so that the impression was one of rather flat affect, the frame-by-frame playback revealed that Frank was approaching each word with a different dramatic emphasis. It was as if he was tasting the ballad syllable by syllable—the way an actor savors the manifold shifts in feeling in each scene. It was all very subtle, of course, invisible until slow motion revealed it, but it was clear that Frank Warner was recalling sound by sound just how each model singer had handled each turn of tune and phrase. This was not imitation; it was dynamic recreation of the art of ballad singing that Warner's sensitivity allowed us to share.

One felt, watching him, that Frank Warner hardly needed a recording machine. His vocal memory was so accurate that he reproduced the best performances in himself. Bob Copper, the English ballad singer, once said of Frank's singing:

> . . . I am astonished to find how well the English traditional singing style survived the journey across the Atlantic and the passing of the years. . . . If for some unaccountable reason all the documentary evidence of the historical links between the U.K. and the U.S.A. disappeared overnight, then these songs and the way Frank sings them would re-establish the facts beyond question.

When Frank was preparing to sing, you would note the delight rising in him. You could see his eyes glowing with fun, the corners of his mouth twitching. He was remembering the person whole, getting ready to relive the strange fantasy of the ballad story, to play the part for you in the multilevel way he had, so that the original singer was there, presented through Frank. Thus the drama of the ballad was heightened, and you were taken into a lumbercamp, onto the deck of a canal barge, into a gold miner's cabin, through the lonesome coves and hollers of the southern mountains or to a Civil War campfire. And when the audience joined in the singing, Frank would smile and say, "Isn't that fine, now . . . just listen to that, would you!"

Through Frank you heard Yankee John Galusha sing the dirge for General Wolfe, the continent's first military hero, with the deep sorrow of young America choking his voice. Through Frank you heard the ballad of Tom Dooley as it was sung by the man who heard wicked Tom himself composing it in his cell before the hanging. In his concerts (and in this book) America in its early fanciful and rambunctious days appears. Sandburg, who used to spend time with the Warners in New York whenever he could, called Frank "maybe the best of all our American singers." When they got together, it was usually Frank who sang and Carl who listened.

For many years the Warners spent every vacation and every scrap of spare cash on their recording trips. It was a continuous act of unpaid, tender devotion to American folk song and a life-long love affair with the people who remembered the ballads. Out of this experience comes this ballad hunter's adventure story—rich in the stories of how the songs were found and who the singers were. Their voices and their stories cause American history to resound from these pages—a history of the struggles of working people.

A woman, singing songs of the revolutionary period, says:

My name is Lena Bourne Fish, and I was born of a race of soldiers. . . . An uncle of my grandmother's . . . was killed at the Battle of Bunker Hill.

Another singer remembered songs his brother brought back from the Civil War:

I had another brother that served three years and was in thirteen battles and never got a scratch. . . . I heard that the boys used to whistle back and forth across the lines. . . . They wondered what in Old Harry they was fightin' for.

And they sang:

Old Abe's in the White House, taking a snooze,
Gen'ral Grant is a-busting his gut with his booze,
While we're out in the snow, and we got no shoes,
But's let's keep a-marching on.

A North Carolina lady with songs from her courting days, recalls:

I couldn't let them [the boys] see the prints of my toes in the sand! . . . Let 'em court someone else that's got shoes on—grown wimmin. I don't claim myself to be grown till I have some shoes.

A man recollects his own experiences in a log drive in New York State:

I used to like breaking log jams. They would pay $1 a day more for a log jam breaker who would go out on the logs instead of just working from the shore. . . . I took a Frenchie out with me once. . . . We was out on the jam, and he went ahead and when I overtook him he began to run, sayin' the logs was moving. The boss was hollerin' from the shore, "Swim! swim!" I got took down to the bottom and sent back upstream. . . . I tried to make the shore, but I would go under again and again. When I come to they was a-knockin' water out of me.

Frank and Anne Warner were doing intensive biographic studies of single singers and their repertoire long before this was advocated as the latest wrinkle in folklore science. In the process they documented hundreds of the most valuable of Anglo-American song variants, and from this wonderful collection they have put together a remarkable anthology. Most collections have a handful of beautiful pieces, but the Warner book, the fruit of forty years of gleaning, is all gold. A number of its songs have become nationally known — "Tom Dooley," "He's Got the Whole World in His Hand," "The Days of Forty-Nine," "The Jolly Roving Tar." I warrant many others will become equally popular, for the Warners mined the most pristine American song terrain — the eastern seaboard, where the old songs still retained the flavor of England, Scotland, and Ireland, and where the new American songs grew in the very springtime of our national saga.

Many of the pieces they found will be unfamiliar even to professionals, because the Warners probed deeply in areas other collectors had overlooked. They found pockets of old songs not far from New York on Long Island and in the Adirondacks. They explored the colonies of early settlers along the Outer Banks of the Carolinas, and their visits in the southern mountains were in the highest valleys above Boone, where tales are told and songs are sung that one hardly finds elsewhere. The result is a collection of rarities and beauties that spans the whole of the Anglo-American repertoire.

New York, N.Y.   ALAN LOMAX
Spring 1984

Preface

OUR SONG COLLECTING began inadvertently in the late 1930s, but it soon became a major interest and an important part of our lives. Very soon we felt the urge to share our discoveries and our feelings about the people and their songs. Frank did this increasingly over the years through his concerts and lectures, but we always hoped that the collection could one day be published so that it could be a permanent part of the library of folk song.

The provenance of the songs in the collection is, roughly, the eastern seaboard of the United States—the area which once comprised the original thirteen colonies. Probably for that reason there are many old world ballads and colonial songs, ballads of immigration, many sea songs, many songs commemorating early historical events—and no cowboy songs at all.

The songs are arranged in geographical clusters, by singers, by the individuals who gave them to us, rather than by the usual categories such as work songs, love songs, songs of the sea, etc. In each division the Child ballads, if there are any, come first, followed by other ballads of British origin, then by ballads native to America, and finally by songs that are not ballads. This order, which is also roughly chronological, follows the example of some other collections. The notes preceding each song show its probable origin and history, and the citations at the foot of the notes list some important collections in which the song, or versions of it, appear. (The abbreviations and shortened references are explained in the bibliography.) The songs are numbered sequentially throughout the book in order to make it easy to refer to them.

We knew some of our singers for many years. With Frank Proffitt, particularly, we had a long and close friendship and years of correspondence. With others we had only one or two brief visits. World War II, or distance and lack of time and money, made travel impossible for a number of years, so that some of our friends died before we could get back to see them. We hope, however, that in their profiles we have been able in every case to give a glimpse into the personality and background of the singer.

The first chapter explains how and why we became interested in traditional folk songs and in the people who remembered and sang them. In the discovery of what was then to us a new world, we were surprised by joy. I well remember the exhilaration of waking—the first time we stayed with the Hicks family on Beech Mountain— to hear an early banjo picker welcoming the dawn. We had entered a world new to us but one in which we felt excitingly at home. One experience after another—our trips north and south, a mountain girl's visit with us in New York City during the war, the letters we exchanged—combined to cement lifelong friendships and to give us a new understanding of our country.

This compilation was begun before Frank's death in February of 1978. It was to be a joint undertaking, culled from our memories and notes. Although I have had to complete the project which Frank and I had planned, I feel it still is a joint effort—the result of our years of song collecting, the research we did together, the experiences and friendships we shared.

Frank would join me in dedicating the book to our sons Jeff and Gerret, and to all those who sing and remember the old songs.

Old Brookville, N.Y.   A.W.
Spring 1984

Music Editor's Preface

IT IS A SUBJECT of constant debate among transcribers of rural singers how much to attempt to get down on paper. It is a cliché that the essence of the traditional singer's art involves nuances of rhythm and decoration which can never be completely captured in notation. Folklorists from time to time have evolved various systems designed to notate as much as possible for the purpose of making very fine distinctions of regional style and historical evolution of the material. The difficulty with such notational schemes is that they render the material unusable by the more casual consumer who may want to *sing* the songs. It has been my consistent goal to convey the information that would be most useful to a reader who wishes to sing the songs.

When considering ornamentation, I have tried to put down ornamentation which seemed to be an essential part of the tune that the singer was hearing—ornamentation that would be pretty much consistent from verse to verse and would be unlikely to be much different the next time he sang the song. In the case of the early recordings on disk, this requires some judgment (one might say guesswork), since often only one or two verses was recorded. I cannot prove that my guesses are correct, but at least the ornamentation shown should give some idea of the style and be useful to the singer. It is not intended, of course, that a potential singer *must* use the ornamentation shown, but it is worth knowing that a particular song had a particular decoration consistently. A singer can then choose to incorporate it or not, depending on his or her own inclinations and abilities.

Sometimes judgments have had to be made about the base tune itself. This has *not* occurred when the singer is simply varying the tune for reasons of narrative; it *has* occurred where the singer was simply not sure of the tune. Some of the singers were clearly recollecting, at the urging of the Warners, songs that they may not have sung for a very long time; confusion in some of these cases is clearly audible. In such cases, extensive consultation with the Warners, using all of our combined backgrounds and experience, has produced our best judgment as to what the underlying tune is.

I have not added guitar chords except in cases where the source played guitar chords. For many of these songs—particularly the older ones—guitar chords cannot be added without violating the essential character of the tune, either the melodic or rhythmic essence. I encourage the reader to sing these songs as they were sung to the Warners—unaccompanied.

In some songs, generally those from black sources or of clearly black origin, the use of quarter-tones, generally at the third scale degree, is an essential part of the melodic style. This quarter-tone leaves the major-minor feeling of the tune ambiguous, and the impact of the song as the source sang it cannot be realized without including the quarter-tone. I have notated this with a "double accidental"; that is, in the key of D for example, I would show both a ♯ and a ♮ in front of the note F or on the F-line in the key signature. The symbol indicates the quarter-tone between F-natural and F-sharp. Thus:

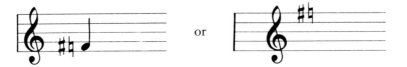

I have generally tried to transpose the tunes into keys that would be comfortable for the "average" singer, again in the hope that the maximum number of readers will want to *sing* these songs. Yankee John generally sang quite high, often higher than he was able to manage, probably an indication of what his range was at an earlier age. His songs have generally been taken down one or two tones. Mrs. Fish, on the other hand, had a very low voice for a woman. Her material has been transposed up at least a fourth and in one case as much as an octave. The Proffitt material is an interesting case, since the Warners knew Frank Proffitt for twenty-five years, during which time his range and singing style changed drastically. As one example, the song *Tom Dooley* was recorded in 1940 in the key of G and on the guitar; it was again recorded in 1960 on the banjo and in the key of B-flat—a full sixth lower! Generally the earlier keys are more accessible to the average singer. For the other singers, generally a change of no more than a third has been necessary, and I have used keys that did not require large numbers of accidentals in the key signature.

Jackson Heights, N.Y.   Dr. Jerome S. Epstein
Spring 1984

Acknowledgments

THE NECESSARY RESEARCH and the preparation of this work was made possible through the assistance of a research grant from the National Endowment for the Humanities. We are indeed grateful to the Endowment for this all-important support.

We are indebted, too, to the Library of Congress for accepting all of our field recordings (the early ones on small disks) and for transferring the entire collection to reel-to-reel tape—one copy for the Library and one copy for us. Without this step the transcription of the tunes would have been nearly impossible.

I would like also to express our gratitude to many individuals who have helped us in our endeavor. First, of course, to all the people who so generously and willingly shared their songs and stories with us. I hope our gratitude to them is apparent in the following pages.

We are immeasurably indebted to our friends Carl Carmer and his wife, Elizabeth Black Carmer, for their enthusiastic support and encouragement in the early years of our collecting. Carl was an authority on Americana (as is witnessed by his many books on regional history and folklore), and he aided and abetted us in every possible way. The Carmers were responsible for our meeting both John Galusha and Lena Bourne Fish, two of our most important singers.

We owe Alan Lomax, our long-time friend, much gratitude for his continuing enthusiasm for our work (as well as for Frank's singing), for his insistence that our collection should be in print, for his advice and help through the years, and for his foreword to this volume.

Many others encouraged and helped and advised us: John Farrar and Stanley Rinehart, the publishers, who gave us our first disk recording machine; Carl Sandburg, who inspired us and whom we grew to love as well as admire; David Grimes of Philco, who made for us a battery-powered portable disk recording machine; William Rose Benét, the poet, and his wife, Marjorie Flack Benét, for their enthusiasm about our collecting and their warm friendship; Harold W. Thompson, author of *Body, Boots & Britches,* who went through our collection in its early stages and shared his knowledge of the songs' background and importance; Samuel F. Bayard, the authority on folk tunes, who also advised us in the early days and who later supplied a tune for one of our songs; Arthur Schrader, long time Music Director of Old Sturbridge Village, and his wife, Penn Elizabeth Schrader, who supplied information about the history of many of our songs; Alan C. Buechner of Queens College, an authority on early American religious music, who found for me the origin of a number of religious songs from the southern mountains; William Main Doerflinger, author of *Songs of the Sailor and Lumberman,* who gave us important advice on many occasions; Louis C. Jones of the New York State Historical Association, for including us year after year on the faculty of the Seminars on American Culture at Cooperstown, where we absorbed much important information about history and folklore; Charles L. Todd of Hamilton College, companion collector and long-time friend, for his advice and support; Wayland C. Hand of the University of California at Los Angeles, editor of Volumes 6 and 7 of the *Frank C. Brown Collection of North Carolina Folklore,* who gave me important advice about the original draft of this manuscript and unexcelled encouragement; Joseph Hickerson, Head, Archive of Folk Culture of the Library of Congress, and Gerald Parsons, Reference Librarian in the same department, who gave us a great deal of time and enormous help in researching the songs in the collection; John Langstaff, creator and director of "The Revels" (among his many accomplishments), who introduced us to Pinewoods Camp which, over the years, has greatly enriched our knowledge and understanding of traditional song and dance; Jac Holzman, founder of Elektra Records (now chairman of Panavision), who published three albums of Frank Warner singing songs from the collection, and who has given us encouragement and support over the years; Amy Kotkin of the Smithsonian Institution, for her advice and important assistance on several occasions; and, for their long-time interest, friendship, and support, Peter Kennedy, author of *Folk Songs of Britain and Ireland;* John Anthony Scott, author of *The Ballad of America;* Bess Lomax Hawes of the National Endowment for the Arts; and three Long Island friends: Eugenia Heimer, and Alfred and Roma Connable.

I am grateful to Jerome Epstein, who so skillfully and carefully transcribed all the tunes from our sometimes very rough field recordings. His comments are found in Appendix C. I am grateful also to Carolyn Rabson, author of *Songbook of the American Revolution,* and Mary Peterson Moore who did the musical artwork.

I had indispensable help from Jeff Warner, who, drawing on his publishing experience and his knowledge of folk music, did months of research on background notes for the songs at the Library of Congress, and gave me invaluable editorial assistance. Gerret Warner, and his wife Mimi Gredy, also gave me important advice, and Gerret, who has training and experience in photography, gave me great help in choosing and reprocessing our photographs. All of the photographs are by Frank Warner except those otherwise noted.

I should like also to thank the Indiana Historical Society for permission to reprint from Leah Jackson Wolford's *The Play-Party in Indiana* the dance instructions to accompany "Chimbley Sweeper" (Song No. 189) given to us by Rebecca King Jones.

To all the other individuals and groups who have helped us along the way—too numerous a company to list here—I offer, also, my deep thanks.

A word about copyright: after our experience with the song "Tom Dooley" (see the sketch about Frank Proffitt for a discussion of this episode), Frank Warner was advised to copyright those of our collected songs which were included in his record albums. That is why there is a special copyright credit line on the pages where these songs appear. The other songs included herein are covered by the general copyright on the book. Should any future royalties be received they would be shared with the original singer or a descendant (if such a person is known to us), as our royalties on "Tom Dooley" have been shared equally with the Proffitts.

A.W.

Traditional American Folk Songs
from the Anne and Frank Warner Collection

When a nation goes down and never comes back, when a society or a civilization perishes, one condition may always be found. They forgot where they came from. They lost sight of what brought them along.

Carl Sandburg, *Remembrance Rock*

Ben Davis told me the way he knew the age of a song was by the way it made him feel. "The old ones make you feel good, the new ones don't make you feel anything."

Lydia Parrish, *Slave Songs of the Georgia Sea Islands*

How the Collection Began

FRANK PROFFITT, our Blue Ridge Mountain friend, once wrote:

My earlyest recalection is of waking on a cold winter morning in a log cabin on old Beaver Dam and hearing the sad haunting tune of Tom Dooly picked by my father (Wiley) along with the frying of meat on the little stepstove and the noise of the little coffeemill grinding the Arbuckle [coffee]. What better world could they be for a small boy who was hungry for the fried meat and biscuit, and hungry allso to make sounds like grown up on a curley walnut banjer.

In thouse days after the crop was laid by folks went a-visiting. Dad would hang the banjer around his neck, [take] a rifle and lantern and we would go to see the folks. As they gathered around the fireplace with a pine knot burning, us younguns would get a place down on the floor and listen to Tom Dooly and other songs being played. Then they would stop and tell us how Tom rode a-courting, a-picking [his banjo] up and down the roads . . . and even picked once in the churchyard whilst the preacher was a-preaching.

I started soon to trying to pick the banjer. Soon the happy day came when Dad said, "I declare you air just about got Tom Dooly a-goin'." . . . Soon when the men came to get [watches and] things fixed I went to singing Tom for them . . . and other songs. Along the road to school to the mill with my brother as at the store, they had me a-singing. They would say, that boy know all of that Tom Dooly. . . . I married into another singing family of Nathan Hicks . . . and went on with the kind of life I loved. . . .

Then Frank Warner come to the mountains and in him I saw a addgicated person who made me feel like somebody and I open my heart to him and gave him the old songs of my people. His eyes sparkled as I sing Tom Dooly to him and told him of my Grandmaw Proffitt knowing Tom and Laura. . . . I told him of my people and he and Anne didn't seem to notice that we was pore and didn't know big words. They bragged on our new calf, our little two room cabin, and brought store stuff for us all to eat. I walked on air for days after they left. . . .

We had met Frank Proffitt, a young mountain man of twenty-five, on our first visit to Beech Mountain in western North Carolina in 1938. That was the day he first sang us "Tom Dooley." It was a day that changed our lives, and his.

We begin with Frank Proffitt because our conscious song collecting began with him and because over the years he became our close and valued friend.[1]

Our collecting, then, began in 1938, and a great deal of it was done during the early 1940s; but after World War II we began again, and continued whenever an occasion arose. The collecting may be said to cover approximately a forty-year period.

E.B. White says in the foreword to his collection of *Essays*[2] that "The essayist is . . . sustained by the childish belief that everything he thinks about, everything that happens to him, is of general interest." Perhaps, in this chapter, we share that belief. If any folk song enthusiast isn't interested in such a personal accounting, he or she may skip the following pages with a free conscience. As Carl Sandburg used to say at the close of a lecture as he picked up his guitar, "Now I'm going to sing a few songs. If nobody wants to listen, I don't mind at all. I'd be doing the same thing at home by myself if I wasn't here."

Frank Warner was born in the South, in the natural habitat of spirituals, ballads, and work songs, and he learned songs from his earliest childhood. His first years, to the age of six, were spent in Selma, Alabama. His father, G. Frank Warner, was a Yankee from Pittsburgh who went to Selma to be the Secretary of the YMCA, and there married Mabel Preston, aged nineteen, a member of his Sunday School class in the Alabama Avenue Presbyterian Church. During their years in Selma they lived with Mabel Warner's parents, James and Hannah—or Annie—(Moreland) Preston, on Sylvan Street, where James Preston ran a general store and a woodyard. There Frank was born, and there his early playmates were black children who lived nearby. Just down the street was a large Negro church, and Frank could always recall the glorious sound pouring out from the church on a Sunday morning when the black congregation raised their voices to praise the Lord. Although his mother had a beautiful, trained voice (later she was contralto soloist with the Duke University Chapel Choir), the earliest song Frank remembered was sung by a black woman washing clothes in the backyard and stirring them in a large black iron pot over the fire:

> Hallelujah, when the morning comes,
> All the saints of God come gatherin' home,
> Tell the story, how they overcome,
> We'll understand it better by and by.

---

1. Our article describing this long relationship, "Frank Noah Proffitt: Good Times and Hard Times on the Beaver Dam Road," appeared in the Autumn 1973 issue of *Appalachian Journal.*
2. E. B. White, *Essays* (New York: Harper & Row, 1977).

From Selma the Warners moved to Jackson, Tennessee, and then to Durham, North Carolina, when Frank was twelve. He began his first conscious interest in traditional music when he was a student at Duke University under Dr. Frank C. Brown, the noted North Carolina collector. At Duke, Frank sang in and directed the Glee Club, led the music in chapel, was a member of an award-winning quartet, and was one of the students asked to sing folk songs to illustrate Dr. Brown's lectures on state folklore. There he also was influenced by Professor Newman Ivey White, a Shelley scholar who was a collector of Negro folk songs.

After his graduation from Duke, Frank had a job in Greensboro, North Carolina, for a number of years directing boys' work for the local YMCA, establishing Hi-Y clubs around the county and building and directing a summer camp. Incidentally, he was singing. For several years he had a weekly "request" program on radio station WBIG. He sang popular songs, traditional songs, funny songs—anything requested by a ready-made audience of his boys and their families, and the girls on the campuses of the local colleges—UNC Woman's College and Greensboro College—where he sang periodically. WBIG had to supply two or three people with note pads to take down the requests.

When he moved to New York City in 1931 to direct program for the Grand Central YMCA, now the Vanderbilt Y, Frank still sang as occasions arose. As time went on he found that most of the people for whom he sang showed special interest in his traditional songs, the ones he had picked up as a child, or those he had learned through Dr. Brown at Duke. He began to concentrate on traditional songs and to look around for more.

I, Anne Locher, was born in St. Louis, Missouri, still half-southern in its culture, and grew up in the Middle West, attending Northwestern University before moving with my family to New York.

In 1938 Frank and I were recently married and were living on West 10th Street in Greenwich Village in New York City. In the spring of that year, through Ralph Fuller, a high school and college friend of Frank's, we met a professor from South Carolina, Maurice Matteson, who had just come to New York from a song-collecting trip in the southern mountains. He had brought back with him a dulcimer made by Nathan Hicks of Beech Mountain, North Carolina. Schirmer later published a small book called *Beech Mountain Ballads and Folksongs,* edited by Maurice Matteson and Mellinger Henry.

We wanted very much to have a dulcimer, so we wrote to Nathan Hicks to see if he would make one for us, which he did. So began our relationship with the Hicks family which continues to this day, to the second and third generations. Nathan's wife Rena wrote us about their ten living children and the three who had died. "I've had thirteen children," she wrote, "and bad luck [miscarriages] four times." Their three oldest were married, and their baby, Jack, was just two months old. They were proud people, but they wrote of their struggles and their great need. "When it's blue cool hear, the stove heats the house just enough to live." That spring all their cabbages froze so they couldn't sell any. Though they would have sold for only fifty cents a hundred pounds, that "would have been better than nothen." Mrs. Hicks's letter were spelled phonetically and were filled with archaic words and phrases.[3] "Can you-uns come to see us?" "The things you sent has hope us so much." We decided to go to visit the family as soon as we could. And we began to badger our friends to give us clothes and bedding to send them.

In June of 1938, we made our first trip to Beech Mountain. I kept a journal of that two weeks' trip, as if I somehow knew it would be the most important milestone in our lives. Excerpts from that journal give an interesting view of that faraway time just before World War II, before super-highways changed the face of America:

Friday, June 3 [1938]   Left New York at 6:50 and drove over the Pulaski Skyway with a wonderful flaming sunset overhead. Found ourselves in real country in twenty minutes . . . but drove on through the Pennsylvania hills under the moon. . . .

Sunday, June 5   We started [from Pulaski, Virginia, where we had spent the night] on a beautiful morning and got into the mountains almost at once. We crossed the state line in about 70 miles. Carolina in the morning! Had breakfast in Galax, Va., first, though, at the Hotel Bluemont. . . . Such a cool spacious dining room. Outside the church bells were ringing. We reached Boone toward noon. . . . To our amazement the town was crowded with people, the streets lined with old cars and trucks and wagons—on a Sunday! . . . We had happened on a "county sing" and everybody in the county was on hand for the festivities. We never hope to see so many mountain people together again. They look different, and sound different. They are almost all thin with rather narrow faces and high cheekbones and straight noses. But so many have bad teeth. . . .

We worked our way up to the Courthouse. Its front yard and porch were filled with people. By degrees we got upstairs and into the courtroom where the "sing" was in process. . . . A mixed group was singing when we came in—about twelve, old and young. They sang hymns, but with a strange rhythm, marvelous to hear. When they finished there was no applause, hardly a change of expression.

The next group was a male quartet . . . the tenor who took the lead sang entirely through his nose, hardly opening his mouth. A young girl, (in the audience) bent down to hide her face and laugh, and came up again without even a smile.

3. Speech experts (including Dr. Cratis Williams of Appalachian State University) have determined that the speech pattern common in parts of Appalachia, and particularly on Beech Mountain, is the closest living example of the English spoken by the settlers of this region in the early 1700s. It is being modified or is disappearing in these days of universal schooling, but Nathan's son Ray, who still lives on the Beech and who is a fine teller of Jack Tales (ancient folk tales still told in the mountains—see Richard Chase in the bibliography), still talks in the old way, with glottal stops that leave the last syllable of a word largely to the imagination of the listener.

In the preface to the first edition of Vance Randolph's *Ozark Folk Songs* (Columbia, Mo.: State Historical Society, 1946–47), Floyd C. Shoemaker and Frances G. Emberson say, "Characteristic of Mr. Randolph's work is the painstaking accuracy with which the dialectical peculiarities have been preserved. The collector has scrupulously avoided any touching up or adding to the texts as the singers sang them; no missing words or forgotten lines have been supplied, but the exact wording and pronunciation have been reproduced with fidelity. Hence the texts give the impression of being fresh from the lips of the singers and true to life, as nearly phonographic as the printed word can be."

We have endeavored, in reproducing the words of our singers, to follow Vance Randolph's example as closely as we could—both in quoting conversations and in the song texts themselves.

We began enquiring about for Nathan. Some people knew him but no one had seen him and we began to think we had kept him waiting for us at home. But finally we talked to a man who knew him well and who said he'd never seen Nathan at one of these things. "He don't come out," is what he said. So we got directions for finding his house and set out. . . . I don't think I've ever been so stared at as we were in Boone that morning. . . .

From Boone we took a state road to Vilas and Valle Crucis and wound up and up for nearly ten miles, then the "durt" road Nathan spoke of. It was nothing but a wagon road, two ruts with boulders and deep mud holes, just wide enough for one car—barely wide enough. It wound up, almost straight up sometimes. Way below us we could see miniature houses and tiny sheep and cows. It was a glorious day and it was breathtakingly beautiful to be so high in the mountains. There were flowers everywhere and the sun was warm and as far as the eye could reach were mountains, rising one beyond the other. But the road! Most of the way we went in low, creeping over the rocks, fording two or three mountain streams. It took us 45 minutes to go five miles. Halfway there we stopped at a house to ask the people on the porch the way, and a man and a boy came down, pointed it out, and allowed they'd go along with us. They'd been waiting, the man said, for the preacher who came up to preach every two weeks at a little Presbyterian church on the "mounting." We hadn't any room but they hung on the running board, the boy leaning down to look in now and then. There were mudholes in the road because they'd had "a right smart bit o'rain here lately." . . .

So at last we could see the Hicks house down in a little cove, and our friends left us and took the road on up. We had to take down the bars of a cattle gate before we could get through and the car rested eventually between two rocks with a stream running underneath. Then we saw Nathan . . . who said he was "shore pleased" to see us and we went down into the house which seemed overflowing with people. I never did completely sort out the family from the neighbors. It was a fairly nice looking, sizable house, but the inside was poverty-stricken. In the main room was a big bed, completely covered by people sitting on it; another cot, similarly occupied, a stove, and a number of rickety chairs with the seats falling out. Mrs. Hicks has a sweet face and a sweet friendly manner. She was so interested in everything, in spite of little Mr. Jack bouncing on her knee (he was 5 months old that day) and another little Hicks on the way? "I couldn't hardly think you'd really come," she said to me. "Those chairs aren't very good," she said when they asked us to sit down, so Frank said, "I have to be careful when I sit down in any chair." "How much do you weigh?" asked Nathan . . . and when Frank asked him to guess, he guessed exactly, to everyone's delight. And when Frank said, "I can see you've been weighing hogs," the last shreds of restraint vanished.

We brought down the guitar and the dulcimer, and the bags of toys and clothes—which were politely set aside unopened, and Nathan got out his "dulcimoor." . . . Frank Proffitt was there, Nathan's oldest son-in-law, with his guitar. He knew a lot of songs and sang them well, in a shy but dignified way. Three of them he said over for me so I could take them down—"Hang Down Your Head, Tom Dooley," "Moonshine," and "Dan Doo." He'd walked over for the occasion from his own place 8 miles away and he was walking home that night. Then Frank [Warner] sang some songs for them . . . they loved "Way Out West in Kansas." The neighbor boys out on the porch nearly knocked each other down over "the old mule coming down the path." . . .

[This was the verse about the mule:

Nathan and Rena Hicks, and Nell—one of their thirteen children—on the south Pinnacle of Beech Mountain, above their house, 1938.

> The sun's so hot the eggs all hatch,
> Way out West in Kansas,
> It popped the corn in the popcorn patch
> Way out West in Kansas,
>
> An old mule coming down the path
> Saw the corn and lost his breath,
> He thought 'twas snow, and froze to death!
> Way out West in Kansas.]

We took pictures, many of them . . . and looked through the binoculars, everyone taking turns. The view from the back of the house is the most glorious I've ever seen—

Ben Hicks, Nathan's father, with the four little singing girls, 1938. Frank and Bessie Proffitt are behind them.

sweeping down into the valley and then rising to range after range of mountains way into Virginia and Tennessee. . . . Frank Proffitt said he could see his cornfield through the glasses, and then, with one of his rare smiles, "I don't see nobody hoein' in it, though." Down the mountain came an old man leaning on a stick, but hale and hearty—Nathan's father, Ben Hicks, together with four little girls as shy as they could be. They wouldn't smile or speak, but presently, when we were all doing something else, they lined up on the porch and commenced to sing, verse after verse: "There'll be no sorrow in heaven, in heaven where all is love," looking up or down or to one side, but not at anybody. . . . I asked Mrs. Hicks some questions. Most of the children go to school two miles away, if they can get shoes for them. . . . The baby looks bright and well. She hasn't enough milk

Some of the Nathan Hicks family behind their house on Beech Mountain in June 1938; (left to right) Ray; Willis, holding Betty; Mary, Lewis's wife, holding Roger; Nathan; Rena; Nell; Anna; N.A.; Lewis.

for him, so he has to have some other feedings. They lost their baby last year because they couldn't afford to buy dextrose for his milk. She makes hooked mats and chair seats when she's too sick to do anything else. They are lovely. She gave me one.

Nathan gave Frank a present too. He had a bear paw nailed up on the porch and when Frank admired it he took out his knife and cut off one claw for him! He shot the bear (a 350-lb. one) right out in the road near the house.

So, toward 6 o'clock, we got ready to go. Mrs. Hicks said she wished we'd stay the night. . . . We did hate to leave. There seemed a bond somehow. . . . They have never been out of the mountains. Mrs. Hicks said, "I'd like to go somewhere. I ain't never been anywheres 'cept to Boone once. . . ."

Like the proverbial stone tossed into still water, our first visit to the Beech caused ever-widening circles—not just in our lives, but in the lives of many mountain people and, in a sense, the world—since some twenty years later the song, "Tom Dooley," which Frank Proffitt sang to us that first day, would spark the world-wide interest in American folk music which was so much a part of the sixties and beyond.[4]

Part of the group on that first day, besides Frank Proffitt, was Frank's wife, Bessie, and their son, Oliver. Bessie was Nathan's and Rena's oldest daughter. In ensuing years we became more knowledgeable about the family, so we know that there too that day were the other Hicks children: Lewis and his wife, Mary, and their baby, Roger; Mae and her husband, Linzy; Ray; N.A.; Anna; Willis; Nell; Betty; and little Jack. Roby Monroe Hicks, Nathan's uncle, was there (Linzy was his son), as well as Nathan's father, Ben—Roby's brother. In years to come Roby and his wife, Buna, became our good friends.

Everyone was making music that afternoon. The sound, and the people, gave us a feeling we have never lost. It was the beginning of our lifelong interest in traditional music and the people who remember it. We had not come with the idea of collecting songs, but our collecting began at that moment. We went back to the Beech every year until the war and gasoline rationing, and then the lack of a car stopped our traveling for a number of years.

At Christmas time in 1938 we sent a box of clothes and toys and goodies for all the children, and to our delight we received a box of greens freshly picked on the mountainside—galax leaves and wintergreen and running cedar. A box of greens has come every Christmas since that time—for forty-five years. They are sent now by the next generations—Ray and Rosa Hicks and their sons.

By 1940 we had acquired a recording machine—a Wilcox Gay Recordio. This was a contribution toward the cause from John Farrar and Stanley Rinehart, the publishers, who had become interested in what we were doing. 1940 was pre-tape days, and the machine cut grooves with a stylus on small disks. There was no electricity then on Beech Mountain or in Pick Britches Valley where Frank Proffitt lived, so that year we took as many of the family as we could get in the station wagon and went down the mountain to Matney, to the home of friends named Rominger, who did have "the electric." Another day we went to a filling station on the highway. None of this was satisfactory, but we did record some good songs and Nathan's story of a bear hunt.

That winter our friend David Grimes, who was vice-president of Philco, asked Frank Warner to do some experimental television shows for Philco in Philadelphia during a six-week period. After that David created for us in the Philco laboratory a battery-powered portable recording machine. In the summer of 1941 we spent several days with the Proffitts—Frank and Bessie and Oliver—in the two-room cabin Frank built when he and Bessie were married. People in the mountains went to bed early then, since they

---

4. After Frank Warner had sung "Tom Dooley" across the country for twenty years and recorded it for Elektra in 1952, it was recorded by the Kingston Trio in 1958. More than three million copies of their record were sold, and the song went around the world.

Roby Monroe Hicks, Nathan's uncle, who wandered down the mountain to meet us on our first afternoon, 1938.

Everyone making music on Beech Mountain; (left to right) Frank Proffitt, Roby Hicks (with back to camera), Frank Warner, Nathan Hicks, Sam Hicks, Vance Presnell, Linzy Hicks. Ray Hicks (lying down) is just listening, 1939. Photo by Anne Warner.

would get up before dawn, but during our visit Frank sat up with us each night until midnight, talking about his boyhood and his people and asking us questions about New York and "the beyont" in general. "The other world," he called it in later years, after he had been out in it himself.

We had, in our early visits, convinced Frank that the songs and stories he grew up with and loved were important not just to him but to others—to people outside the mountains. Remembering them, and passing them on, became a very important part of his life. Some years later he wrote us: "I so much desire to only be a representitive of my kind of people, neaver to just exault myself."

Anne Warner recording Frank Proffitt on the steps of the cabin he built when he and Bessie Hicks were married in Pick Britches Valley, Watauga County, North Carolina, 1941. The battery-powered recording machine was made for us by Philco.

Frank, Oliver, and Bessie Proffitt, 1941.

Frank Proffitt gave us an understanding of the strength and glory of pioneer America. He grew up in a situation very little changed from pioneer times. His life was hard and full of disappointments and frustrations—a drought that threatened his crops or a flood that washed them all away. Sometimes there seemed no way to feed his family. He would leave home for temporary jobs when he had to—road work or carpentry. But the mountains were in his soul, and he didn't think of leaving them. He was generous, sensitive, uncommonly intelligent, stubborn, and, often, full of humor.

We first met Buna Vista Hicks, known as "Buny"[5] to her kin and neighbors, on our second visit to Beech Mountain in 1939. She and her husband Roby played fiddle and banjo interchangeably, Roby having made both the instruments with loving skill.

We have on tape a very long interview with Roby, shared part of the time by Lee Monroe Presnell, a cousin and a wonderful old-time singer. They didn't encourage each other to sing—"Roby cain't sing like he used to"—but they do tell about the early days in the mountains and the firstcomers, who cleared the steep slopes and planted crops and settled down. Each family brought a gun, an axe, some salt, and "sody." Usually they brought a Bible, whether or not a member of the family could read, and always, in their minds and hearts, a storehouse of old-world songs and ballads and stories— their only literature or entertainment.

Buna soon became one of our favorite people in this world. She was wonderfully unspoiled by modernity. On one visit, before we had seen her, we asked Rosa, Ray Hicks's wife, "How is Aunt Buny?" and Rosie said, "Oh, she's just so gaily."

One time when we visited Beech Mountain we decided to take enough beef and onions and carrots and potatoes to make a really good beef stew for everybody. We thought it would be a treat, knowing how seldom meat was available, and forgetting that people like what they are used to.

Rena was polite about our plans, but she went ahead with her own preparations for the meal: fried eggs—in two inches of grease—cabbage, boiled potatoes, mashed potatoes, rice, biscuits, and cornbread.

So I made the stew, and we put it on the table. Most everybody tried some, and most everybody was polite. Nobody had ever had any before. Lewis said, "I reckon I could eat this every day!" (It was Lewis who once said, when told there were eight million people in New York, "I reckon if that many folks tuck out after you, they'd shore catch you!")

Finally everybody had had a bit of stew except N.A., one of the teenaged Hicks boys. "Come on, N.A.," the others urged, "try some." And, finally, having eaten his fill of everything else, N.A. did try some. "Ain't that good?" said his mother. "How about it?" from the others. N.A. was frank and clear, as he had every right to be. "Hit

5. In the mountains this pronunciation is true of almost all names ending in *a*: "Rosie" for Rosa, "Reny" for Rena, "Wataugy" for Watauga County, and, of course, "Tom Dooley" for Tom Dula. This occurs, we have found, in other rural districts. Local people in the Adirondacks in New York State always referred to the town of Minerva as "Minervy."

Buna Hicks and her husband, Roby Hicks, Beech Mountain, 1939.

don't please me," he said. So was born a bit of family folklore—used by all the Warners at appropriate moments ever since.

One spring Nathan borrowed money for seed and planted a field of cabbages—his cash crop. When the plants were just above ground a hard rain came along and washed all the plants and the top soil down into the valley. Nathan took his dulcimer under his arm, Rena told us later, and walked ten miles over to Frank Proffitt's "to play the misery out of his soul."

We didn't know about this, but just about that time we sent a note to Nathan and Rena to say we would arrive two days later for our annual visit. When we got to the house on a rainy Sunday afternoon Rena met us on the porch. Our letter had come the day before, after Nathan had gone. "I knowed how Nathan would hate to miss seein' you," she said, "and I jist prayed all night that he'd get the message to come home." There was no physical way to send a message—no telephone, no car, no one ready to walk a twenty-mile round trip.

After we'd chatted awhile and the rain had stopped, Frank went up to the car to get some packages and food we had brought, and there was Nathan, with his dulcimer, coming up the road. "Well," he said, "I was a-goin' to stay a week, but it jist kep' a-comin' to my mind to come on home."

Neither Nathan nor Rena seemed surprised—just pleased.

In September of 1938, through a young neighbor in our eighteenth-century house on West 10th Street, we met Betty and Carl Carmer. We had read Carl's *Stars Fell on Alabama*[6] some years before and admired it. This was the first regional book of Americana which included both the history and folklore of a particular state, and since Frank was born in Alabama it interested us particularly. Scores of books of this genre have been written since. Carl began it all. He was an "appleknocker" from upstate New York with a gift for words—written or spoken—and he was a great storyteller. Betty was from New Orleans. Together, or separately, the Carmers were irresistible.

A couple of weeks later, on September 18, we had dinner with the Carmers for the first time in their elegant Victorian duplex apartment at 144 West 12th Street. (In 1940 we moved from 10th Street to the ground floor apartment at 144 West 12th—underneath the Carmers—where we lived for a dozen years.) We remember the date because it was the night of the first devastating hurricane to hit the Northeast. We were quite unaware of that, though, until later. Also at the Carmers' that evening were Marjorie Flack, the writer and illustrator of children's books, and a delightful man named Bill, whose other name we didn't catch. When he was out of the room later in the evening I asked Carl, "What does Bill do?" "Well," said Carl kindly, "he is one of America's

6. The Tin Pan Alley song by that title which was published later had nothing to do with the book. Probably the song writer just borrowed the book's title, which is a phrase from an Alabama legend: In the memories of the oldest slaves was a story about "the year the stars fell"—a shower of stars that changed the land's destiny and made Alabama into a state different from all others. Carl wrote the book on Alabama after teaching for six years at the State University in Tuscaloosa.

leading poets." He was William Rose Benét, author of many books of poetry, later to win a Pulitzer Prize for his autobiography in verse, *The Dust Which is God.* He and Margie Flack were married in 1941.

In 1939 a New York *Herald-Tribune* Book and Author Luncheon was held, as usual, at the Hotel Astor just above Times Square. In those days one still could associate elegance with Times Square. The authors to be honored were Raymond Gram Swing, a well-known and popular journalist and war correspondent, for his book *How War Came;* Carl Carmer, for *The Hudson;* and Carl Sandburg, whose final four volumes of his Lincoln biography, *The War Years,* had just been published. Irita Van Doren, editor of the *Herald-Tribune Books,* presided knowledgeably and charmingly. Carl Carmer had asked Frank to accompany him and sing a few Hudson Valley songs, so we met Carl Sandburg for the first time.

Just a few days before the luncheon Frank had received from Nathan Hicks the wooden banjo Nathan had made for him because Frank so admired one we saw hanging on Nathan's wall. It was a masterpiece of folk craft, and Frank took it with him to show to the two Carls. They admired it mightily, and on an impulse Frank said to Sandburg, "Why don't you sign the head for me?" So he did: "Carl Sandburg, 1939." Since then the banjo has acquired some 265 signatures of people well known and not so well known in the fields of folklore and American history, from Woody Guthrie and Leadbelly and Big Bill Broonzy and Pete Seeger and Burl Ives to Allan Nevins and Carl Van Doren and John and Alan Lomax. Even Andrés Segovia — because Carl Sandburg knew him well and took us to spend an afternoon at his apartment. Frank carried the banjo and sang with it from Hollywood to the British Isles and everywhere in between.

Carl Sandburg published one of the earliest collections of American folk songs in 1927, *The American Songbag,* and he gave many a song program himself. He liked folk songs to sound as they did in their natural habitat. After hearing Frank that day at the Astor he said, "Frank, it's plain that your voice has never been ruined by a conservatory!"

In 1938, when Carl Carmer was finishing his book on the Hudson River[7] and was doing research in upstate New York, he met a former lumberman in the Adirondacks who knew songs. "Next time you have some vacation," Carl said to us, "you should go see 'Yankee John' Galusha." In the summer of 1939, we did. John Galusha, who lived in Minerva, New York, near North Creek, where the mighty Hudson is a wadeable trout stream, was eighty years old that year. He was born in 1859, before the Civil War. Yankee John became perhaps our most important source of early songs, since he was a singer who knew historical ballads seldom found in oral tradition, as well as lumbering songs, Erie Canal songs, and many an Irish ditty.

Carl had told us to go to Aiden Lair, a country inn run by the Cronin family

7. This is one of the *Rivers of America* series of which Carl was later the editor for many years.

The head of Frank Warner's banjo, made by Nathan Hicks, signed by folksingers, folklorists, and others, 1965. Photo by Frank Woerner.

on Route 28 N, northwest of Minerva. It stood alone, one house on the road, yet it was on the road map. Perhaps that was because Matt Cronin had been one of the drivers in 1901 who took Theodore Roosevelt—on the night President McKinley died—by buckboard, over corduroy roads, from Mount Marcy where he had been camping, to North Creek to catch a train for Albany and Buffalo, for his informal swearing-in ceremony there. In 1939 Matt Cronin's widow and her family were running the inn, which was more like a boarding house with guests treated as members of the family. The youngest daughter, Eloise, with black hair and beautiful blue eyes, who taught in the local high school, was our guide and became our friend. She took us to meet Yankee John, persuading him to go home from the tavern where he was drinking with some companions. He was reluctant at first. Some years before he had sung a great many songs for a Professor Gray and had never heard from him again. Finally, he did sing several memorable songs that cool August night, sitting in his kitchen by the wood-burning stove: "The British Soldier," "The Ballad of Blue Mountain Lake," and "The Irishtown Crew." We knew that we wanted to know Yankee John for himself, as well as for his songs. His friendship was increasingly important in the eleven years we knew him.

When we got to Minerva the next year, in 1940, we had our newly acquired recording machine. We found that the Galushas' daughter, who lived with them, and worked for the local telephone company, had just died. They were in their eighties, both the Galushas, and this left them alone. They were heartbroken, and we were distressed and gave up all idea of singing. We went to see them, of course, and Yankee John, to our surprise, volunteered to sing a few things. He started on "The Ballad of Montcalm and Wolfe," but couldn't get beyond the first stanza:

> Bad news has come to town, bad news is carried,
> Some says my love is dead, others says she's married.
> As I was a-pond'ring on this, I took to weeping.
> They stole my love away whilst I was sleeping.

The words were moving, especially that morning, and the tune was strange to us and beautiful. It haunted us all winter. The next year we were grateful to find that Yankee John's pioneer resilience had carried him over his sorrow and that he was looking forward to a song-swapping session. That year he gave us the rest of that ballad and many other songs.

In 1940, before going back to Yankee John's, we went first to see the Carmers, who were spending the summer at the MacDowell Colony in Peterborough, New Hampshire, a haven for writers and artists and musicians. When we arrived Carl said, "The afternoon is young and shouldn't be wasted. I've heard that there is a lady in East Jaffrey who knows dozens of songs. Her name is Mrs. Fish."

Lena Bourne Fish using our newly acquired Wilcox Gay Recordio in her home in East Jaffrey, New Hampshire, July 4, 1940.

So, on the afternoon of July 4, having inquired at Mr. Duncan's Drug Store in East Jaffrey the day before and having learned that Mrs. Fish lived with her son, Charles, who was foreman of a lumber mill on the outskirts of town, we knocked on the door of a pleasant white frame house across from the lumberyard and were greeted by "Grammy" Fish herself, Mrs. Lena Bourne Fish. She was delighted to welcome anyone interested in songs.

That afternoon we had our first recording experience. We knew nothing then about the art of collecting and of recording. We had had no academic training in folk-lore, and there was no general knowledge of its existence, as there is today. The Wil-cox Gay Recordio with which we worked, compared to a cassette or a reel-to-reel re-corder, was indescribably difficult. When turned on, a stylus cut a groove in the acetate coating the small paper disk. As the stylus or needle cut the groove, a thread of the acetate often would wind itself around the needle, interfering with the cutting. There was a great deal of surface noise. And if the singer was not ready when the machine was turned on, or if he or she forgot the words and stopped to think, the disk could be used up without anything on it. There was no way to go back and rerecord, as there is on tape. Of course a collector should record every verse of a song, since a traditional singer may make variations in the tune from stanza to stanza. It is good, too, to in-clude some discussion of a song, where it was learned, and what the singer knows of its history. However, we had very little money to invest in this new overriding interest, and we didn't have many disks at any given time. So, in most instances in those early days, we recorded only two or three verses of any song, getting three songs to each side of a small disk. This Frank did, just to have a record of the tune. The words were up to me, and I put into my notebooks all the words of all the songs. There was one advantage to this, since I took down the words when I was with our singers and could verify a word that might be in doubt. This made for a much more accurate record than is possible in transcribing old recordings from an informant who may not have spo-ken clearly.

We spent the next day with Grammy Fish too, and two days the following year, and recorded from her memory ninety-six songs.

In August of 1940—with our new recording machine—we returned to one of our fa-vorite places, the Outer Banks of North Carolina. During that visit we met John and Alwilda Culpeper at Nag's Head. We visited them in their house among the sand dunes and recorded some of their songs: Captain John's "The Boston Burglar," among them, and Miss Alwildie's "The Gypsy's Warning." The Culpepers told us about "Tink" (C. K.) Tillett, who lived on Roanoke Island, down the beach and across the sound, who "used to know lots of songs." Then Frank remembered that he'd had a friend at Duke, P. D. (Peleg Dameron) Midgette, who had talked about an Uncle Tink Tillett, and that Dr. Frank Brown had gone to see him. We didn't have a lot of time, since we had arranged to meet Frank's brother later that afternoon. He would be waiting for us with his boat on the Alligator River to take us for a visit to Durant's Island, and there was no way to get word to him. We packed the car, to save time, and set off for Roanoke Island—not to Manteo, site of the Lost Colony, but to Wanchese, the island's other village. The few streets in Wanchese don't have names. They still don't. Every-one knows everyone. By asking anyone we met we soon found the Tilletts'—a pleasant house looking over inlets and marsh to the water. Tink was in the yard with his thirty-one-year-old bank pony, Lemon. They both won our hearts. Tink said he'd be happy to sing, so we brought in the recording machine, hooked it up to an overhead light,

Mr. C. K. Tillett with his thirty-one-year-old bank pony, Lemon, Roanoke Island, North Carolina, 1940.

and set to work. After all these years it is hard to believe that Tink sang to us that day—in such a short time—eleven songs, all of them important. We were fast friends in a few minutes and full of joy at our meeting. And then we had to leave. "Come back next year and spend a week with us," Tink said. We couldn't think of anything we would rather do. Unfortunately, Tink died in the spring, before we could get back to the Banks.

The war years were busy. I was deeply involved in my work at the Council on Foreign Relations and their war studies. Frank was running an enormous USO for service men in connection with his work at the YMCA.

In the spring of 1943 I took a few months off for the birth of Jonathan Francis, who immediately turned into Jeff when Frank wrote a paean to him, our first born, patterning it somewhat after the ballad of John Henry, the legendary black steel-driving railroad worker. The morning John Henry was born, they say, "the Mississippi River run *up*stream for a hundred and fifty miles!" Frank turned the initials "J.F." into "Little Jeff," since "Jonathan" didn't fit the southern black idiom he had in mind. Bill Benét published the verses in his department, "The Phoenix Nest," in the *Saturday Review of Literature* for April 10, 1943. Jonathan has been called Jeff ever since. In introducing the verses Bill said:

I have known, in my time, some proud fathers, and even officiated as one myself; but the most inspiriting canticle of joy I have recently run across was rendered the other day by my friend Frank Warner of West 12th Street, for longtime a fine singer of other folks' ballads, and an erudite collector of the same. The occasion was the birth of the first child and the son and heir of the Warner *maison.* Frank says the first verse came to him while riding on a bus to the hospital, and he worked out the rest from there. I should like to hear Frank sing it to his *gui*tar (with the accent on the ee!) I think it mighty fine.

Well, on the mornin' little Jeff was born, Lawd, Lawd,
Well, the mornin' little Jeff was born,
Well, New York town swang 'round and 'round,
And the subway run plumb out'n the ground,
And the great big buildin's bowed low down—
On the mornin' little Jeff was born.

On the mornin' little Jeff was born, Lawd, Lawd,
The mornin' little Jeff was born,
Gabriel blowed his trumpet to beat the band
And the angels danced 'round hand-in-hand,
And the Lawd said, "Jeff, you's a natchel man!"
On the mornin' little Jeff was born.

On the mornin' little Jeff was born, Lawd, Lawd,
The mornin' little Jeff was born,
He stretched his legs in the mornin' sun
An' he said, "Jest look what the Lawd's done done!"
An' he said, "God A'Mighty! I'm your lovin' son."
On the mornin' little Jeff was born.

One night around midnight, in 1944, when Frank was out of town and when Jeff was a year old, the telephone rang and a voice straight off Beech Mountain said, "Hello, Mis' Anne? This is Mis' Hicks's girl, and I'm up here at the bus station, and I want you to come up and git me." It turned out to be Mae—married to her cousin Linzy Hicks. I couldn't leave Jeff, so I told Mae to get someone to put her into a taxi.

23

Mae Hicks of Beech Mountain, North Carolina, outside our apartment in New York City, 1944.

She had to come only from 40th Street, the bus terminal, down to 12th Street. When she arrived she said, "Linzy's goin' overseas, and I jist had to come and git one more sweet kiss afore he goes."

"But where is he?"

"I've got his address," Mae said. "Hit's in care of the postmaster, so I thought I'd go to see the postmaster and ask him where Linzy is at."

It was an APO address, and he had already gone. I verified this the next day through my nephew Bill Dane, who then was stationed at the New York City Army Post Office, along with Oscar Brand, incidentally, whom we came to know a bit later.

We decided to keep Mae with us for a week, knowing she probably would never see New York again, as indeed she has not. She bore up well when things were going on, but if left to herself she would sit and cry quietly. I was working again, and we had a black friend, Maud Setzer, who came in by the day to take care of Jeff. Mae and Maud got on well. They both were from North Carolina.

Mae went to the grocery store on 12th Street and 6th Avenue several times a day. It was such a novelty to her to have a store so near. People there took an interest in her. She said they would ask her where she was from and she would say, "from the North." I asked her why she said that. "I meant from North Carolina," she said. She would buy a layer cake and eat half of it for breakfast. Everything was strange to her. She had never used a knife and fork at home, just a spoon. They seldom could afford meat, in any case. We showed her how to use a knife and fork when we had pork chops one night, and she did very well, although she said, "Hit seems like a lot of trouble."

Most people who have never been in New York are familiar with it through movies. Mae had never been to a movie, since Linzy, a Primitive Baptist, considered them sinful. She let me take her to Radio City Music Hall on the weekend, though. She found the carpet in the lobby "like walking on cotton" and was baffled by the Rockettes ("Is them real people up thar, or jist picturs?"), and by their seeming to be all the same size. Also she couldn't figure out how lights could turn everyone blue. But she was transported with awe and joy to see the whole orchestra rise on its platform out of the pit. "I never thought there could be anything like that. Hit's the purtiest thing I ever did see."

Even more interesting was a trip to the Central Park Zoo. Mae had never even heard of most of the animals there. She said her mother had a can of shortening with a picture of a seal on it, but she didn't know it was a real animal. Since Linzy had been in the army and she got his allotment checks ($50 a month was unheard-of riches to a mountain girl) she had acquired a battery-powered radio so she could listen to the news, and she had been hearing about guerrilla fighting here and there. There was a bit of explaining to do when we reached the gorilla cage.

One day Frank got his secretary to take Mae for a day's outing, and they rode the Staten Island Ferry (the first time she had seen a boat, or a large expanse of water) and then visited the top of the Empire State Building. When they got home in time for dinner Mae called out, "Honey, we shore did see a swee-ee-eet time!"

She was very brave. I asked her what she would have done if she had got to New York and hadn't found us. She said, "I'd a-bought me a room." We found that she had earlier taken a bus out to "Nebrasky" to see Linzy in camp there. She said, "I'd take dog's fare to git to see Linzy." When we put her on the bus to go home Frank asked her if she had enough money, and she said she had a "right smart bit"—a hundred dollars. It was more than we had at the time.

Mae's visit was a unique experience in our lives. Everything was so new to her. It was as if she had been raised on another planet. Yet throughout the visit she remained completely herself, never losing her mountain dignity, unself-conscious about her lack of knowledge of what we considered commonplace, unashamed to show her sorrow, but always brave. We realize that it was a confrontation of cultures that, in these days of instant communication, is unlikely ever to happen again.

Linzy came home two years later, in good shape. Mae's mother Rena wrote that he "hadn't changed a bit." The mountains make strong characters.

Our second son, Gerret Preston, was born in November of 1945, and when he was eight months old or thereabouts, we managed to borrow a car so that we could go to Minerva to see Yankee John and Mrs. Galusha. It was the only time Mrs. Galusha ever let us take her picture—with Yankee, and Jeff, who was three and a half. We had a splendid visit. The Galushas were delighted to see the children. And Yankee John sang us a number of songs we hadn't heard before, including a prize-fighting song, "The British-American Fight."

We didn't get back to see him again until 1950. Mrs. Galusha had died the year before, and he had been quite ill. He was in good spirits, though, and happy to see us, and eager to try out our new *tape* recording machine, a Pentron. He and Frank talked, on tape, for a long time, about Yankee's boyhood and the lumber camps and the Civil War. Yankee John—"the Adirondack Eagle" he was called in his younger days—died a few months later.

In the late thirties we met two young instructors at The College of the City of New York who had been collecting folk songs for the Library of Congress during their free summer months—Charles Lafayette Todd and Robert Sonkin. We spent many happy hours with Lafe and Bob during a number of years, comparing notes and recordings. We have kept in touch with Lafe and have seen him whenever it could be arranged.

In the early forties, through Lafe, who by that time was teaching at Columbia University, we got to know Leadbelly—Huddie Ledbetter, of Louisiana and Texas, "King of the Twelve-String Guitar," first of the true folksingers to win national fame. John and Alan Lomax had first heard Leadbelly sing in a Texas penitentiary where they had received permission to record Negro blues. Leadbelly was Huddie's prison name (his cellmate was called "Iron Head"), but he kept it all his life. When he was pardoned by an outgoing governor the Lomaxes gave him a job as their driver and eventually brought him to New York and introduced him to a startled world.

By the forties Leadbelly was living in New York City on Avenue A with his wife Martha. Around this time Lafe invited us to an evening at his apartment on Morningside Heights to meet a group of Columbia faculty, and to hear Leadbelly sing. It was a memorable evening, dominated by Leadbelly. All he needed was a jug of Mission Bell wine and there was no stopping him. He had a sense of what was fitting. Before singing his great song about the ox named "God-damn"—"Who made the back-band, whoa God-damn!" he would say, "Mr. Todd, is this a Cunnin'ham crowd?" Because if so, he would amend the song to "Who made the back-band, whoa Cunnin'ham!"

Mr. and Mrs. John Galusha with Jeff Warner, Minerva, New York, 1946.

"TAKE THIS HAMMER" MEMORIAL CONCERT
SATURDAY JANUARY 28 1950 TOWN HALL NEW YORK

LEAD BELLY

Presented by the Lead Belly Memorial Concert
Committee

Produced by Alan Lomax,
assisted by Francis Martin

Stage manager Vernon Enoch

P R O G R A M

I. Ballads and Folk Songs

Sam Gary - Alan Lomax - The Varieteers
"Blues for Lead Belly", recited by Bill Robinson,
  accompanied by Sammy Price
Edith Allaire - Frank Warner - Tony Kraber
Rev. Gary Davis - Jean Ritchie - Oscar Brand
Tom Glazer - Prof. Harold Thompson - W. C. Handy
Woody Guthrie and Tom Paley - Lord Invader
Hally Wood - Ensemble

II. Blues

Sonny Terry - Brownie McGhee - Sticks McGhee
Billy Taylor - Dan Burley -
Brownie McGhee's "He's Gone Away" Blues.
Mary Moore, singing "Lord, I Tried."

III. Jazz and Ragtime

Bill Dillard, narrator.
Eubie Blake and his ragtime piano.
All-Star Band with Sidney Bechet, Count Basie,
  Bill Dillard, Billy Taylor and others.
Hot Lips Page and His Band.
Programed by George Avakian, Charles Edward
  Smith, Bob Maltz.

IV. Lead Belly Memorial

Voice of Lead Belly.
Introduction of Ledbetter family.
"Take This Hammer", filmstrip about
Huddie Ledbetter –
  Produced by Fran Dellorca, assisted
  by Al Helb, Irving Toorchin -
  Written by Alan Lomax.
Peter Seeger and The Weavers and the
Good Neighbor Chorus, Laura Duncan.

Concert accompanist, Sam Price

Photographs courtesy Sid Grossman,
  Van Fisher, Betty Little, Skippy
  Adelman, Jean Evans

PRODUCTION COMMITTEE

Naome Walsh, Arrangements
  Edith Allaire
  Greer Johnson
  Robin Roberts
  Paul Walsh

Cover and inside of the program for the "Take
This Hammer" Leadbelly Memorial Concert,
1950.

In 1946 a joint meeting of the New York State Historical Association and the New York Folklore Society was held in Elmira, New York. On the program for the "Evening of Ballads" were Alan Lomax, Leadbelly, and Frank Warner. After the meeting Frank drove Lead and Alan back to New York City, Alan sleeping on the back seat, and Leadbelly recounting, during all the hours it took to drive down state, the hair-raising tales of his boyhood and younger days in New Orleans, playing piano and guitar in whorehouses, drinking, fighting, even killing. As he said, "The man was comin' at me with a knife. I *had* to shoot him."

Leadbelly died at the end of 1949. In January of 1950 Alan Lomax and a Sponsoring Committee organized a Leadbelly Memorial Concert, "Take This Hammer," held at Town Hall in New York City at midnight on a Saturday night. Town Hall was filled—even all the standing room. The list of those who participated was remarkable. Frank was proud to be among them.

In 1954 *Record Changer* magazine asked Frank for a brief statement about Leadbelly in connection with the issuance of some of his recordings. This is part of what he wrote at that time:

> Leadbelly never lost his primitive power. . . . In the years I knew him, listened to him, sang and talked with him, this is what he came to mean to me: At his best—with his guitar organically fused into himself and his wild uninhibited voice in full cry—Leadbelly brought a spine-tingling, hair-raising impact to people who had never listened to unadulterated back-street, rock-breaking, swamp-grown Negro singing. He translated a way of life into music. He spoke it true.

In 1941 we had a letter from Alan Lomax from Washington. He said he had heard of our work through Lafe Todd and hoped we could get together and compare notes. He was then head of the Folk Archives which he and his father, John Lomax, had established at the Library of Congress. After Alan came to New York we became close friends, and we have cherished his friendship ever since. He lived on Perry Street, just a few blocks from us. During the war when Alan was with the Special Services Branch of the Army and preparing broadcasts for the Armed Forces Radio Service for the troops overseas, he got Frank to participate in some of these programs, along with Leadbelly, Woody Guthrie, Burl Ives, Sonny Terry, and Brownie McGhee. After the war Frank also took part in some of Alan's "Columbia Workshop Series" called "This is Singing Country."

Through Alan we met Moe Asch who had a recording company then called Disc. This was before Asch started Folkways. Under the Disc label in 1946 Moe brought out Frank's first album—a set of three 78 rpm records called "Hudson Valley Songs." Playing behind Frank are Bess Lomax Hawes, mandolin; Baldwin (Butch) Hawes, guitar; and Peter Seeger, banjo. We had first met Pete the year before when he was just out of the Army, and Margot Mayo, founder and director of the American Square Dance Group (she was connected also with The Little Red Schoolhouse and with Mills

College, both in Greenwich Village), had brought him around to see us. Pete was just developing his famous banjo style, and we shared Margot's enthusiasm for his talents. No one knew then that he would sing and play his way around the country and the world to become, as Studs Terkel once said, "America's tuning fork." Our paths and Pete's have crossed constantly over the years from the hootenanies of the forties to Newport and other festivals.

Through the Carmers we came to know Dr. Louis C. Jones, former professor of folklore at Albany State College, and the recently appointed Director of the New York State Historical Association at Cooperstown, New York. He was, and is, an innovative scholar and a storyteller full of wit and charm. In 1948 he organized the first of the Seminars on American Culture, offering "to local historians, collectors, writers, teachers, museum workers, librarians, folklorists, and Americana enthusiasts generally an opportunity to study with others who share their interests and with distiguished specialists in the areas of their enthusiasms," as an early program states. Beginning that first year and continuing without a break for eight years, and then intermittently on some eight or ten additional occasions, Frank was on the Seminars faculty, participating in the courses on folklore and singing an evening concert. The Seminars were a heady experience in those early days for anyone interested in American history, primitive art, crafts, pioneer life, or folklore. In the early years Dr. Harold Thompson of Cornell (author of *Body, Boots, & Britches,* the definitive book about New York State folklore) led the folklore course. He was a scholar, a collector, a musician, and a marvelous companion. Samuel Hopkins Adams (author of *Canal Town* and *Grandfather Stories,* and many other books) professed to care little for folk music but recorded for us several songs he had learned in the Georgia Sea Islands. He was full of lore about the Erie Canal and upstate New York. There we came to know Dick Dorson, Dr. Richard Dorson, for many years head of the Folklore Department at Indiana University, who was to become famous for his books of field-collected folklore, and as the conscience of academic folklorists.

At Cooperstown we re-established our friendship with Henry Beston, author of *Outermost House,* and thereafter we had a warm correspondence with him. His letters were full of the ideas and anecdotes which make his *Northern Farm* so interesting.

In October of 1957 he wrote us:

Nobleboro, Maine

Dear Frank and Anne —
    After having trailed it like Sherlock Holmes, I have just seen *Run of the Arrow*[8] and this comes to congratulate Frank on a splendid piece of work. When he began to strum

---

8. In 1956 Sam Fuller, who had written the script for a movie about the Civil War and who was directing and producing it for RKO, heard one of Frank's early Elektra records on which he sings "The Old Rebel Soldier" (No. 193). As a result, Frank went to Hollywood and was a part of "Run of the Arrow," starring Rod Steiger. Frank sang the song and had a speaking part as well in the opening scenes of the movie. It still turns up on the late late show.

Carl Carmer and Frank Warner at Fenimore House, Cooperstown, New York, ca. 1957.
Photo by Anne Warner.

his banjo and sing, I almost stood up in the movie theatre and shouted "Hello! Frank!!"
. . . I saw the picture in good old Portland, at the best theatre.

It is the late autumn, the season of mince pies, cider, and open fires, and we are
enjoying it to the full. I sometimes think that Americans need more such simple pleasures;
complicated pleasures often end up in fatigue. My own pet bear has just returned to his
dugout, and I shall presently wish him a cosy winter. He is a very likeable bear, and once
stood on hind legs and waved to me.

So Viva! "Run of the Arrow" and its best actor! With warmest best regards and all
affection to all the house.

Ever faithfully, your rustic colleague,

s/ Henry

Also, in Cooperstown, we learned much about folk art and absorbed a feeling
for it from the great collection at Fenimore House; about pioneer life from the Farm-

Rod Steiger, Frank Warner, and Olive Carey in the RKO picture "Run of the Arrow," 1956. Photo by Oliver Sigurdson, RKO Radio Pictures.

er's Museum and its curator, George Campbell; about the Iroquois people from Dr. Arthur Parker, author of numerous books on the Iroquois Confederacy and himself an Iroquois; about jazz and its folk roots from Marshall Stearns, our Greenwich Village neighbor who was an authority on Chaucer (which he taught at Hunter College) as well as on jazz.[9]

9. One morning, after Frank's concert the night before, Marshall Stearns joined us for breakfast in the hotel dining room. "Frank," he said, "no white man can get those sounds in his voice. Your mother was a slave!"

Cooperstown, named for the family of James Fenimore Cooper, is a beautiful unspoiled village at the foot of Otsego Lake—the Glimmerglass of Cooper's novels. For all the Warners, our brief sojourn there each summer came to have a special aura that set it quite apart from the rest of the year. The Otesaga Hotel, with its immensely high ceilings, its spacious and beautiful dining room, its wide veranda overlooking the lake, was a noble example of late nineteenth- or early twentieth-century America, but the excitement came from combining that setting with the intellectual repast of the Seminars. Never again would a vacation that offered only swimming, tennis, sunbathing, or sightseeing have any appeal for us.

One summer after the dust bowl years Lafe Todd and his colleague Bob Sonkin were recording in an Okie camp in California. They heard a man playing a banjo and singing, while sitting on the tailgate of an old Ford truck. His name was Henry King, and he was singing what we think is the ultimate version of "Springfield Mountain" (No. 23),[10] though he knew nothing about that. He didn't mind their recording him for the Library of Congress, so that is how we first heard "Fod." It was a favorite with Frank's audiences. It won't be in this book because we didn't collect it, but it is on a Library of Congress recording—Album No. II of "American Folk Songs." (Frank Warner sings "Fod" on his Elektra Album EKL-153, "America's Singing Heritage.") One verse goes:

As I went down to the mowing field,
    Hoori, toori, fodalinka dido,
As I went down to the mowing field,
    Fod.
As I went down to the mowing field,
A big black snake took me by the heel!
    Too rally day.

"Fod" was a favorite of Carl Sandburg's after he'd heard Frank sing it. Once we had a postcard from him, though he didn't often communicate in writing at this point in his life, saying just "Fod—C.S." One musical and conversational evening in our West 12th Street apartment, after Frank had responded to a request to sing "Fod," Carl said, "Now, there's a useful word. Fod! Semicolon or colon, as you wish. Period, if you like. Where are you going? I'm going where I want to go. Won't you tell me where you're going? No . . . Fod. When are you coming home? Can't you tell me when you're coming home? No, I'm not going to tell you that either. Fod. Will you write? I don't know. Fod."

I had answered the phone one day in the spring of 1950 and heard a deep voice with its unmistakably Scandinavian inflection say, "This is Carl Sandburg. I thought

10. "Springfield Mountain" is an early American ballad about an event that took place in Massachusetts in 1761 when a young man died as the result of a rattlesnake's bite. See songs Nos. 23 and 65.

Frank Warner, Carl Sandburg, and Jean Ritchie at the Warners' apartment, 1950. Photo by George Pickow.

I'd like to get together with Frank again, to swap some songs and conversation. Could I come down to see you Sunday evening?" He could indeed. Could he bring anything? Not a thing in the world. This was the first of many visits.

Carl was spending some months in New York that year, doing the final work on his *Complete Poems.* Happily for us, there was something about our Greenwich Village apartment where there was informality, young children, a fire in the fireplace, a cat, a pot of coffee always ready (Carl had a true Scandinavian fondness for coffee), and shared interest in the people, that he found a relief from crowds and adulation. "This isn't New York City," he used to say. "It could be Indiana or Illinois or anywhere except New York."

Carl sometimes left us with a heart-warming, truly Sandburgian goodbye: "Frank and Anne Warner are not what is wrong with this country!"

In the spring of 1950 Frank stopped by one day for the first time at Peter Carbone's String Shop on Bleecker Street in the Village. As he walked in, Peter, who had photographs of folk music people all around his walls, said, "Frank, where have you been?" Peter sold and mended instruments and passed on information and provided a meeting place for folk enthusiasts. Israel Young's Folklore Center came to the Village a bit later. That day Frank met at the String Shop a tall rather gangling youth named Jac Holzman, recently converted — a few months before — to traditional music. Jac came by to see us, and we soon became firm friends. He had dropped out of St. John's College in Annapolis, and had broken temporarily with his family to pursue his own course. He had rented a room somewhere in the Village, and some space in a shop called "The Record Loft," while he put together his plans for a recording company. So began Elektra Records. Jac had just turned twenty-one, but it was obvious that he was on his way to something important. He was a recording engineer almost by osmosis, having been doing technically difficult recording jobs for big recording companies since he was sixteen. He began dropping by regularly, usually at dinner time, since his funds were low, and we were happy to make him a part of the household. Elektra, in time, became an international recording company, introducing such stars as Jean Ritchie, Cynthia Gooding, Susan Reed, Theodore Bikel, Ed McCurdy, Judy Collins, and — later — The Doors, Harry Chapin,[11] Carly Simon, and many others. Jac also founded Nonesuch Records.

Elektra Records had been in Jac's mind while he was at St. John's, and he had produced EKL-1 then, though we never heard much about it. In 1952 he produced EKL-2, by Jean Ritchie, and later that year EKL-3, "Frank Warner Sings Folk Songs and Ballads." Frank recorded two additional albums for Elektra: "Songs of America's Wars," in 1954 (EKL-13), and "America's Singing Heritage" (EKL-153) in 1958.

Early in 1950 we had met Jean Ritchie, the entrancing traditional singer from the Cumberland Mountains in Kentucky. She married George Pickow that year, and they lived around the corner from us on Seventh Avenue. Jean and George, and in due course their two sons, Peter and Jonathan, have been our good friends ever since.

Early in the war years, in 1942, we had been introduced to a young soldier named John (Jack) Langstaff[12] by Jeanne Behrend, the concert pianist. She had been a fellow student with Jack at the Curtis Institute, and she knew Frank and Jack would share an interest in traditional music — as indeed they did.

We hadn't been in touch with Jack for a number of years when, in the spring of 1956 (by this time Frank had become Director of the YMCAs of Nassau and Suffolk Counties and we had moved to Long Island), he wrote about the plans for a week in August that year devoted to traditional folk music at Pinewoods Camp near Cape Cod, conducted by the Country Dance and Song Society of America. Thus began an

11. Harry Chapin and Jeff Warner were fourth-grade classmates at P.S. 41 in Greenwich Village when we first knew Jac Holzman.

12. John Langstaff, in addition to being an international concert artist, has produced a number of recordings and books. He is the creator and director of the Christmas Revels — a celebration of Christmas, the New Year, and the winter solstice through carols, songs, rituals, and dances. During the past dozen years the Christmas Revels — and the Spring Revels too — have themselves become a tradition in Cambridge, Massachusetts, and have been presented since 1979 in New York as well.

association with Pinewoods which has continued ever since. It has brought us friendships with innumerable musicians, dancers, singers, and scholars from Great Britain as well as America, and has given us an expanded understanding of and familiarity with the world of traditional music and dance.

Frank Proffitt, from Pick Britches Valley, was with us at Pinewoods in 1961 and 1962. He brought to everyone there his music, his humor, his warmth. In 1961 we all met Douglas and Helen Kennedy, leading British folklorists. Evelyn Wells, author of *The Ballad Tree,* taped a conversation between Douglas Kennedy, Frank Proffitt, and Frank Warner, with some songs by Frank Proffitt. Douglas used the tape later in his lectures in Britain. He said of Frank Proffitt, "The hills of Scotland are full of faces like his."

That summer at Pinewoods three distinct cultures came together, demonstrated how they had blended, and rejoiced in each other: Douglas Kennedy, Scottish by origin, British by training and experience; Frank Proffitt of an earlier British culture, preserving many of its features as in a time warp; and, of course, the Americans all around them—Americans with a special interest in what each of the others represented.

We have left out a great many friends and experiences and events—all stemming from our interest in folk music: the years of the Newport Folk Festivals; the festivals in Berkeley and Chicago; the joy we have had in introducing traditional folk music to students at innumerable schools and colleges; our visits to the St. Regis Reservation on the Canadian border where we collected Mohawk lore and were initiated into membership in the tribe; the pleasure of sharing American folk music with British audiences.

But here, from our collection, are some of the best stories we can tell of our singing friends, and some of their songs. Through these friends we feel we have discovered America.

New York State

THE ADIRONDACK MOUNTAIN region embraces the largest state forest preserve in the United States—2,179,556 acres of state land, open to camping, hiking, mountain climbing, fishing, and, in proper seasons, hunting. The mountains constitute a series of high peaks at the center, gradually lowering on all sides—from Mount Marcy's height of 5,344 feet to 100 feet at the shores of Lake Champlain. In the northeast and northwest the land levels off into rolling country and high plateaus.

The Adirondack Mountains are not high to people who know the Alps or the Rockies. Their summits are rounded and worn and are covered with pine and fir trees—not high rocky crags perpetually wreathed in clouds. Little farming has ever been done on their rocky sides, which makes them look very different from the Appalachians. The region is distinguished, too, by the enormous number of lakes which it encompasses—1,345 named lakes and many more that are nameless. The largest lake within the preserve is Lake George, which is of spectacular beauty—thirty miles long, dotted with wooded islands, with the mountainous eastern shore "forever wild."

Sometimes called America's original vacation land, the Adirondack region, during its gilded age—from 1875 to 1910—could boast of huge luxurious resort hotels such as the Fort William Henry or the mighty Prospect House on Blue Mountain Lake which could house 500 or 600 guests and did so, in spite of being thirty miles from the nearest railway. Here such statesmen as Theodore Roosevelt and many of the socially elite—the Tiffanys, the Astors, Stuyvesants and Biddles, with their guests from London, Paris, St. Petersburg, and all the fashionable capitals of Europe—strolled in their finery along broad piazzas twenty-seven feet high. Besides the hotels, the area contained fabulous summer places—one- or two-thousand acre estates called "camps," as the marble palaces in Newport were called "cottages." There was "Camp Pine Knot," owned by Collis P. Huntington; J. P. Morgan's "Camp Uncas," with a fieldstone fireplace as big as some Manhattan apartments; and Francis P. Garvan's "Kamp Kill Kare"—a strange name for the most stylish of the camps.

Famous in the area too, from the earliest days, were the Adirondack guides who knew the woods and all their lore and who often were rustic philosophers besides. William Chapman White quotes one of the first of these Adirondack guides, John Cheney, who, in 1837, put into simple and beautiful words his description of the view from Mount Marcy:

It makes a man feel what it is to have all creation under his feet. There are woods there which it would take a lifetime to hunt over, mountains that seem shouldering each other to boost the one whereon you stand up and away, heaven knows where. Thousands of little lakes among them so light and clean. Old Champlain, though fifty miles away, glistens below you like a strip of white birch when slicked up by the moon on a frosty night, and the Green Mountains of Vermont beyond it fade and fade away until they disappear as gradually as a cold scent when the dew rises.[1]

JOHN GALUSHA

It was in August of 1939 that we first met Yankee John Galusha. He was eighty years old, somewhat bent with the weight of years, but vigorous and hearty. He had spent his life in the North Country—the Adirondack Mountains of New York State—as a logger, game and fishing guide, forest ranger (Vanderwhacker Mountain was his last charge), and farmer. In 1941, when he was eighty-two, he told us he had cut five tons of hay that summer, kept his cattle, and raised a vegetable garden. He and Mrs. Galusha, his "Lizzie," were living in a farmhouse on Fourteenth Road in Minerva, a village some miles northwest of North Creek.

On our second visit the following year (1940) we had our first recording machine, an early Wilcox Gay Recordio, and a supply of small acetate-coated paper disks. On to these, during that and subsequent visits, Yankee John sang many songs, some of them rarely found in oral tradition. We had many a long talk with him during our visits, and he became a dear and valued friend.

Over the years we had some correspondence with the Galushas—Mrs. Galusha doing the writing.

Oct. 2, 1941

Dear Mr and Mrs Warner
—Dear Friends . . . am I pardoned for keeping you waiting and not answering your letter before? All the excuse is that I am lazy. We have been very well. John has had a hard cold is on the gain just now. The weather has been very nice . . . John received the pic-

---

1. Quoted in *Adirondack Country,* by William Chapman White (New York: Duell, Sloan and Pearce, 1837; Boston: Little, Brown, 1954), p. 14.

John Galusha, Minerva, New York, 1939.

John Galusha and Flash, with Jeff Warner, 1946.

tures and is enjoying them very much. That was a wonderful trip for him [we had taken him on a visit to Thurman, N.Y., where he grew up]. I hope you are both well and of course working hard. Hoping to hear from you again.

Love from John and I

Mrs. John Galusha

Dec 30 1943

Dear Friends,

I was glad to hear from you. I've wondered what you were doing in the war. By the news on radio it is not finished yet. . . .

Thanks for your kind rememberances. . . . I think you might hear John singing. . . .

I was pleased to get your boy's picture. I hope he is well also you and Frank. I am very well only getting too old to write very good. . . . John has had a cold. We are alone this winter as Vincent got married and works in Albany and is home only weekends. It is cold this morning, 8 below, not much snow. . . .

Love and kisses for my baby,
Mr & Mrs John Galusha

"Flash" was the name of John's dog. We have one postcard from Minerva (with a view of Sleeping Giant Mountain) that just says "Thanks. Flash" We can't remember what we did to earn his gratitude.

In 1941 we took Yankee John for a day's visit to Thurman, New York, where he had been born and raised, He had not been back in forty years, though it was only some thirty miles away. "I don't recognize nawthen around here," he said. He did meet one old friend, Truman Smith, born in 1861. Turned out he'd been deputy sheriff for fifty years. Yankee said, "We used to be boys together." "Well," said Truman Smith, "You live right in Minervy and ain't been back in all this time? You ought to been dead years ago!"

Some of his boyhood friends Yankee found in the burying ground. Talking of them Yankee John said, "Well, it makes me happy to think I've beat all those old codgers! . . . You know, I used to dread death, but now it don't mean *that* to me. I've had a good life, and I'll die as I have lived."

As we passed one headstone, "There's Dick Cameron, seventy-five years old. I used to go to school with him." And, "Why there's Guy Brookes, born 1795, died 1879. He was no good. Used to sell spinning wheels. The children made up rhymes about him. Old G.B.:

Old Guy Brookes, Lord how he looks!
He would lie and cheat and swindle . . .
He would sell a lady a spinning wheel
And cheat her out of the spindle!

There also were stones marking the graves of Yankee's mother and father and of his brother Stillman, who died of wounds received at Cold Harbor.

Yankee was in high spirits during much of that afternoon. He talked about the Adirondack Dog Dude Ranch that had been launched in a nearby community—full of girls "with nothin' on but goggles and garters." He recited an Irish toast:

Here's to you and your folks and me and my folks
If you and your folks thought as much of me and my folks
As me and my folks think of you and your folks
There wouldn't be such folks since folks was folks.

And an epitaph:

> Among those gray rocks
> Enclosed in a box
> Lies Mr. John Cox
> Who died of smallpox.

And finally something moved him to tell us of a small incident he'd never forgotten, and one that told us so much of Yankee's real nature: "I had a cow once named Blackie. One day when I went to milk her she hit me in the eye with her horn. I used to be real flashy—quick tempered. She didn't mean it. She was a regular pet. But it hurt, and I hit her with the bucket. I was never so sorry for anything in my life. I threw that pail out, and I went and put my arms around her neck, and she put her face up against me just as innocent . . . I even told her I was sorry."

That trip to Thurman was a day to remember.

In 1950 we owned a car once more and planned a visit to Minerva. We knew Mrs. Galusha had died the year before and that Yankee John had not been well, and we had written for his birthday in February. The next month we had a letter from the Mountain Ridge Nursing Home in Minerva:

3/5/50

Dear Frank,

Mrs. Bennett will write for me, to let you know that I received your letter and was very glad to hear from you. Many thanks for your birthday dollars but instead of tobacco I bought candy as I don't smoke a pipe in bed. . . . I am confined to my bed most of the time. . . . I had a pretty severe heart spell the 4th of Feb. . . . Some days I feel pretty good and I sing when I feel like it. . . . My legs sort of went back on me . . . I eat quite good most of the time and I'll enjoy the candy and think of you while eating it.

I hope you and your family do get up this way this summer. I'd enjoy seeing you again. My best to Anne, the boys and yourself. . . .

Yankee John

In July of that year—1950—we saw Yankee John for the last time, shortly before his death at the age of ninety-one. He was dressed and sitting in the kitchen of the house in Olmstedville, near Minerva, where he was staying with his great niece and nephew, Margaret and Jack O'Donnell. It was a moving, and happy, reunion.

We had just acquired our first tape recorder, and we mentioned it just as a matter of interest. Yankee John said he would like to see it, so we brought the machine in and hooked it up, and Frank began to ask John some questions about his early memories. What follows is a transcription from this tape with the questions omitted because they break the flow of the narrative. We call it, for obvious reasons, "That's the Way They Lived."[2]

I was born in 1859. February 6th, 1859. . . .

I can remember when we used to farm it and raise all the stuff that we consumed mostly on our farm—everything like eggs and butter and cheese, and flour—we would have our grain ground into flour and bring it home and use it, as they go to the stores and buy it today. . . .

I can remember as long ago as when I wore dresses . . . little boys wore dresses, lots of them, until they was, oh, five or six years old, and then they would go into their pants and you ought to see 'em strut around when they got their pants on! They could thrash buckwheat then as good as a man, almost. Boys would wear their hair sometimes as long as a girl [while they were in dresses] . . . and then they would go straight along up to farm work. That's the way they lived.

We had horses . . . and we used to use lots of oxen too. But they always had horses . . . they brought horses into the country with them. I couldn't tell you when that was [the first coming]. My folks come in pretty early. . . . I guess Galushas are all over the United States. . . .

They say the first Galusha that ever came into the United States was kidnapped— what they call "shanghaied." The British used to shanghai men out of Ireland and put them on the ships and send them out. They would send press gangs to take a lot of men and put them to work on vessels in them days. . . . [Yankee John's grandfather fought in the War of 1812, so the Galushas came over long before the wave of Irish immigrants that resulted from the potato famine.]

I lived in several different places, but for quite a few years we lived in Thurman. My father[3] . . . I stayed with my father until I was old enough to go out to work. He farmed it. He worked in the lumber woods in the winter time for other people . . . lots of people did that. They farmed it in the summer and worked in the wintry woods in the winter . . . that's the way they lived. . . .

When I was a boy there was an old couple that came around . . . they had a horse and a wagon, a covered wagon . . . big enough, I guess, that they lived in it most of the time . . . traveling all around the country. Their name [the man's name] was Yankee Annan. I used to mimic people, when I was a kid, that I'd hear singing. I began to mimic him, and people named me "Yankee" after him. . . . I was possibly somewhere between eight and ten years old. . . . I know I learned songs from him, but I can't remember what they were to save my life. He tried to get my father to let me go with him . . . but my father wouldn't let me go. I had work to do . . . that was the time when people wanted children to work. That's the way they lived. . . .

I can remember when my father went to the South and got my brother[4] that was

2. This transcription of Yankee John's recording was printed under the above title in the *New York Folklore Quarterly* (June 1966): 104.

3. R. M. Galusha, 1822–1892. *His* father fought in the War of 1812. Yankee's mother was Catherine Wilsey. Her father, John Wilsey, was born in 1801 and died in 1885.

4. Stillman Galusha, born May 4, 1844, died March 10, 1865. He was a member of Company 1, 96th New York Infantry.

wounded in the battle of Cold Harbor . . . and he lived from in May until the next March. He died sometime in March from the effects of the wounds. He was hit twice . . . shot on top of the breastworks . . . he fell back and laid there from quite early in the morning until after dark . . . he had a broken leg just above the knee and a bullet right through just above his hip. My father went down and got him . . . carried him in his arms between the stations. He had to change cars coming home, and there was no conveyance they could get and he had to carry him. A wagon was sent to meet them at North Creek. . . .

I had another brother that served three years and was in thirteen different battles and never got a scratch. His term of enlistment expired and he was discharged and come home . . . then they called for volunteers again and offered a $1,000 bounty to them that would enlist, and he turned right around and enlisted again and got back just in time to get into the fight at Appomattox Courthouse and got his $1,000 and came back home again. He had a streak of luck. . . .

I heard that the boys used to whistle back and forth across the lines, and how they swapped hardtack for tobacco. The southern boys wanted the hardtack, and the northern boys wanted tobacco. The Yanks called the Rebels "Johnny Grayback," and the southerners used to call the northern boys "Billy Yank." They say they was quite friendly. . . . The time they had that epidemic that the blackberries did such good—the southerners and the northern boys would be right out there together picking berries. I have heard three different soldiers tell of that—I heard Bill Hangsen and I heard my brother tell of it, and . . . Cameron . . . I forgot his given name. They wondered what in Old Harry they was fightin' for. They swapped songs too. . . .

I knew a rebel colonel—I guided him, fishing. Every time I looked at him I thought of my brother lying on his bed, groaning . . . and I wanted to kill him. I didn't like him . . . but he was an all right fellow. The southern people are a generous race of people, if you can believe what you read and what other people tell you.

You know, I have been fixed for death. . . . I am a Catholic, you know [he told us years before that he had become a Catholic when he married Lizzie], and I have been annointed for death twice this spring . . . and now it is summer . . . I've got another one to go. . . .

Well, goodbye . . . God bless you . . . and thanks for your blessing.

Marjorie Lansing Porter, our good and long-time friend, was from the North Country, Essex County, herself. She was a local historian, a newspaper editor and writer, and a collector of folklore and folk songs. She knew Yankee John well and recorded for her archives many of his songs and his stories of the old days and ways. Here are some excerpts from her news story about Yankee John's death, written for the *Record-Post*, Au Sable Forks, New York, on September 28, 1950:

John Galusha was born February 6, 1859, in the town of Thurman, Warren County, New York, the son of Reuben M. Galusha, farmer. John was sixteen when he answered the call of the Adirondack woods, close at hand, and became a tenderfoot lumberjack. Life in the woods offered good wages and adventure. . . . In addition the profession of Ad-

St. Mary's Church (1848) in Irishtown, New York, 1955.

irondack guide was open to men like Yankee. Consequently, for many years he derived both his living and a reasonable satisfaction with life from these two occupations, guiding (and sometimes farming) during the summer seasons and lumberjacking the other two-thirds of each year. Later, for sixteen seasons, he acted as fire observer on Vanderwhacker Mountain for the New York State Conservation Department. . . . As a guide, John Galusha felt his life enriched since he met and worked for "great big high folks" such as the President of the United States, the Governor of New York State, members of the Tahawus Club at the old "Upper Works" of the McIntyre Iron Company, and men prominent in various walks of life. . . . Yankee was a bachelor until his late twenties, yet he and his wife were privileged to spend over sixty years together at Minerva before she died at the home of their son, Vincent, in the winter of 1948–49.

The Galushas lie side by side now in the burying ground of St. Mary's Church in Irishtown, and share one headstone:

John Galusha   Elizabeth Galusha

1859–1950   1859–1949

Yankee John's "Cabin Boy" is called by Laws "The Maid in Sorrow." It is a less sophisticated and more tender story than the better known "The Handsome Cabin Boy" (Laws *ABBB,* N-13) where the pretty female dresses in sailor's clothing and goes to sea in search of adventure.

Mrs. Lena Bourne Fish, in New Hampshire, sang us a version of "The Maid in Sorrow," little changed from the broadside, which she also called "Cabin Boy," No. 48. The tunes for these two versions are very different from each other.

See: Gardner, 401; Greenleaf, 100; Laws, *ABBB,* N-12, 208

CABIN BOY

Oh, once I had a sweet-heart, Young— Jim-my was— his name, And it's
for the — sake of Jim-my That— I — crossed o'er — the main. And—
if I nev-er do find — him, I will mourn con-stant-lie, All
for the — sake of Jim-my A — maid I will live — and die.

Short jacket and sailor's breeches
This fair one she put on,
And like a brave young sailor
She boldly marched along.
She bargained with a sea captain
Her passage to be free,
And she would be his true companion
While crossing the raging sea.

One night as they were talking,
A-going to their bed,
The captain to her bravely said,
"I wish you was a maid,
For your cherry cheeks and ruby lips
Have so enchanted me
That I do wish with all my heart
That you was a maid for me."

46

"O hold your tongue now, Captain,
Such talk is all in vain,
And if the sailors hear you,
They will laugh and make you game.
But wait until we do reach the shore
And two pretty maids we will find
For you and me to sport and play
And with them drink our wine."

It happened a few days after,
This gallant ship did land,
And as she stepped off on the dock
She waved her lily-white hand,
Saying, "Once I was a sailor on board your ship
But a maid I am on shore.
Adieu, adieu now, Captain,
Adieu for evermore."

"If you'll come back, my pretty maid,
And if you will marry me,
I have a large fortune
That I will assign to thee,
Ten thousand guineas in bright gold
That I will assign to thee,
If you will come back, my pretty maid,
And say you will marry me."

"No, for once I had a sweetheart,
Young Jimmy was his name,
And it's for the sake of Jimmy
That I have crossed o'er the main.
And if I never do find him,
I will mourn constant-lie,
All for the sake of Jimmy
A maid I will live and die."

2. The *Flying Cloud*   John Galusha, 1941

Yankee John sang this song straight through — all sixteen verses — without hesitation. He didn't tell us where he had learned it and, unfortunately, as in so many other instances, we failed to ask him. In his younger days, he told us, he could hear a long song once, and remember it word for word.

Laws, in his *ABBB,* says that "The *Flying Cloud*" is one of a small but select group of pirate ballads found in American oral tradition which "seem usually to have been composed in England and to deal with both British pirates and the British ships they encountered. The best of these ballads, 'The Flying Cloud,' is unique in its length, its wealth of detail, and its dealing with both slavery and piracy. . . . The story of a young man's career in crime seems too vivid not to have been based to some extent on actual events, but so far the origin of the piece has proved elusive" (p. 10). There is no record of an actual *Flying Cloud,* or of a Captain Moore.

Horace Beck cites Franz Rickaby: "at one time the ability to sing this song was a prerequisite to being allowed to work in Michigan lumber camps" (p. 223). Beck questions the song's British origin, since only one version has been found in the British Isles and versions are widespread from Ontario and Maine and throughout the Middle West.

Beck says that a ship called the *Flying Cloud* was built in 1851 in Boston by David McKay, but it was never a pirate ship and the song is earlier. William Doerflinger says it may have originated as early as 1830.

See: Beck, *JAF* 66, p. 123; Belden, 128; Cazden II, 429;
Doerflinger, 136; Laws, *ABBB,* K-28, 154; Thompson, 39

My name is Ed-ward Hall-a-han, I would have you to un-der-stand. I was born in the town of Wa-ter-ford In — dear old Er-in's land. When I was young and in my — prime And — for-tune on me smiled, My par-ents do-ted on —— me For — I was their on-ly child.

My father bound me to a trade
In Waterford's fair town.
He bound me to a cooper
By the name of Willie Brown.
I served my master faithfully
For fourteen months or more,
When we shipped on board of the *Ocean Queen*
Bound for Valparaiso's shore.

When we arrived in Valparaiso,
I fell in with Captain Moore,
Commander of the *Flying Cloud*
That sailed from old Trimore.
He kindly invited me
A-slaving voyage to go—
To the burning sands of Africay
Where the sugar cane does grow.

Now the *Flying Cloud* is a Spanish brig
Of five hundred tons or more.
She could easily sail around anything
That sailed from old Trimore.
Her sails are as white as the 'riven snow
And on them not a stain.
The eighteen brass nine-pounder guns
She carried astern her main.

Now the *Flying Cloud* is as fine a ship
As ever swam the seas,
Or ever spread a maintop sail
Before a lively breeze.
I have oft-times seen her in a gale
Blown on her weather beam,
With her main royal flying aloft
Running eighteen off the reel.

48

And in just ten days sailing
We reached the African shores.
Five hundred odd of those poor souls
From their native soil we bore.
We marched them out along our decks
And stowed them down below.
Scarce eighteen inches to the man
Was all that we could allow.

And then we put to sea again
With our cargo of slaves,
It would have been better for those poor souls
Had they been in their graves.
For the plague and fever came on board,
Swept half their lives away.
We hove their bodies up on deck
And tossed them in the waves.

And in just ten days after
We reached Bermudia's shore,
Where we sold them to the planters
To be slaves forever more—
The royal coffee fields to hoe
Beneath the broiling sun,
For to lead a hard and a wretched life
Until their career was run.

And when our money it was all gone,
We put to sea again.
When Captain Moore he came on board
And he says to us, his men,
"There's gold and silver to be had
If me you will sustain.
We'll hoist a lofty pirate flag,
We'll scour the Spanish Main."

Then they all agreed, but five young lads,
And they ordered us them to land.
Two of them were Boston boys
And two from Newfoundland.

The other was an Irish lad
From the county of Trimore.
How I wish to God I'd joined those lads
And went with them on shore.

For we were chased by many's the ship,
By liners and frigates too,
But all in vain astern of us
Their volleyed thunder flew.
'Twas all in vain astern of us
Their cannon roared so loud.
Yes, all in vain down on the main
For to catch the *Flying Cloud*.

Till a Yankee ship, a man o' war,
The *Dungeon,* she hove in view,
And she fired a shot across our bows
'Twas a signal to lay to.
We answered not that signal shot,
But we flew before the wind.
When a chain shot cut our mainmast off
We were forced to fall behind.

Then we cleared our decks for action
And she ranged up alongside,
And short across our quarterdecks
There ran a crimson tide.
We fought till Captain Moore was slain
And eighty of his men,
When a bombshell set our ship on fire,
We were forced to surrender then.

It was back to Newgate I was borne,
Bound down in heavy chains,
For the robbing and plundering of many's the ship
Down on the Spanish Main.
We had caused their crews to walk the plank,
Gave them a watery grave,
For the motto of our captain was
That a dead man tells no tales.

Now it's fare you well, old Ireland,
It's the place that I adore.
And twice farewell to my mother dear,
I ne'er shall see you more.
It was whiskey and bad company
That made a rake of me.
O youths, beware of my sad fate
And a curse on piracy.

Now farewell you shady groves
And the girl that I love so dear.
No more your voice like music sweet
Will sound all in my ear.
No more I'll press your ruby lips
Nor kiss your lily white hand,
For today I die a scornful death
All in a foreign land.

3. The Bonny Bunch of Roses-O   John Galusha, 1941

This song appeared on broadsides and in *The Forget Me Not Songster* and other songsters in the early nineteenth century. Versions in oral tradition have been found by Mackenzie and Creighton in Nova Scotia, by Greenleaf in Newfoundland, by Christie (p. 232) and Grieg in Scotland (*Folk-Songs of the North-East,* p. xciv), and by Baring-Gould (p. 56) in England. Although we collected the song only from Yankee John, we know that it was sung by Charles Tillett on the Outer Banks of North Carolina. After his death Mrs. Tillett told us that her husband used to sing "Bonny Bunch of Roses-O." Mrs. Galusha told us that her father used to sing "that song about the roses."

Laws says that the roses are England, Ireland, and Scotland, and notes that traditional singers always took great pains to stress this meaning.

Kenneth Peacock says, "The Napoleon of this song is the Emperor's son by his second marriage to Marie Louise of Austria . . . [who] was kept a virtual prisoner in the Austrian Court at Vienna . . . he died of TB at the age of 21." He notes a broadside "patterned after older broadsides, called 'The Bunch of Rushes.'"

See: Creighton, *Songs and Ballads from Nova Scotia,* 140; Greenleaf, 170; Huntington, 207; Laws, *ABBB,* J-5, 131; Mackenzie, 188; Peacock, Vol. 3, 988

THE BONNY BUNCH OF ROSES-O

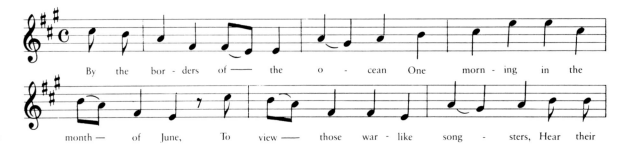

By the bor-ders of — the o - cean One morn-ing in the month — of June, To view — those war - like song - sters, Hear their

50

mer - ry notes and sweet - lie tunes, I — o - ver - heard — a — fe - male talk -
ing, She seemed to be in grief and woe, Con - vers - ing with young
Bon - a - parte Con - cern - ing the bon - ny bunch of ros - es - o.

When next I saw Napoleon,
Down on his bended knees was he,
Asking the pardon of his mother,
Who granted it most mournfully.
He says, "I'll take an army
And through tremenjous dangers I will go.
In spite of all the universe
I'll conquer the bonny bunch of roses-o."

"No, Son, don't talk so venturesome,
For England has the hearts of oak.
There's England, Ireland, and Scotland—
Their unity has ne'er been broke.
O Son, think on your father's fate,
On the Isle of St. Helene his body lies low,
And you will soon follow after.
Beware of the bonny bunch of roses-o."

Then he took one hundred thousand men,
And kings likewise to bear his train.
He was so well provided for
He thought to sweep this earth alone.
But when he arrived in Moscow,
He was overpowered by the driven snow.
When Moscow was a-blazing, there
He lost his bonny bunch of roses-o.

"O Mother, now believe me,
For I am on my dying bed.
If I had lived I would have been clever,
But now I droop my weary head.
And when my body lies mouldering,
And weeping willows o'er me grow,
The deeds of great Napoleon
Will sting the bonny bunch of roses-o."

4. Lass of Glenshee   John Galusha, 1941

Many of Yankee John's songs were Irish in origin or sung to an Irish tune, but a few, like this one, were purely Scottish. On this side of the water it has been found in Michigan, Vermont, the Catskills, and on a number of broadsides. Ford and Ord report it from Scotland.

Laws quotes Ord: "I do not know a more popular song than this. It has been sung in nearly every farmhouse, cottage, and bothy in Scotland for the past 70 or 80 years. The author of it was a shoemaker named Andrew Sharpe, a native of Perth, who died there on 5th February, 1817."

See: Cazden I, 113 (with extensive notes); Cazden II, 120; Flanders *VFSB*, 131; Ford, *Vagabond Songs and Ballads of Scotland*, Ser. 1, 12; Gardner, 202; Laws, *ABBB*, O-6, 229; Ord, 75

LASS OF GLENSHEE

One bright summer's morning as the fields they were a-dawning, Bright Phoebus arose and shone over the lee. I espied a fair maid, as I homeward was riding, A-herding her sheep on the braes of Glenshee.

Her cheeks were like the roses, and under them
    was a dimple,
And keen was the blink of her bonny blue ee.
She was neat, tall, and handsome, her voice so
    enchanting,
That my heart soon belonged to the lass of Glenshee.

I stood in amaze, and says, "Aye, bonny lassie,
If you will only consent to go to Jamestown with me,
No other in this world will set foot in my castle,
There none that will go clothed more finer
    than thee."

"Fine carriages you will have for to ride in at leisure.
When the people do speak, they will say 'ma'am'
    unto thee.
Fine servants you will have for to go at your
    bidding.
I will make you my lady, the lass of Glenshee."

"I care not at all for your carriages to ride in,
Nor I don't care at all for your great grandeury.
I would rather be here in my homespun little
    cottage,
A-herding my flocks on the braes of Glenshee."

"Come leave off your nonsense, don't cause me to blunder.
Don't cause all the gentry to laugh at me.
There are many up in numbers, both old and young, yonder,
That are pointing this moment toward the lass of Glenshee."

"Come leave off your nonsense and get on behind me.
As the sun it rolls 'round, my fair bride you will be.
No other in this world will be mistress of my castle!"
She smiled, and consented—I took her with me!

Many years have rolled 'round since we were united,
Many seasons have changed, but there's no change in me.
My love, she's as fair as the robes in the morning
That are hung out to bleach on the hills of Glenshee.

May the lark forget to arise in the morning,
Caledonia's dark waters flow back from the sea,
But never will I, while that I have my senses,
Forget to be kind to the lass of Glenshee.

5. Plains of Baltimore   John Galusha, 1941

This nineteenth-century ballad of Irish emigration with its splendidly happy ending is obviously Irish and speaks in the traditional idiom. It is hard to believe that we have not come across it in any other collection. Harold Thompson told us some years ago that he had never seen or heard it anywhere. Unfortunately we did not ask Yankee John where he had learned it.

PLAINS OF BALTIMORE

It's of a rich mer-chant's daugh-ter —— in Lon-don did re-side. She vowed and swore —— she loved me —— and wished to be —— my bride. She knew the night I was go-ing a-way, she

wrung her hands —— and cried, "O Wil - lie, —— are you go - ing a - way for to leave —— your love —— be - hind?"

"This very night I am ready, along with you
    to go,
If it's even through the Chiney seas or Greenland's
    hills of snow.
I am ready to adventure with you while Atlantic
    billows roar."
And she smiled on fortune's cruelties in the land of
    Baltimore.

It was early next morning, just as the dawn did
    appear,
Our journey we pursued it, me and Eliza dear.
In silk my love was dressed, most rare to behold,
And in her belt her fortune took, ten thousand
    pounds in gold.

When we arrived in Belfast, some hours before it
    was day,
My true love she got ready our passage for
    to pay.
We paid our passage from Belfast, bid adieu to the
    shamrock's shore,
And with a swift and gentle gale we sailed
    for Baltimore.

When we arrived in Baltimore, we took up on
    some plains,
We cleared the timber from the land and soon we
    made it pay.
And now we drink good coffee and tea, both brandy,
    ale, and wine,
And here's success to old Ireland and the girls we
    left behind.

I wrote my father-in-law a letter, as you shall
    plainly see,
That if he was not satisfied, his money I'd send
    to him.
He wrote me back an answer, and this to me did say,
Five thousand more you will receive on your first
    son's birthday.

Now to conclude and finish, my pen I will lay down.
Here's a health to all good-hearted girls through city
    or through town—
Here's a health to all good-hearted girls with riches
    and money in store—
May they prosper now I've finished, on the Plains
    of Baltimore!

6. The St. Albans Murder   John Galusha, 1941

Laws lists this ballad under the title "James McDonald." The story is the one
found in so many murder ballads—"Omie Wise," "Pretty Polly," and "The Wexford
Girl" (which Yankee John sang, No. 7), for instance. James promises Annie, who is
about to bear his child, that he will take her to Longford and marry her. Instead, he
takes her to a lonely place and fatally wounds her. Thinking her dead, he leaves her;

but she is still alive when found the next morning and so tells what was done to her. James is arrested and sentenced to death.

In Creighton and Flanders-Barry the song is listed as an Irish street ballad.

The ballad was recorded for the Library of Congress by Philip Cohen in Ripton, Vermont, in 1941 from the singing of Grandpa Dragon.

Yankee John always put feeling into the singing of his ballads. After singing the last line, "And when I'm on the gallows tree, good Christians for me pray," Yankee John said to us, "I'd pray for him. I'd pray for him to burn in hell!"

See: Creighton, *Songs and Ballads from Nova Scotia*, 42; Flanders-Barry, *NGMS*, 71; Harvard Catalogue, (B) Bebbington, 1x, 150; Laws, *ABBB*, P-38, 270; Library of Congress field recording AFS, 5218 B 1; Ord, 477

THE ST. ALBANS MURDER

Come all — my — good Chris - tians, I pray — you lend an ear, — It's of as foul a mur - der as — ev - er you — did hear, — Con - cern - ing of one Ann O' - Brien who was scarce - ly — six - teen, — Her — beau - ty bright did me de - light un - til Sa - tan temp - ted me. —

* 2nd verse

She being a farmer's daughter, and I a
  merchant's son,
It was down in the town of Longford convenient
  to Athlone.
I kept this fair one's company until I did her
  beguile,
And then to take her precious life I planned it in
  this style.

It was on a Monday's morning, as you shall
  plainly see,
I wrote to her a letter and soon she came to me,
Saying, "Ann, if you will go with me to Longford
  we will go,
And you and I will be married, I'm sure there will
  no one know."

Then she gave her consent and away we went across
  the country fair,
[one line missing]
As I was going to murder her I made her this
  reply,
Saying, "Ann, you will go no further for here you
  have got to die."

"O James, think of my infant and don't give me
  a scare,
Nor don't commit a murder upon this night so
  drear.
I vow to God on my bended knees if you'll only
  spare my life,
That I will no longer trouble you nor endeavor to
  be your wife."

I heeded not her pleading as you will plainly
  know.
With my heavily loaded riding whip her body I
  laid low.
Her blood and brains did descend like rain, and her
  cries would pierce your heart.
I thought that I had her murdered before I did
  depart.

But she was alive next morning just at the dawn
  of day,
When a shepherd's only daughter by chance there
  came that way.
She saw her lying in her gore, and she ran to
  her relief,
Saying, "Anna dear, you are dying, shall I send for
  you the priest?"

A priest was quickly sent for, and the doctor came
  likewise,
And also a detective that went off in disguise.
She knew the road I'd taken, and she placed them
  on my trail,
And a prisoner I was taken and locked up in
  St. Albans jail.

As I lay there awaiting, all for the judgment day,
The stern old judge to sentence me, these words to
  me did say,
"For the murdering of young Ann O'Brien, as you
  shall plainly see,
On the seventeenth day of next August you will
  swing on the gallows tree."

Now my name it's James McDonald, my life and I must part.
For the murder of young Ann O'Brien I am sorry to my heart.
I hope that God will pardon me while on the judgment day,
And when I'm on the gallows tree, good Christians for me pray.

7. The Waxford Girl   John Galusha, 1941

Laws says that "The Wexford Girl," or "Waxford," as Yankee John sang it, is related to "The Oxford Girl," "The Lexington, or Knoxville, Girl," and other ballads of like nature. "The Wexford Girl" is "one of the most widely known ballads in America. . . . About fifty texts of this ballad have been printed from American tradition. . . . Three different broadside versions are available. . . . The oldest of these and presumably the original is 'The Berkshire Tragedy, or The Wittam Miller,' an 18th century broadside included in The Roxburghe Collection" (Harvard University).

See: Laws, *ABBB*, P-35, 104, 267.

THE WAXFORD GIRL

It was in the town — of Wax - ford — where I did live — and dwell, — It was in the town — of Wick - low — I owned a flour — mill. It's there — I met — this Wax - ford girl with her dark and roll - ing eye, I — asked her to — walk out with me, — my wish - es to — com - ply.

* 2nd verse

I went down to her mother's house about eight
      o'clock that night,
I asked her to walk out with me our wedding day
      to appoint.
We walked and talked along the road until we came
      to level ground,
When from the hedge I drew a stake and knocked
      this fair one down.

She fell all onto her bended knees, for mercy she
      did cry.
"O Willie, do not kill me here for I'm not prepared
      to die!"
I heeded not one word she said but I beat her all
      the more,
Until the ground around her was covered o'er
      with gore.

Then I took her by the yellow locks and dragged her
      o'er the ground,
And threw her into the water that runs through
      Waxford town.
Lie there, lie there, you Waxford girl who thought
      to be my bride,
Lie there, lie there, you Waxford girl, to me you'll
      never be tied.

Returning home that evening about twelve o'clock
      at night,
My mother being nervous, she woke all in a fright,
Saying, "Son, dear son, what have you done to
      bloody your hands and clothes?"
And the answer that I made her was bleeding at
      the nose.

I called for a candle to light myself to bed,
Likewise for a handkerchief to tie my aching
      head.
I rolled and I tumbled, no comfort could I find,
For the flames of hell was around me and before my
      eyes did shine.

About three days after, this fair one she was
      found,
A-floating in the river that runs through
      Wicklow town.
And everyone who saw her said she was a beauty
      bright,
Fit for any nobleman, or any lord or knight.

I was taken on suspicion, locked up in Wicklow
      jail.
There was none to intercede for me, no one to go
      my bail.
Her sister swore my life away without either fear
      or doubt,
She swore I was the same young man who took her
      sister out.

Come all you false true-lovers, a warning take
      by me,
Don't never treat your own true love to such
      severity.
For if you do, you sure will rue, and be the same
      as I,
For hanged you'll be all on the tree, and a murderer
      you will die.

8. The Ballad of Blue Mountain Lake   John Galusha, 1939

Yankee John worked at lumbering "in the wintry woods" in his early days, and
when he and Mrs. Galusha were first married she worked with him—as a cook—in
a lumber camp for a few years. She told us she went to school with some of the boys

58

mentioned in this boisterous, wonderfully singable, local ballad about life among the shanty boys. Carl Carmer, who led us to Yankee John, prints the words of Yankee's version in his book, *The Hudson* (1939), and two versions are printed in *The New Green Mountain Songster* (Flanders-Barry), the shorter one from Vermont and the longer one—very similar to Yankee John's—from Glens Falls, New York.

Harold K. Hochschild, in his *Lumberjacks and Rivermen in the Central Adirondacks, 1850–1950* in the chapter on "Township 34," says:

> Township 34 may justly lay sisterly claim to a folk song, "The Rackets Round Blue Mountain Lake," which commemorates the doings of lumberjacks and log drivers just across the line in Township 19. . . . The song probably dates from the 1870s. . . . What is probably the authentic song . . . appeared in *The Hudson* by Carl Carmer. . . . Will and Shang (Dennis) Sullivan, the brothers mentioned in the second stanza, served as members of the crews of W. W. Durant's steamboats during the 1880s. . . . Jimmy Lou, not remembered by any other name, was a tough woodsman from Minerva. Dandy Pat was Patrick Moynehan, then a young lumberjack, who rose to wealth and power. The boss was George Griffin. . . . Bill Mitchell was a well-known Blue Mountain laker. The incomparable Nellie was Ella Plumley, who married her fellow-villager, Walter Hammer.

Carl Carmer, in discussing the song, quotes Yankee John: It "happened over at Blue Mountain Lake near Eagle's Nest and Towahloondah . . . after we'd cut the sides of Big and Little Pisgah mountains. All that stuff come down the Hudson. It's the same tune as some of the lakers used to sing called 'Red Iron Ore' but I tell 'em we was cuttin' trees and singin' it here long before they heard of iron dust near the big lakes." Towahloondah was the Indian name of Blue Mountain, Carl tells us.

The tune, according to Flanders-Barry (p. 178), is "King John and the Abbot of Canterbury," to which "The Little Brown Bulls" also is sung.

See: Carmer, *The Hudson,* 372; "Flanders-Barry, *NGMS,* 176; Hochschild, Chapter 34; Laws, *NAB,* C-20, 156; Thompson, 267 (one stanza)

THE BALLAD OF BLUE MOUNTAIN LAKE

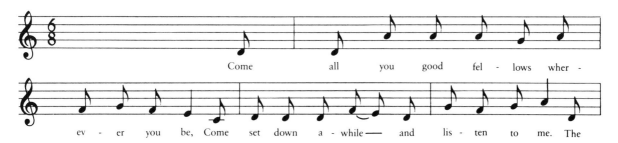

Come all you good fel-lows wher-ev-er you be, Come set down a-while—— and lis-ten to me. The

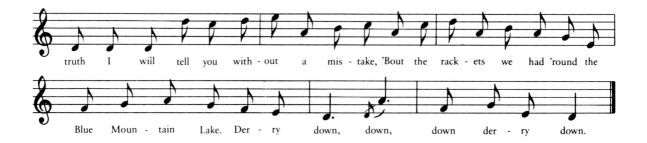

truth I will tell you with-out a mis-take, 'Bout the rack-ets we had 'round the Blue Moun-tain Lake. Der-ry down, down, down der-ry down.

There's the Sullivan brothers and Big Jimmy Lou,
And Old Mose Gilbert and Dandy Pat too.
A good lot of fellows as ever was seen,
And they all worked for Griffin on Township
  Nineteen.
Derry down, down, down derry down.

Bill Mitchell, you know, he kept our shantee,
And as mean a damn man as you ever did see.
He'd lay 'round the shanty from morning to night,
And if a man said a word he was ready to fight.
Derry down, down, down derry down.

One morning 'fore daylight Jim Lou he got mad.
He knocked hell out of Mitchell, and the boys was
  all glad.
And his wife, she stood there, and the truth I will tell,
She was tickled to death to see Mitchell catch hell!
Derry down, down, down derry down.

Bill Potter stood there with a queer-looking grin,
A-shiverin' with fright for fear someone'd
  plug him.
He ran into the shanty a-shakin' with fear,
"They can fight and be damned, I'll not interfere!"
Derry down, down, down derry down.

Old Griffin stood there, the crabby old drake,
A hand in the racket we thought he would take.
When some of the boys came and took him away,
"Becripes," said Old Griffin, "I've nothing to say."
Derry down, down, down derry down.

You can talk of your fashions and styles to be
  seen,
But none can compare with the cook of Nineteen.
She's short, thick, and stout without a mistake,
And the boys call her Nellie, the belle of Long Lake.
Derry down, down, down derry down.

And now my good fellows, adieu to you all,
For Christmas is coming, I'm going to Glens Falls.
And when I get there I'll go out on a spree,
For you know when I've money the divil's in me!
Derry down, down, down derry down.

"Blue Mountain Lake"
Words and Music Collected, Adapted and Arranged by Frank Warner
TRO—© Copyright 1971 and 1984 Melody Trails, Inc., New York, N.Y. Used by Permission

9. The British-American Fight John Galusha, 1946

Yankee John put this song on a disk for us in 1946—the one year that, because of small children in tow, I didn't write down all the words to the recorded songs. Our recording machine wasn't doing too well on that occasion, and when we came to transcribe the words there were difficulties. It was nearly thirty years before we got the whole song transcribed—through the help of our English friend David Jones (a fine singer of traditional songs) who had done some boxing in England in his early years.

The song, also known as "Heenan and Sayers," and "The Brave Benicia Boy" (since Heenan came originally from Benicia, California), relates the story of an epic fight between the champion of England, Tom Sayers, and his challenger from America, John C. Heenan. It took place on April 17, 1860, at Farnborough in Hampshire, and though boxing was illegal in Britain at that time, two special trains for the fighters, their entourages, and hundreds of enthusiasts—including many members of Parliament —left London in the predawn of that day for the site of the match. The fight began at 7 A.M. The usual "rules" were observed: bare knuckles, no holds barred, no time limit. A round ended when a man was down, and the fight ended when one fighter could not get up. This one went on for two hours and twenty minutes, through forty-two grueling rounds, when it was stopped and so ended in a draw. It was the first international heavyweight championship match. It was the last of the bare knuckle fights and the most famous boxing match of modern times.

In 1977, 116 years after the match, Coward McCann and Geoghegan published a book by Alan Lloyd called *The Great Prize Fight,* which describes the era, the fighters, and the event in great and effective detail. In a review of the book in *Newsday,* the Long Island newspaper, William J. Garry says: "Extracting his information from contemporary press accounts, Lloyd does a splendid job of recreating the bloodthirsty swagger of the Victorian prize ring." Yankee John's song, in much more compact form, creates the same effect.

We have a copy of an English version, which is very different, sent to us by our friend Peter Kennedy in Devon. In this connection it is interesting that Laws says: "I was uncertain whether to include this [and two other ballads about prize fights] in *Native American Balladry* or in *American Balladry from British Broadsides* . . . but since the heroes were Americans and since the ballads have been reported from tradition only in America, I have decided to give them here" (p. 239). We now have an English version, but I have left the song with the ballads native to America.

See: Beck, *The Folklore of Maine,* 267; Finger, 48; Hubbard, 362;
Laws, *NAB,* H-20, 240; Rickaby, 177

It was in the mer-ry En - gland, that home of John - ny Bull, Great Brit - ain filled her glass - es —— and filled them brim - ming full. Says, "There's a toast to Drake, —— like - wise to Brit - ons brave, For the cham - pi - ons we are on the land and the wave."

* etc. if one syllable   ** etc. if two syllables

Then up rose Uncle Sam, and he looked far o'er
    the main,
"Is that the British Bull that's a-bellowing again?
Has he so soon forgotten the giant on the plain
That was always playing lightning when his day's
    work was done?"

"Or does he yet remember the Bunker Hill
    of old,
Or once upon Lake Erie with Perry brave
    and bold,
Or the bold charge at Yorktown when we caused
    him for to sigh?
Beware of Yankee muscle, Johnny Bull, mind
    your eyes!"

It was in the merry England, all in the bloom
    of spring,
When Britain's noble champion stood stripped all
    in the ring
To meet our noble Heenan, the galliant son
    of Troy,
To try his British muscle on our bold Benicia boy.

There was two heavy flags that floated o'er the ring—
And the Briton's was the lion, just ready for
    to spring,
And the Yankee's was the eagle, and a noble bird
    she was,
For she carried a bunch of thunderbolts in each of
    her claws.

Now the coppers they were tendered as the milling match began.
To the one on bold Sayers the bets came rolling in,
They fought like noble heroes, till one received a blow,
And the red crimson tide from our Yankee's nose did flow.

"First blood!" cried Johnny, "Let England shout for joy!"
They cheered their British bully whilst our bold Benicia boy
Says, "Let the tiger entertain them," and lightning flashed his eyes,
Saying, "Smile away old England, but Johnny mind your eyes."

The grand round of all, boys, this world has never beat.
He grabbed their English boy, and he hurled him from his feet,
His followers they cheered him as he held him in the air,
And from his grasp he flung him, which made the Britons stare.

Now come all ye jolly young men who'd friends and fortune make,
Come look upon the eagle, and never be afraid.
May our Union stand forever, and our flag will be unfurled,
And the Star Spangled Banner will float 'round the world.

10. The British Soldier (or, The Dying British Sergeant)   John Galusha, 1939

Yankee John's version of this song, usually called "The Dying British Sergeant," is, so far as we can find, the only complete version found in oral tradition. Flanders-Barry in *The New Green Mountain Songster,* print four lines of the song, with a different tune, collected from a Mrs. Ellen Nye Lawrence in Montpelier, Vermont, and add a full text of the words from "a Vermont journal as taken from an old manuscript." The other known versions are on broadsides or ballad prints. It is included in the Isaiah Thomas Collection of early American broadsides in the American Antiquarian Society in Worcester, Massachusetts.

The soldier who here received his "death-lie wound" must have been one of those Englishmen who sympathized with the American fight for freedom in spite of his own loyalty to the crown. It seems to us one of the few Revolutionary War songs (usually so wordy and with a stage flavor) in which the emotions of that time seem real. In 1939 Yankee John told us, "The first time I heard that song Will Munn sang it on the bank of Newcomb Lake fifty years ago."

See: Flanders-Barry, *NGMS,* 118; Laws, *NAB,* dA 29, 258; Thos. Coll., 1, 33

THE BRITISH SOLDIER (or, THE DYING BRITISH SERGEANT)

Come all you good peo-ple, wher-e'er you be, Who walk by the land— or— sail— by the sea, Come lis-ten to the words of a dy-ing man, I think you will— re-mem-ber them. It was in De-cem-ber, the eigh-teen day, When our fleet set sail for A-mer-i-cay, Our drums and trum-pets loud did sound, And then for Bos-ton— we— were bound.

And when to Boston we did come,
We thought by the aid of our British guns
We could make those Yankees own our king,
And daily tribute to him bring.
They said it was a garden place
And that our armies could with ease
Tear down their walls, lay waste their lands,
In spite of all their boasted bands.

We found a garden place indeed,
But in it grew many a bitter weed
Which soon cut off our highest hopes,
And sorely wound[ed] the British troops.

For to our sad and sore surprise
We saw men like grasshoppers rise,
Freedom or death! was all their cry,
Believe, they did not fear to die.

When I received my death-lie wound,
I bade farewell to England's ground.
My wife and children will mourn for me,
Whilst I lie cold in Amerikee.
Fight on! America's noble sons,
Fear not great Britain's thundering guns.
Maintain your rights from year to year,
God's on your side, you need not fear.

"The British Soldier"
Words and Music Collected, Adapted and Arranged by Frank Warner
TRO – © Copyright 1971 and 1984 Melody Trails, Inc., New York, N.Y. Used by Permission

11. The *Cumberland* and the *Merrimac*   John Galusha, 1941

On March 8, 1862, in Hampton Roads (Chesapeake Bay), Virginia, the Confederate warship *Merrimac* (a northern ship captured, rebuilt as an ironclad, and renamed the *Virginia*) arrived off Newport News to meet a federal squadron consisting of the *Cumberland,* the *Congress,* and the *St. Lawrence* (sailing ships), and the steam frigates *Minnesota* and *Roanoke.* The Union ships carried some 200 guns and more than 2,200 men. Forty minutes after the *Merrimac* began her attack, the *Cumberland* sank. There were sixty casualties on the southern side, four hundred on the Union side.

It was a crushing defeat for the Union. But the very next day, March 9, the *Monitor*—the Union ironclad sometimes called "a cheesebox on a raft," arrived from New York and fought the *Merrimac* to a draw. Confederate ironclads were never again a threat to the Union blockade.

Yankee John sang this song to us in 1941. It has been found on broadsides, but as far as we know, only three other times in oral tradition: once by Helen Creighton in Nova Scotia (known there as "Maggie Mac"), and once by Frank C. Brown at Nag's Head, North Carolina. Neither of these versions is clear or complete. A version very similar to Yankee John's (minus the first verse) is included in Irwin Silber's *Songs of the Civil War,* collected by Ellen Stekert from Ezra ("Fuzzy") Barhight—also in upstate New York.

See: Brown, Vol. 2, 530; Cazden II, 85; Creighton, *Songs and Ballads from Nova Scotia,* 282;
Silber, *Songs of the Civil War,* 237

THE *CUMBERLAND* AND THE *MERRIMAC*

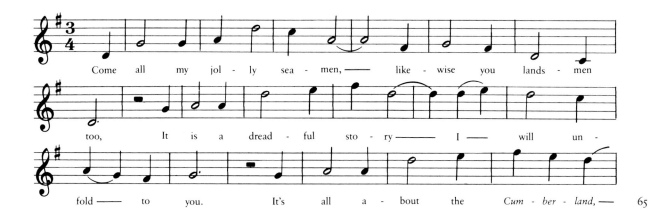

Come all my jol-ly sea-men,—— like-wise you lands-men too, It is a dread-ful sto-ry—— I—— will un-fold—— to you. It's all a-bout the Cum-ber-land,——

the ship so true and brave, And it's man-y's the
loy-al sea-man——— that met a wat-'ry grave.

It was early in the morning, just at the break
of day,
When our good ship the *Cumberland* lay anchored
in the bay,
When the man from on the lookout down to the
rest did say,
"There is something like a housetop, to the larboard
she does lay."

Then our captain took his telescope, and he gazed
far o'er the blue.
Turning 'round he said as follows to his brave and
loyal crew:
"That thing you see over yonder just like a turtle's
back,
Is that cursed Rebel steamer they call the
Merrimac!"

Then our decks were cleared for action, each gun
was pointed true,
But still that Rebel steamer came steaming o'er
the blue.
And on she kept a-coming till no distance did
us part,
When she sent a ball a-humming that stilled the beat
of many's the heart.

In vain we poured our broadsides into her ribs
of steel,
But still no breach was in her, no damage did
she feel.
Up stepped the Rebel commander, in a voice of
thunder spoke,
"Pull down your flying colors, or I'll sink your
Yankee boat!"

Then our captain's eyes did glisten, his face grew pale
with rage,
And in a voice of thunder to the Rebel commander
said,
"My crew is brave and loyal, and by me they will
stand,
And before I'll strike my colors you can sink me and
be damned!"

Then this ironclad she left us a hundred yards
or more,
The screeching and screaming of her balls our
wooden sides she tore.
She struck us right amidships, her ram went crashing
through,
And the waters they came pouring in on the brave
and loyal crew.

Then our captain turned unto his men and unto
    them did say,

"I'll not leave the *Cumberland* while she does ride
    the wave,

It's you, my loyal comrades, may seek your lives
    to save,

But I'll go down with my gallant ship for to meet a
    watery grave."

They swore that they'd not leave her, and manned
    the guns afresh,

And broadside after broadside poured, till the waters
    reached their breasts.

And as they down went sinking, down in the briny
    deep,

The Stars and Stripes still floated from the maintop's
    highest peak!

12. The Days of Forty-Nine   John Galusha, 1941

According to Professor William L. Alderson of Reed College ["The Days of '49, Reprise," *Northwest Folklore* 1 (1965): 5–10], the first appearance of this song in print was in *The Great New Popular Songster* (San Francisco, 1872) where it was described as "sung with great success by [Billy] Emerson's Minstrels at the Alhambra Theatre in San Francisco."

Professor Alderson says, "In the Lomax edited anthology *Folk Song U.S.A.* . . . that work employs a tune collected by Frank Warner from Yankee John Galusha, but of that text only a 'portion,' determinably rather small, came from that source" [Galusha].

Alderson (who happens to be wrong in his assumption, since Yankee John sang us five verses and the chorus) was arguing against the song's being a folk song since he had found it only in fragmentary texts, or in printed texts similar to that printed in the book noted above. Yankee John's version, however, like all his songs, he had learned through oral transmission. Of course he could have learned it from someone who had a printed source.

Professor Alderson says the original song probably was written by banjo artist Charles Bensell (stage name: Charley Rhoades) who died in June 1877. It is "certainly a minstrel song par excellence." It was published in many songsters of the seventies and eighties, including, we are sure, "Old Put's Golden Songster" in its later editions.

"The Days of Forty-Nine" was one of many songs that came out of the Gold Rush days when on Long Island, for instance, not a boat was left that was capable of sailing to Panama or around the Horn. Though it began as a stage song, we think it was kept alive by communities that saw their sons strike out for the West to seek their fortunes, and then saw them come home, often, broke and broken. Old Tom Moore is an example of the returning forty-niner, the disillusioned seeker of that elusive pot of gold. That we found this version of the song in upper New York State shows that the composer told a tale that was real to his hearers.

Folk Songs of the Catskills (Cazden II) has a similar and longer version of the song given to the editors by George Edwards. Cazden's notes further explore the song's history and transmission.

See: Cazden II, 341; Laws, *NAB*, Appendix 3, 277; Lingenfelter, 196; Lomax, *Cowboy Songs,* 378; Lomax, *FSUSA,* 180; Randolph, Vol. 1, 221

I'm old Tom Moore from the bum-mer's shore In the good old gold-en days. They
call me a bum-mer and a gin sot too, But what care I for praise? I
wan-der 'round from town to town Just like a rov-ing sign, And the
Chorus
peo-ple all say, "There goes Tom Moore Of the days of for-ty-nine!" In the
days of old, in the days of gold, How oft-times I re-pine For the
days of old when we dug up the gold, In the days of for-ty-nine.

There was Nantuck Bill, I knew him well,
A fellow that was fond of tricks.
At a poker game he was always there
And heavy with his bricks.
He would ante up and draw his cards
And go in a hat-full blind.
In a game of bluff Bill lost his breath
In the days of forty-nine.
          Chorus

There was New York Jake, a butcher boy,
He was always getting tight.
And every time that he'd get full
He was always hunting a fight.
One night he run up against a knife
In the hands of old Bob Kline,
And over Jake they held a wake,
In the days of forty-nine.
          Chorus

"The Days of Forty-Nine"
Collected, Adapted and Arranged by Frank Warner, John A. Lomax and Alan Lomax
TRO—© Copyright 1947 (renewed 1975) Ludlow Music, Inc., New York, N.Y. Used by Permission

There was poor old Jess, the old lame cuss,
He never would relent.
He never was known to miss a drink
Or ever spend a cent.
At length old Jess, like all the rest
Who never would decline,
All in his bloom went up the flume
In the days of forty-nine.
            Chorus

There was roaring Bill from Buffalo,
I never will forget—
He would roar all day and he'd roar all night,
And I guess he's a-roaring yet.
One night he fell into a prospecter's hole
In a roaring bad design,
And in that hole roared out his soul,
In the days of forty-nine.
            Chorus

13. General Scott and the Veteran   John Galusha, 1941

    This is another of Yankee John's historical ballads which, to our knowledge, has
not been found elsewhere in oral tradition. The only reference we have found is in a
small songster arranged and edited by Frank Moore. Moore's Foreword says: "This
volume contains a selection from the best political and personal ballads that have appeared since the commencement of the present Rebellion. They have been gathered
from various sources, Rebel as well as National, and are presented to the reader without note or comment."
    General Winfield Scott was a hero of the War of 1812, a native son of Virginia
who chose to side with the Union in the War between the States. According to Moore,
"Gen. Scott and the Veteran" was written by Bayard Taylor on May 13, 1861. He prints
ten verses. Yankee John gave us six, in somewhat different order, but they tell the
same story.
    In this same little book (which has only words, no music), on page 42, is "Song
on Gen. Scott" from a Rebel's point of view. It is by "N.B.I. Tune: 'Poor Old Horse,
Let Him Die.'" The first verse (of four) reads:

    Virginia had a son
    Who gathered up some fame.
    He many battles won
    And thereby won a name.
    But now he is growing old,
    And nature doth decay.
    Virginia she does scold—
    And all can hear her say:
            Poor old Scott, let him die.

See: Moore, *Personal and Political Ballads*, 105   69

An old and crip-pled vet-er-an to the War De-part-ment came. He saw the chief who led him through man-y's the field of pain, The chief who shout-ed, "For-ward!"—wher'-er our ban-ner rose, And held the Stars and Stripes a-loft—be-hind the fly-ing foes.

"I'm ready, General, so you'll let a post to me
    be given,
Where Washington can see me as he looks from
    highest heaven.
And say to Putnam at his side, or maybe General
    Wayne,
There goes old Billy Johnson who fought at Lundy's
    Lane."

"If he should fire on Pickens, let the colonel in
    command
Put me out on the rampart with a flagstaff in
    my hand.
No odds how hot the cannon smoke or how the
    bullets may fly,
I will hold them Stars and Stripes aloft and hold
    'em till I die."

"I'm not so weak but I can strike, and I've got a
    good old gun.
Put me in range of traitors' hearts, and I'll pick
    'em one by one!
Your mini rifles and such arms I ain't worthwhile
    to try,
I couldn't get the hang of them nor keep my
    powder dry."

"But when the fire is hottest, just before the
    traitors fly,
When shells and balls are screeching and bursting
    in the sky,
If any stray shot should hit me and lay me on
    my face,
My soul would go to Washington, and not to
    Arnold's place!"

"God bless you, Comrade," said the chief, "God bless your loyal heart.
There are younger men in the field would claim to have their part.
We will plant our sacred banner in each rebellious town,
And woe henceforth to any hand that dares to pull it down."

14. The Irish Sixty-Ninth   John Galusha, 1941

Yankee John's antecedents were Irish, though they were early arrivals in the New
World, unlike those of most of his Irish neighbors, many of whom emigrated because
of the potato famine of the 1840s. Because of his neighbors, and his forebears, he knew
many an Irish song, a number of them being concerned with the American Civil War.
One of Yankee John's most notable contributions to our singing repertoire was a song
of which he could remember only one verse. This, in itself, was most unusual. It appears, with its tune later in this book (No. 25) but since it is so short we quote it here
because of its tribute to the Irish:

This day will be remembered by America's noble sons!
If it hadn't been for Irishmen, what would our Union done?
It was hand-to-hand we fought 'em, all in the broiling sun.
Stripped to the pants we did advance in the Battle of Bull Run!

In August of 1955 we had a letter from a friend named Thomas Larremore, a
graduate of Yale, a professor, a musician and glee club conductor, long interested in
our song collecting. He wrote:

Dear Frank,
    Just this evening I have stumbled upon something that seems so important that I
must pass it along to you . . . glancing again through Prof. Robert Taft's book, *Photography and the American Scene*, p. 228, I came across the following very significant passage, describing the experiences of the Union photographers, particularly Matthew Brady,
at the first battle of Bull Run (Manassas, I suppose, to you): "Brady has shown more pluck
than many of the officers and soldiers who were in the fight. He went—not exactly like
the 'Sixty-ninth,' stripped to the pants—but with his sleeves tucked up and his big camera
directed upon every point of interest in the field."
    The significant passage, of course, is "stripped to the pants," and the reference . . . to
the "Sixty-ninth." What all this means to me is that "stripped to the pants" may . . . turn
out to come from some regiment bearing the numerals "69th" that took part in the Battle
of Bull Run. One such strong possibility is the old 69th of New York, the "Fighting Irish"
regiment, now the 369th.

When he wrote that letter Tom Larremore was not familiar with Yankee John's "The Irish Sixty-Ninth," or he would have been even more interested. We have not been able to find any specific reference to this song.

In reading the songs about the Irish fighting for the Union the feeling is strong that the Union is and will be a friend to Ireland, that the English may come in against the Union, in which case the Irish-American would be fighting against the English. In any case, the Irish are learning how to fight, and that would be useful in a future war against England. This all could be a reflection of soldiers' feelings, or it might be the projection of actors' and songwriters' feelings, or it might be just an attempt to rouse the Irish public with propaganda from the stage.

See: Wright, *Irish Immigrant Ballads and Songs* for similar songs, such as "The Gallant 69th Regiment," "The New York Volunteers," "Dedicated to the Brave 69th," and "Colonel Owen's Gallant Irish Volunteers," etc.

THE IRISH SIXTY-NINTH

Ye Er-in sons of hill and plain, Come lis-ten to my fee-ble strain, Per-haps you'll think it all a dream, Though ev-'ry line is true. I'll sing to you of our long cam-paign Through sum-mer sun and win-ter's rain, To Rich-mond's gates and back a-gain, I will re-late to you.

It was in August, sixty-one,
When Colonel Owens took command,
And brought us into Maryland
Where let it rain or shine.
He drilled us—every day we rose
To learn us how to thrash our foes,
And more than once they felt the blows
Of the Irish Sixty-ninth.

In February, sixty-two,
While passing in a grand review,
We were told our foes we would pursue
And Richmond overthrow.
To Washington we went straight way,
And sailed in steamers down the bay
Until we were forced next day
To land at Fort Monroe.

72

At Hampton then we camped around,
Until brave Little Mac came down
And ordered us up to Yorktown
Our strength there to combine.
And there we worked both night and day,
And drove the Rebel hordes away,
And marching through the town next day
Went the gallant Sixty-ninth.

From Yorktown then we sailed away,
And landed at West Point next day,
And gaily marched along the way,
And camped among the pines.
And there we stayed three weeks or more,
Until we heard the cannons roar
And musketry come like a shower
Along the Rebel lines.

Then double quick away we went,
Across the river we were sent
To drive the Rebels back we meant,
No man fell out of line.
Where Philadelphia's noble sons
Had nobly spotted Pickett's guns,
And when away the Rebels run,
Cheered the gallant Sixty-ninth.

Then on Antietam's field again
We boldly faced the iron rain.
Some of our boys upon the plain
They found a bloody grave,

Where our brave general, Little Mac,
Made boastingly to clear the track
And to send the ragged Rebels back
Across the Potomac's waves.

At Fairoaks then long weeks we lay,
Had picket fighting night and day,
I've seen our brave boys borne away
And some in death grow pale.
And in that seven days' fight, going back
Over bloody fields we left our track
Where other regiments they fell back,
We stood as at Glendale.

Next day out on the battle field,
Old veterans they were forced to yield,
For the Rebels had a stone wall shield
Protecting front and rear.
[They gave us constant] shot and shell.
It was like the gaping jaws of hell,
And many's the brave man round us fell.
We boldly did our share.

O'Keen, our colonel, nobly stood
Where the grass was turning red with blood,
And growing to a crimson flood.
We still kept in our line,
And many got a bloody shroud,
Though Philadelphia's sons were proud
And sang of deeds in praises loud
Of the gallant Sixty-ninth.

15. The Irishtown Crew   John Galusha, 1939

This is one of the first songs Yankee John sang to us on our first visit with him.[5]
Yankee John's family was Irish, but they came to America in the 1700s. Yankee's grand-

    5. There is an article on Yankee John and "The Irishtown Crew" (and the song itself) in the *New York Folklore Quarterly* (June 1966): 110, by Frank and Anne Warner.

father fought in the War of 1812. This is a purely local song, but purely Irish too—in the style of "Uncle Tom Cobleigh and All."

Irishtown, in 1939, was a deserted village some three miles from Minerva, but it was obviously flourishing at the time the song was written, and when we last saw it in 1975 it was rebuilt and flourishing once more, full now of respected and respectable families. But young Irishmen were noted for their willingness to go on a spree now and then, and they no doubt brought the trait over the water. The song may show a bit of wishful thinking too, but that is part of the fun.

Ratigan's was a bar in Irishtown where the adventures of the evening began. "The Corners" was another pub run by a blind man named Gibney. Yankee John said that Gibney, since he could not see, measured out the whiskey by putting his thumb over the edge of the glass and pouring up to his thumb. This explains the last two lines of the song.

In St. Mary's churchyard in Irishtown we have found gravestones bearing the names of a dozen or more of the boys named in the song.

THE IRISHTOWN CREW

On the first day of A-pril, I'll nev-er for-get, The I-rish-town boys ——— at Rat-i-gan's met. They filled up their glass-es and swore sol-emn-ly That that ver-y day they'd go out on a spree! Sing

Chorus

fol the dol lad-die Ri tol the dol lad-die Sing fol the dol lad-die Ri tol the lo day!

74

There was Holland and Blucher and Williams
and Brinn,
And one Mack and Ernie that drives the gray
team.
There was Isaac and Letty and Paddy and Joe,
And one Micky Connors that lived down below.
Chorus

They filled themselves up on Ratigan's beer,
And straight for the Corners they quickly did
steer,
Resolved before morning they'd finish their spree
And spend a few hours with young Tommy Mee.
Chorus

Arriving at the Corners, they met more of the boys:
There was Early and Duffy and Jimmy McCoy,
Yankee, Neely, Cub, and Tom Flynn,
Joe Burto, Pete Lindsay, and one Danny Lynn.
Chorus

There was Nelson Burto, a dear friend of mine,
He used to go courting one black Angeline,
With Tucker the mason that plastered our wall,
And Black Pete Mitchell, the pride of them all.
Chorus

Money being plenty, the drinks they went 'round,
And glass after glass of the spirits went down.
In less than an hour not a man was in sight
But was drunker'n a fiddler and wanted to fight!
Chorus

Tucker in the kitchen his way he did make,
There sit Wallace Plumly, all the way from
Long Lake.
Says Gibney, "I'd have you my house to respect,
This gentleman's here my house to protect."
Chorus

"I ask no odds of your house, I'd have you to know,
For this Long Lake pup you have up here for show."
So Plumly he quickly jumped out on the floor,
And Tucker he kicked him right bang through
the door!
Chorus

Then out in the street Plumly run like a pup
You couldn't see his coattails for the dust he
kicked up,
Saying, "I think myself I got in the wrong pew,
For the divil himself couldn't match such a crew!"
Chorus

Gibney he bolted and barred up his door,
For love or for money wouldn't sell one drop more.
"You're all drunk now, and you'll get no more."
When slam! went the panels right out of his door!
Chorus

Some built a big bonfire to keep themselves warm,
And others crawled off into Butler's barn,
And some under Sullivan's shed went to sleep,
And them that was *too* drunk, laid out in the street.
Chorus

For to conclude and to finish my song,
Here's a health to Pat Ratigan, may he live long.
To hell with you, Gibney, you're blind and can't see,
And you'll never thumb no more whiskey for me!
Chorus

16. The Jam on Gerrion's Rock John Galusha, 1941

Yankee John had helped break many a log jam in his day, and he sang this song with feeling. It tells the story of six young Canadian boys (their foreman being James Monroe) who, in spite of a general belief that it was wrong to work on Sunday, undertook to break a jam and were all killed in the attempt. Clara Benson, Monroe's sweetheart, dies of grief shortly thereafter and is buried beside him near the river.

In *Lumbering Songs from the North Woods,* Edith Fowke says that this is the "most widespread of shanty songs."

Laws, in *NAB,* says that "one might suppose falling trees and branches would be the great hazard of lumbering, but I have found only one traditional ballad on that subject. . . . Death by drowning was apparently much more common, to judge by the ballads, in eleven of which lumbermen met that fate. The most widely known of these [is] 'The Jam on Gerry's Rock.'"

Although the ballad seems to recount an actual event and gives the name of the principal character and the location of the tragedy, scholars have not been able to find the actual place or date of the occurrence. Fannie Hardy Eckstorm spent more than twenty years (1904–27) in a search for the origin of the ballad without definite results. See her chapter "The Pursuit of a Ballad Myth" in *Minstrelsy of Maine,* pp. 176–98.

We collected another, very similar, version of this ballad from Steve Wadsworth in Northville, New York.

Folk Songs of the Catskills (Cazden II) prints three versions of the ballad and has extensive notes.

See: Brown, Vol. 2, 501; Cazden I, 6; Cazden II, 46; Doerflinger, 238; Eckstorm, 87; Fowke, *Lumbering Songs from the North Woods,* 98; Laws, *NAB,* C-1, 147 (long list of sources); Thompson, 259

THE JAM ON GERRION'S ROCK

Come all you bold shan-ty boys, wher-ev-er you may be, I

hope you'll pay at-ten-tion and lis-ten un-to me. It's

of some jo-vial shan-ty boys, so man-y true and—— brave, All
at the jam on Ger-ri-on's Rock they—— met with a wat-'ry grave.

It was on one Sunday's morning as you will
plainly see,
Our logs were piling mountains high, we could not
keep them clear.
When at length our boss cried out, "My boys, with
hearts void of fear
We will break that jam on Gerrion's rock and for
Saginaw town we'll steer."

Some of them were willing, whilst others did hang
back,
All for to work on Sunday, they did not think it was
right.
Until six bold Canadian boys did volunteer and go
For to break the jam on Gerrion's rock with their
foreman, young Monroe.

They had not rolled off many logs when the boss
unto them did say,
"I would have you to be on your guard for this jam
will soon give way."
No sooner had he spoke those words when the jam
did break and go,
And it washed away those six bold youths and the
foreman, young Monroe.

When the rest of the shanty boys those sad tidings
came to hear,
To search for their brave comrades for the river they
did steer.

And one of the headless bodies found to their sad
grief and woe
All cut and mangled on the beach lay the foreman,
young Monroe.

They took him from the water, smoothed down his
raven curls.
There was found some among them whose cries did
rend the earth.
There was one found among them, a girl from
Saginaw town,
Her moans and cries did pierce the skies, for her
true love was drowned.

Young Clary was a noble girl, likewise a raftsman's
friend.
Her mother was a widow dwelled by the river side.
The wages of her own true love the boys to her did
pay,
And a larger subscription she received from the
shanty boys next day.

Come all ye bold shanty boys, for your comrades
now pray.
They buried him quite decently all on the first of
May.
On a tall pine tree by the river side there stands in
letters to show
The day and the date of the drowning of our hero,
young Monroe.

Young Clary did not serve life long, to her sad
    trouble and woe.
In less than six months after, she was called
    to go,
In less than six months after, she was called
    to go,
And her dying request was granted, to be buried by
    young Monroe.

Now come all my bold shanty boys who wish to go
    that way,
By those two little mounds by the river side there
    stands that tall pine tree.
The shanty boys cut the words all around, two lovers
    there lay low:
"Her name was Clary Benson, and her true love,
    Jack Monroe."

17. James Bird   John Galusha, 1941

This long and tragic ballad about a brave fighter who was nevertheless shot for desertion—after the Battle of Lake Erie in 1814—was written by Charles Miner and published in his newspaper, *The Gleaner,* at Wilkes-Barre, Pennsylvania, in 1814.

Laws says that "this ballad is far from extinct. The Library of Congress collection, for example, contains recordings made between 1937 and 1939 by singers in New Jersey, Ohio, Michigan, and California." He quotes Professor Franz Rickaby (p. xxxv):

> Mr. Miner was a Congressman, an editor, a man of affairs, of good education and possessing considerable literary sense—all of which qualities would normally be set down as inimical to any feeling for popular balladry. Yet in "James Bird" he composed a ballad which clung in the hearts of the American folk for nearly a century; a ballad which, in my experience at least, varies less in its countless folk-versions than any other popular song. No detail in it has seemed superfluous, no stanza unnecessary, no sentiment false to the emotional realities of the thousands who heard, learned, sung, and believed it.

Harold Thompson gives both the folk explanation of Bird's fate and the official one. He says the song "follows rather closely Bird's last letter to his parents, in which he makes no excuses but warns others to avoid his fate. It was a gallant, undisciplined, and penitent young man who was made to serve as example to troops which had the frontier's dislike for regimentation."

Yankee John did not comment on this song as he did on many others, but he knew it all.

Seven verses of this ballad are in *Folk Songs of the Catskills* (Cazden II) with notes.

See: Belden, 296; Cazden II, 67; Laws, *NAB*, A-5, 41, 121; Thomson, 344;
Thompson and Cutting, 125

Sons of plea - sure, — lis - ten to — me. —
And ye — daugh - ters too, give — ear. You a sad and
mourn - ful sto - ry — As was ev - er — told shall hear.
*2nd verse
**2nd verse

Hull, you know, his troops surrendered
And defenseless left the west.
Then our forces quick assembled
The invader to resist.

Among the troops that marched to Erie
Were the Kingston volunteers.
Captain Thomas them commanded
To protect our west frontiers.

Tender were the scenes of parting,
Mothers wrung their hands and cried,
Maidens wept their loves in secret,
Fathers strove their tears to hide.

But there's one among that number
Tall and graceful in his mien,
Firm his step, his look undaunted,
Ne'er a bolder youth was seen.

One sweet kiss he stole from Mary,
Craved his mother's prayers once more,

Pressed his father's hand, then left him
For Lake Erie's distant shore.

Mary tried to say, "Farewell, James,"
Waved her hand but nothing spoke,
Goodbye Bird, may heaven protect you
From the rest at parting broke.

Soon they came where noble Perry
Had assembled all his fleet.
There the gallant Bird enlisted
Hoping soon the foe to meet.

Where is Bird? The battle rages.
Is he in the strife or no?
Now the cannon roar tremendous.
Dare he meet the furious foe?

Aye, behold him, see, with Perry,
In the selfsame ship they fight.
Though his messmates fall around him
Nothing can his soul affright.

79

But behold a ball has struck him,
See the crimson current flow!
"Leave the deck!" exclaimed brave Perry.
"No," cried Bird, "I will not go."

"Here on deck I took my station,
Here will Bird his colors fly.
I'll stand by you, noble Captain,
Till we conquer or we die."

So he fought, though faint and bleeding,
Till our Stars and Stripes arose.
Victory having crowned our efforts
All triumphant o'er our foes.

And did Bird receive a pension?
Was he to his friends restored?
No, nor ever to his bosom
Clasped the maid his heart adored.

But there came most dismal tidings
From Lake Erie's distant shore.
Better if poor Bird had perished
'Midst the battle's awful roar.

"Dearest Parents," said this letter,
"This will bring sad news to you.
Do not mourn your first beloved,
Though this brings his last adieu."

"I must suffer for deserting
From the brig *Niagory* [Niagara].
Read this letter, Brothers, Sisters,
'Tis the last you'll have from me."

Sad and gloomy was the morning
Bird was ordered out to die.
Where's the breast not dead to pity
But for him will heave a sigh?

Oh, he fought so brave at Erie,
Freely bled and nobly dared.
Let his courage plead for mercy,
Let his precious life be spared.

See him march, hear his fetters,
Harsh they clank upon the ear.
But his step is firm and manly
For his breast ne'er harbored fear.

See he kneels upon his coffin,
Sure his death can do no good.
Spare him! Hark, O God, they've shot him!
Oh, his bosom streams with blood.

Farewell, Bird, farewell forever,
Friends and home he'll see no more.
But his mangled corpse lies buried
On Lake Erie's distant shore.

18. Jamie Judge (or, Bonshee River)   John Galusha, 1941

This elegy for a young woodsman who, like many of his compatriots, died in a log jam, was a favorite of Yankee John's and of ours. Referring to the last verse, Yankee said, "I can remember when the boys wore their hair way down on their neck." At the time he said that—1941—it seemed strange indeed. He told us, "I sang this song in a bar room once, and there was a man there named McDonald, from Canady. He looked kind of downhearted, seemed to be thinking of something, so I asked him what was the matter. He says, 'It's that song you just sang. Jamie Judge was my nephew, and I raised him.'"

Laws calls the song "Jimmie Judd (The Beau Shai River)" and mentions E. C. Beck, Barry, and Gardner. Beck suggests that the ballad was taken to Michigan from New Brunswick or Maine, but Barry (whose version, like Yankee John's, mentions the Bonshee River), says the river referred to is the Bonnichere (Bonne Chère?) in Renfrew County, Ontario.

See: Beck, *Songs of the Michigan Lumberjacks*, 145; *Bulletin*, No. 10, 20; Gardner, 277; Laws, *NAB*, C-4, 149

JAMIE JUDGE (or, BONSHEE RIVER)

It was on yon Bonshee River
One mile below Renfrew,
Where we went out to break a jam
And with the jam went through.
In vain was his activity
His precious life to save,
In spite of his exertions
He met with a watery grave.

It was early the next morning
The drivers all did join
To go in search of this young man
His body for to find.
They searched the deep on every side
Where the seething torrents fly,
Till a fisher boy, as I've been told,
His floating corpse espied.

"Jamie Judge"
Collected and Arranged by Frank Warner
TRO—© Copyright 1959 and 1984 Hollis Music, Inc., New York, N.Y. Used by Permission

When they took him from the water,
It would grieve your heart full sore,
To see his handsome features
By the rocks all cut and tore,
To see so fine a young man
Cut down in all his bloom.
It was on yon Bonshee River
He met with an awful doom.

To see his aged father,
It would grieve your heart full sore,
And to see his aged mother
While her gray hair she tore.

To see the girl that loved him
Bowed down with grief full sore,
Saying, "He was my only true love,
No other will I adore."

This young man's name was James A. Judge,
I mean to let you know.
I mean to sound his praises
Wherever I do go.
His hair hung down in ringulets,
His skin was white as snow,
And he was admired by all the girls
Wherever he did go.

19. Jump Her, Juberju John Galusha, 1939
20. The _Bigler_ Florentine Vincent, 1948

Our good friend Marjorie Porter, the North Country historian and collector who knew Yankee John and had more time to spend with him than we did (our vacations—our only song-collecting time—were all too short), has told us that Yankee, as a lumberjack on the Boreas, the Hudson, and the Beaver rivers, aimed for the highest wages, which meant being in charge of a "jam boat." The pay for this job in the late 1800s was $4 a day, compared to shore pay of $1.50 a day. A bowsman, a steersman, and an oarsman manned the heavy skiffs which were used when a log jam could not be broken by men working from the river banks. The bowsman, who held a bow pole seven or eight feet long with a hook on the end, would jump from the boat onto the jam, striking his hook into the key log to pry it loose. Then, he hoped, he would have time to jump back into the boat.

One time, Yankee John told Mrs. Porter, there was a jam on the Boreas River at Dan Lynch Falls. Yankee took his boat up close and had almost finished his job, he thought, when one log shot up and knocked an oar out of its socket. The boat tipped over and floated away downstream. Yankee John said "he swam that falls for nearly half a mile, fighting every inch of the way to a sand bar at the foot of the falls where another jam had formed." He knew he had to get ashore, so he swam for it and jumped onto the logs. But when he looked back at the foaming mass of water down which he had fought his way, his knees buckled and he fell flat and had to be carried off the jam.

This song, which Yankee sang with great gusto, comes from "The _Bigler_," or "The _Bigler_'s Crew," a song about a schooner on the Great Lakes, and its slow trip from Milwaukee to Buffalo. The Lomaxes, in _Our Singing Country_, print a version from

Captain Axel Trueblood, who told them, "I've walked the old *Bigler*'s decks many times. . . . She was supposed to be the slowest vessel in the fleet." They also quote Ivan H. Walton of the University of Michigan: "The 'juberju' mentioned in the chorus has been variously described as the jib boom, the raffee yard, and the crossfire, upon which the sailors at times climbed to ride the halliard down to the deck." The "rigging" mentioned in the last verse was carried over to Yankee John's song, since there is no rigging in a lumberman's boat, unless the term is taken to mean "gear."

In our file of clippings about folk songs we find an article by Horace Reynolds, who wrote many fine articles on this subject, entitled "Some Folksong Mysteries" from the *Christian Science Monitor* of April 25, 1945. It includes this paragraph: "Juba, a common classical name for a Negro, became also the word for a noisy, rollicking dance formerly popular with the Negroes. As a word for the dance, it became corrupted to juber-jew, Jubal Jew, and, in a phrase from a lumberjack ballad, still another syllable is added: 'Watch her! Catch Her! / Jump in her jujubaju!'"

The Lomaxes, in their *American Ballads and Folk Songs* (published seven years before *Our Singing Country*), pp. 28–29, print two short versions of a song called "Ten Thousand Miles From Home." Version "A" they say, was sung by a "seventy-one-year-old ex-jailbird Negro in New Orleans." Version "B" is a Kentucky version from Harvey H. Fuson's *Ballads of the Kentucky Highlands.* They are both hobo songs about "riding the next freight train." Surprisingly, the chorus to "A" is:

Watch her an' catch her an' jump her ju-ber-ju
Release the brakes and let 'er go,
The bums will ride her through.

Ewen MacColl, in *The Singing Island,* includes a song called "The Dogger Bank," which he says is "almost certainly an English sailor's parody of an American . . . song." This is the chorus:

So watch her, trigger, the proper ju-ber-ju
Give her sheet and let her rip
We're the boys to put her through,
You ought to have seen us rally,
The wind a-blowing free
A passage from the Dogger Bank
To Great Grimsby.

The thirteen-stanza version of "The *Bigler*" which follows the Galusha song was given to us in 1948 by Florentine Vincent of Cape Vincent, New York. She was eighty-one then and was called "Tinnie" by everyone who knew her. She said that Cal McKee, the captain, was from Clayton, New York.

See: Creighton, *Maritime Folk Songs,* 141; Laws, NAB, D-8, 165 ("The *Bigler*'s Crew");
Library of Congress field recordings 2323 B 2, 2324 A 1; Lomax, *FSUSA,* 148;
Lomax, *Our Singing Country,* 220; Rickaby, 168; Sandburg, *The American Songbag,* 175

JUMP HER, JUBERJU

He said he'd been a boat-man for six-teen years or more, He'd run the Hud-son Riv-er where the thun-der-ing tor-rents pour, He dread nor feared no dan-ger while in his own ca-noe, He'd run the Hud-son Riv-er and the In-di-an Riv-er too.

Chorus

Watch her, catch her, jump her, ju-ber-ju, Give her the wind and let her go if Joe can shove her through! You ought to heard 'em howl-in' as they went a-float-in' by, With a face the col-or of snow, my boys, and a tear in ev-ery eye!

It was on a Sunday morning just at the hour
   of ten,
Joe Thomas and his boat crew their business did
   begin.
He slammed his boat against the jam and split her
   bow in two,
And soon she filled with water and washed away
   his crew!
   Chorus

I guess she done some business that kept him busy
   there,
For she turned a handsome somersault and her bow
   stood in the air!
The current was swift and nimble, from the jam she
   swept away,
And spite of all that Joe could do for the cellar she
   made away.
   Chorus

He'd bothered Norton all the spring to let him run
   the boat,
I guess he got his fill of her when from him she
   did float.
For his boat lays on the bottom, and her rigging's
   cast away,
Joe's breaking jams along the shore for a dollar 'n'
   a half a day!
   Chorus

THE *BIGLER*

Now my friends, if you will listen, I will sing you
   a little song.
I'm sure it will please you, and I'll not detain
   you long.
At Milwaukee, in October, where I chanced to
   get a sight
In the timber drover *Bigler,* a-hailing from Detroit.

   Chorus
   Watch 'er, catch 'er, jump up in a juber-ju,
   Give 'er sheet and let her go, we're the boys to
      crowd her through.
   You ought to have seen us howling, the wind
      a-blowing free,
   On our passage down to Buffalo from
      Milwaukee.

It was a Friday morning about the hour of ten,
The *Robert Emmet* towed us into Lake Michigan.
We set sail where she left us in the middle of the fleet,
And the wind was to the southward, so we had to
   give her sheet.
   Chorus

At night the wind had hauled around which blew
      both stiff and strong,
And swiftly through Lake Michigan the *Bigler*
   plowed on.
And far before her foaming bows the fiery waves
   would fling,
With every stitch of canvas set, her course was wing
   and wing.
   Chorus

85

But the wind it hauled ahead before we reached the
   Manitous,
And two and a half a day just suited the *Bigler*'s
   crew.
From there unto the Beavers we steered her
   full by,
We steered her to the wind just as close as she
   would lie.
   Chorus

We made Skillagallee and Waugeshanks, the entrance
   to the strait,
We might have passed the fleet ahead if they'd hove
   to and wait.
But we drove them on before us, the handiest you
   ever saw,
Clear down to Lake Huron from the Straits of
   Mackinac. [pronounced Mackinaw]
   Chorus

When on Lake Huron we passed Presque Isle, and
   then we bore away,
And shortly we passed the Isle of Thunder Bay.
Across Saginaw Bay the night was awful dark,
We kept a good lookout ahead for the light of Point
   a-Barque.
   Chorus

We made one mile and kept in sight of Michigan's
   east shore,
A-booming for the river, as we'd oftimes done
   before.
When off Port Huron Light, our anchors we
   let go,
And the *Sweepstakes* came along and took the *Bigler*
   in tow.
   Chorus

The *Sweepstakes* took eight of us, and all of us fore
   and aft,
She towed us down on Lake St. Claire and stuck us
   on the flat.

86

She parted the *Hunter*'s towline, trying to give us
   some relief,
And the *Bigler* went astern and smashed into the
   Maple Leaf.
   Chorus

Oh, the tug she left us, outside the river light,
Lake Erie to roam and the blustering winds to
   fight.
She let go our towline, and we paddled our own
   canoe,
Her nose pointing for the dummy on her way to
   Buffalo.
   Chorus

We made the O, flew past Long Point, the wind
   blew fresh and free,
We hauled along the Canada shore, Port Colburn on
   our lee.
What's that looms in the distance? We all knew as
   we drew near,
For like a blazing star shone the light on Buffalo
   pier.
   Chorus

And now we all are safe in Buffalo Creek at last,
And under Read's elevator the *Bigler* she's made fast,
And in Tim Doyle's saloon we'll take a social
   glass,
For we are jolly shipmates, and we'll let the bottle
   pass.
   Chorus

We soon received our papers from our skipper
   Cal McKee,
And with our baggage jumped ashore, but not for
   on a spree,
For Garson's we started, where we arrived in quiet
   repose,
And the boys they rigged us out in a splendid suit
   of clothes.
   Chorus

Oh, now my song is ended, and I hope it pleases you.
Here's to the *Bigler,* her officers, and crew.
I hope she'll sail till fall, in command of Cal McKee,
Between the ports of Buffalo and Milwaukee.
Chorus

21. The Ballad of Montcalm and Wolfe   John Galusha, 1940, 1941, 1946

This ballad (more commonly known as "Brave Wolfe") commemorates the Battle of Quebec on September 18, 1759, which decided whether the North American continent should be English or French. The French, under General Louis Montcalm, were entrenched in a fort on a bluff above the St. Lawrence River on the eastern edge of the Plains of Abraham. General James Wolfe (a native of Greenwich, England, where monuments and references to him abound) was sent to dislodge them and to take over Quebec. It seemed an impossible assignment, but Wolfe took his ships upriver far beyond the city, and under cover of darkness took his whole army down river in small boats to a point where they climbed up the steep banks without being discovered. In the morning, there stood the British troops in battle formation on the Plains of Abraham.

Standing there ourselves a few years ago, we found it hard to imagine why the French left the safety of the fort and came out to do battle. But they did—and in a few minutes it was all over. Both generals were dead, and the British were the victors.

Edith Fowke, in writing of this ballad, says that Wolfe "had become engaged to Katherine Lowther shortly before leaving for America. . . . The parley between Wolfe and Montcalm is imaginary, and Wolfe was not on horseback when he was shot." Mrs. Fowke also tells us that "when Pitt appointed him to lead the Canadian campaign, a courtier complained to King George II that Wolfe was mad. 'Mad, is he?' said the King. 'Then I hope he'll bite some of my other generals.'"

Laws says, in his *NAB,* "With the possible exception of 'Springfield Mountain,' 'Brave Wolfe' is apparently the only native ballad to have survived in tradition from colonial times" (p. 115). The ballad was popular for perhaps a hundred years. It is found in eighteenth-century broadsides and in songsters published in the 1840s. Then it was gradually forgotten except by scholars and a few oldtime singers like John Galusha.

Yankee John pronounced the second syllable of *Montcalm* with a flat *a* like the *a* in "dam."

I was interested to see a version of this ballad in Bob Copper's book about his early boyhood in Sussex, England (*Early to Rise,* p. 235). It is called "Bold General Wolfe" and is a song from the Copper family repertoire.

See: Damon, "Series of Old American Songs," Harris Collection, Brown University; *The Forget Me Not Songster,* 100; Fowke, *Folk Songs of Canada,* 46; Laws, *NAB, A-1,* 119; Lomax, *FSNA,* 42 (Galusha version); Randolph, Vol. 4, 101; Thos. Coll., 3, 69; Thompson, 323

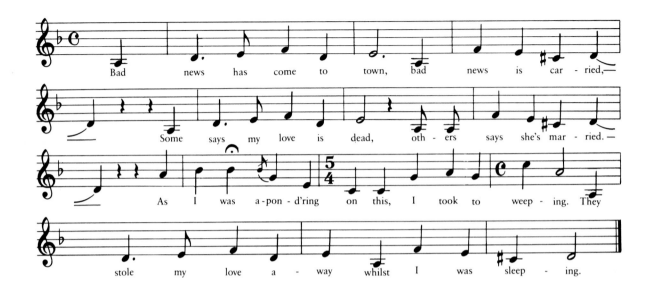

Bad news has come to town, bad news is car - ried,—
Some says my love is dead, oth - ers says she's mar - ried. —
As I was a-pon-d'ring on this, I took to weep - ing. They
stole my love a - way whilst I was sleep - ing.

Love, here's a ring of gold, long years I've kept it.
Madame, it's for your sake, will you accept it?
When you the posy read, pray think on the giver.
Madame, remember me, for I'm undone forever.

Then away went this brave youth, and embarked all
    on the ocean,
To free Americay was his intention.
He landed in Quebec with all his party,
The city to attack, being brave and hearty.

He drew his army up in lines so pretty
On the Plains of Abraham back of the city,
At a distance from the town where the French would
    meet him,
In double numbers, who resolved to beat him.

Montcalm and this brave youth together walkéd,
Between two armies they like brothers talkéd.
Till each one took his post and did retire.
It was then these numerous hosts commenced their
    fire.

Little did he think death was so near him.
[one line missing]
When shot down from his horse was this our hero.
We'll long lament his loss in tears of sorrow.

He raiséd up his head where the cannons did rattle,
And to his aide he said, "How goes the battle?"
His aide-de-camp replied, "It's ending in our favor."
"Then," says this brave youth, "I quit this earth
    with pleasure."

"Ballad of Montcalm and Wolfe"
Words and Music Collected, Adapted and Arranged by Frank Warner
TRO—© Copyright 1971 and 1984 Melody Trails, Inc., New York, N.Y. Used by Permission

[A variation on the last verse—sung by John Galusha in 1946]
He raiséd up his head where the cannon did rattle,
And to his aide he said, "How goes the battle?"
His aide-de-camp replied, "It's ending in our favor,
Quebec is in our hands, nothing can save her."
"Then," says this brave youth, "I quit this earth with pleasure."

22. The Red, White, and Red   John Galusha, 1946

On a visit to Minerva in 1946 Yankee John got to talking about his brothers' experiences during the Civil War (when he himself was a small boy), and how often, during a lull in the fighting a few Yanks and a few Rebels would meet between the picket lines. They would swap hardtack for tobacco, and would swap songs and stories too, as he told us in our last talk with him in 1950 (p. 44).

This fine Confederate song was learned by Yankee John's brother from a Rebel soldier on one of these occasions. The flag referred to was the first battle flag of the Confederacy, "a red field with a white stripe in the middle third and a blue jack with a circle of white stars." There were seven stars, for the seven states of the Confederacy. The familiar flag known as the "Stars and Bars" came later in the war. We have been unable to find any Confederate flag that was just red and white, but Civil War experts say the "jack" is superimposed on the field, and that frequent reference is made in song and poetry to "the triple-barred banner," showing that the bars were considered the important part of that early flag. We have come across incidental references in novels or poems confirming the fact that red and white were considered the colors of the Confederacy. In Winston Churchill's novel *The Crisis* (this was the American novelist, a distant cousin of the English Winston Churchill), there are three references to the colors of the Confederacy as red and white. On our last visit to Yankee John we mentioned the problem to him. His solution was interesting. He said, "The fact that there was some blue on all of their flags shows that underneath they knew we were right!"

The song can be found in Brown, though there the fragmentary text seems to be a recomposition of the song Yankee John sang to fit a later battle, "On the Plains of Manassas."

The battle referred to in the song as having taken place "on the 10th of last June" was the southern victory at Big Bethel on the Virginia peninsula in 1861. The contending generals were General John Bankhead Magruder, C.S.A., and Major General Ben F. Butler, U.S.A., known as "old Picayune."

See: Broadside in Dr. Charles T. Abell Collection, Harvard Library; Brown, Vol. 2, 529;
Laws, *NAB*, dA 36, 258

On the banks of the Po - to - mac there's an ar - my so grand, Its ob - jects are sub - jects of Dix - ie's fair land. They say that they've split our great Un - ion in two And al - tered the col - ors of the Red, White, and Blue.

Chorus
Hur - ray, hur - rah, we're a na - tion to dread, We'll stand by our col - ors, the Red, White, and Red!

'Twas a nice little fight on the tenth day of
    June,
Old Bethel Magruder licked old Picayune.
It commenced in the morning and fought till they
    fled,
And victory waved over the Red, White, and Red.
    Chorus

On the banks of the Potomac the Yankees
    we met,
And we gave them such a licking they'll never
    forget.

They started for Richmond and thought they'd get
    through,
But we made them skedaddle, with their Red, White,
    and Blue.
    Chorus

They never will subdue us, that you will see.
While there's Davis, Bragg, Beauregard, Johnson,
    and Lee,
Magruder and Stonewall and others ahead,
We'll all die defending the Red, White, and Red!
    Chorus

"The Red, White, and Red"
Adapted and Arranged by Frank Warner
TRO — © Copyright 1961 and 1984 Melody Trails, Inc., New York, N.Y. Used by Permission

23. Springfield Mountain   John Galusha, 1940

The song tells the story of a farmer's son who was bitten by a rattlesnake while mowing his father's field and died as a result. It happened in Wilbraham, Massachusetts, formerly known as Springfield Mountain, in the year 1761. The name Myrick appears in many versions, but the name Curtis is used in other versions, and the name Merrill in a version collected by Helen Hartness Flanders. Yankee John sang "Lieutenant Cushman." Years later we met a native of Wilbraham who told us that Cushman was one of the oldest family names in that region.

Laws says that "Springfield Mountain" "may be the oldest of native ballads now current to have originated with the folk." He says it is one of the two colonial ballads to have survived in oral tradition. The other is "Brave Wolfe," also sung to us by Yankee John (No. 21).

Mark Tristram Coffin says that Phillips Barry discovered an 1849 manuscript (words only) that is the earliest known printed text of the ballad. However, Laws says, "My belief is that this ballad, like many others, was locally composed soon after the tragedy it recounts."

The ballad spread across the entire country, but it is found usually in one of the comic forms it acquired after rattlesnakes became less of a problem. S. Foster Damon, in his notes for the Brown University "Series of Old American Songs," noting the changes that occurred in the song, says that "about 1838 it began to be sung on the stage; the vogue of the Yankee was then in its prime; and the ancient tragedy became excellent comedy when stammered or nasalized by George Gaines Spear, Yankee Hill, or Judson Hutchinson." The comic version sheet music was first published in 1840 by George P. Reed of Boston.

Yankee John sang this version to us with dignity and feeling and a sense of tragedy. We feel it must have been close to the way it was originally sung.

See: Belden, 299; Brown, Vol. 2, 489; Bulletin, No. 7, 5; Coffin, *American Narrative Obituary Verse and Native American Balladry,* 103; Flanders, *VFSB,* 15; Laws, *NAB,* G-16, 220; Lomax, *FSNA,* 13; Randolph, Vol. 3, 167

SPRINGFIELD MOUNTAIN

On — Spring - field Moun - tain — there did dwell —— A — like - lie youth——

who was known full well. Lieu - ten - ant— Cush - man's, his on - ly

son,— A — like - lie youth — scarce — twen - ty - one.

One Monday's morning he did go	His voice was heard both far and near,
Down in the meadow for to mow.	But none of his friends did there appear.
He mowed around till he did feel	Thinking that he some workman called,
A p'izen serpent bite his heel.	Poor boy alone at last did fall.

When he received his death-lie wound
He laid his scythe down on the ground.
To return home was his intent,
Crying aloud long as he went.

It was in the year seventeen hundred and sixty-one
When this sad accident was done.
May this a warning be to all
To be prepared when God doth call.

"Springfield Mountain"
Collected, Adapted and Arranged by Frank Warner
TRO—© Copyright 1976 and 1984 Devon Music, Inc., New York, N.Y. Used by Permission

24. Virginia's Bloody Soil   John Galusha, 1939

This moving Civil War ballad was sung to us by Yankee John on our first visit with him. As we have said, Yankee felt deeply about the Civil War. We were conscious of that as he sang this song. It is a local song, written, he said, by James McCoy of Minerva, New York, about a local hero, Captain Dennis Barnes, who was killed in the Battle of the Wilderness.

The author moved Fort Sumter into Virginia, but that doesn't really matter. We consider this one of the most important songs Yankee John gave us.

Laws lists "Virginia's Bloody Soil" among "Native ballads of doubtful currency in tradition" (p. 258). This may well be an accurate description, since the ballad was written by a Minerva man and sung to us by a man from the same village. Perhaps it did not travel at all. Lomax prints the Galusha/Warner version in *The Folk Songs of North America*, p. 99, as does Irwin Silber in his *Songs of the Civil War*, p. 259. In describing the Battle of the Wilderness, Silber says: "A quiet, sweet-smelling wooded area in northern Virginia, not too many miles below the Rapidan River on the road to Richmond from Washington, was the scene of one of the fiercest battles of the Civil

War . . . which took place early in May of 1864 . . . [and] raged for three full days, from May 5 through May 7, with losses in killed, wounded, and missing estimated at some 17,000 for each side."

I have come across some notes I took when Yankee John was talking about the Civil War. "Have you heard about Sheridan's oath?" he said. "Well, there was a man up in Newcomb who was with Sheridan. He told me how a captain come up to Sheridan in the middle of a battle and said, 'We're whipped, General, we can't stop 'em.' Sheridan said, 'You may be whipped, but the men ain't. I'll water my horse in Wilson's Creek tonight, or I'll water him in hell!' Then he got the army turned and started back and they went to fightin' and drove the Rebels back and licked 'em. That one man turned the tide of battle. Harrison (that was the man's name who told me) said that was Sheridan's oath. He told me too that Sheridan said, 'If you see a crow going over the Shenandoah Valley, tell him to take his rations with him.'"

See: Laws, *NAB,* dA 35, 258

VIRGINIA'S BLOODY SOIL

"Virginia's Bloody Soil"
Adapted and Arranged by Frank Warner
TRO—© Copyright 1961 and 1984 Melody Trails, Inc., New York, N.Y. Used by Permission

When our good old flag, the Stars and Stripes, from Sumter's walls was hurled,
And high o'er head on the forrardest walls the Rebels their flag unfurled,
It aroused each loyal northern man and caused his blood to boil,
For to see that flag—Secession's rag—float o'er Virginia's soil.

Then from o'er the hills and mountain tops there came that wild alarm:
Rise up! ye gallant sons of North, our country calls to arms,
Come from the plains o'er hill and dale, ye hardy sons of toil,
For our flag is trampled in the dust on Virginia's bloody soil.

And thousands left their native homes, some never to return,
And many's the wife and family dear were left behind to mourn.
There was one who went among them who from danger would ne'er recoil.
Now his bones lie bleaching on the fields of Virginia's bloody soil.

When on the field of battle, he never was afraid,
Where cannons loud would rattle, he stood there undismayed.
When bullets rained around him he stood there with a smile,
Saying, "We'll conquer, boys, or leave our bones on Virginia's bloody soil."

In the great fight of The Wilderness, where's many the brave man fell,
He boldly led his comrades on through Rebel shot and shell.
The wounded 'round they strewed the ground, the dead lay heaped in piles,
The comrades weltered in their blood on Virginia's bloody soil.

The Rebels fought like fury, or tigers drove to bay.
They knew full well, if the truth they'd tell, they could not win the day.
It was hand to hand they fought 'em, the struggle was fierce and wild,
Till a bullet pierced our captain's brain, on Virginia's bloody soil.

But above that din of battle, what means that dreadful cry?
The woods are all afire, where our dead and wounded lie.
The sight to behold next morning would make the stoutest heart recoil,
To see the charred remains of thousands on Virginia's bloody soil.

And now our hero's sleeping with thousands of the brave,
No marble slab does mark the place that shows where he was laid.
He died to save our Union, he's free from care and toil,
Thank God! the Stars and Stripes still wave above Virginia's soil!

25. This Day (or, The Battle of Bull Run)   John Galusha, 1941

Bull Run was the first great battle of the Civil War. It took place on Sunday, July 21, 1861, near Manassas, Virginia (to the Confederates it was always "The Battle of Manassas"), and west of the stream called Bull Run. The Union forces were commanded by Brigadier-General Irvin McDowell, the Confederates by General Joseph E. Johnston. At first a Union victory seemed assured, but eventually, because of maneuvers by the southern armies, the northern forces first retreated and then withdrew in panic.

Yankee John, who could remember seventeen or eighteen stanzas of "The *Flying Cloud*" (No. 2) and ten of "The Irish Sixty-Ninth"[6] (No. 14), could recall only one verse of this piece commemorating Bull Run—and incidentally glorifying the Irish. Brief as it is (Yankee John would have called it "a snatch of a song"), we have always considered it a gem. Southerners have been known to remark that the next to last line is appropriate, since the Yankees lost their shirts in the battle.

We have not found the song anywhere else.

THIS DAY (or, THE BATTLE OF BULL RUN)

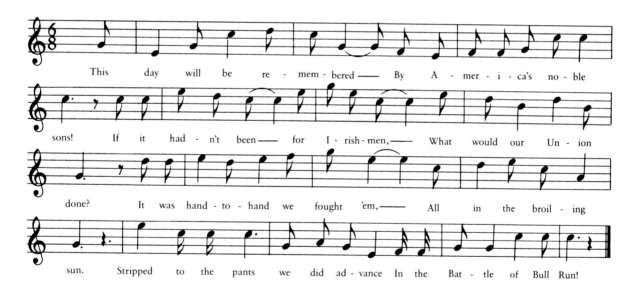

This day will be re-mem-bered —— By A-mer-i-ca's no-ble sons! If it had-n't been—— for I-rish-men, —— What would our Un-ion done? It was hand-to-hand we fought 'em, —— All in the broil-ing sun. Stripped to the pants we did ad-vance In the Bat-tle of Bull Run!

"The Battle of Bull Run"
Adapted and Arranged by Frank Warner
TRO—© Copyright 1961 and 1984 Melody Trails, Inc., New York, N.Y. Used by Permission

6. See note for "The Irish Sixty-Ninth," No. 14, with reference to this song.

26. Down in a Coal Mine   John Galusha, 1941
27. In the Pit from Sin Set Free   Benjamin S. Davies, 1948

It is interesting that Yankee John, in the woods of northern New York, knew this coal-mining song through oral tradition—proving that songs, and people, crossed state lines frequently and that a good song was assimilated easily, whatever its subject.

Edith Fowke and Joe Glazer, in their *Songs of Work and Protest,* say that the song "was originally a stage song written by American comedian J. B. Geoghegan in 1872. It was soon adopted by the coalminers and became the best known of all miners' songs, particularly in the anthracite fields of Pennsylvania. It also crossed over to Britain where it became widely popular and is still sung today" (p. 47).

See *Coal Dust on the Fiddle* by George Korson (1943) and Korson's *Minstrels of the Mine Patch* (1938). Korson gives a different tune from Yankee John's. He includes a great verse:

> Then cheer up lads and make ye much of every joy ye can.
> But let your mirth be always sich as best becomes a man.
> However fortune turns about we'll still be jovial souls,
> For what would America be without the lads that look for coals.

Archie Green, in his *Only a Miner,* says, "To my knowledge the very first coal song recorded in the United States was 'Down in a Coal Mine,' placed on Edison Cylinder 9818 in 1908 by the Edison Concert Band. However, the earliest actual recordings by working miners on home ground were obtained by George Korson and Melvin Le Man in Pennsylvania's anthracite region during 1935."

Samuel Bayard of Pennsylvania State University has told us that he has often heard singers say that in southwest Pennsylvania this song could not be sung openly for fear of mine police, since it was a sort of rallying song for Union men and striking groups.

See: Green, 132; Korson, *Coal Dust on the Fiddle,* 153; Korson, *Minstrels of the Mine Patch,* 277

Because he knew of our interest in the song "Down in a Coal Mine," Benjamin S. Davies, a friend and associate of Frank's (he was the General Secretary of the Pittsburgh and Lake Erie Railroad YMCA in Campbell, Ohio), sent us the words to this song ("In the Pit from Sin Set Free") in 1948 with the following note: "The coal mine song we talked about is given herewith as well as I can remember it. I heard it about 40 years ago from a part-time preacher in a small coal-mining community. His name was John Muir. I do not recall hearing it from anyone else at any time, but for some strange reason it has stuck with me." We have found no reference to the song anywhere. In 1974 we sent it to Sam Bayard (author of *Hill Country Tunes*) at Pennsylvania State University, hoping he might give us a lead or suggest a tune. He replied:

Dear Frank,

    . . . No, I don't know the song you sent . . . though it is a most characteristic product. The only tune in my knowledge which might fit it is the one enclosed. I admit the tune is rather on the trashy side, but it, or one of its ilk, is rendered inevitable by the meter the composer chose. . . .

    This tune, which strikes me as being related to "When Time Shall Be No More," and to a melody sung to a re-make of "Poor Omie." . . . I got accompanying a religious piece telling the story of Jonah and the whale. . . . The chorus is:

    Over there, over there, in that land so bright and fair
    He will tell us all about it over there
    In that hallelujah land we'll take Jony by the hand
    And he'll tell us all about it over there.

The tune has its religious associations, as you see . . . With all the best to you and yours,
                                                                Sincerely,
                                                                Sam

DOWN IN A COAL MINE

Oh, I'm a jo - vial col - lier lad, As blithe as blithe can be. And wheth - er this world goes good or bad, It's all the same to me. It's lit - tle of the world I know, And I care less for its ways, For where the dog star nev - er glows I wear a - way my days.
Chorus
Down in - to a coal mine, Down in un - der - ground, Where no rain or

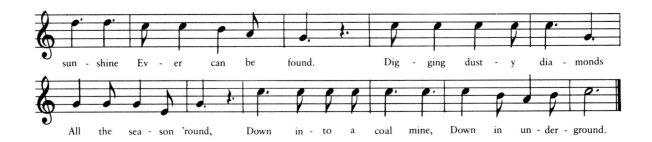

sun - shine Ev - er can be found. Dig - ging dust - y dia - monds

All the sea - son 'round, Down in - to a coal mine, Down in un - der - ground.

My hands are horny, hard, and black
While working in the vein,
And like the clothes upon my back
My speech is rough and plain.
And if I stumble with my tongue,
I've one excuse to say,
It's not the collier's heart that's wrong,
It's his head that goes astray!
Chorus

Oh, it's little do the great ones care,
Who sit at home secure,
What hidden danger colliers dare,
What hardships they endure.
The fire their very mansions boast
To cheer themselves and wives
Perhaps were kindled at the cost
Of jovial colliers' lives.
Chorus

IN THE PIT FROM SIN SET FREE

In the pit from sin set free, Sud - den death would glo - ry be. That is
why I sing with glee, — Je - sus saves. We black dia - monds for them get, Though they
force us hard to sweat. There's sal - va - tion for them yet, Je - sus saves.

Chorus
Je - sus saves, Je - sus saves, Je - sus saves, — Je - sus saves, From the

fear of pit ex-plo-sion, Je-sus saves. When our work on earth is done, we will rise to wear a crown, And go sing-ing 'round the throne, Je-sus saves.

Where in spite of all their rubs,
And the deputy who snubs,
As we wait for empty tubs,
Jesus saves.

Whether the coal be soft or hard,
Working by the day or yard,
Perfect peace is my reward,
Jesus saves.
Chorus

28. Longshoreman's Strike John Galusha, 1941

John Greenway, in his *American Folk Songs of Protest* says that this song, with one more verse, has been found only on a broadside by Wehman in the Harris Collection at Brown University.

However, Cazden now says (Cazden II) that the words to "The Longshoreman's Strike," also known as "The Poor Man's Family," were written by Edward Harrigan, "leader of the successful stage team Harrigan and Hart," with music by Dave Braham, and that the lines of the song were first printed in 1875 in a Harrigan and Hart songster. The text appeared also in W. H. Arnold's *Billy's Request Songster* of 1880, p. 15. Obviously a song of the New York waterfront (though perhaps first a stage song), it somehow traveled up the Hudson to Yankee John's neck of the woods.

In the verse about "the white man's children," the "Chineyman" refers to the many Asiatics who were crossing into the States illegally from Mexico—"from the South"—during the late nineteenth century.

Cazden includes "The Poor Man's Family" as sung by George Edwards. It differs from Yankee John's song but shares many of the same words and the same conclusion. Cazden's notes discuss the history of the song, adaptations of it, and similar songs which appeared around the same period, as well as a discussion of the various tunes used for songs of this genre.

Peter Kennedy tells us that he knows the tune used by Yankee John as the one in Britain used for "The Bucket of Mountain Dew."

See: Cazden II, 377; Damon, "Series of Old American Songs," Harris Collection, Brown University; Greenway, 236; *People's Song Bulletin* 3, nos. 6–7 (July–August 1948)

They'll bring their Eye-talians o'er the sea,
And the Chineyman in from the south,
Thinking they can do our work,
Take the bread from out our mouths.
Whilst the white man's children they must starve!
Sure, we will never agree,
For to be put down like a worm in the ground
And starve our family.
Chorus

29. Nothing's Too Good for the Irish   John Galusha, 1940

Here is another Irish comic song—obviously a stage song originally—sung by Irish comedians before becoming known to the folk. Versions may be found in *Irish Immigrant Ballads and Songs,* p. 496. Robert L. Wright, the editor, learned the song from Michael L. Dean's *The Flying Cloud and 150 Other Old Time Songs and Ballads of Outdoor Men, Sailors, Lumberjacks, Men of the Great Lakes, etc.* There are oral tradition changes in the words and no tune is given.

Yankee John, Irish himself, said to us with a twinkle in his eye, "Some people end the song, 'Hanging's too good for the Irish!'"

NOTHING'S TOO GOOD FOR THE IRISH

I'll tell to you a sto-ry that was told to me— A good old sto-ry,—— Gra-ma-chree. When my moth-er she was dy-ing,—— "My lad," says she, "Noth-in's—— too good for the I-rish!" When we come o-ver, me and my broth-er Dan, Says

I, "We will do the best that we can." They made me a
cop - per, and him an al - der - man Noth - in's too good for the

Chorus

I - rish. Dutch - men were made for to car - ry coal and shov - el snow, I -
tal - ians for or - gans, the En - glish - men to mash, Chi - nese for
wash - ing, the Japs for a jug - gling show, Ne - groes to white - wash, the
Jews were made for cash, Cu - bans for cig - a - rettes, the Por - tu - gees to
sail the seas, Scotch - men for bak - ers, the French were made for style,
Roo - shians for min - ing, A - mer - i - cans for lib - er - ty, But men made for
boss - es are sons of Er - in's Isle! Hip hip hur - rah!
Er - in go bragh! Noth - in's too good for the I - rish!

There's none of our clan, boys, that'd ever work
    hard:
There's my father-in-law on the boulevard,
Cousin Tim, he's a foreman in the old pipe yard.
Nothing's too good for the Irish!

There's old Uncle Dan, sure he's no one's fool,
Guards ice in the summertime to see it's kept cool,
And my sister Mary Helen? Sure she teaches school.
Nothing's too good for the Irish!
    Chorus

30. An Old Indian   John Galusha, 1941

This song is an example of a genre which goes back to 1787 when "The Death Song of a Cherokee Indian" was published, and later was ascribed to Philip Freneau. Austin E. Fife and Francesca Redden discuss the "Indian Song" in detail. The songs reflect the "noble savage" motif of romantic literature in the United States and Great Britain.

William Rose Benét says: "the noble savage . . . supposedly lived under just and reasonable laws which, when compared to European authoritarian governments, were made to seem infinitely more desirable. Literally hundreds of travel books describing such utopias were extremely popular from the 16th to 19th centuries and gave impetus to emigration from Europe to the new world. . . . Chateaubriand's novels dealing with the American Indian . . . portray the romantic, sentimentalized aspects of this myth; its influence is also to be found in the Indian novels of James Fenimore Cooper."

This song of Yankee John's we have found in only one other collection—E. C. Beck's. Beck indicates that the song, which he calls "The Indian's Lament," was widely sung in lumbering camps in the Great Lakes region. The Michigan version has an interesting last verse:

O when shall we meet in that bright happy land?
The paleface then will take us by the hand,
For the Great Spirit promised, and his words are not in vain,
That the Indian and white man would be friends again.

See: Beck, *Lore of the Lumber Camps,* 281; Benét, 718; Fife, 379

AN OLD INDIAN

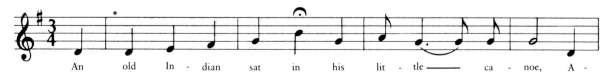

An old In - dian sat in his lit - tle —— ca - noe, A -

float - ing a - long o'er the wa - ter so — blue. He

sang of the days when these lands were their own, Be

fore the pale — fa - ces a - mong them were known.

*2nd verse

There was a time when the red men was lords of
    this soil,
They lived there at ease, free from sorrow and toil.
They hunted the beaver, the panther and deer,
For they knew in their own wood they had nothing
    to fear.

The time when the white man first came to their land,
We used them like brothers, we gave them our hand.
We knew they were weary, we gave them repose,
Not dreaming those white men would ever prove
    foes.

But soon they began to encroach on our rights,
Their numbers increasing, they put us to flight.
They have driven us away from our own happy
    shores,
And the fires of our councils they burn no more.

Oh, where is the tall pine and cedar now gone?
The tall pine and cedar their axe has laid low.
The beaver, the panther, the huntsmen have
    slain,
And the red deer is driven far over the plain.

They have built their large cities all over our land,
And on our rich meadows their farms now stand.
They claim all our country from Texas to Maine,
And the red man may seek for his wigwam
    in vain.

Oh, where are the graves of our forefathers now?
They are rudely roamed over and tilled by
    the plow.
Their children, e'er needy, rejected and poor,
And the homes of their fathers they'll visit
    no more.

31. Once More A-Lumbering Go   John Galusha, 1946

Like "The Ballad of Blue Mountain Lake," this song is a wonderfully singable
song from the lumber camps.

Edith Fowke prints a version with a different tune. She says it is related to a Maine song, "The Logger's Roast," which was first printed in 1851.

Lawrence Older, a long-time friend who told us many stories of his days in the lumber woods of New York State, used the title of the song as a symbol for the story of his life in his article by that title in the *New York Folklore Quarterly*.

Duncan Emrich includes the words of a version on Library of Congress record LP 56, recorded by Alan Lomax from the singing of Carl Lathrop at St. Louis, Michigan, in 1938. It is very similar except that place names are changed to fit the new locale; "Come all you roving lumberjacks that run the Saginaw stream / We'll cross the Tittabawassee where the mighty waters flow," etc. And there is an additional stanza:

When our youthful days are ended and our stories are growing old
We'll take to us each man a wife and settle on the farm
We'll have enough to eat and drink, contented we will go
We will tell our wives of our hard times, and no more a-lumbering go.

See: Emrich, *American Folk Poetry*, 531; Fowke, *Lumbering Songs from the Northern Woods*, 31;
Library of Congress recording LP 56; Older, 96

ONCE MORE A-LUMBERING GO

Come all you sons of free-dom, who 'round the moun-tains range, Come all you jol-ly lum-ber boys, and lis-ten to my song. By the banks of the sweet Sar-a-nac, where its lim-pid wat-ers flow, We'll range the wild woods o-ver and once

Chorus

more a-lum-bering go, And once more a-lum-bering go, We'll

range the wild woods o-ver And once more a-lum-bering go.

To the music of our axes we'll make the woods resound,
And many a tall and lofty pine come tumbling to the ground.
At night 'round our good campfires
We'll sing while cold winds blow, and
Chorus

You may sing about your parties, your parties and your plays,
But pity us poor lumber boys go jouncing on our sleighs.

But we ask no better pastime
Than to hunt the buck and doe, and
Chorus

When winter it is over, and ice-bound streams are free,
We'll drive to our logs to Glens Falls, and we'll haste the girls to see.
With plenty to eat and plenty to drink
Back to the world we'll go, and
Chorus

32. Paddle the Road with Me John Galusha, 1950

During a taped conversation with Yankee John Galusha on our last visit with him in 1950 he suddenly said, "Now, I'm going to sing you a song." This is the song. We had never heard it before, and so far as we know it has never been found elsewhere in this country. Peter Kennedy tells us that there are versions (with words only) in the two Lowland Scots collections of John Ord and Gavin Greig. Ord has four verses. The first and second are similar to those of Yankee John but do not contain his third verse. Here are the third and fourth verses from Ord:

O never mind cold winter, love,
The spring will follow soon.
Come sit you down beside me,
And I'll sing you a nice song—
I'll sing to you a nice song
While I diddle you on my knee,
For you are the bonnie lassie
That's to pad the road wi me.

So she has donned her hose and shoon,
And to the kirk they've gan.
And lang, aye, lang ere morning
That couple were made as ane—
And lang, lang ere morning
Her troubles they were set free.
For she's the bonnie lassie
That's to pad the road wi me.

Greig (*Folk-Song of the North-East,* No. 68) has six verses. The first two are similar to Ord and Yankee John. He mentions that the tune is a variant of that used for "The Irish Girl" as given by Joyce in *Irish Peasant Songs*. He asks readers of the newspaper to send in any more verses, and two more appear in no. 70—one of them very similar to the third verse sung by Yankee John:

Perhaps the one that you may choose
Will be of some graceless clan—
He may beat you and abuse you,
And pull your courage down.
Aye he'll pull your courage down,
And gar ye to rue the day.
So you'll better be the bonnie lass
That'll pad the road wi me.

PADDLE THE ROAD WITH ME

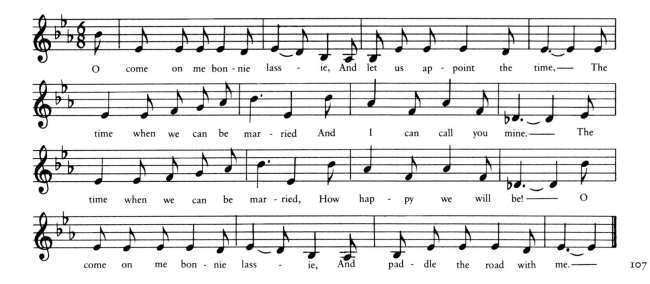

O come on me bon-nie lass - ie, And let us ap-point the time,—— The
time when we can be mar-ried And I can call you mine.—— The
time when we can be mar-ried, How hap-py we will be!—— O
come on me bon-nie lass - ie, And pad-dle the road with me.——

To paddle the road with you, kind sir,
Cold winter is coming on;
Likewise my aged parents,
They have no child but one.
Besides, my aged parents,
They have no child but me;
Wherein my dad, he has picked out a lad
To paddle the road with me.

The lad your dad he has picked out,
He is nought but a country clown.
He'll torment you and abuse you,
And tear your beauty down.
He will cause you for to curse the day
That him you ever did see;
So, come on me bonnie lassie,
And paddle the road with me.

Now this young couple are married,
They live in yonders town.
They are happy as their neighbors,
Their neighbors all around,
They are happy as their neighbors,
Their neighbors where'er they be;
Wherein, she blesses the day she happened that way
To paddle the road with me.

33. Shanty Boy, Farmer Boy   John Galusha, 1941

We collected two versions of this conversation between two girls about the relative merits of the farmer's way of life and the shanty boy's. The other one (with a different tune) is from Lena Bourne Fish in New Hampshire. The shanty boy, "manly, tough, and hearty," wins over the farmer's son, "so green that the cows would eat for hay!" But Franz Rickaby says that although the shanty boy's experience was rugged and daring he knew that "the 'mossback' . . . was the better off," with more security, more time with his family, and less danger of tragic accidents. As a matter of fact, most shanty boys, like John Galusha, "farmed it" in the summer months, in any case, and usually ended up as farmers after their lumbering days.

Rickaby says this conversation is "reminiscent of medieval débat," and Edith Fowke says "the form [of the song is] patterned on such British 'debates' as 'The Husbandman and the Searvingman,' . . . or soldiers and sailors" (p. 183).

Alan Lomax includes a version of the song in his *The Folk Songs of North America.*

This same tune usually is used for the song "Peter Emberly." Norman Cazden once told us that the tune is the one used for the Irish "Foggy Dew."

    See: Fowke, *Lumbering Songs from the Northern Woods,* 183; Lomax, *FSNA,* 109; Rickaby, 52, 201

As I ram-bled out one—eve-ning as the sun was go-ing down, I ram-bled to a place called Pe-ters-bor-ough town. I heard two girls con-vers-ing, as I was pass-ing by, One said she loved a—farm-er's son and the oth-er a shan-ty boy.

The one loved the farmer's son, these words I heard her say:
The reason why she loved him was because at home he'd stay.
He'd stay at home all winter, nor lumbering would he go,
And when the spring it did come in, his lands he'd plow and sow.

All for to plow and sow your ground, the other one did say—
If your crops would be a failure, your debts you could not pay.
If your crops would be a failure and the grain market be low,
The bailiff would have to sell you out to pay the debts you owe.

If the bailiff would have to sell us out, I am sure it would do no harm—
For there's no use in going in debt when you are upon a farm.
You can raise your bread from off the soil, without toil through snow and rain,
While the shanty boy must work each day his family to maintain.

How I love my shanty boy, he'll go out in the fall.
He's manly, tough, and hearty, he's able to stand the squalls.
How happy I'll receive him in the springtime when he comes—
While his money's free he'll share with me when your farmer boy has none.

You can talk about your farmer's son, this girl she did say—

Your farmer's sons that are so green that the cows would eat for hay!

How easy you can tell one of them when they drive into town,

The small kids they'll run up to them saying: Johnny, why did you come down?

What I have said about your shanty boy, I hope you will excuse me.

If ever I get free from a farmer, with a shanty boy I'll be.

If ever I get free from him, for a shanty boy I'll go,

I will leave him broken-hearted, his lands for to plow and sow.

34. The Shanty Man   John Galusha, 1941

Yankee John was a shanty man in his younger days, and he sang this song with great feeling. Beck says it is "the commonest recitation of the lumberjack hardships." Doerflinger notes that the song (he calls it "A Shantyman's Life") dates from 1860 or later when liquor had been banned in almost all camps.

Frank once met a Mr. C. T. Ethridge at Rouse's Point, New York. He was the druggist there, and President of the local YMCA. He came from North Creek and had known Yankee John. He gave Frank this verse which is somehow memorable:

Did you ever go into a lumberman's shanty
Where food was scarce but bedbugs were plenty
Where they eat with their fingers and fight with their knives
To keep the red devils from taking their lives?

See: Beck, *Lore of the Lumber Camps,* 33; Cazden I, 121; Cazden II, 39; Doerflinger, 211; Thompson, 256

THE SHANTY MAN

The shan-ty man leads a — drea-ri-some — life, Though — some — think it free from — care. It's wield-ing an

axe from morn-ing till night In the mid-dle of — for-ests — drear. Ly-ing in the shan-ty, bleak— and — cold, Where the storm-y winds— do — blow, And as soon as the morn-ing's day-light ap-pears To the wild— woods we must go.

* 2nd verse

Transported I am from the haunts of man
On the banks of the Hudson stream,
Where the wolves and the owls with their terrible howls
Disturb our nightly dreams.
At two o'clock our noisy old cook
Sings out, "'Tis the break of day!"
While in broken slumbers we do pass
Those cold winter nights away.

Had we ale, wine, or beer, our courage for to cheer,
While in those dreary wilds,
Or a glass of any shone, while in the woods alone,
We would forget old Erin's Isle.
But remote from the glass or the smiles of the lass
We lead but a drearisome life,
Whilst others live at ease, contented for to please
A brawling and a scolding wife.

When the spring it does come, double hardships begin,
When the waters are so piercing cold.
Dripping wet are our clothes, and our limbs are almost froze,
And our pike poles we scarcely can hold.
While the rocks, shores, and jams gives employment to all hands
And our well-banded rafts we do steer,
While the rapids that we run seem to us but only fun,
We avoid all slavish fear.

Though the shanty man is the one that I love best,
And I never will deny the same,
My heart scorns those few city foppish boys
Who think it a disgraceful name.
You can boast about your farms, give the shanty boy his charms,
So far they surpass them all.
Until death it doth us part, we'll enjoy each other's heart,
Let our riches be great or small.

111

35. A Trip on the Erie   John Galusha, 1941

The Erie Canal, running more than 350 miles from Lake Erie to the Hudson River at Albany, was officially opened on October 26, 1825. The Erie made New York "the Empire State," with more people and more business than any other state in the Union. It opened the route for commerce, so that furs could be brought out of the interior and material and manufactured products could be taken in, and it also opened the way for settlers in the Midwest.

Canals, where they operated successfully, put the stagecoach and the Conestoga wagon out of business, and before they in turn were replaced by the railroads, they created a colorful era in our history. Those who lived along the Erie Canal and those who made their living on it, the "canawlers," were a special breed. It was a hard rough life but it had its fascinations, and it called up many a song—"The E-Ri-E," "Life on the Raging Canawl" (the longstanding joke was to picture the narrow, shallow ditch as the scene of wild storms and angry waves), "Boatin' on a Bull-Head," etc. It is interesting that the best-known canal song, "Low Bridge, Everybody Down," was written and published in 1913 by Thomas S. Allen, long after the canal days were over. Its title, of course, was taken from the cry often heard in canal days when the barges passed under bridges and anyone standing on their decks would be knocked into the water.

The Lomaxes include three versions of this song—without music—from various sources. However, the American Folksong Archive recording of "A Trip on the Erie" sung by Captain Pearl R. Nye, Akron, Ohio, on November 3, 1937, has at least twenty verses, with a music hall tune.

The tune in the Gordon recording is much closer to Yankee John's song than the stage song sung by Captain Nye.

See: Library of Congress, American Folk Life Archive, #1604 A and B, and #1605 A (collected by Alan and Elizabeth Lomax); Library of Congress, American Folk Life Archive, "California 30," recording in 1922 or 1923 by R. W. Gordon from a singer named Desmond; Lomax, *ABF,* 462

A TRIP ON THE ERIE

You can talk of your pic-nics and trips on the lake, But a trip on the E-rie you bet takes the cake! With the

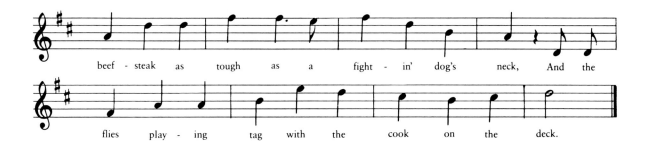

beef - steak as tough as a fight - in' dog's neck, And the

flies play - ing tag with the cook on the deck.

Chorus
Haul in your towlines and take in your slack,
Take a reef in your britches and straighten
    your back.
Mind what I tell you and don't you forget
To tap the mules gently when the cook's on
    the deck.

Now the cook she's a daisy, she's dead gone on me,
With her fiery red head, and she's twice twenty-
    three.
She's knock-kneed and freckled, a dumpling, and
    a pet,
And we use her for a headlight at night on the deck!
    Chorus

"A Trip on the Erie"
Words and Music Adapted and Arranged by Frank Warner
TRO—© Copyright 1977 and 1984 Devon Music, Inc., New York, N.Y. Used by Permission

36. The Twenty-Third   John Galusha, 1941

This, really, is just a fragment of a song, one of the few that Yankee John didn't
remember in its entirety; but it is a favorite of ours. With its spirit, its use of actual
names, its colloquial expressions, it gives us the actual *feel* of this period of the Civil
War from the Union side. We wish we knew more of it. On the other hand, this is
enough.

We have been unable to find any reference to the song in other collections.

THE TWENTY-THIRD

The Twen - ty - Third was drawn in line And rea - dy for the

113

strife. Each man for his coun - try Would free - ly give his life. The first vol - ley that they fired on us, They shot our flag a - way,—— And gal - liant Boggs fell cheer - ing us on, On the thir - ty - first of May— In the Shen - an - do - ah low - lands, low - lands, low, In the Shen - an - do - ah low - lands low.

Here's health and prosperity
To gallant Colonel Neal.
Likewise our other officers,
Their hearts were true as steel.
Here's a health to every private

Who stood by them that day,
And nobly fought for their colors
On the thirty-first of May—
In the Shenandoah lowlands, lowlands low,
In the Shenandoah lowlands low.

"The 23rd"
Adapted and Arranged by Frank Warner
TRO—© Copyright 1961 and 1984 Melody Trails, Inc., New York, N.Y. Used by Permission

STEVE WADSWORTH

In the spring of 1969 Charles and Margaret Coffin—old friends from the Cooperstown Seminars where Marg for several years had taught a course in the history of hand-

Steve Wadsworth, Northville, New York, 1969.

painted tinware—invited us to spend Memorial Day weekend with them at their home in Northville, in upstate New York, on the Sacandaga Reservoir. It would be a long-delayed reunion and, besides, they said, they knew a former logger who might well know some songs.

So we met and spent an afternoon with Steve Wadsworth, recording two cassettes full of conversation and songs. Steve was seventy-three that spring. A year earlier he had had the dreadful experience of having his legs severely burned in a gasoline explosion that occurred when he and a mate were burning road tar off their shovels and there was a sudden shift in the wind. He had come through it remarkably, and was even walking quite well at last, but he claimed he had nearly lost his mind and that his memory was gone. Nevertheless, before the afternoon was over he had sung a complete version of "The Jam on Gerrion's Rock," "Cole Younger," "The Farmer's Boy," and "Curly Head of Hair," as well as "The Ballad of Blue Mountain Lake" with some variations from the Yankee John Galusha version.

Here are some excerpts from a very long recording of Steve's reminiscences:

I was born in November of 1895. . . . When I was a boy my father and mother were up against the hard part of life. I started work at thirteen and a half as a "handy-andy" in a hotel in Hobe where I got seventy-five cents a day for doing all sorts of chores, and sometimes I was washin' dishes at nine o'clock at night. I had to get up early too, since I went to school half a day, and I had four cows to milk night and morning. My mother took half of my weekly wages, but I couldn't blame her for that. There was seven kids in the family, and my father's wages on the road was $1.75 a day. My mother made gloves for the glove people in Gloversville. If she hadn't, I guess we all would've starved. I can remember her sewing gloves sometimes at 1:30 in the morning.

When I was nearly fifteen a feller I'd known in school who was a little older than I was got me to run away with him and go into the woods to saw logs. The boss up the Lawrence there was named Matt McCoy, and he says to me, "What can you do?"

"Anythin' you want me to," I says.

"You look pretty light to me," he says, "but I can't let Joe Wadsworth's boy down." He knew my father, you see.

He told us John Fisher had some men cutting logs and that he would put us with men who knowed how to work . . . so he put us to sawin' logs with the men. We used a cross-cut saw . . . this was peeled timber—we was just cuttin' it up into logs. We had to cut 200 of the spruce and hemlock logs a day, and we was gettin' $35 a month for 26 work days from 6 in the morning until 6 at night. I was so homesick at first I nearly died. Every time I'd hear the train whistle blow off somewhere I would wish I was back washin' dishes. . . . I had some bad times, but . . . I got used to it, and I worked there about a year altogether. For a time I worked as a skidder, making skid trails to skid the logs into piles after the trees was felled. They were big spruce and hemlock, virgin timber, some of 'em three or four feet in diameter.

The food in camp wasn't too good. For breakfast we'd have pork rolled in flour and fried and flapjacks and black coffee—no milk. At work we would knock off about twelve o'clock. We usually carried our lunch in a pack basket—smoked ham or bacon, bread and butter, baked beans, potatoes—the potatoes was usually brought in hot. No fruit or other vegetables, and no fresh meat. Sometimes on Sunday the men would go fishin', and then we'd have fish to eat.

After that I worked up to Canada Lake, and I worked over near Newcomb. . . .

I used to like breaking log jams. They would pay $1 a day more for a log jam breaker who would go out on the logs instead of just working from the shore. They'd give you a peavy stick about six feet long and you would get out on the jam and pull free the log causing the jam (you got to wear Clark shoes so your toes wouldn't get caught between the logs), and then you got to run along the logs to get to the shore before the logs got loose and throwed you. . . .

I took a Frenchie out with me once who was a good logger—we was workin' for Jack Donohue. Sometimes, if the logs was stopped by rocks, if you hit the key log it would swing away from the rocks and catch you and you couldn't get off—and that's what we got. . . . We was out on the jam, and he went ahead and when I overtook him he began to run, sayin' the logs was moving. The boss was hollerin' from the shore, "Swim! Swim!" I jumped in and got took down to the bottom and sent back upstream. When I come up there was about forty feet of that swift current. . . . I tried to make the shore, but I would go under again and again. When I come to they was a-knockin' the water out of me. But both of us got out.

There was a man named Woods up on the Hudson River. . . . On a Sunday he might sing forty songs. Most of the songs I knew I learned from him, I think. . . .

My wife died twenty-three years ago when my youngest daughter was just three months old. But we had eleven children, and the older ones took care of the younger ones. . . . One son was killed a couple of years ago in the woods—a tree fell on him. . . . That's another mark on me. It pretty near killed me. You lose your power through them things. You think of those things happening . . . and the feeling stays with you. I grieved a year and a half over that. That's why I always cry when I sing "Gerrion's Rock." I know what them things is like. . . .

37. The Farmer's Boy   Steve Wadsworth, 1969

We were pleased to find this English song in New York's north country. It is the unusually happy story of an itinerant farm boy who stops at a farmer's house seeking work and as Yankee John Galusha used to say "had a streak o'luck."

The song appears a number of times on both sides of the Atlantic. Peter Kennedy includes a version from Galloway, Scotland, and notes that it has been found in Lincolnshire, Shropshire, Somerset, Hampshire, Sussex, and Yorkshire. The version in Kennedy lacks the next-to-last verse of this version—having only four verses instead of five.

The song has been reported in this country from Vermont, Iowa, Ohio, and Wyoming. Belden prints a version from Missouri very similar to this and notes that in the early eighteenth century it was popular all over England. Belden quotes

from Robert Bell's *Ancient Poems, Ballads, and Songs of the Peasantry of England.*
Steve Wadsworth learned the song from his mother.

See: Belden, 272; Flanders, *VFSB*, 118; Huntington, 216; Kennedy, 555; Laws, *ABBB*, Q-30, 287

THE FARMER'S BOY

The sun was sink-ing in the west, When cold - ly blew the wind, When ti - red and lame a poor boy came Un - to a farm-er's door, Say-ing, "Is there an - y - one with-in Who would give to me em - ploy? To plow, to sow, to reap, to mow, And be a farm-er's boy?"

"And if you cannot hire me,
One favor I would ask.
Would you give me one night's lodging
From this cold and wintry blast?
And early in the morning
I'll go wandering for employ,
To plow, to sow, to reap, to mow,
And be a farmer's boy."

"My father's dead, my mother's living,
With six little children small.
And the worst of it is for my poor mother
I'm the oldest of them all.
And the worst of it is for my poor mother
I'm the oldest of them all,
To plow, to sow, to reap, to mow,
And be a farmer's boy."

"Oh, hire him," the woman replied,
"No farther let him go!"
"Oh yes," cried their only daughter dear,
While the tears down her cheeks did flow.
"For a boy that is willing to earn his bread
Should not wander for employ,
To plow, to sow, to reap, to mow,
And be a farmer's boy."

'Twas but a few years after,
This good old farmer died,
Left him fifty acres of good land
And his daughter for his bride.
His friends they all wished him luck,
While the neighbors wished him joy.
'Twas a lucky day he passed that way
To be a farmer's boy.

38. Cole Younger   Steve Wadsworth, 1969

Steve had trouble singing this song and resorted to recitation in the last verses, but it was interesting to find it in his repertoire. It has been found infrequently in oral tradition.

The song appeared in the original edition of John Lomax's *Cowboy Songs* (p. 106), and Alan Lomax, in *The Folk Songs of North America,* includes the song and tune as sung by Edward L. Crain on Folkways Disc No. 15. He says Edward Crain apparently learned the song word for word from *Cowboy Songs* and set his own tune. Randolph tells us: "Cole Younger was a Missourian who rode with Quantrell's guerrillas, and became a captain in Shelby's Missouri Cavalry toward the end of the Civil War. He and his brothers turned outlaw and robbed trains and banks with the James boys. Captured while trying to loot a bank at Northfield, Minnesota, in 1876, Cole was sent to prison for murder. Pardoned in 1901, he joined his old comrade Frank James in a Wild West Show venture."

In Appendix 2 ("Other Songs in the Repertoire," p. 180) in *A Singer and Her Songs,* edited by Roger Abrahams, Almeda Riddle notes that she knows "Cole Younger" in seven double stanzas. She says it "has been in the hills as long as I remember."

This was not just a song to Steve Wadsworth. He was concerned about Cole Younger as an actual person and about the reasons for his erratic behavior and his downfall.

Norm Cohen, in *Long Steel Rail,* has extensive notes on the history of the Younger brothers and their exploits and of the ballad and many references to articles and recordings.

See: Cohen, 117; Laws, *NAB,* E-3, 177; Lomax, *FSNA,* 350; Randolph, Vol. 1, 425

I am a not-ed high-way-man,—— Cole Young-er
is my name. I've c'm-mit-ted man-y a dep-re-
da-tion, which brings my par-ents shame. I'm the rob-ber
of —— the North-field Bank, the same I'll ne'er de-ny, Which
leaves me now a pris-'ner in —— Still-wa-ter Jail to lie.

Now the first of my depredations, I mean to let
you know,
'Twas of a gold miner, I robbed him of his
gold.
I robbed him of his gold, me boys, and that with-
out delay,
And on our way returning home, my brother
Frank did say,

"Cole, we will get fast horses, together you
and I,
We will fight them as guerrillas, Cole, until the
day we die.
We will have revenge on our father's death, together you and I,"
Which leaves me now a prisoner in Stillwater Jail
to lie.

The Union Pacific Railroad train was the next we did
surprise.
To see the dead and wounded would bring tears to
your eyes.
But we will get fast horses together you and I [this
is garbled]
And still we'll have revenge on our father's death
before the day we die.

Then we mounted on our horses, my brother Frank
and I,
And all along the roads there, the crimson gore did fly.
It was on a Nebraska prairie the James boys we did
meet,
With shining knives and revolvers we all sat down
to play,
With plenty of good old whiskey to while the time away.

My plans was on the Northfield Bank when Jesse James did say,

Saying,. "Cole, if you undertake that job you will never get away."

Saying, "Cole, if you undertake that job you will never get away,"

Which leaves me now a prisoner in Stillwater Jail to lie.

Then we mounted on our horses and rode to the southern bounds of town.

It was there that we dismounted and to council we sat down.

And then we mounted and rode straightway to the bank for that terrible haul.

[The rest of the lines were spoken, not sung:]

It was just before the counter I dealt that terrible blow, saying, "We are that noted guerrilla band that gives no time to play. Hand out all your money."

It was at the very first volley, that Joe Cadwell he went down.

And there was where my brother Jim received his deathly

We mounted on our horses and rode away from town.

When up came riding Jesse James, saying, "Boys, we are surprised.

You'd better get rid of your brother or you'll never get away."

"The first man who touches my brother will die."

"You see his brother was wounded, and they said he'd have to leave him but he wouldn't do that, so he was captured and spent the rest of his life in the Stillwater Jail. He said he'd shoot the first man that took his brother's life. Their father was an outlaw that got shot and they was avengin' their father's life."

39. Curly Head of Hair   Steve Wadsworth, 1969

Steve told us that he used to have curly hair himself when he was a boy, and that the girls sitting behind him in school would run their hands through it. He didn't seem to mind remembering that! No doubt that is why he sang this song with a great deal of zest and humor.

The only reference to it we have found is a Library of Congress field recording—AFS, 5223 A 1—recorded in Ripton, Vermont, in 1941 by Philip Cohen from the singing of Grandpa Dragon. The words are different in a number of places, and the last verse is:

Now I've adopted a new plan
I think it is the best
For to go unto some barber shop
Get my hair and whiskers dressed

But the girls they will laugh at me
And strangers at me stare
Saying, you look like hell and damnation
Since you lost your curly hair.

See: Library of Congress field recording AFS, 5223 A 1

CURLY HEAD OF HAIR

You asked me for to sing a song, I'll see what I can do. I
don't care what I sing a-bout, If it on-ly pleas-es you. And
now I sing — to you my song, — Please don't on me stare, For there's
noth-ing half so hand-some As a cur-ly head of hair.

I know my hair is beautiful,
It gets me into scrapes.
The other night at the menagerie
I was ogled by the apes!
And in making my escape from there
I was jostled by a bear,
[spoken] Which mistook me for one of her cubs
      With my curly head of hair.

Now I am a jolly good fellow,
But I've got a scolding wife.
And if things don't go to suit
She'll often rip and tear,
[spoken] And then she'll twist her fingers
      In my curly head of hair.

So I'll go unto some barber
And have my hair and whiskers dressed.
And when I do come back again
The people will on me stare,
[spoken] Saying, "You look like all creation
      Since you lost your curly hair."

New Hampshire

LENA BOURNE FISH

NEW HAMPSHIRE is, of course, one of the original thirteen states. It was named for Hampshire, England, by virtue of the royal grant in 1629 to Captain John Mason of that shire. It has high mountains, by eastern United States standards, more than thirteen hundred ponds and lakes, large wooded areas, and a seacoast eighteen miles in length. The White Mountains are famous for their beauty and for their picturesque chasms and notches, including Franconia Notch with its "Old Man of the Mountains"—a high peak which forms the profile of a man's face.

The southeastern section of the state, which includes East Jaffrey, is known generally as the Monadnock region since, in addition to its fertile valleys and chain of hills, it has three lofty peaks of hard rock known as monadnocks: Monadnock, Cardigan, and Kearsarge.

It is a gentle land, and seemed particularly so on the early July day in 1940 when we drove into Peterborough. We secured a room at the Peterborough Inn and then went in search of Carl and Betty Carmer at the MacDowell Colony in the nearby woods. The Colony, founded by the widow of Edward MacDowell, the American composer, was, and is, a retreat for qualified artists, writers, and composers. There are a main house and lodge and small working studios scattered through the woods, far from each other. Here the artists may spend their days, free from interruptions or distractions. A box lunch is delivered at noon to each studio—dropped off at the door. The Carmers had asked us to come by, hoping that Frank would give the Colony an evening of folk music, and we were more than happy to do so.

We arrived in mid-afternoon, and Carl sent us off in search of a lady he had heard about who was said to live in East Jaffrey and who also was said to know dozens of songs. Her name was Mrs. Fish. East Jaffrey was only a few miles away, so we set off without delay.

The following statement is transcribed from the small disk on which Mrs. Fish recorded for us these four brief paragraphs about her background and her early life.

My name is Lena Bourne Fish, and I was born of a race of soldiers. A man by the name of Gordon Miles, who was killed at the Battle of Quebec in the French and Indian War, was a member of my great-great-grandmother's family. An uncle of my grandmother's by the name of Henry Hutchins was a Color Sergeant and was killed at the Battle of Bunker Hill. My grandmother was born at an army fort somewhere in the State of Vermont, and my [great] grandfather Bourne was also a Revolutionary War soldier, as well as my mother's grandfather, Michael McSergeant.

My father's ancestors came from Scotland in the early days of 1700 and settled in Rhode Island, and later moved to the town of Bourne on the Cape [Cod], which town was named for the family. My mother's grandfather was Colonel Ryder, an officer in the British Army.

I was born in the beautiful Adirondack section of New York State about sixteen miles from Plattsburgh in a small iron-manufacturing place called Black Brook.

This collection of old songs has been kept in my family for more than two hundred years.

Mrs. Fish was born in April 1873, the daughter of Stratton Bourne and Cynthia Abel Bourne. Her father was a native of northern Vermont. He was a lumber salesman in the Adirondacks, supplying wood for charcoal which was used in the iron mines. Lena Bourne grew up in Black Brook, New York, where she was born, and for a while taught school in Wilmington, New York, but found she did not like teaching. Perhaps because of this she answered an advertisement she saw in a newspaper: A Mrs. Fish in Temple, New Hampshire, wanted a housekeeper, since she herself was a busy midwife. It is interesting to know that as a professional midwife she would deliver a baby at the mother's home and then stay for a week, caring for mother and child and cooking for the whole family—all for the sum of $10. Lena Bourne, then, moved to Temple, New Hampshire, when she was twenty-four years old, and a year later married her employer's son, John Fish, aged twenty-one, a farmer with his father. When John Fish died in 1918 at the age of forty-one, Lena Fish and her seven younger children moved to East Jaffrey, where her eldest son, Charles Horace Fish, had a job in a lumber mill.

When we first knocked on Mrs. Fish's door, we said tentatively, "We have heard you are interested in the old time songs?" "Come right in," she said. And before we knew it we were all seated around our nearly untried recording machine, and Grammy was singing. She was not to be stopped, either. Someone knocked, and in the middle of a verse one can still hear her (on the disk) call to her granddaughter in another room, "Go't the door!" This was our first recording session, and Mrs. Fish was singing the sort of songs we had hoped to hear.

By 1940, in her nearly seventy years, Grammy Fish—as she was known to everyone—had collected hundreds of songs. From whom she learned them is something of a mystery. Some she learned from her father, especially the Irish songs; and some she

Lena Bourne Fish, East Jaffrey, New Hampshire, 1940.

must have learned from the men who worked with her father in the north woods. Charles Fish believes she learned some from her uncle Butler Bourne who, in his last years, lived alone on Whiteface Mountain in the Adirondacks near Black Brook, making small birchbark canoes and other artifacts which he sold to interested tourists. Charles Fish said that Uncle Butler "knew a lot of songs and he kept them in a chest which he passed on to Aunt Sophia [Lena's sister]. I think she gave them to Mother. I don't know how she knew the tunes."

In four recording sessions with Grammy Fish she gave us nearly a hundred songs. Fifty of these, for some reason, were never given to the only other collector of her songs, Helen Hartness Flanders, who visited Grammy in 1940 just two months before our visit, and again in 1942 and 1943. We don't know why Grammy never mentioned Mrs. Flanders to us. Mrs. Flanders published thirteen of Mrs. Fish's Child ballads in her *Ancient Ballads Traditionally Sung in New England,* but only three of Grammy's other songs, in either collection, have been published until now. The three are "Whiskey in the Jar" (called "Gilgarrah Mountain" by Mrs. Fish), "Felix the Soldier," and "Get Up Jack" (called "The Jolly Roving Tar" by Mrs. Fish). They are in Alan Lomax's *The Folk Songs of North America,* contributed from our collection.

Many of the songs Mrs. Fish knew have not been found among traditional singers elsewhere on this side of the Atlantic. They include "The Jolly Roving Tar," "The Press Gang Sailor," and "The Rambler from Claire." Many of her songs are variants, unique in both text and tune, of commonly found songs: "The Castle by the Sea" ("Lady Isabel and the Elf Knight"), and "The Sailor Boy." ("Sailor Boy II" is the title Laws gives to Mrs. Fish's "The Young Prince of Spain," No. 61.)

Mrs. Fish deserves recognition as a preserver of her own New York and New England tradition, and as one of the most important informants of the Northeast. We feel a great sense of gratitude to her, not only for the important and interesting songs which she so generously shared with us, but for the evidence she gave of what an interest in traditional music can mean to an individual.

In 1976 we were able to spend several hours with Charles Fish, the son with whom Grammy lived when we visited her so long ago. He even remembered our visits. He and his daughter, Ruth Quinn, with whom he then was living and who had been in high school in the early 1940s, told us some things about Mrs. Fish's background and family, but they could not tell us much about her music. Grammy had eight children, but not one of them learned any of her songs. Mr. Fish did tell us that as his mother grew older she became fearful for her health and was often ill—until Mrs. Flanders, and we, and then local people became interested in her singing. After that she sang for Red Cross meetings and Boy Scout dinners and church suppers. With her granddaughter's help she started a little mimeographed sheet about songs which she called "The Dreamer," including in it the words of some of her old songs and also some of her own composition. Her granddaughter distributed the paper around the village to anyone who was interested. After these activities developed, Grammy's fears and ill health faded away, and the last years of her life were busy and happy.

In August of 1940 she wrote us:

My dear Mrs. Warner,
Your nice letter and picture received and I thank you both so much for it. I have framed it and every time I look at it it reminds me of you.

Last Saturday I went up to Bread Loaf School of Middlebury College, Vt., and put on a program of old songs. They came after me and brought me back and gave me $5. I rode over 200 miles and had such a pleasant trip . . . so it seems as though I should have to keep singing my way through life.

Lena Bourne Fish

And in September of 1940:

My dear Mr. and Mrs. Warner,
    I wish to thank you so much for the beautiful hooked mat you so kindly sent me. [This was made by Rena Hicks, our North Carolina mountain friend.] . . .
    I hope if you come to New Hampshire again next year you will look me up and perhaps I can hunt up a few more old songs. Did you ever hear of an old song called "The Weeping Willow Tree?" This was the name of a ship that was built in Virginia in the days of Sir Walter Raleigh. . . . I guess songs are like friends, the old ones are always the best. . . .
    Thanking you again for the beautiful mat, I remain your friend and well wisher,

Mrs. Lena Bourne Fish

Our last visit with Grammy Fish was in 1941. The war made travel impossible. We had no more leisurely vacations, and, in any case, gasoline was so severely rationed that we sold our car in 1943. Grammy died in December of 1945.

In addition to some copies of her mimeographed newsletter we have several notebooks which she gave us with copies of old songs, copies of some songs she herself wrote for special occasions, and her own observations on the songs and on life. One important paragraph, in her own handwriting, is an introduction to a group of Irish songs:

With what tender memories my heart was filled as I wrote down these old songs. Many of them I have heard my honored father and other dear old friends of my childhood sing at banquets and other gatherings where old songs were often sung. As you review the songs of long ago . . . I think you will find they will compare favorably in both rhythm and rhyme to the modern song and verse. May they fill many hearts with tender memories of childhood is the sincere wish of

Lena Bourne Fish

Lena Bourne Fish, with friend, 1940.

40. Barbara Allen   Lena Bourne Fish, 1941

In one of her notebooks which Grammy Fish gave us she had written these comments about "Barbara Allen":

. . . I am not in accord with the sentiments of this song, as I do not believe that a false
and fickle love is worth dying for. Although dying of love is said to have been a very common occurrence in the early days of our country. It is genealy [generally] believed that
women were more susaptable to this complaint than men were; but according to this old
ballad, men sometimes died of this fatal malady. But I am thankful that the men and women
of our generation take their love affairs more calmly, as life is too short to work ourselves
up into a fever and die of either love or pride. That is a coward's way out of dificulties;
and I have never this far been a coward.

Belden, in his notes on this ballad, says, "Whether originally a stage song (as
might be conjectured from Pepys's entry of January, 1666) or not, 'Barbara Allen' has
become, and remains, the most widely known and sung of all the ballads admitted
by Child to his collection." Belden prints two versions from Missouri and mentions
fourteen others, known variously as "Barbery Allen," "Barbara Allen's Cruelty," "Barbara Ellen," "Bonny Barbara Allen" (Child's title), etc.

Versions of the ballad words do not vary greatly, indicating that printed texts
were widespread. The time of year mentioned is occasionally changed. Usually "the
merry month of May / When the green buds they are swelling," occasionally is changed
to "Martinmas, when the leaves are falling." Belden says that "The taunt about leaving her [Barbara Allen] out in the drinking of healths, found in Child A, in Ord [Scot-
land], and a Hampshire text, is almost unfailing in American copies; and so is the rose
and briar ending, which does not appear in the Child versions," or in Mrs. Fish's version.

We have heard fragments of this ballad from a number of our singers and another complete version (and two tunes) from Rebecca King Jones in North Carolina
(No. 187).

See: Belden, 60; Child No. 84, 180 ("Bonny Barbara Allen"); Coffin and Renwick, 82, 239

BARBARA ALLEN

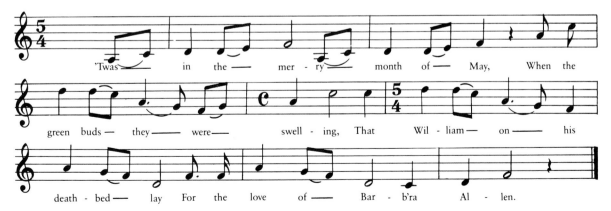

'Twas in the mer-ry month of May, When the
green buds they were swell-ing, That Wil-liam on his
death-bed lay For the love of Bar-b'ra Al-len.

He sent his servant off in haste
To the place where she was dwelling,
Saying, "William's sick and calls for you.
Please come, dear Barbara Allen."

She walked out with a lordly air,
Although she felt like crying.
But all she said when she got there
Was, "Young man, I fear you're dying."

"Oh, I am sick, so very sick,
With fever I am shaking.
If you will only smile on me,
It will keep my heart from breaking."

"O mind you not, young man," said she,
"When the gay May bells were knelling,
You drank a toast to the ladies all,
But slighted Barbara Allen?"

"I know you're sick, and very sick,
And death is with you dealing,
But I will never smile on you
Nor will I be your healing."

He bade this cruel world adieu,
When she turned coldly from him,
And walked away with an air of pride,
Hard-hearted Barbara Allen.

Before she reached her dwelling place
She heard the death bell knelling.
And every peal the death bell gave
Meant woe to Barbara Allen.

"O Mother dear," she sobbed and said,
"My heart is filled with sorrow.
As my love has died for me today,
I'll die for him tomorrow."

They laid her at rest by his side
While the violet buds were swelling,
For her poor William died of love
But of pride died Barbara Allen.

41. The Castle by the Sea   Lena Bourne Fish, 1940

This ballad is a version of Child No. 4, "Lady Isabel and the Elf Knight," which some scholars trace back to a ballad of the twelfth century in the Lower Rhine region. As is usually the case in American versions, the supernatural nature of the lover has been forgotten or is not mentioned. This element of the supernatural, present in so many ancient ballads, did not travel over the water. We do not really know why.

The editors of the Frank C. Brown North Carolina collection say that this ballad is a favorite among the singers of that state, and they include seven versions—each under a different title: "Pretty Polly," "The Seven Sisters," "The Seventh King's Daughter," "Pretty Cold Rain," "Sweet William," and "The Six Fair Maids." We have collected a North Carolina version, known as "Pretty Polly," from Rebecca King Jones in the Piedmont section of the state. A confusing thing about Mrs. Jones's version is that in it both the lady and the parrot are called "Polly." Her chorus, though, is clear:

Hush, hush, pretty parriot bird.
Pray, don't you tell no tales on me,
For your cage shall be lined
With the brightest links of gold,
Swing here on this green willow tree, tree
Swing here on this green willow tree.

Mrs. Fish's version does not mention the talking parrot which is so prominently featured in most versions.

Another version of the ballad was given to us by Mrs. Murphy of Hogansburg, New York. It does include a reference to the intelligent parrot who protected her lady's honor by telling a tale to account for her absence before daylight, and it tells a more complete story. These are the last five verses of Mrs. Murphy's version, picking up the story after the lady has disposed of the false knight:

She mounted on her milk white steed
And led the dappled gray.
She rode till she came to her father's gate
Three long hours before it was day.

The parrot being up in the tall willow tree
Began to flutter and cry,
Saying, "What is the matter pretty Polly
You are out so long before day?"

The maid being up in the chamber so high
Raised the window to see
Says, "What is the matter pretty Polly
You are calling so long before day?"

"There was a bold cat came to my cage door
And he was determined to stay,
And I have been calling pretty Polly
To drive the bold cat away."

"Well done, well done, my pretty Polly,
Well done, well done," said she,
"Your cage shall be lined with glittering gold
To swing high in the tall willow tree."

Mrs. Murphy was born in 1858. She learned this song from her grandmother when she herself was a little girl going to the district school five miles from Hogansburg on the edge of the St. Regis Indian Reservation in upper New York State.

See: Coffin and Renwick, 25, 211, for a complete list of where this ballad may be found.

A - rise, O a - rise, my la - dy fair, For you my bride shall be, ———— And we will dwell in a syl - van bow'r In my cas - tle by the sea. ————

And bring along your marriage fee,
Which you can claim today,
And also take your swiftest steeds,
The milk white and the grey.

The lady mounted her white steed,
He rode the turban grey.
They took the path by the wild sea shore,
Or so I've heard them say.

As she saw the walls of the castle high
That looked so black and cold,
She wished she'd remained in Boston town
With her ten thousand pounds in gold.

He halted by the wild sea shore,
"My bride you shall never be!
For six fair maidens I have drowned here,
The seventh you shall be."

"Take off, take off, your scarlet robes,
And lay them down by me.
They are too rich and too costly
To rot in the briny sea."

"Then turn your face to the water's side,
And your back to yonder tree.
For it is a disgrace for any man
An unclothed woman to see."

He turned his face to the water's side,
And his back to the lofty tree.
The lady took him in her arms,
And flung him into the sea.

"Lie there, lie there, you false young man,
And drown in place of me.
If six fair maidens you drowned here,
Go keep them company."

She then did mount her milk white steed,
And led the turban grey,
And rode until she came to Boston town
Two hours before it was day.

42. Gypsy Davy   Lena Bourne Fish, 1941

Child says that in "the earliest edition of the ballad styles the gypsy Johny Faa . . . was a prominent and frequent name among the gypsies. Johnnë Faa's right and title as lord and earl of Little Egypt were recognized by James V [of Scotland] in 1540. But in the next year Egyptians were ordered to quit the realm within thirty days on pain of death." During the ensuing sixty years succeeding generations of an Egyptian named Johnë Faa were sentenced to be hanged, and a hanging appears to have taken place in 1624. This event resulted, presumably, in the popular ballad, and Faa, says Child "became a personage to whom any adventure might plausibly be imputed."

The ballad was first printed in Scotland (according to Child) in 1740, but the English version may have been printed earlier.

Frank Warner learned a version of this ballad, called "Black Jack Davy," when he was working with Dr. Frank C. Brown at Duke University, and which he sang frequently thereafter. Somehow it is not included among the many variants in the printed Brown collection.

We collected a very different version from Frank Proffitt in North Carolina called "Gyps of David." He sings this on his first Folk-Legacy record.

Both Belden, and Coffin and Renwick have interesting notes about the ballad.

In Mrs. Fish's version it is indeed "a gypsy king" who comes to ask the lady to be his wife, and the problem seems to be that "They tell me to marry beneath my rank / Is nothing short of danger." It is only in the final stanza (a verse that is standard in most versions) that there is any suggestion of her being already married. But there is no pursuit and no overtaking as in so many versions.

See: Belden, 73; Brown, Vol. 2, 161; Child, No. 200, 483 ("The Gypsy Laddie");
Coffin and Renwick, 119, 254

GYPSY DAVY

A gyp-sy king came o-ver the hill, De-fy-ing storm and dan-ger. It seemed to be my — lot to fall In love with the dark-eyed stran-ger.

He has asked me to be his wife,
To be his honored lady.
Has asked me to leave my home and kin
And follow Gypsy Davy.

I do not envy our honored queen
Or any titled lady.
I'd rather be a gypsy queen,
The bride of black-eyed Davy.

They tell me to marry beneath my rank
Is nothing short of danger.
But title and gold cannot compare
With my love for the dark-eyed stranger.

Last night I slept in a down-feather bed,
An honored titled lady.
Tonight I'll sleep in the green, green field
By the side of Gypsy Davy.

So when the lord came here at night
Inquiring for his lady,
The servants made him this reply,
"She's gone with Gypsy Davy."

43. Lord Bateman   Lena Bourne Fish, 1940

This ballad is called "Young Beichen" by Child, who collected fifteen versions in the British Isles, all but one from Scotland. It tells the story of an English nobleman who sails around the world and is eventually captured by the Turks and put in prison. The daughter of the king (in this version Susan Frier) steals the key to the prison and sets the prisoner free upon his promise to give her "houses and lands" and to marry her within seven years. After seven years she follows him to England, and there they are joyously married. In some versions, though not in this one, Susan arrives on the day Lord Bateman is marrying another lady, whom he instantly rejects in favor of his Turkish love.

Child mentions the widespread legend that the English nobleman was the father of Thomas à Becket, and his mother a Saracen princess, but says the facts do not bear this out.

Versions of the ballad (sometimes known as "The Turkish Lady") are widespread among the folk. The editors of the Frank C. Brown collection question whether it became popular because of its frequent appearance on broadsides and in songsters, or whether ballad printers used it because it was known to be a favorite. Versions have been found in recent times in Scotland and various parts of England, in the Bahamas, in Newfoundland, and in the United States from Maine through the South and the Middle West.

Roby Monroe Hicks in the North Carolina mountains sang us an interesting version which he called "Young Beeham."

See: Brown, Vol. 2, 50; Child No. 53, 95 ("Young Beichen"); Coffin and Renwick, 58, 226; Hudson, 75; Sharp, *English Folksongs of the Southern Appalachians*, Vol. 1, 77

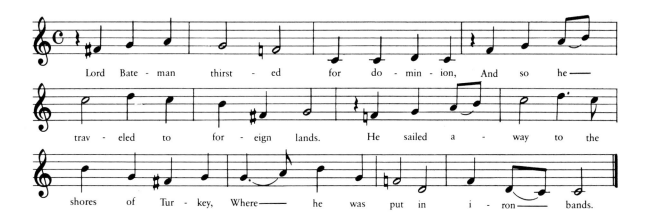

Lord Bate - man thirst - ed for do - min - ion, And so he —
trav - eled to for - eign lands. He sailed a - way to the
shores of Tur - key, Where —— he was put in i - ron —— bands.

The Turkish king had but one daughter,
A charming maiden and fair to see.
She stole the keys of her daddy's prison,
And vowed Lord Bateman she would set free.

"Have you houses and have you lands,
And have you livings of high degree?
Will you share them with a Turkish princess,
If from this prison she will set you free?"

"Oh I have castles and I have lands,
And I have livings of high degree.
All of these will I give to you, my princess,
If from this prison you will set me free."

She took him then to her daddy's parlor,
Gave him freely of a wine so strong,
And every health she drink to Bateman,
She heartily wished that he was her own.

"Let's make a pledge and a solemn vow,
For seven long years it shall extend,
That you shall wed no other maiden,
And I will wed no other man."

Seven long years soon had passed,
And eight and nine had passed away.
Still Bateman waited for a princess,
Although his locks were turning grey.

One day a lady came to his castle,
And asked if Lord Bateman dwelt therein.
"Oh, yes," replied the brisk young porter,
"I will call him, please wait within."

"Please ask him if he has forgotten
The Turkish princess that set him free,
And that my vows are not forgotten,
I'm waiting still his bride to be."

He took her by the lily white hand
And led her over the marble stone.
She is known no more as Susan Friar
But is now the wife of Lord Bateman.

44. The Old Wether's Skin   Lena Bourne Fish, 1941

This ballad is Child No. 277 and is one of the two versions we collected—the other, very different—from Frank Proffitt in North Carolina called "Dan Doo" (No. 103). Versions have been found in all parts of the British Isles and throughout the United States. It goes back to the sixteenth century. Shakespeare is thought to have used its theme for his "The Taming of the Shrew."

A version, almost the same as Mrs. Fish's, is in the Carrie B. Grover collection, *A Heritage of Songs*. Coffin and Renwick have interesting notes about the ballad's provenance and usage. Belden says that the "Rosemary" and "Dan Doo" refrains are found only in America—the first "the preferred New England form," the second found usually in the South.

The "wether" is the bellwether of the flock of sheep, the leader. A common way to tan sheep's hide was beating it with hickory switches.

See: Belden, 92; Cazden II, 503; Child No. 277, 603 ("The Wife Wrapt in Wether's Skin");
Coffin and Renwick, 146, 274; Flanders, *Ancient Ballads Traditionally Sung in New England*,
Vol. 4, 77; Grover, 68

THE OLD WETHER'S SKIN

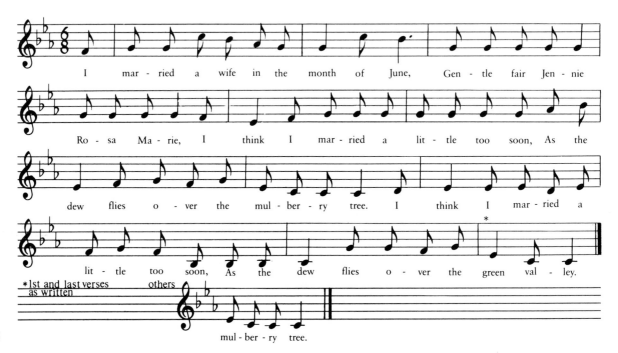

She would not card, and she would not spin,
Refrain
Afraid of soiling her lily white skin,
Refrain
Afraid of soiling her lily white skin,
Refrain

So while I was tilling my meadow and lands,
She sat in the parlor with folded hands,

One day I came home from jogging the plow,
Saying, "Good wife is my dinner done now?"

"There's bread and there's cheese upon the shelf,"
"If you want any dinner, go get it yourself,"

Down to the sheep pen I went with haste,
And I killed the bellwether without any waste,

Then I took out my knife and went rip, rip, rip,
And off went the wether's pelt strip, strip, strip,

I then threw the hide upon my wife's back,
And with two sticks I went whickety whack,

I will tell my brother and all of my kin,
For to wallop your wife is surely a sin!

You may tell your brother and all of your kin,
But I'm bound to tan my old wether's skin,

She then cooked my dinner and set up the board,
With "Yes, Sir," and "No, Sir," at every word,

She cooked my food well, she did card and spin,
Since the day that I tanned my old wether's skin,

45. The Ship Carpenter   Lena Bourne Fish, 1941

Child calls this ballad "James Harris" or "The Daemon Lover." In most American versions it is known as "The House Carpenter," and in some "The Ship's Carpenter," but the text remains much the same. It has been found in almost every state in the United States. Belden has interesting notes which trace its origins at least as far back as the seventeenth century. The supernatural element present in early Scottish texts from oral tradition is missing in American versions.

Coffin and Renwick include a most interesting discussion of the variation in ballads and how it comes about.

We collected three other complete texts of this ballad, called in each case "The House Carpenter"—from Roby Hicks on Beech Mountain, North Carolina, from Frank Proffitt in the Beaver Dam Section of Watauga County, North Carolina, and from Rebecca King Jones of Crab Tree Creek, also in North Carolina. Each one tells the same story, but each differs from the others in wording and in the arrangement of verses.

See: Belden, 79; Child No. 243, 543 ("James Harris" or "The Daemon Lover");
Coffin and Renwick, 137, 263

"Well met, well met, my pret-ty fair— maid." "Not so
ve-ry well met," said— she. For— I am mar-ried to a
ship car-pen-ter,— And a ve-ry fine— man is— he."

"If you will forsake your ship carpenter
And go along with me,
I will take you where the grass grows green
On the banks of a sweet valee."

"If I forsake my ship carpenter,
And go along with thee,
What have you there to entertain me on,
To keep me from slavery?"

"I have ships all in the bay,
And plenty more upon land,
Five hundred and ten of as fine young men,
They are all at your command."

She took her babe all in her arms,
And gave him kisses three.
"Stay at home, stay at home with your father dear,
For he is good company."

She had not sailed six weeks on the sea,
I know not more than three,
Before this fair lady began for to mourn,
And she mourned most pitifully.

"Now do you mourn for gold," he said,
"Or do you mourn for me?
Or do you mourn for your ship carpenter
That you left to follow me?"

"I do not mourn for gold," she cries,
"Nor do I mourn for thee!
But I do mourn for my ship carpenter
And my pretty sweet babee."

In the heavens there rose a big storm cloud,
And how the waves did roar!
At the bottom of the ship there sprang a leak
And her mourning was heard no more.

46. The Battle with the Ladle   Lena Bourne Fish, 1941

Eloise Hubbard Linscott, in her *Folksongs of Old New England,* includes a bal-
ladlike song called "The Ladle Song," collected in Weston, Massachusetts. Like Mrs.

Fish's song, it has six verses, and although both songs tell the same story the words are quite different. We have not found it in any other United States collections, but a version is in Patrick Weston Joyce's *Old Irish Folk Music and Song* and in Frank Kidson's *Traditional Tunes*.

See: Joyce, 111; Kidson, 92; Linscott, 227

THE BATTLE WITH THE LADLE

A rich old mi-ser mar-ried me, His age it was three score and three, My age it was but sev-en-teen, I wish that rogue I nev-er had seen.

If from home that I should go,
To see a friend, a friend or so,
If any man should speak to me,
'Twould much arouse his jealousy.

Those bitter griefs I could not bear,
And so one morning I do declare,
As he was sleeping in his bed,
With my ladle I rapped his head.

He jumped up like brave man stout,
And 'round the house he ran about,

But not a single moment's rest,
Until that rogue I had well dressed.

Then he fell down upon his knees,
And vowed he never would me displease,
My old man I did subdue,
With my ladle—and so may you.

So all young girls about to wed,
Listen to the words I've said,
Don't be abused by any man,
And always have a ladle on hand.

47. Bill the Weaver   Lena Bourne Fish, 1941

More commonly known as "Will the Weaver," this ballad is found in the United States on broadsides of the early nineteenth century—including those in the Isaiah Thomas Collection in the library of the American Antiquarian Society in Worcester, Massachusetts. This collection consists, as Thomas himself said, of "Songs, Ballads, etc. Purchased from a Ballad Printer and Seller in Boston, 1813. Bound up for Preserva-

tion, to show what articles of this kind are in vogue with the Vulgar of this time, 1814"
(quoted by Laws, *ABBB*, "The Origin and Distribution of Broadside Ballads," 46).

W. Roy Mackenzie says the song was current in England and Scotland in the eighteenth century and cites song books and broadsides from 1739 on.

See: Cazden II, 517; Henry, *Folksongs from the Southern Highlands*, 304; Laws, *ABBB*, Q-9, 277;
Mackenzie, 328; Sharp, *English Folksongs of the Southern Appalachians*, Vol. 2, 207;
Shoemaker, 135; Thos. Coll., 1, 22

BILL THE WEAVER

"Moth-er, Moth-er, now I'm mar-ried, And I wish that I had tar-ried!
For my wife she does de-clare That the britch-es she will wear."

"Now, dear son, go home and love her,
Unto me no faults uncover.
Give my daughter what's her due,
Let me hear no more from you."

Going home a neighbor met him,
Told him something that did fret him.
"Neighbor, Neighbor, I will tell you
Who I saw at your house just now."

"Who was there but Bill the weaver.
He and your wife sat close together.
They went in and shut the door,
Unto you I'll tell no more."

He went home like one in wonder,
On the door he rapped like thunder,
"Who is there?" the weaver cried.
"It's my husband, you must hide!"

Then up the chimney hole he ventured,
As the door her husband entered.
She began to sign and moan,
"Why did you leave me alone?"

"Wife, dear wife, don't be in a passion,
But please follow my directions.
Draw some beer for I am dry."
Like a good wife, she did comply.

While she was gone he did endeavor
To hunt out this Bill the weaver.
He hunted the chambers 'round and 'round,
But not a soul was to be found.

Then up the chimney hole he saw him,
And a brilliant thought came to him.
As he sat black as a coal
A-straddle of the trammel pole.

140

He then built up a roaring fire,
Much against his wife's desire.
She screamed, she cried, "List' to your wife.
Take him down and spare his life!"

Then from the trammel pole he took him,
And so heartily he shook him.
Crying out at every stroke,
"Come no more to stop my smoke!"

48. Cabin Boy   Lena Bourne Fish, 1940

Grammy Fish's "Cabin Boy" tells the same story as the one Yankee John gave us (No. 1), but in very different words and with a different tune. Laws calls this song "The Maid in Sorrow." It is found on broadsides and has been collected in Michigan and in Newfoundland, where it is called "Short Jacket."

Mrs. Fish said, "This old Irish song was written over one hundred years ago."

See: Gardner, 401; Greenleaf, 100; Laws, *ABBB*, N-12, 208

CABIN BOY

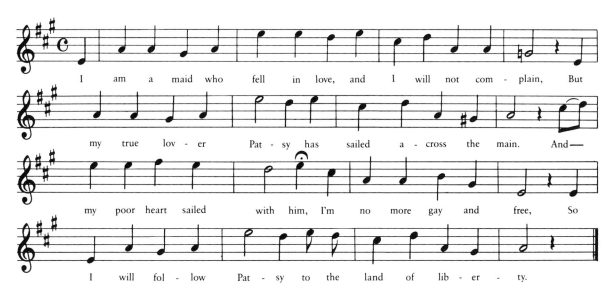

I am a maid who fell in love, and I will not com-plain, But
my true lov-er Pat-sy has sailed a-cross the main. And—
my poor heart sailed with him, I'm no more gay and free, So
I will fol-low Pat-sy to the land of lib-er-ty.

141

My curly locks I did cut off, and man's clothes I
  put on,
I dressed as a servant sailor and sailed at early
  dawn,
And hired to the captain to work my passage
  fee,
To be his loved companion to the land of
  liberty.

"What foolish talk, dear Captain, such talk is all
  in vain,
If the sailor boys should hear you they would laugh
  and make game.
But when we reach America, some pretty girls we'll
  find,
We'll love them and embrace them, for we know
  they will incline."

One night as we were talking, and many things
  were said,
He smiled and said, "My dear, I wish you were
  a maid.
Your Irish eyes a-dancing, they seem to conquer
  me,
And give me this desire that you were a maid
  for me."

About three weeks or after, our ship arrived
  on shore,
"Goodbye, dear jolly sailors, goodbye for
  evermore!
Once I was a cabin boy, but now am a maid
  on shore,
And wish our kindly captain good luck for
  evermore."

49. Captain John   Lena Bourne Fish, 1941

Also known as "Johnny the Sailor," or "Green Beds" (and as "Jack Tar" on some
of the broadside versions), variants of this song have been found in both England and
Scotland and on broadsides in the collection at Harvard. In various versions it is widespread on this side of the ocean from Nova Scotia through the middle western and
southern states of the United States. Mackenzie links it to "The Saucy Sailor" and a
host of other songs "popular both in the fo'c's'le and in the cottage," dealing with a
sailor's testing his welcome ashore—by the ladies and others—by pretending that he
has no money and then proving that he has. In Grammy Fish's version some elements
of the usual story are missing: the sailor never does meet the daughter he has asked
to see, and no mention is made of any retributive action as a result of the treatment
he has received.

The ballad is thought to be from the early nineteenth century.

See: Belden, 160; Brown, Vol. 2, 335; Hudson, 156; Laws, *ABBB*, K-36, 159; Mackenzie, 245; Randolph,
Vol. 1, 250; Sandburg, *The American Songbag*, 430

I'll tell you of a sail-or whose name was Cap-tain John, They re-port-ed him a fail-ure, with ship and car-go gone. He spent his mon-ey free-ly and did-n't count the cost, So in a for-eign har-bor his for-tune was lost.

His ship drove into port, and he landed at the quay.
But no one came to meet him, or so I've heard them say.
Yet with his old-time courage he did sing a merry song,
But no one had a greeting for the failure Captain John.

He then called at a pub where he often did lodge in,
But no one bade him welcome as he boldly entered in.
He bade the kindly landlord, as brisk as brisk could be,
"Call down your daughter, Polly, and set her down by me."

"Have you forgot your reckonings to me, Captain John?
And for the gold you owe me I've surely waited long.
My daughter Polly's busy, John, and cannot come today,
And little in your company she likes for to stay."

Then Johnny being weary, he hung down his head,
And then called for a candle to light him to bed.
"My beds they are not empty, John, nor won't be for a week,
So for some other quarters, poor Johnny, you must seek."

"Tell to me your reckonings, and then they shall be paid.
That I'll not pay my reckonings you need not be afraid."
"It is five and twenty shillings, John, as I have often told,
And now it must be paid, in silver or in gold."

John put his hands in his pocket, pulled them out full of gold.
It is the same old story that often has been told,
The sight of the money made the old barter rue,
He says, "A kindly greeting, John, I spoke in jest to you."

143

50. Felix the Soldier   Lena Bourne Fish, 1940

Grammy Fish told us that this was a song of the French and Indian War, and that seems to be true. We don't know any more than that about it. It is typically Irish in its humor—broad and flippant enough to cover every situation—and in its tune. We haven't found it anywhere else.

Laws, in *ABBB*, lists a song called "The True Paddy's Song" or "The Kerry Recruit," which tells a somewhat similar story—without mentioning the French—but we don't believe it is the same song. "Felix" seems older. Lomax's *Our Singing Country*, p. 200, also includes "The True Paddy's Song."

Alan Lomax includes the Fish version of this song in his *The Folk Songs of North America*, p. 45. In writing of it he says: "If soldier folk songs were the only evidence, it would seem that the armies that fought in early American wars were composed entirely of Irishmen. The finest folk ballads of [these wars] . . . all had Irish tunes, and perhaps our best soldiers' folk songs are these two pieces ["Felix" and another song called "The Wars of America"] sung by Irish recruits who marched with the redcoats in the French and Indian Wars. They speak for the many poor Irish lads forced by privation to become mercenary soldiers."

In O'Lochlainn's *Irish Street Ballads*, p. 143, there is a song called "Mrs. McGrath," which is not this song though it tells a similar story of an Irish soldier who lost both his legs in a sea battle, and whose mother makes a similar exclamation upon seeing him:

Oh then were ye drunk or were ye blind
That ye left yer two fine legs behind
Or was it walking upon the sea
Wore yer two fine legs from the knees away?

"Noble Lads of Canada," heard on R. W. Gordon cylinder "California 10" at the Library of Congress, uses the same tune Mrs. Fish used for this song. No singer or other information is given.

FELIX THE SOLDIER

They   took   a - way   my   brogues,   And   they   robbed   me   of   my   spade,   They

put me in the ar - my, And a sol - dier of me made. But I could - n't beat a drum, And I could - n't play the flute, So they hand - ed me a mus - ket, And they taught me how to shoot.

But the Injuns they were sly,
And the Frenchies they were coy,
So they shot off the left leg
Of this poor Irish boy.

We had a bloody fight
After we had scaled the wall,
And the divil a bit of mercy
Did the Frenchies show at all.

Then they put me on a ship,
And they sent me home again,
With all my army training,
After battle's strife and din.

They headed for the Downs,
And we landed at the quay,

My mother came to meet me,
And these words to me did say,

"O Felix, are you drunk,
Or Felix are you mad?
And whatever has become
Of the two legs you had?"

I will bid my spade adieu,
For I cannot dig the bog,
But I still can play the fiddle,
And I still can drink my grog.

I have learned to smoke a pipe
And I've learned to fire a gun,
To the divil with the fighting,
I am glad the war is done.

"Felix the Soldier"
Words and Music Collected, Adapted and Arranged by Frank Warner
TRO — © Copyright 1971 and 1984 Melody Trails, Inc., New York, N.Y. Used by Permission

51. Gilgarrah Mountain Lena Bourne Fish, 1941

This song of Mrs. Fish's about an Irish rogue and robber has long been a favorite of ours. A somewhat different version known as "Darlin' Sportin' Jenny" has had wide popularity in this country since the mid 1960s—first introduced, we believe, by performer Bob Gibson. "Gilgarrah" is frequently pronounced as "Gilgarry," and Mrs. Fish so pronounced it.

Law's version "A" (or variants of it) has been collected in Ireland (Joyce, p. 345), tune only, and O'Lochlainn, printed in *Journal of American Folklore* 25, p. 152, in Nova Scotia (Creighton, *Songs and Ballads from Nova Scotia*, p. 192), and in West Virginia, where it is called "Captain Kelly." It may be found also on a number of broadsides. O'Lochlainn's chorus is slightly different from Mrs. Fish's:

Whack fol the diddle, O,
Whack fol the diddle, O,
There's whiskey in the jar.

Versions of "B" appear in two Flanders collections: "McCollister" in Flanders, *VFSB*, p. 139; and "Lovel the Robber" in Flanders-Barry, *NGMS*, p. 245.

A version is found in Robert W. Gordon collection (*Adventure Magazine, 1933*)—two verses and a different chorus:

And there's whiskey in the jar
And there's more behind the bar
And touch it if you dar'
Says the bold sojer boy.

All versions of the ballad indicate the perfidy of the robber's lady, who usually is said to have loaded his pistols with water . . . surely a difficult thing to do. Only in the Fish version does Polly fire off the pistols and load them with pepper. That is a more plausible act, if just as disloyal.

See: Laws, *ABBB*, L-13 A ("Whiskey in the Jar" and "The Irish Robber" A), 173;
Laws, *ABBB*, L-13 B ("The Irish Robber" B or "McCollister")

GILGARRAH MOUNTAIN

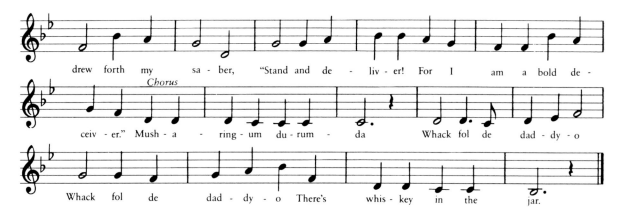

drew forth my sa - ber, "Stand and de - liv - er! For I am a bold de -
Chorus
ceiv - er." Mush - a - ring - um du - rum - da Whack fol de dad - dy - o
Whack fol de dad - dy - o There's whis - key in the jar.

The shining golden coins did sure look bright and jolly,
I took the money home and gave it to my Molly.
She promised and vowed she never would deceive me,
But the divil's in the women, and they never can be easy.
Chorus

I returned to my cave in the Gilgarrah Mountain,
And left my sweetheart Molly the money a-counting.
As I was soundly sleeping, the divil sure may take her,
She fired off my pistols, and she loaded them with pepper.
Chorus

She told Colonel Pepper where I was a-hiding,
And led them to my cave in the right early morning.
O Molly, you've deceived me, although I loved you dearly,
But you never cared for me, I can see it bright and clearly.
Chorus

When I awakened between six and seven,
Guards were around me in numbers odd and even.
I flew to my pistols, but alas I was mistaken,
For I fired off my pistols, and a prisoner was taken.
Chorus

They put me in jail, without judge or writing
For robbing Colonel Pepper on Gilgarrah Mountain.
But they didn't take my fists, so I knocked the sentry down,
And I bade a long farewell to the jail in Sligo town.
Chorus

Some take delight in fishing and bowling,
Others take delight in the carriages a-rolling,
But I take delight in the juice of the barley,
Courting pretty girls in the morning so early.
Chorus

"Gilgarry Mountain" ("Darlin' Sportin' Jenny")
Collected, Adapted and Arranged by Bob Gibson, Bob Camp and Frank Warner
TRO—© Copyright 1961 and 1963 Melody Trails, Inc., New York, N.Y. Used by Permission

147

52. Hi Rinky Dum   Lena Bourne Fish, 1940

This is a version of "The Milkmaid," sometimes known as "Seventeen Come Sunday." Laws mentions that it has been found in Virginia, West Virginia, Ohio, and Nova Scotia. Cox gives its title as "My Pretty Maid," and also prints a song called "The Milkmaid," to which it is certainly linked. Of "The Milkmaid," he says, "No song is better known in America."

For informative notes, see Cazden I, and also Cazden II.

"Hi Rinky Dum" may have many neighbors in American collections, but Mrs. Fish's tune is certainly unique, with an intriguing refrain that has an ambiguous tonic.

Another version of this song was given us by Mrs. Colin Westcott in Manteo, North Carolina. She called her song "Where Are You Going, Pretty Maid?" It has just three verses, but a very pretty tune.

See: Cazden I, 122; Cazden II, 479; Cox, 394; Creighton and Senior, 164; Eddy, 188; Laws, *ABBB*, O-17, 234; Sharp, *English Folksongs of the Southern Appalachians*, Vol. 2, 156

HI RINKY DUM

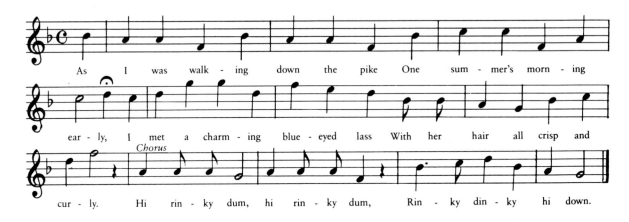

"Where are you going, my pretty maid,
My little blue-eyed daisy?"
"I am not going very far,
For really I am lazy."
    Chorus

"I'm in love with you, my pretty maid,
What is your age, my honey?"
She replied with a bewitching smile,
"I'll be seventeen next Sunday."
    Chorus

"Are you not tired of the single life,
Will you be the wife of Sammy?"
She answered me regretfully,
"I cannot leave my mammy."
Chorus

"Yet I should like to be your wife,
For you are so good looking,
But I will never wash your shirts
Or never do your cooking."
Chorus

"Then you shall never be my wife
For you've not learned life's lesson."
"I never asked to be your wife,
'Twas you that popped the question."
Chorus

53. I'll Sit Down and Write a Song   Lena Bourne Fish, 1940

Laws entitles this song "Sailor Boy I." He says it is seldom found in the northeast United States though it is widely found in the South and Middle West. Belden says, "I have not found it reported from the North Atlantic States," though Barry prints a version compiled from various sources in Maine. Mrs. Fish's version, unlike most others, does not have the girl's father build her a boat in which she goes to seek her love: "I'll hire me a little boat." Nor does the girl kill herself from grief at the end. Her cry in the last verse is almost more moving: "Oh, who can fathom my despair!"

We collected three additional versions of "Sailor Boy I" (all from North Carolina): from Lee Monroe Presnell on Beech Mountain, a song he called "My Sweet Soldier Boy," from Martha Ann Midgette in Mann's Harbor, called "Captain, Captain" or "The Sweetest Boy that Ever Sailed," and a third from Roby Monroe Hicks on Beech Mountain called "A Soldier's Trade."

See: Barry, *The Maine Woods Songster,* 58; Belden, 186; Laws, *ABBB,* K-12, 146; Randolph, Vol. 1, 297

I'LL SIT DOWN AND WRITE A SONG

I'll   sit   down ——— and   write   a   song,   I'll ———   149

write it short, and I'll write it strong. At ev - ery word I'll let

fall a tear, Will end — my song, —— fare - well my —— dear.

It was early, early in the spring,
My love was sent to serve the king.
A sad misfortune attended him
By the angry sea and the stormy wind.

I'll hire me a little boat,
And in the harbor I'll set float.
When that ship anchors I'll say, "Ahoy!
Have you brought back my sailor boy?"

I had not sailed scarce a mile or three
Before that vessel I chanced to see.
"O Captain, Captain, tell me true,
Does my dear William sail with you?"

"My lass, your William is not here,
Your lover's drowned I deeply fear.
On yon green isle as I passed by,
There I lost sight of a sailor boy."

Oh, who can fathom my despair!
My sorrow is more than I can bear.
All my fond hopes so bright and free
Lie buried in the deep blue sea.

"I'll Sit Down and Write a Song"
Collected, Adapted and Arranged by Frank Warner
TRO — © Copyright 1973 and 1984 Melody Trails, Inc., New York, N.Y. Used by Permission

54. Johnny Sands   Lena Bourne Fish, 1941

Herein is the story of the wife who drives her husband to the point of wishing to drown himself, who offers to help by tying his arms and pushing him into the water, but who, in the end, is tricked into falling in herself. He, of course, cannot help her because she has tied his arms. This form of the story usually is called "Johnny Sands." George Lyman Kittredge, in the *Journal of American Folklore* 29, p. 179, says that the song, although based on a folk tale, "is literary and hardly older than the 40s of the 19th century," and that it is found in so many places — in some fifteen states — because it was sung by the Hutchinson Family of New Hampshire and other singing troupes. The S. Foster Damon–Brown University "Series of Old American Songs" includes a reproduction of the sheet music of this song, dated 1842, which gives the author as

John Sinclair, who was born in Scotland in 1790 and who began his American stage career c. 1830. But the Harvard Library has an Irish broadside of the song and at least two British ballad sheets.

Another form of the story seems to be older. Perhaps Sinclair reworked it to create the story of Johnny Sands. It goes back to a song called "The Old Woman of Slapsadam," but with many other titles: "The Wily Auld Carle," "The Old Woman of Dover," etc. Here the old woman feeds her husband marrow bones "to make him blind," and he then asks her to help him drown himself, with the same result as in the other song. The marrow-bones-blindness motif usually is missing from American versions, except in one text included in Randolph (Vol. 4, 246), and in a version which we collected from Frank Proffitt in North Carolina, "There Was an Old Roman." *Folk Songs of the Catskills* (Cazden II) has a version from Grant Rogers called "The Old Woman from Boston."

See: Belden, 238; Brown, Vol. 2, 448; Cazden II, 518; Hudson, 198; Kennedy, 415 (English version: "The Old Woman of Blighter Town"); Laws, *ABBB,* Q-2, Q-3, 274

JOHNNY SANDS

A man whose name was John - ny Sands Had mar - ried Bet - ty Hague, And though she brought him gold and lands, She proved a dread - ful plague. For, oh, she was a scold - ing wife, Full of ca - price and whim, He said that he was tired of life, And she was tired of him.

Said he, "Then I will drown myself,
The river runs below."
Said she, "Pray do, you silly elf,
I have wished it long ago."

Said he, "Upon the bank I'll stand,
Do you run down the hill,
And push and push with all your might."
Said she, "My dear, I will."

151

"For fear that I should courage lack,
And try to save my life,
Pray tie my hands behind my back."
"I will," replied his wife.
She tied them fast as you may think,
And when securely done,
"Now stand," said she, "upon the bank,
And I'll prepare to run."

So down the hill his loving bride,
Now run with all her force,
To push him in—he stepped aside,
And she fell in, of course.
So, splashing, darting, like a fish,
"O save me, Johnny Sands."
"I can't, my dear, though much I wish,
For you have tied my hands."

55. Only a Soldier   Lena Bourne Fish, 1941

This ballad about the "Bold Soldier" (which is the title Laws gives the song) is extremely widespread on both sides of the Atlantic. Laws takes a long paragraph to list the collections in which it is included. In England the ballad is known as "The Bold Dragoon" or "Come All You Maids of Honor."

Belden says, "The likeness of the story here told to that of 'Erlinton,' Child No. 8, has been noted by previous collectors," and he notes that Davis includes the ballad as an appendix to "Earl Brand," Child No. 7. Norman Cazden, calling the song "The Bold Soldier of Yarrow" (*Journal of American Folklore* 68, pp. 201–209) relates the piece to Child No. 214 and No. 215. But Laws himself says "Even a hasty comparison of texts will show that [this ballad] . . . is entitled to separate identity" (p. 102).

There is a broadside of this ballad, Arthur Schrader tells us, in the Old Sturbridge Village Museum Library which is dated sometime before 1814. Norman Cazden (Cazden I) says that there is a broadside of it as early as 1679. He also separates this ballad from Child No. 7, "Earl Brand," and No. 8, "Erlinton."

See: Belden, 103; Cazden I, 42, 108; Cazden II, 183; Chappell, *Folksongs of Roanoke and the Albemarle*, 88; Davis, *Traditional Ballads of Virginia*, 92; Flanders, *VFSB*, 232; Laws, *ABBB*, M-27, 193; Randolph, Vol. 1, 303

ONLY A SOLDIER

I'll tell you of a sol-dier who late-ly came from war. He—
court-ed a la-dy who had rich-es laid in store. Her—

rich - es were so great——— that they scarce - ly could be told, But still she loved her sol - dier for he was brave and bold.

She said, "My honored soldier, I fain would be
    your wife,
But my old Tory father would take away my life."
He took his sword and pistols and hung them by
    his side
And vowed that he would marry her, whatever
    might betide.

As they had been to church and were coming home
    again,
They met her cruel father, with seven well-armed
    men.
"Let's flee," said the lady, "for I fear we shall be
    slain!"
"Fear nothing," said the soldier to his charmer
    again.

Her father addressed her and unto her did say,
"What sort of behavior is this your wedding day?
Now since you've been so foolish as to be a soldier's
    wife,
All in this lonely valley I will end your happy life."

The soldier replied, "Sir, you know not what you
    say.
I've never been defeated nor shall not be today."
He then drew his broad sword, his pistols they did
    rattle,
And the lady held the horse while the soldier fought
    the battle.

The first man he came to he quickly had him
    slain;
And the next one he came to he run him through
    the same.
"Let us flee," said the rest, "we shall surely all be
    slain,
To fight a valliant soldier is all together vain."

The old man said, "You butcher, you make my
    blood run cold.
You shall have my daughter and a thousand pounds
    in gold."
"Fight on," said the lady, "our portion is too small."
"O stay your hand, bold soldier, and you shall have
    it all."

Her father took him home and acknowledged him
    his heir,
Not for the love he had for him but just through
    dread and fear.
There never was a soldier that was fit to carry
    a gun
That would ever flinch a hair till the battle
    was won.

Never despise a soldier because he may be poor,
He truly is a knight as he was in days of yore.
And he's bold, brisk, and jolly, both sociable and
    free,
He'd as soon fight for love as to fight for liberty.   153

56. The Ploughboy of the Lowlands   Lena Bourne Fish, 1940

The ballad known as "Edwin (Edmond, Edward, etc.) in the Lowlands Low," of which this seems to be a variant, tells the story of the girl whose father runs a public house. When her lover returns from sea with the fortune he had amassed her father murders him for his gold. The girl informs against her father, and he is hanged for the deed. According to Laws the ballad is widespread and is to be found in almost every collection in England, Ireland, Scotland, and the United States.

But in Mrs. Fish's ballad the girl is the daughter of a lord whose father does not wish her to marry beneath her station. She insists that she is not interested in titles or wealth and that she will have no one but her ploughboy—until her lover, returning home one night from town, is shot down by a robber. Seven years later the girl receives a letter "from a dying man in Perth," confessing that her father had hired him to pose as a robber and shoot her ploughboy. She then informed against her father, and he was hanged. She vows she never will wed, for "My heart is with Edmund Dale that ploughed the lowlands low."

Peter Kennedy from Devon tells us that this "is a most unusual version" of the Edmund story.

See: Belden, 127; Brown, Vol. 2, 267; Cazden II, 190; Cox, 345; Laws, *ABBB*, M-34, 197; Randolph, Vol. 2, 59

THE PLOUGHBOY OF THE LOWLANDS

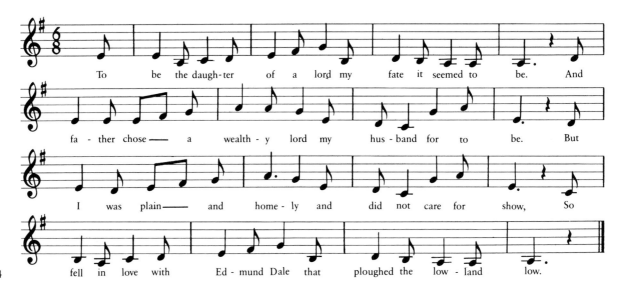

To be the daugh-ter of a lord my fate it seemed to be. And
fa - ther chose —— a wealth - y lord my hus - band for to be. But
I was plain —— and home - ly and did not care for show, So
fell in love with Ed - mund Dale that ploughed the low - land low.

My father said, "My daughter dear, you make my
    proud heart ache.
To wed beneath your station is surely a mistake."
I replied, "What is a title? and I do not care for
    show,
So I will wed my Edmund Dale that ploughs the
    lowlands low.

One day as my ploughboy lover was returning home
    from town,
A robber laid in wait for him and boldly shot him
    down.
My father with much weeping did now bemoan his
    fate,
But bitter tears did not avail, his pity came too late.

So after seven lonely years I still remain unwed,
Though I had many lovers my vows were still
    unsaid.
One day a letter came to me from a dying man in
    Perth,
Who said he must his sin confess before he left this
    earth.

He said my cruel father with many coins in gold
Hired him to shoot my lover, to play the robber
    bold.
This letter to my father I quickly then did show,
And my lover was avengéd who plowed the
    lowlands low.

My father was condemned to die and died a public
    show,
For murdering of my sweetheart that ploughed the
    lowlands low.
By many I've been asked to wed, but I'll see them
    come and go,
My heart is with my Edmund Dale that ploughed
    the lowlands low.

57. The Press Gang Sailor   Lena Bourne Fish, 1940

Mrs. Fish's "The Press Gang Sailor," known in England as "The Valiant Sailor"
or "Polly on the Shore," is the only version of the song collected in North America.
The melody has some similarities to the tune sung by George "Pop" Maynard of Sussex, England, reported in the *Journal of the English Folk Dance and Song Society* for
December 1963. Arthur Schrader, long Director of Music at Old Sturbridge Village,
has sent us a facsimile of "The Valiant Sailor" as printed in Edinburgh in 1744 in a
small songster or chapbook called *The Irish Boy's Garland*. He says the songster is
part of the Harding collection of old English music now in the Bodleian Library at
Oxford.

Mrs. Fish said to us, "This is an old song that has been in my family since the
French and Indian War." The verses are almost identical to English texts, though less
complete than several.

A sailor's life was hard in the old days, and pay was scanty. Often shanghai methods—the press gang—was a captain's (or the Royal Navy's) only means of getting a crew. The press gang was feared and hated, but it seems to have been accepted, in this song, without too much rebellion. The singer blames only himself for his misfortune, and when the battle is joined he is English to the core. Pausing only briefly for a tender thought about his Polly and her charms, he ends with a ringing cheer for the English cause. These may be the sentiments, of course, of a song writer who had never been to sea.

We are told by a navy man that the "bloody flag" was the red battle flag, raised to fly under the English flag whenever an enemy is engaged.

THE PRESS GANG SAILOR

Come all you wild young men, And a warn-ing—— take by me,
Nev-er to lead your-self a-stray In-to no bad com-pa-ny.

As I myself have done,
In the pleasant month of May,
When I was seized by a press master
Of a warship at anchor in the bay.

As we were sailing along,
A-sailing along so high,
Who did we meet but a French man-of-war,
And to them we did draw nigh.

As we hoisted the English flag,
We did a bloody flag let fly.
Let every man stand firm to his gun,
For the Lord knows who must die.

The deck was sprinkled with blood,
And the big guns so loudly did roar.
How I did wish myself safe at home,
And along with my Polly on the shore.

She's a tall and slender lass,
With a dark and a rolling eye,
As I lay bleeding on the deck,
'Tis for your sweet sake I'll die.

May the Union Jack be unfurled
Over every land and clime,
And the brave deeds by our sailor boys
Be extolled till the end of time.

"The Press Gang Sailor"
Words and Music Collected, Adapted and Arranged by Frank Warner
TRO—© Copyright 1971 and 1984 Melody Trails, Inc., New York, N.Y. Used by Permission

58. Pretty Sylvia   Lena Bourne Fish, 1940

"Pretty Sylvia" seems to be known in most other versions as "The Female High-wayman," but they all tell of the girl who disguises herself as a highwayman to test her lover. He gives her his watch and his gold but refuses to give up the diamond ring which she herself had given him, so he passes the test to her satisfaction. She later confesses, and the story ends on a note of love and happiness.

There are a number of broadsides of this ballad in England, where it is known also as "Sylvia's Request and William's Denial," and as "Sovay, Sovay." Hammond recorded a version in Long Burton in 1906 which was published in the *Journal of the Folk-Song Society* 3 (1908–1909): 128, which includes a final verse:

Oh! then this couple married were
And they did live a happy pair
The bells did ring and the music play
Now they've got pleasure both night and day.

Child ballad No. 105, "The Bailiff's Daughter of Islington," tells a very similar story about a lady who tested her lover by accosting him on the highway. That ballad, also, has a happy ending.

Peter Kennedy, author of *Folk Songs of Britain and Ireland,* says that Mrs. Fish's version of this song is "old fashioned and rare."

See: Flanders, *VFSB,* 133; Greenleaf, 61; Kennedy, 722 ("Sylvia"); Laws, *ABBB,* N-21, 213 ("The Female Highwayman"); Mackenzie, 318

PRETTY SYLVIA

Pret - ty Syl - vi - a on a sum - mer's day, She — dressed her - self in — man's ar-
ray, With sword and pis - tol hung by her side To — rob her lov - er she did ride.

She met her lover on the plain,
And boldly bade her lover stand,
"Stand and deliver, without no strife,
Or in one moment I'll end your life."

After he had given her his gold,
She said, "I ask for one thing you hold,
That diamond ring that you proudly wear,
Deliver that, and your life I'll spare."

"That diamond ring is a pledge of love,
Gave by that's constant as a dove,
Of all my gold I will freely share,
My life I'll lose, but the ring I'll spare."

As they did walk in the garden green,
A fairer couple was never seen,
He saw his watch hanging by her clothes,
Which made him blush like a blooming rose.

Away she rode from her own true love,
For she was harmless as a dove,
Love or gold to see which was best,
Her valiant lover had stood the test.

"Why do you blush at a deed so bold,
I'll freely give back your watch and gold,
And since your love has proved to me true,
Nothing but death parts me from you."

59. The Rambler from Claire   Lena Bourne Fish, 1941

Reporting the collection of this song in Sussex, England, Lucy Broadwood, in the *Journal of the Folk-Song Society,* notes "as the broadside is so well known . . . missing lines have been inserted in brackets" (p. 149). She also says, "According to Dr. (P. W.) Joyce's version, 'The Rambler from Claire' commands the 'united men' (i.e., the 'united Irishmen,' that widely spread secret society by which the Rebellion of 1798 was chiefly directed). After some successful battles, he finds himself obliged to escape to America" (p. 151). This explains the third verse of Mrs. Fish's version.

Wright's source is a broadside, no imprint, in the Cambridge University Library. The tune given is from Patrick Weston Joyce's *Old Irish Folk Music and Song,* p. 194.

We have not found a reference to the song elsewhere in this country.

See: *JFSS* 5 (1911): Part 19, 149–51 (Lucy Broadwood); Wright, *Irish Immigrant Ballads and Songs,* 205

THE RAMBLER FROM CLAIRE

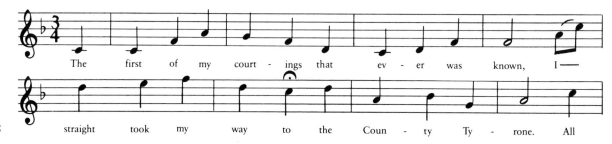

The first of my court - ings that ev - er was known, I —
straight took my way to the Coun - ty Ty - rone. All

of the fair maid - ens they used me well there, They——
called me the stran - ger, the —— ram - bler from Claire.

I then took my way to the town of Tralee,
And there made acquaintance with Sally McGee.
I first gained her favor, and then left her there,
And now they are searching for the rambler from
    Claire.

Now I have the title of a united man,
I can't stay at home in my own native land.
It is off to America I have to repair,
I'll indeed be a stranger, the rambler from Claire.

I never will marry, will not settle down,
For I am a rambler from town unto town.
Though ladies may please me when rosy and fair,
I will still be the stranger, the rambler from Claire.

Here's luck to my mother, wherever I be,
Likewise to my sweetheart, dear Sally McGee.
The ship is now ready, and the winds they blow fair,
He is gone, God be with him, the rambler from
    Claire.

60. Young but Daily Growing   Lena Bourne Fish, 1940

Laws calls this ballad simply "A-Growing," and it is sometimes known as "The Trees They Do Grow Tall." Laws gives a paragraph of other sources of the song, most of them English, from: Somerset, Surrey, Devon, Essex, Yorkshire, Dorset, Hertford, and Lancashire. Both Christie and Ord print versions from Scotland. It is found less frequently on this side of the water, in Nova Scotia, Kentucky, Connecticut, and Vermont.

The Penguin Book of English Folk Songs, edited by R. Vaughn Williams and A. L. Lloyd, says: "It is sometimes said that the ballad is based on the actual marriage of the juvenile laird of Craigton to a girl several years his senior, the laird dying three years later, in 1634. But in fact the ballad may be older; indeed, there is no clear evidence that it is Scottish in origin. Child marriages for the consolidation of family fortunes were not unusual in the Middle Ages and in some parts the custom persisted far into the seventeenth century."

Laws says that this song is "a fine old ballad generally considered worthy of a place in the Child collection" (p. 20).

See: Creighton and Senior, 108; Flanders and Olney, 196; Laws, *ABBB,* O-35, 242;
Sharp, *English Folksongs of the Southern Appalachians,* Vol. 1, 410; Sturgis, 3

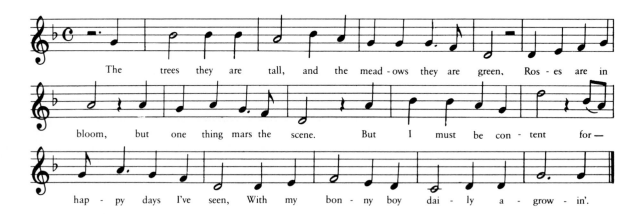

The trees they are tall, and the mead-ows they are green, Ros-es are in bloom, but one thing mars the scene. But I must be con-tent for— hap-py days I've seen, With my bon-ny boy dai-ly a-grow-in'.

"Father, father, much harm have you done,
Four long years have passed since I was twenty-one.
A lover of twelve years is surely much too young,
Only just a school boy a-growing."

"Daughter, dear daughter, no harm have I done,
I have promised you to a rich lord's son.
He will make a bed for you to rock upon,
He is young, but daily a-growing."

She made a shirt of the finest of lawn,
Made it for her boyish lover to put on.

She sighed as she longed for her wedding day to
    come,
With her bonny boy daily a-growing.

As she sat a-sewing in her father's castle hall,
She saw him with the young boys playing at the ball.
And smiled, as she said, "He's the flower of them all.
He's young but daily a-growing."

At thirteen he was a married man,
And at fourteen the father of a son.
But at sixteen his grave it was green,
He died in the youth of his growing.

61. The Young Prince of Spain   Lena Bourne Fish, 1940

Laws calls this song "The Prince of Morocco," or "Sailor Boy II." In addition to the sources noted below, it may be found on broadsides at Harvard in several collections.

John Galusha sang a version of this song, telling the same story but in very different words. He was much amused by the trick played on the hard-hearted father.

See: Brown, Vol. 2, 232; Flanders-Barry, *NGMS*, 38; Laws, *ABBB*, N-18, 211; Randolph, Vol. 1, 354

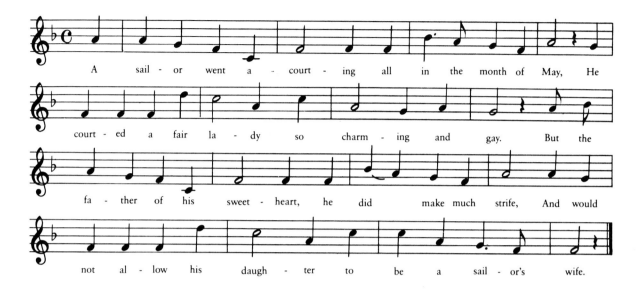

A sail-or went a-court-ing all in the month of May, He
court-ed a fair la-dy so charm-ing and gay. But the
fa-ther of his sweet-heart, he did make much strife, And would
not al-low his daugh-ter to be a sail-or's wife.

The sailor sailed away to the far off coast of
Spain,
In hopes of some good fortune or riches to
gain.
He bought a prince's robe with a star upon his
breast,
And sailed away back home to the girl he loved
best.

He landed at the wharf, so I have heard them say,
After he had been absent five years and a day,
With the stay upon his breast, he went to see his
love again,
And her father was pleased with the young prince
of Spain.

He made a great feast, as the wedding day drew
near,
Of the young prince of Spain and his daughter
so dear.
And while the social glasses passed merrily
around,
He paid off his daughter with ten thousand
pounds.

Then up spoke the sailor, "This is my happy day,
For I'm the jolly sailor you once turned away.
And by such good fortune you've now crowned
my life,
I have ten thousand pounds and a beautiful
wife!"

"You may go to the devil," her father replied,
"I wish you had been drowned in the ocean so wide.
If I had mistrusted that this was your plot,
Not one single farthing from me would you have
got."

62. Imaginary Trouble   Lena Bourne Fish, 1940

More often known as "The Crying Family," a version under that title was collected by Mrs. Flanders in Vermont. The Vermont version has a refrain which Mrs. Fish did not use. The story line is very much the same except for Mrs. Fish's last two lines: "Each night the ghost doth come / And cries upon the water." Since the babe whom they are all lamenting has not yet been born, the "ghost" seems well ahead of its time.

Mrs. Flanders compares the song to Grimm's folk tale No. 34, "Clever Else." The story is remarkably the same except that the death of the child is to come about, it is feared, from a pickaxe left sticking in a beam in the cellar ceiling, rather than by drowning.

Grammy Fish, though she did not give us the source of her information, told us that this song was "often sung in Revolutionary War camps."

See: Flanders-Barry, *NGMS,* 14

IMAGINARY TROUBLE

There lived, as I've heard say, Down by a running water, An old man and his wife Who had a charming daughter.

One night said Kate to John,
"I've had a troubled fancy,
I heard the waters roar
And thought upon our Nancy."

"If Tom and Nance should wed,
And such a thing there may be,
Their marriage might bring about
A prattling little baby."

"When that dear babe could walk,
And just begin to waddle,

Perchance he might come here
And in the water paddle."

"I know he will be drowned,
I hear those waters calling,
'O pretty sweet baby.'"
And both began a-bawling.

No doubt but it was fate
That brought those lovers walking
To where old John and Kate
Were a-sighing and a-talking.

They all sat on the green,
While Katie told her fancy.
How they did weep and wail,
Tom, old man, Kate, and Nancy.

They all went crying home,
Tom, old man, wife, and daughter.
Each night the ghost doth come
And cries upon the water.

63. Joe Bowers   Lena Bourne Fish, 1940

Laws, in *NAB*, notes that this ballad has been found throughout the South, the Middle West, and the Southwest. It does not seem to have been collected in New England except for this version from Mrs. Fish.

For a full discussion of the possible authorship of the ballad Laws refers the reader to Louise Pound, *Western Folklore* 16 (1957): 111–20, "Yet Another Joe Bowers." Miss Pound accepts John A. Stone, the Old Put of *Put's Golden Songster,* as the author of "Joe Bowers," as well as of "Sweet Betsy from Pike," and, possibly, "Days of Forty-Nine" (No. 12). Stone crossed the plains from Pike County, Missouri, in 1849, and died January 23, 1864.

Belden calls "Joe Bowers" "the best-known relic of the gold fever of '49" (p. 341), and quotes Lomax (*Journal of American Folklore* 28, p. 5) as calling it "one of the popular songs among the Confederate soldiers of the Civil War."

See: Belden, 342; Brown, Vol. 2, 607; Laws, *NAB*, B-14, 139; Lomax, *ABF*, 422

JOE BOWERS

My name it is Joe Bowers, And I have a brother Ike. I came from old Missouri, All the way from Pike. I'll tell you why I left there And how I came to roam, To leave my poor old mammy So far away from home.

I fell in love with a girl back there,
Her name was Sally Black,
I asked if she would be my wife,
She said it was a whack.
Said she to me, to me, "Joe Bower,
I have no man but you,
And never will deceive you.
I'll be faithful kind and true."

"O Sally, my dearest Sally,
Sally just for your sake
I'm going to Colorado
And try to raise a stake."
Said she to me, "Joe Bower,
You are the man to win.
Here's a kiss to bind the bargain,"
And she hove a dozen in.

So I came to Colorado
To try to strike it rich.
Came down upon the bolsters [boulders?]
Just like a thousand bricks.
I worked both late and early
Through all the rain and snow,
I was working for my Sally,
'Twas all the same to Joe.

In a few short weeks a letter came
From my dear brother Ike.
It came from old Missouri,
All the way from Pike.
It brought to me the darndest news
That ever you did hear.
My heart is almost bursting,
So please excuse a tear.

It said that Sal was false to me,
Her love for me had fled,
That Sal had married a butcher,
And the butcher's hair was red.
More than that the letter said,
'Twas enough to make me swear,
That Sally had a baby,
And the baby had red hair!

Goodbye dear old Missouri,
My friends and early home.
I'll forever be a stranger
And wander sad and lone.
For Sally has deceived me
And has caught me in her snare.
I don't see how that babe of Sal's
Could really have red hair.

64. Richmond on the James   Lena Bourne Fish, 1941

This Civil War song may be said to be related to "The Dying Soldier" found in Doerflinger, and therefore to "The Dying Ranger," a Southern variant noted by Laws, *NAB,* A-14. It seems to be related also to Laws, *NAB,* A-13, called "The Battle of Mill Springs," and also to a song Almeda Riddle sings called "A Soldier of the Legion." Roger Abrahams (*A Singer and Her Songs,* p. 72) says that this song of Mrs. Riddle's is "Bingen on the Rhine" by Caroline E. Norton, Lady Maxwell. Mrs. Fish's tune, however, is not the tune of "Bingen on the Rhine."

In spite of the similarity of its theme to that of the songs mentioned, "Richmond on the James" has too many differences not to be accepted as a separate and distinct song.

See: Belden, 397; Doerflinger, 274; Laws, *NAB,* A-13 and A-14, 125; Randolph, Vol. 2, 264

RICHMOND ON THE JAMES

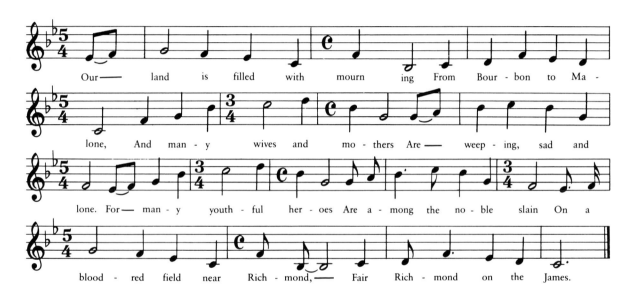

Our land is filled with mourn ing From Bour - bon to Ma - lone, And man - y wives and mo - thers Are weep - ing, sad and lone. For man - y youth - ful her - oes Are a - mong the no - ble slain On a blood - red field near Rich - mond, Fair Rich - mond on the James.

A soldier boy at Richmond
Lay gasping on the field.
The battle strife was over,
And the foe was forced to yield.
But there fell one noble hero
Before the foe-man's aim
On that blood-stained field at Richmond,
Fair Richmond on the James.

A comrade stood beside him,
As his life blood ebbed away.
They had been chums together
Since boyhood's early day.

Together they had struggled
'Mid strife and grief and pain,
But to part that night at Richmond,
Fair Richmond on the James.

He said, "My noble comrade,
You will miss me for awhile,
But the faces that once loved us
Again on you will smile.
Again you will be foremost
In all the village games,
While I lie here at Richmond,
Fair Richmond on the James."

165

"Take the sword home to my brother,
And the star upon my breast
To my young and gentle sister,
The one I loved the best.
A brown lock from my forehead
To my mother who still dreams
Of the safe return of her soldier boy
From Richmond on the James."

"Now, my loving comrade,
On my breast is a dark brown braid.
It is of one of the fairest
Of all the village maids.
We were to be married,
But death the bridegroom claims,
While she is far that loves me
From Richmond on the James."

"I know that she is praying,
While her blessed heart still dreams,
Of the safe return of her soldier
From Richmond on the James."

65. On Springfield Mountain   Lena Bourne Fish, 1941

We have collected at least four versions of this colonial ballad about an actual event that took place in 1761 in Springfield Mountain, now Wilbraham, Massachusetts. The one from John Galusha (No. 23) must be very close to the original serious ballad. Later the ballad was widely popular in a number of comic versions both on the stage and among college students. This was after urbanization had made rattlesnakes less of a problem. This version from Mrs. Fish is not the serious original, nor is it one of the ridiculous versions that poke fun at a country bumpkin. It falls somewhere in between, ending with a biblical allusion to the snake in the Garden of Eden. The eighth verse has the interesting lines: "Poor Billy died, gave up the ghost / And away he went to the painted post." Could this be a reference to the sexton, who conducted funerals and who usually was also the barber of the community, with a red and white painted pole, or post? There is a town in western New York State named Painted Post, but I don't believe it has anything to do with this song.

There is a long discussion of this song by Phillips Barry in two issues of *Bulletin of the Folk-Song Society of the Northeast*. In No. 7 he quotes a verse found on a tombstone in Deacon Adams Cemetery in Wilbraham:

Here lies ye Body of Mr. Timothy Mirick, Son of
Lieut. Thomas & Mrs. Mirick Who died August
7th 1761 in ye 23rd Year of his Age. "He cometh
forth like a flower and is cut down He fleeeth
also as a Shadow and continueth not" (Job XIV, 2)

And in No. 8:

This youth he soon gave up the ghost
And up to Abraham's bosom did post.

The Fish version is close to (but not exactly like) a stage version published as early as 1840 and copyrighted by George Gaines Spear, "The Pesky Sarpent: A Pathetic Ballad," included in the "Series of Old American Songs," Harris Collection, Brown University.

See: Brown, Vol. 2, 489; *Bulletin, No. 7*, 4–5; *Bulletin,* No. 8, 3–6; Eddy, 248; Laws, *NAB,* G-16, 220; Library of Congress field recording 3755 A; Lomax, *FSNA,* 13

ON SPRINGFIELD MOUNTAIN

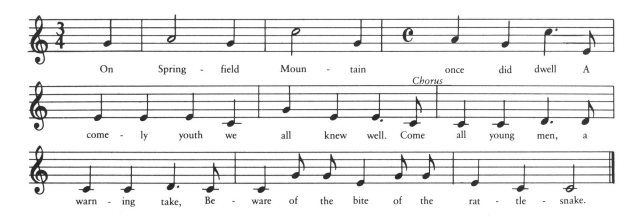

On Spring - field Moun - tain once did dwell A

Chorus

come - ly youth we all knew well. Come all young men, a

warn - ing take, Be - ware of the bite of the rat - tle - snake.

He lived in peace and homely cheer, With his charming wife, sweet Molly dear. *Chorus*	He raised his scythe, and with one blow He laid the pesky serpent low. *Chorus*
One sunny morning he did go Down in the meadow for to mow. *Chorus*	He carried it home to his Molly dear, She sighed and looked so very queer. *Chorus*
He had not mowed scarce 'round the field, Before a rattler bit him on the heel. *Chorus*	"O Billy dear, why did you go Down in the meadow for to mow?" *Chorus*

Poor Billy died, gave up the ghost,
And away he went to the painted post.
Chorus

Since Eden's days the snake hath planned
To rid the world of mortal man.
Chorus

A hatred for him he doth feel,
So he creeps up and bites his heel.
Chorus

66. William the Sailor   Lena Bourne Fish, 1941

We have found no references to this story of the sailor and the rich young lady who meet so fortuitously and to such a happy end. Perhaps this song, too, was a stage song in its original form.

WILLIAM THE SAILOR

As—— Wil - liam the sail - or was walk - ing one day, He met a fair maid - en both charm - ing—— and—— gay, Who asked him his name and his place—— of—— a - bode, And al - so asked why he was trav - l'ing that road.

*2nd verse

168

"My name it is William, a sailor by trade,
All the ports of America I've already surveyed.
In the township of Danville I make my abode,
So I think there's no harm in my traveling this road."

"A sailor's a rover," this fair maid replied,
"So they love to wander to ports far and wide.
Though they may seem friendly, they've an un-
    stable mind,
And so they a mistress in every port find."

"Now I am a rover," the sailor replied,
"But have never yet taken a mistress or bride.
I'm alone in the world and without kith or kin,
So to be a sailor I think is no sin."

"I've sailed to home ports and to lands far away,
But have not been in love till I met you today.
So when I've made a fortune in lands far and wide
I'll return and will ask you to be my fair bride."

"O William, my William, do not sail away,
But forget distant harbors and lands far away!
For I have great riches and am also alone,
So please share my future, my lands, and my home."

Then William consented to be the bridegroom,
The parson was sent for the next afternoon.
A happier couple none ever did see
Than the jolly young sailor and his fine lady.

67. The Bonny Bay of Biscay-O   Lena Bourne Fish, 1941

We have been able to find no information in print about this song. English friends
have told us that this is one of the folk songs blandly thrust upon small English school
children, with no information about its origin or usage. There is a version of the "Gypsy
Laddie" (Child No. 200) in which the chorus says: "Some sang high and some sang
low, and some sang the 'Bonny Bay of Biscay-o.'" The song has not been found elsewhere in America, although a song of the same name appears (words only)—with very
different words—on page 515 of *American Folk Poetry,* edited by Duncan Emrich. That
song may be heard on Library of Congress field recording AFS, 4464 B as recorded
by Alan Lomax from the singing of Mrs. Carrie Grover of Gorham, Maine, in 1941.
Mrs. Grover's song is about a terrible storm at sea and the British ship that was nearly
destroyed in the Bay of Biscay-o.

THE BONNY BAY OF BISCAY-O

Of   all   the   har - bors   east   or   west,   There   is   one   place   that   169

I — love — best. So which - ev - er way the wind doth blow, I'll
steer for the bon - ny Bay of Bis - cay - o.

Chorus
For the girl I love is waiting there,
With her eyes of blue and her golden hair.
So it's eastward hi, and westward ho,
But return to the bonny Bay of Biscay-o.

At night in my hammock I will sleep,
As we sail upon the briny deep.
Though the tempests rage and the wild winds blow,
I will dream of the bonny Bay of Biscay-o.
    Chorus

In one more year I will settle down
With my bride in this fair seaport town.
She is sweeter and dearer by far, I know,
Than the winds of the bonny Bay of Biscay-o.
    Chorus

"Bay of Biscayo"
Collected and Arranged by Frank Warner
TRO — © Copyright 1971 and 1984 Hollis Music, Inc., New York, N.Y. Used by Permission

68. The Bull Frog   Lena Bourne Fish, 1941

This song (also known as "The Frog in the Spring"), with its wonderful nonsense refrain, and "The Frog and the Mouse" ("The Frog He Would A-Wooing Go") — and sometimes a conscious or unconscious combination of the two — may be said to be, as Combs noted, "the most universal of all traditional songs surviving in the English-speaking world." Combs, as a matter of fact, does not differentiate between the two songs. Randolph does separate them: Vol. 1, pp. 402–410 for "The Frog's Courtship" or "The Frog and the Mouse," and pp. 362–65 for "There Was an Old Frog." Of the latter he says: "This piece was sung by several of the early blackface minstrels. . . . It is based upon an English nonsense rhyme, according to Kittredge."

Arthur Schrader of Old Sturbridge Village tells us that in 1695 in London a song was known called "Great Lord Frog and Lady Mouse," and that in New Haven in 1787 "The Bull Frog" was turned into a parody of an Italian opera.

Aside from all that the song is great fun to sing and children love it.

See: Combs, 67, 218; Randolph, Vol. 1, 402–410

Oh, I took him out and laid him on the ground,
Sing song Polly won't you ky-me-o.
The bull frog winked and looked all around,
Sing song Polly won't you ky-me-o.
    Chorus

He rode away to get him a bride,
Sing song Polly won't you ky-me-o.
With a sword and a pistol by his side,
Sing song Polly won't you ky-me-o.
    Chorus

But the sun shone bright for there was no rain,
Sing song Polly won't you ky-me-o.
So the bull frog jumped in the pond again,
Sing song Polly won't you ky-me-o.
    Chorus

69. The Captain with His Whiskers   Lena Bourne Fish, 1941

This song of Mrs. Fish's is older than she realized. Old Sturbridge Village has
issued a small recording called "Parlor Ballads in America 1790–1840," and one of its

songs is "O! They March'd Thro' the Town," with the note that its words were written by "the fashionable early nineteenth-century English poet Thomas Haynes Bayly (who wrote "Long, Long Ago"), whose main creative period was the 1820s, and a tune by Sidney Nelson, a London music teacher and ballad composer." The notes go on to say that the song "came into popularity about the mid-1830s," and has survived in oral tradition. The song is much the same as Mrs. Fish's, as its first verse shows:

Oh! they march'd thro' the town with their banners so gay,
To my casement I ran just to hear the band play;
And I peep'd thro the blind very cautiously then,
Lest the neighbours should say that I look'd at the men.
Oh! I heard not the tune tho' the music was sweet,
For my eyes at the time had a much greater treat,
For the troop was the finest that e'er I did see,
And the Captain by chance caught a sly glimpse of me.

I understand that whiskers became popular among military men during the 1850s and somewhat later among civilians. In the 1850s "The Captain with His Whiskers" took over Bayly's version in the songsters and songbooks in which it may be found. Joseph Hickerson, head of the Folk Archives at the Library of Congress, says that "The Captain" is to be found in many late nineteenth-century collections.

Mrs. Fish did not know that whiskers would again become popular with men of another generation. When she gave us this song she added these comments:

This is an old army song which, according to my records, was writtten about eighty years ago [1860]. Of course I realize that it is strictly out of date, as no man of this day and age could ever hope to find a girl to dance or keep company with him if his face was covered with whiskers. But in the good old days whiskers were deemed to be an emblem of strength and manhood. So if a girl had a lover well bewhiskered it was considered a thing to take pride in. It is a song that retained its popularity for a good many years, for I can remember when I was a child of hearing it played at big events.

See: *New Comic Songster;* Randolph, Vol. 2, 281

THE CAPTAIN WITH HIS WHISKERS

172   As they marched through the town with their ban - ners so gay I —

went to the win - dow to hear — the band play, And I
peeped through the blinds ve - ry cau - tious - ly then, Lest the
neigh - bors should say — I was look - ing at the men. I heard — the drum
beat and the mu - sic so sweet, But my eyes at that mo - ment caught a
much — great - er treat, For the troop was the first that — ev - er I did
see, And the cap - tain with his whisk - ers took a sly — glance at me.

When we met at the ball, I of course thought it
   right
To pretend that we never had met till that night.
But he knew me at once, I perceived at a glance,
So I hung down my head when he asked me
   to dance.
He sat by my side at the end of the set,
And the sweet words he told me, I never can forget.
For my heart was enlisted and could not get free
When the captain with his whiskers took a sly
   glance at me.

Though he marched from the town, and I saw him
   no more,
Yet I think of him still and the whiskers he wore.
I dream all the night, and I talk all the day
Of the love of a captain who has gone far away.

I remember with superabundant delight
When we met in the street, and we danced all
   the night,
And I keep in my mind how my heart jumped with
   glee
When the captain with his whiskers took a sly glance
   at me.

But there's hope for a friend just ten minutes ago
Said the captain had returned from the war, and
   I know
He'll be looking for me with considerable zest,
And when he has found me you all know the rest.
Perhaps he is here, let me look 'round the house,
Keep still every one of you, as still as a mouse.
For if that dear captain is here he will be
With his whiskers a-taking a sly glance at me.

173

70. Ho Boys Ho   Lena Bourne Fish, 1941

This rousing, singable song from the Gold Rush days of '49 has an interesting history.

In 1850 the minstrel song "De Camptown Races," composed by Stephen Foster, was an immediate success, and people were singing it on every hand. Doerflinger gives three versions of a shanty, "Sacramento," used aboard the clipper ships sailing for California by way of Cape Horn. He says that the "tune and short refrains of Foster's song are combined in the shanty with the chorus of one introduced by the Hutchinson Family, a famous New England concert troupe, 'in honor of a band of overland emigrants, who left Massachusetts in the spring of 1849.' 'Ho for California!' ran:

> Then, ho! Brothers ho!
> To California go,
> There's plenty of gold in the world, we're told
> On the banks of the Sacramento."

Mrs. Fish's chorus is the same as that of the Hutchinson family song, but all of her verses are different. We believe, however, that the Fish song, like the shanty, must be a reworking of the Hutchinson Family song.

Doerflinger gives other sources of the shanty, including Colcord, Sandburg, and Sharp. He also quotes John Tasker Howard (*Stephen Foster: America's Troubadour*) as saying that "the chorus air [of "Camptown Races"] is that of the English ballad, 'Ten Thousand Miles Away' ('The Capital Ship')." It is even possible that "Ten Thousand Miles Away" became a black shanty, heard and reworked by Foster into "Camptown Races."

Irwin Silber and Earl Robinson, in *Songs of the Great American West,* say that part of the Hutchinson tune for "Ho For California" was taken from Dan Emmett's song, "De Boatman's Dance," published in 1843.

See: Doerflinger, 67, 351; Gordon, 95

HO BOYS HO

174

Cal - i - for - ni - a go. There's plen - ty of gold in the world we're told, On the banks of the Sac - ra - men - to.

We'll walk down the trail through heat and cold,	No dainty fare we gold diggers know,
For we know at the end we will find gold,	For our bannocks are made of sour dough,
Chorus	*Chorus*

Through the sands of the desert hot and dry,	At night on the ground we'll all sleep sound,
With never a sound but the coyote's cry,	Except when the wolves come prowling 'round,
Chorus	*Chorus*

We will hit the trail back home some day,
When gold and good fortune comes our way,
Chorus

71. The Jolly Roving Tar   Lena Bourne Fish, 1940

Mrs. Fish told us that she learned this song from an old man who used to sail on a whaling ship. It carries the roll and flavor of the sea, and the chorus is designed for rowdy singing.

There is a good version of the song (without a tune) in Lomax's *American Ballads and Folk Songs.* Lomax says, "This song was sung and written down by John Thomas, a Welsh sailor on the *Philadelphia* in 1896."

So far as we have been able to discover, it has not been found elsewhere in America. Nor, for that matter, have we heard of its appearing in tradition in the British Isles, although it is no doubt of English origin.

See: Lomax, *ABF,* 493.

Ships may come and ships may go As long as the sea doth roll. Each sail - or lad just like his dad, He loves the flow - ing bowl. A trip a - shore he does a - dore With a girl that's plump and round. When your mon - ey's gone it's the same old song, Get up, Jack, John sit down. Come a - long, come a - long, you jol - ly brave boys, There's lots of grog in the jar. We'll plow the bri - ny o - cean With the — jol - ly — rov - ing tar.

When Jack gets in it's then he steers
For some old boarding house.
He's welcomed in with rum and gin,
They feed him on pork souse.
He'll lend and spend and not offend
Till he lies drunk on the ground.
When your money's gone it's the same old song,
Get up, Jack, John sit down.
Chorus

He then will sail aboard some ship
For India or Japan,
In Asia there the ladies fair
All love the sailorman.
He'll go ashore and on a tear
And buy some girl a gown.
When your money's gone it's the same old song,
Get up, Jack, John sit down.
Chorus

"The Jolly Roving Tar"
Collected and Arranged by Frank Warner
TRO — © Copyright 1959 and 1984 Hollis Music, Inc., New York, N.Y. Used by Permission

176

When Jack gets old and weather-beat,
Too old to roam about,
In some rum shop they'll let him stop
Till eight bells calls him out.
He'll raise his eyes up to the skies,
Saying, "Boys, we're homeward bound!"
When your money's gone it's the same old song,
Get up, Jack, John sit down.
      Chorus

72. The Jolly Tinker   Lena Bourne Fish, 1940

In view of the important role which the tinker or the traveling peddler played in pioneer America, we are surprised that we have not found this song in any of the collections or heard it from anyone but Mrs. Fish. To our colonial forebears, often living isolated lives far from neighbors or a town, having no way to hear any news or any new songs, or any place to shop for small items of necessity or luxury, the tinker must have been a most important individual who was looked for with expectancy and cordially welcomed.

See: Laws, *NAB,* F-24, 203 ("The Peddler and His Wife")

THE JOLLY TINKER

I am a jolly tinker That goes from town to town. I will mend your pots and kettles If you'll only bring them 'round. Tu-ra lad-dy, tu-ra lad-dy, tu-ra lad-dy hi row.

I know how to solder,
And I can mend a pot.
I can also stop a hole
So it will not leak a drop.
Tura laddy, tura laddy, tura laddy, hi row.

I can mend umbrellas,
And I can tinker clocks.
The housewives are all smiles
When they see the tinker stop.
Tura laddy, tura laddy, tura laddy, hi row.

A tinker never marries,
Has a girl in every town,
And they shower me with kisses
As they bring their kettles down.
Tura laddy, tura laddy, tura laddy, hi row.

They feast me and regale me
With choicest meat and wine,
And whatever house I stop at,
I can always sup and dine.
Tura laddy, tura laddy, tura laddy, hi row.

So many wait my coming,
For I have many friends.
I've never stored much gold,
Yet I have a lot to spend.
Tura laddy, tura laddy, tura laddy, hi row.

My life is wild and free,
And I do not seek renown.
I am just a jolly tinker
With a girl in every town.
Tura laddy, tura laddy, tura laddy, hi row.

73. Old Tippecanoe   Lena Bourne Fish, 1940

This is a presidential election campaign song of 1840 to the tune of "The Crusader's Marching Hymn"—also known as "I Won't Be Home Until Morning," or "The Bear Went Over the Mountain." It is in praise of William Henry Harrison, who held a commission under Washington from 1793 to 1798. Upon his appointment he is known to have walked from Philadelphia to Pittsburgh to join his troops. Harrison also served as governor of the Territory of Indiana (which included the present states of Indiana, Illinois, Michigan, Wisconsin, and part of Minnesota) under three presidents—John Adams, Jefferson, and Madison. Harrison was a major general and a hero in the War of 1812, earning the nickname "Tippecanoe" from the battle of that name on November 7, 1811, where he defeated the British and their Indian allies led by Tecumseh. In the campaign of 1840 he won the election over the incumbent president Martin Van Buren.

The Whigs' propaganda in 1840 on Harrison's behalf, obviously, was effective. Using the symbols of a log cabin and hard cider, they turned the patrician William Henry Harrison into the candidate of the people. "There is no evidence to suggest that Harrison ever had much to do with the north end of a plow, but this did not prevent the Whig rhymesters from singing about the 'honest old farmer of North Bend,' or the 'plain-spoken yeoman' in his fields."[1]

1. Irwin Silber, *Songs America Voted By*, p. 34. In his chapter on this campaign (pp. 33–45), Silber notes that the year 1840 was the first time there was a wide use of political songs.

Harrison was sixty-seven when he was elected to the presidency. He was inaugurated, outdoors, on a cold rainy day, standing bareheaded to give his address. He died just thirty-one days later, and John Tyler became president. One of the slogans of the campaign had been "Tippecanoe and Tyler too!"

We have not found the song elsewhere.

OLD TIPPECANOE

The times are bad and want cur - ing, They're get - ting past all en - dur - ing, Let us turn out Mar - tin Van Bur - en, And put in old Tip - pe - ca - noe.

Chorus

So the best thing we can do Is to vote for old Tip - .pe - ca - noe! We've had of their hum - bug a - plen - ty, Now all of our pock - ets are emp - ty, We've not one dol - lar now where we had twen - ty, So we'll vote for old Tip - pe - ca - noe.

He was born in a humble log cabin,
Was raised up on hoe cake and bacon,
But the spirit of valor still dwells in
The heart of old Tippecanoe!
Chorus

Our daring and dauntless brave rider,
His fame's growing deeper and wider,
Let us drink with a glass of hard cider
To the health of old Tippecanoe!
Chorus

179

74. The Prop of the Nation   Lena Bourne Fish, 1941

This song in praise of the working man could be a union song in the light of its subject matter, but we have found no reference to it in any other collections. Mrs. Fish told us it was used as a campaign song by supporters of Rutherford B. Hayes in the presidential campaign of 1877, though we have found no confirmation of her statement. Hayes, a Civil War hero and general, member of Congress, and governor of Ohio, was the nineteenth President of the United States. He stood for sound money and was responsible for trebling the contents of the Library of Congress.

THE PROP OF THE NATION

"Who is the sup-port of our coun-try to-day, The rich or the poor?" you may ask. No, it is the man with the toil-hard-ened hand Who for-ev-er you'll find at his task.

He labors with zeal and earnestly strives
To obtain all the best things of life.
He will give of his substance to brothers in need,
To those who have failed in the strife.

When our land needed soldiers to take up their guns,
And asked them for her right to stand,
The ranks of brave soldiers have ever been filled
From the ranks of the brave working man.

They serve her in peace, and serve her in war,
Will be ever first in the fray,

Though some may be poor, they are true to the core,
Ever ready her laws to obey.

They've founded our country and built up their homes,
Through all the broad scope of our land.
And no deed of justice was ever passed by
By their kindly and toil-hardened hand.

All our lofty buildings in which we take pride,
Our towers and cathedrals so grand,
The first and last stone of those buildings so vast
Were laid by his toil-hardened hand.

75. The Telegraph Wire   Lena Bourne Fish, 1940

This surely is another stage song that moved into tradition. We have not found this particular song, but there were other songs of the stage from around 1900 dealing with the telegraph (invented by Marconi in the 1870s). George M. Cohan, at the age of twenty in 1898, wrote his first big hit entitled "I Guess I'll Have to Telegraph My Baby." David Owen Levy, in *All The Years of American Popular Music,* says that the Cohan song is "one of the earliest popular songs about wireless telegraphy" (p. 211).

We wonder how many people still know that in the last line of the third verse "three or four buffaloes" refers to buffalo lap robes, then a mark of luxury.

The fifth verse, referring to "hoop skirts" does seem to place the date of the song as earlier than 1900.

THE TELEGRAPH WIRE

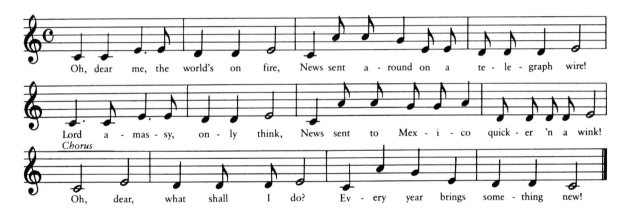

Oh, dear me, the world's on fire, News sent a-round on a te-le-graph wire!
Lord a-mas-sy, on-ly think, News sent to Mex-i-co quick-er 'n a wink!
Chorus
Oh, dear, what shall I do? Ev-ery year brings some-thing new!

Cyrus Field, he won renown
By stretching a cable to London town.
Ben Franklin surely won renown
When he brought that pesky lightning down.
    Chorus

When I was young and went to a ball,
I had to drive an ox team or none at all.
But now they have a horse and sleigh,
Three or four buffaloes—everything gay.
    Chorus

And now the horse is deemed too slow,
The railroad trains are all the go.
Just sit in your seat and ride along,
A ticket can be bought for 'most a song.
    Chorus

With hoop skirts and stays in fashion too,
We poor men know not what to do.
They really set our brain on fire,
So Morse invented the telegraph wire.
    Chorus

76. Touch Not the Cup Lena Bourne Fish, 1940

A great wave of temperance songs crossed the American land, beginning in the 1830s, according to George W. Ewing in his *The Well-Tempered Lyre: Songs and Verse of the Temperance Movement,* which includes this song, to be sung to the air "Long, Long Ago."

Grammy Fish sang three verses to that same air—the only temperance song she gave us. Rowena Peterson, from Ogdensburg, New York, whom we met when we all were attending the Seminars on American Culture conducted by the New York State Historical Association at Cooperstown, New York, gave us a typed copy of "Touch Not the Cup" with four verses. It was taken from *Favorite Songs and Hymns for School and Home,* edited by J. P. McCaskey (American Book Company, c. 1899). James H. Aikman is given as the author of the words, and T. H. Bayly (see notes for No. 69) is given credit for the tune. This is the verse which Mrs. Fish did not sing:

Touch not the cup, young man, in thy pride,
Touch not the cup, touch not the cup.
Hark to the warning of thousands who've died—
Touch not the cup, touch it not.
Go to their lonely and desolate tomb,
Think of their death, of their sorrow and gloom,
Think that perhaps thou may'st share in their doom—
Touch not the cup, touch it not.

Among the early songsters which we have collected over the years is one called *The Temperance Harp: Original and Selected Music for All Temperance Occasions,* by C. J. Warren. It includes all four verses with words by J. H. Aikman. The tune is the same as Grammy's, but no mention is made of the composer.

Randolph prints two verses—Grammy's first two, and he notes that it is also included in the *Franklin Square Song Collection 3* (1885), p. 78.

George Ewing says, "'Touch Not the Cup' is anonymous in twelve collections, credited to J. H. Aikman in one, to Mrs. J. H. Aikman in another, and to Paxton Hood in a third" (p. 11). He found it in an 1844 temperance book, *The Washingtonian Harp* (one year later than our aforementioned songster) and says that the song has lasted virtually unchanged in folk collections since that time.

See: Ewing, 179; Randolph, Vol. 2, 427

TOUCH NOT THE CUP

Touch not the cup, it is death to the soul, Touch not the cup,

touch not the cup. Man-y I know who have quaffed from that bowl,

Touch not the cup, touch it not. Lit-tle they thought that a de-mon was—

there, Blind-ly they drank and were caught in the snare, But of that

death-deal-ing bowl, O be-ware! Touch not the cup, touch it not.

Touch not the cup when the wine glistens bright,
Touch not the cup, touch not the cup,
Though like the ruby it shines in the light,
Touch not the cup, touch it not.
Fangs of the serpent are hid in that bowl,
Deeply its poison will enter the soul,
Soon will it plunge thee beyond thy control,
Touch not the cup, touch it not.

Touch not the cup, friend, O drink not a drop.
Touch not the cup, touch not the cup.
All that thou lovest entreats thee to stop,
Touch not the cup, touch it not.
Stop for the friends that to thee are so near,
Stop for the home that to thee is so dear,
Stop, for thy country is trembling with fear!
Touch not the cup, touch it not.

77. Treat My Daughter Kindly (or, The Little Farm)   Lena Bourne Fish, 1941

This song, which is also known as "The Little Farm" and as "All the Little Chickens in the Garden," was sung to us by Mrs. Fish in 1941. Both Frank and I remember hearing it from other sources—probably when we were children in very different parts of the country. I have not been able to find out very much about it. There is one version in Randolph from Springdale, Arkansas. The story is the same, although the words are quite different from those sung by Mrs. Fish—except for the chorus. Randolph's notes (pp. 111–12) say:

Three stanzas and a chorus entitled "The Farmer's Daughter" appeared in *Hamlin's Wizard Oil Songbook*, Chicago, n.d., c. 1897. A very similar text is quoted by Mark Sullivan (*Our Times*, N.Y., 1927, p. 181) without a title, and described simply as 'a song to a prospective son-in-law.' See also Stout (*Folklore from Iowa*, Memoirs American Folklore Society, Vol. XXIX, 1936, p. 28). Irving Stone, in his biography of Jack London (*Saturday Evening Post*, July 9, 1938, p. 53) says that London sang a song called 'Treat My Daughter

Kind-i-ly' in 1894 or 1895. C. V. Wheat (Aurora, Mo., *Advertiser*, Dec. 5, 1940) prints four stanzas of a text called 'The Farmer's Daughter,' which he describes as 'an old courting song, popular some three generations back.'

Alan Lomax says his mother sang him the song when he was a child—a version almost exactly like the one found in Randolph.

The mention of Yorkshire in Mrs. Fish's first verse has made us wonder if the song could have an English origin—perhaps English music hall. When we found it included on a topic recording by the Watersons we hoped to find that fact established. However, their notes say only: "Martin Carthy and Norma Waterson heard a man named Joe Udal sing this at a shepherds' meet in the Lake District in 1974, and took a fancy to it." We are still wondering.

The song can be heard on a Library of Congress recording called "All the Little Chickens in the Garden." It was recorded in April of 1948 by Herbert Halpert from the singing of Mrs. Prudie Tillman of Hopkinsville, Kentucky.

The recording Mrs. Fish made for us on a small disk in 1941 has been lost. Frank Warner knew the tune, but he is not here to sing it, and I cannot remember it well enough. We print the song, therefore, without a tune.

See: Library of Congress field recording AFS 9741 B 3; Randolph, Vol. 4, 111; Topic Record No. 12 TS 265 ("for pence and spicy ale")

TREAT MY DAUGHTER KINDLY (or, THE LITTLE FARM)

While traveling down in Yorkshire
Not very long ago,
I chanced to fall in love,
With a girl you all must know.
I told her if she'd come with me,
I would see her on her way,
And when I took her to her home
I heard her father say,

Chorus
"Treat my daughter kindly,
Never do her harm.
When I die I'll leave you
My little house and farm,
My horse, my cow, my pig and plow,
And all my cocks and hens,
And all yon little chickens in the garden."

Now when I went a-courting,
I was so blooming shy
I hadn't a blessed word to say,
If folks were passing by.
One night I met her all alone
And asked her to be my bride,
She said she would if I'd remember the words
I'd heard her father say,
    Chorus

But now that we are wed
And keep a little farm,
My wife she is my only pride,
She is my only charm.
And when I tease and squeeze her,
She reminds me of the day
When first I took her home
And heard her father say,
    Chorus

Beech Mountain, North Carolina

AS YOU CLIMB from Boone, North Carolina (where the elevation is 3,000 feet), past Vilas and Valle Crucis, the mountains rise before and about you on every hand. The grade of the road steepens, and the road itself winds and twists and climbs until the feathery tops of trees are below you on one side, while a mountainside rises steeply on the other. Trees abound—wild locust, sourwood, oak, tulip, poplar, pine. Once there were chestnut trees, but not for many a year, since the blight. In the spring there are masses of laurel, like pink clouds, and the more dramatic rhododendron, and always wildflowers everywhere. Mount Mitchell, the tallest peak in the eastern United States (elevation 6,684 feet), is behind you, Grandfather Mountain is impressive on the left, and soon you are heading up the Beech, as Beech Mountain is called by all who live on its slopes.

Beech Mountain is made up of connected ridges which rise to a high outcropping of rock called The Pinnacles. The eastern slopes of the mountain, the side where the Hicks family lives, is in Watauga County. The other side, toward Banner Elk, is in Avery County. We are speaking of the northwestern corner of the state, just a few miles from the Tennessee border. Standing by Nathan Hicks's house, which is below the south Pinnacle, one looks out on a vast sweep of valleys with the mountains stretching away in the distance from North Carolina into both Tennessee and Virginia. It is remarkably beautiful country.

On our first visits to the Beech in the late thirties and early forties—and to the Frank Proffitts' in Pick Britches Valley—before the TVA had brought in electricity, people lived mostly by subsistence farming, raising and canning their own vegetables, picking mountain berries, hunting game—rabbits or squirrels or an occasional bear. They would raise a few chickens, mostly for eggs. Those who could would raise a hog once a year, putting the meat up in jars to last the winter, but this was not general.

What Horace Kephart, in his book *Our Southern Highlanders* said about the mountain people in 1913 was still largely true when we first went to the mountains in the late thirties: "full three-fourths of our mountaineers still live in the eighteenth century, . . . in their far-flung wilderness, away from large rivers and railways, the habits, customs, morals of the people have changed but little from those of our old colonial frontier; in essentials they are closely analogous to what we read of lower-class English and Scottish life in Covenanter and Jacobite times."[1]

Kephart tells us in detail about how the mountains were settled. The Swiss and the Palatine Germans flocked into Pennsylvania about 1682 and were followed into that region by the Scotch-Irish, or Ulstermen of Ireland. James I, in 1607, had confiscated the Irish estates in Ulster and peopled the territory with Scotch and English Presbyterians. These people came to be known as the Scotch-Irish, although the native Irish detested them and there were many bloody battles. Eventually the Ulstermen began leaving Ireland for the new world—settling on land west of the German settlements in Pennsylvania. Here they began to clash with the Indians, and eventually they began to migrate southward into Appalachia.

> So the western piedmont and the mountains were settled neither by Cavaliers nor by poor whites, but by a radically distinct . . . people who are appropriately called the Roundheads of the South. These Roundheads had little or nothing to do with slavery, detested the state church, loathed tithes, and distrusted all authority save that of conspicuous merit and natural justice. The first characteristic that these pioneers developed was an intense individualism. The strong and even violent independence that made them forsake all the comforts of civilization and prefer the wild freedom of the border was fanned at times into turbulence and riot; but it blazed forth at a happy time for this country when our liberties were imperilled. . . . During the Revolution, the Appalachian frontier was held by a double line of the men whom we have been considering: one line east of the mountains, and the other west of them.

Now there is electricity and a TV aerial on every house or cabin. Most of the roads are good, and there are school buses and jobs in Boone or Banner Elk or other places not too far away if one has a car. Most people have a car or truck of some kind. On the other side of Beech Mountain there is a ski run and motels and shops, and an amusement park called "The Land of Oz." We are thankful that "our" side of the Beech still is largely unchanged.

NATHAN AND RENA HICKS

Rena and Nathan Hicks were first cousins. Their fathers were Andrew and Benjamin Hicks, sons of Sam and Becky Hicks. In a taped conversation with Rena in 1951 she told us something of her childhood:

---

1. Horace Kephart, *Our Southern Highlanders* (New York: Macmillan, 1913, 1922; New and Enlarged Edition, 1936), p. 285.

My mother was born in Spice Creek, one of twelve. She and my daddy had fifteen—three died, but twelve are still living. Two brothers and ten sisters.

I was the oldest so I had to do all the work when Mama was sick. I didn't get any chance to go to school—jist three months. My mother taught me up to second grade, and Daddy taught me letters.

Our house had six rooms, three downstairs and three upstairs, but we didn't use the upstairs. . . .

I remember when Mama and Daddy was gone somewhere and I was left with the milking to do and the sow to feed, and the sow put her head in the bucket and the milk spilled so we didn't have any milk that day. I was scared, because Mama always whipped me if I did something wrong . . . and she did that time too, but not too hard. It was good though—helped me to be careful.

There was a store two and a half miles away and another ten miles. We walked when we had to go to the store. There was no other way. We didn't buy much—coffee and sugar and calico to make clothes. Mama made all the clothes for everyone—sewed buttonholes and everything.

We pulled galax leaves to sell—that was all the money we got—for that and other things, herbs. There was a lot of ginseng then, but not much now. We'd gather strawberries and huckleberries, but just to eat or can. We didn't have no horses, just steers (we called 'em) and chickens and pigs. We didn't raise no dogs . . . my Daddy didn't like dogs, and we'd never seen one till a stranger brought one in and scared one of my sisters so bad! When my brothers come along, though, my Daddy let them have a dog.

I used to have to help hoe corn and set traps for birds (deadfall traps). My mother made the triggers. I would pick beans and cook and wash and take care of the babies and make butter. . . .

I was married at thirteen and Nathan was eighteen. We stayed with his daddy for a year, and then Nathan and his daddy and neighbors built this house. Some worked free and some we paid. Bessie was born when I was fifteen. I have three childern dead and ten living—four boys and six girls.

N.A. is named for his daddy and we call him N.A. to tell them apart. . . . Ray lives up the mountain with his family, and we help each other out. And Jack's my baby—he's both a girl and a boy too. He helps me in the house and he farms too—works with his brother. He's thirteen now, and he is going to school for two more years. He gets his pension until eighteen if he stays in school—$27 a month. If he stops school, he doesn't get any money. That's all the cash money we get. It buys his clothes and helps us out. We don't get much of any cash for our farming—just barely make a living. You have to go into debt for fertilizer and then have to pay it all back, so you don't get any money. Jack walks three miles to school, to Cool Spring.

Having heard of Nathan Hicks through Maurice Matteson, we wrote him in February of 1938 to order a dulcimer. His reply was dated February 22:[2]

---

2. The Hickses' spelling was phonetic, and we wouldn't think of correcting it. In any case, spelling in the eighteenth century, even among educated people, and even with regard to personal names, was an individual matter.

Nathan Hicks, standing on the slope of the south Pinnacle of Beech Mountain, North Carolina, above his house, June 1938.

Dear Mr. Warner

I Recived your Letter that you wanted a Dulcimer like Mr Matteson I cant send it unless [I get] some money as Postage and glue and nails cost me money and times are so Hard and my wife is sick most of time and we Have tin chirldern and time are so Hard I cant get much money. . . . Please send me the money and I will have the Dulcimer Redy time I Hear from you. . . .

So thanking you so much for the order wish I war able to make it and send it on but cant. Please ancher soon. You freind, Nathan Hicks.

We responded, and he wrote again on March 3:

Dear Mr. Warner

I Recevied your Letter and Check . . . shore war glad to get your Kind Letter I will have the dulcimer finish in a few days and in the mail for you Hope it will please you and you could get me some more orders as we are in Det so much as I Kneed money so bad. . . . We all war shore glad to Hear that you war going to send us some Clothing and Presents as we all Kneed all the Clothing that we can get as it is verry coole up Heare on this mountain. . . .

Hope this finds you all well and Happy ancher soone

Your friend
Nathan Hicks

So began a correspondence that lasted through the years, occasionally with Nathan until his death in 1945, but particularly with Rena. We have dozens of her letters, telling of her daily activities, her flowers which she grew and loved, her view of life ("I never met anybody who wasn't a friend"), her small pleasures, her needs, her tragedies. Some of the envelopes they used were those they had received, turned inside out and pasted with flour paste. Some of the letters were written on the inside of such unfolded envelopes, or on pieces of wrapping paper. All were full of warmth and friendship.

Before we went to see Nathan and Rena for the first time we sent them a big box of clothes and bedding which we had gathered from all our friends. Who could resist trying to help fill such a need? Not our friends, nor Frank's compatriots and acquaintances at the YMCA, nor anyone over the years to whom we told the Hickses' story. We were grateful to be able to send many boxes during the following years, and to be able to sell Rena's hooked rugs and chair seats and table mats for her in New York—to friends and acquaintances and through various Women's Exchange groups.

The Hickses reciprocated to the best of their ability. Nathan made a cradle for us when my young nephew and his wife had a baby girl in 1941. He carved two hearts connected by a chain of wooden links for us at Christmas one year. Each heart was to be a picture frame for our photographs. When Jeff was born Rena hooked a beautiful oval rug in pink and blue for him, with his name as the central design.

June 22 1939

My Dear Mrs Warner

I want to thank you so much for selling Rugs and mats for me tell Mr Carl Carmer that we thank him for the Check He sent for the Dulcimer; My sweater was just a fit and I thank you for being so Loving to Bring me a Present Hope you Both will gett to come again. . . .

I am so glad we do know each other Better now than eaver and I want to thank you for the Dinner that you brought to us as we did Enjoy it so much and for you Both eatting with us all. . . .

Mrs Nathan Hicks

Anna Hicks, thirteen and just married, taking home some of the clothes we had brought to the family, 1939.

Rena Hicks, and Nell, with a sampling of Rena's hooked rugs, 1941.

August 22, 1939

Dear Mrs. Warner

    I thought I would ancher your Kind and sweet Letter shure war glad to Hear from you . . . I got the check for $33.50 shure war glad to get it as I am all ways in Kneed and I am so glad that you can sell the thangs so quick and can get a little more for them then I can get at Banners Ealk . . . I am so well Pleased that I have found such good freinds out theair . . . I try to give you all many thanks and Blessings at Knight when I goe to Bed. . . . Nathan Has got Frank Bango Redy to send we will mail it to morrow . . . so you all can Be on the Lookout for it . . . it is a Peach it Has a Loud sound He said Frank could see for His self when it arive to Him I hope He will Be pleased. . . .

    This leaves us all well But myself I don't gess I will ever Be well anymore I am prag-

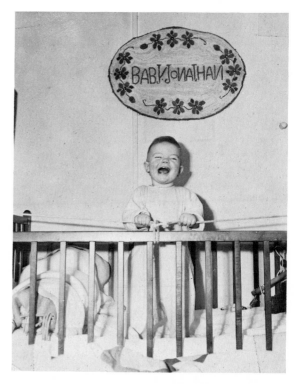

Jeff (Jonathan) Warner, nine months old, with Rena Hicks's rug, 1943.

nent again just the same old truble I feel Very well only when I ame pragnent but then I cant stand on my feet just haft to sit and work. . . .

We all send our Love to you both and your freinds. . . .

Mrs. Nathan Hicks

March 24 1940

Dearest Mrs Warner

While thanking so much of you thought I would ancher both of your sweet letters . . . I have been Past Ritting . . . I lost all of my Blood but the Doctors and nurses give me Blood and Nathan so . . . I have a Little Hope of getting to goe Back to the chirldern . . . Ever one Heare at the Hospittal Has Been so kind and good to me they fix my Baby all Redy for Bureal Heare and our Preacher tuck it home Mr M. G. Murry is His name My Baby was Born thursday . . . it war a Little girl I had Been sick so long till it coulden Live . . .

Send my Love to you Both
Mrs Nathan Hicks

Ray Hicks, fifteen, with his pet groundhog, 1940.

Banner Elk, N.C.
Feb 25 1945

My dearest Friend

    Will ancher your letter Shore was glad to hear from you and do thank you for the check dear I cant work at the Rugs untill everthang wear off Dear I no you will be shock when you Heare the sad newes Mr Nathan Hicks lost his mind Just in a dash and Hing himself on Feb 19 about one mile from Cool Spring Church 4 miles from Home and Funel [funeral] war held in our little Church 22 [on the 22nd] dear I used the Flowers on Him No one never no what is in Front of us dear if any one could have Heard Him Pray and ask the Lord to let Him live would attend church and never get Drunk He ask the Lord to let Him Live and He would goe to Church and not Drank any moore. His dady died on the 7 of this month and the funel war Held on the 9 Like one day bean 2 weeks Between the Funeals and His Mother is taking it so Hard and poor Willis and May seems

Church on Beech Mountain, with some of the Hicks family, 1951.

like they can't stand it But our dear Lord will take us throw it woulden Hurt us so Bad
if He had died a naurtial [natural] death it woulden Hurt us so Bad

Love from us
Mrs. Nathan Hicks

The work Rena mentions in the first part of her letter refers to the rugs and chair
seats and place mats which she made. The flowers she mentions were some artificial

flowers she had asked for and that we had sent along with other things in our Christmas box. She loved flowers and grew them all around the house in the summer time. No flowers were to be had in the mountains in February, so she used the Christmas flowers for the funeral.

September 4 1951

Dearest Freinds

Will ancher your card and letter shure war so Glad to Hear fom you and to no you all war thanking of us as we all are thanking of you all we Shure did Enjoy your visit with us all. . . . Jack shure did like Jeff and Gairreit [Gerret] we got pretty lonely after you all left. . . . Anna war Hurt Beacause she diden get to stay and cook for us and she war going to sing Black Jack David for you and put on a Jack Tale also . . . Jack has started in school today. We kneed Mr Warner Heare to sleep up a storm as He said He did that night it Rain as we not Had any Rain since that night and our Springs is just about dry and our cows are about to starve. . . .

We all send our Love to you all,

Rena Hicks

Rena's son Ray and his family lived just up the mountain. During our visit in 1951 when we taped the interview with Rena, we also taped Ray Hicks telling three or four Jack Tales. Ray uses the old time speech patterns, as his father did, almost swallowing the last syllable of his words. He is a natural story teller. His blue eyes glint with humor, he throws his whole body into the telling, and his obvious delight at Jack's mastery of every situation is infectious. Ray is nearly seven feet tall. His brother-in-law Frank Proffitt used to say that the construction bosses in Boone were happy if they could get Ray to help build a new house because then they didn't have to build any scaffolding.

Mrs. Hicks has written on the back of this envelope: "Letter Edge in Black"

August 11 1952

Dearest Freind,

Will Rite you a few Lines to let you Heare what Happen in our Home the first Sunday in Aug Jack and one of His cousans had Been trying to learn how to Swam and Jack and Him slip off to a Black Hole of watter on Sunday Left heare about 9 o clock and they brought me word at 12 o clock He war dead. . . . the undertaker said he got stringled and scard . . . but Jack is Gone and Left me all alone Ray and Rosa will take care of me But I cant stand the chirldern and noise But I will haft to stand it some way But it Hard to Bear to give up a young youth like Jack I have lost Little Ones and Mr Hicks But it never compair with this Pray for me your Friend

Love to all Mrs Rena Hicks

When Rena was left alone—after the death of young Jack—Ray and Rosa and their two children (later there would be three more) moved down the mountain to live

Ray Hicks and young Jack Hicks, with Jeff and Gerret Warner on the Hicks's horse, Beech Mountain, 1951.

with her. There they still live. Rena died just before Christmas in 1976. We are so glad we got back to see her and all our mountain friends in 1975.

August 13 1959

Dearest Freinds,

    Will ancher your nice letter shure war glad to Hear from you all we all shure did injoy our old time get togather and the Picnic and all that came and Aunt Buna dear it war wonderfull to get togather again and I was so glad you all meet the Presnell Famly . . . dear I shure did have a grand time But it diden seeme Rite unless you all could have stayed 2 or 3 nights with us as you all seemes Like one of us in our family. . . .

    Dear I thank you all moore then I can tell you for ever thang and for the Glasses you Brought me I have them on now Ritting you We all send you our Love

Rena Hicks

In 1940, when we took some of the Hickses down the mountain to Matney, in search of electricity, Nathan recorded for us this story of a bear hunt:

    Well, Hardy Hicks, he come runnin' out, says, "Hey, Nathan, come out here! There's something," says, "hit's foot's as big as both of my hands!" He said, "I b'lieve hit's a ba'r!"
    I said, "No, you know hit ain't no ba'r."

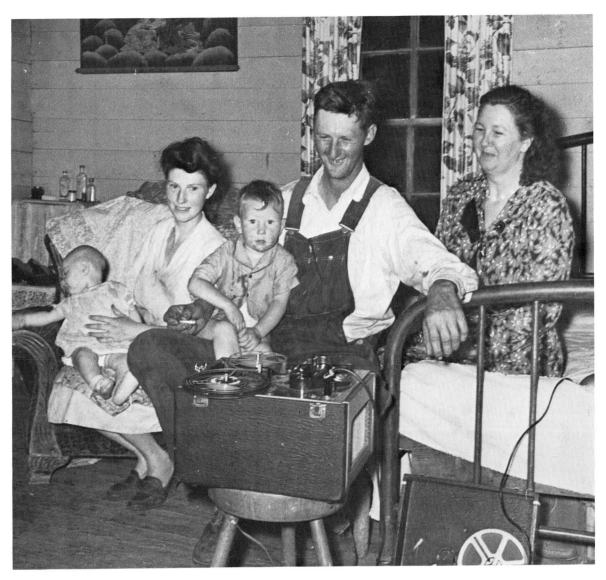

Ray Hicks, listening to the tape he had just made of some of his Jack Tales, with his wife
Rosa holding Jean, Leonard on his knee, and his mother Rena, 1951.

"Come out here and see."

I went out, and sure enough hit was a ba'r . . . we jumped it up. We tracked it across
the mountain, and Winser Hicks come up and said, "Thar's a ba'r up there." He come
with his gun.

A crowd of Nathan Hicks's descendants and other relatives at the Hicks house on Beech Mountain, 1959, listening to the story of the bear hunt that Nathan recorded in 1940. Frank Warner had transferred it to tape from the disk on which it was first recorded.

We tracked it on down to Beech Creek and crossed the Green Br'ar Ridge. Then Winser give out his toe was hurt—he had to go back. . . . [laughter from the audience] He give me his gun—a twelve-gauge shotgun, with buckshot.

Me and Hardy Hicks then went on a-pullin' through the woods. We passed on through to Sherman Presnell's and told him to come out, there was a ba'r. He said, "Aw, hit's no ba'r, jist a big coon. You boys is jist fooled up." He had two little old dogs, and he brung them.

We tracked it on across the mountain, a big mountain of rocks, you know. We sent the dogs in after him and Sherm, he got down and said "Boys, I believe I hear it a-growlin'!" Says, "Look out!" But hit wasn't in there.

We tracked it on into Matney and kep' trackin' him, and we jumped him up. We went through Scaly, and saw his back . . . he was standin' up in the field. I seen hit a-comin', top of the field, and I said, "Yander comes the ba'r!"

Hardy seen it too, you know, and he said, "You go that way and I'll go this way, and you'll meet it right down there!"

Sure enough, I met him, and I shot him with the shotgun—shot him three times. Weighed 400 pounds. He was fat. . . .

In 1983 the Folk Arts Program at the National Endowment for the Arts joined with the Smithsonian Institution's Office of Folk Life Programs to present National Heritage Fellowships to sixteen Americans "who have contributed to the shaping of our artistic traditions and to preserving the cultural diversity of the United States." Among them were two of our friends from Beech Mountain: Ray Hicks, son of Rena and Nathan Hicks, and his cousin Stanley Hicks, son of Buna and Roby Monroe Hicks. Here are excerpts from their citations in the official program issued by NEA:

Ray Hicks: A mountain farmer . . . [who] tells traditional fairy tales and legends that date back hundreds of years. "Used to be," he says, "Whenever we had a long slow job to be done, like a cornhuskin' or something, we'd just gather all the young'uns around and put them to work. Then's when we'd tell the old tales about Jack. Why, them kids would work for hours and never a sound out of them, long as I'd keep telling them tales." . . . Through his masterful storytelling, Ray Hicks has played a major role in preserving and perpetuating one of humankind's most ancient and venerable art forms.

Stanley Hicks: . . . Like his father, Stanley Hicks tells traditional stories and makes finely crafted banjos and dulcimers. . . . He sings the old ballads, too, and when he finds himself unable to sit still any longer, he leaps up to dance in the flat-footed "jumping jack" style he learned long ago. . . . He possesses an unswerving devotion to the traditional ways and customs . . . passed on to him from earlier generations. "You know, back in them days," he says, "we made a lot of stuff. My grandpa made the first pair of shoes I ever wore . . . Daddy sharpened mill rocks and made mills, and made banjos and dulcimers. . . . There's his dulcimer he built years ago—it still lives, it's still here. And same way by myself, when I'm gone, there's some of my stuff for the young'uns . . . you know, it still lives."

Mrs. Hicks gave us this version of "Little Musgrave and Lady Barnard," though she did not know the tune and had to recite it. It is full of phrases which indicate the "mishearing" which often happens in the oral transmission of songs—particularly those with words or phrases whose meaning is not understood either by the singer or those who are listening. Here, in the first line there is "a ravin white," which must be a mishearing of "arrayed in white." In the seond line "Pelat" may be a corruption of "Prelate." In the eighth verse and in the twelfth and thirteenth and later verses "galad" could only be a corruption of "gay lady" which is used so often in ancient ballads.

This very old ballad of adultery and revenge (Child says it is quoted in Beaumont and Fletcher's "Knight of the Burning Pestle" about 1611) has been found with much greater frequency in the United States than in Britain.

See: Brown, Vol. 2, 101; Child No. 81, 172 ("Little Musgrave and Lady Barnard");
Coffin and Renwick, 79, 237; Eddy, 48; Flanders-Barry, *NGMS*, 135

MATHY GROVE

First come in a ravin [arrayed in] white,
Next come in was a Pelat,
Next come in was Lord Donal's wife,
She was the fairest of them all.

Little Mathy Grove was standing by,
On him she placed her eye,
"Come and go home with me
And stay all night."

"If I do, Lord Donal will kill me.
I know by the ring
That you wear on your finger
That you are Lord Donal's wife."

"If I am Lord Donal's wife,
He is not at home.
He is away
At the king's highway working."

Little footspad [footpage] was standing by,
These words he heard.
He buckled up his shoes and he run
Till he come to the broken-down bridge.

He bent his breast and he swam
Till he come to the other side.
He buckled up his shoes and he run
Till he come to Lord Donal's gate.

He dingles at the ring,
And none as ready
As Lord Donal himself
To rise and let him in.

"What news have you brought to me?"
"Little Mathy Grove
Is in the bed
With your galad [gay lady]."

"If this the truth you brought to me,
And true it may be,
To the oldest girl that I got
Married you may be."

"If that's a lie that you brought to me,
And a lie it may be,
On a green shade tree in this old land
A hanged man you may be."

He saddled the old king's horse
And he rode away.
When little Mathy Grove awoke
Lord Donal was at his feet.

"How do you like my blankets?
And how do you like my sheets?
And how do you like my galad
That lies in your arms asleep?"

"Much do I like your blankets,
And much do I like your sheets,
Much better do I like your galad
That lies in my arms asleep."

"Rise up, put on some clothes!
And it never shall be said in old England
That I slew you,
A naked man."

"How can I
When I'm afraid of my life?
You with two swords,
And me not a knife."

"I have these two swords
That cost me deep in the purse.
I will give you the best sword,
And I will take the worse."

"I will give you the first lick,
And strike it like a man.
And if you don't kill me,
I will kill you if I can."

The very first lick
That little Mathy Grove struck,
He wounded
Lord Donal full sore.

The very first lick
That Lord Donal struck,
Little Mathy Grove
Could strike no more.

He took his galad by the hand
He led her over the place and set her on his knee.
"Which do you like the best,
Me or little Mathy Grove?"

"Much do I like your ruby lips,
Much do I like your chin —
Much better do I like little Mathy Grove's finger,
Better than you and all your kin."

He drew his sword from
His right side
And split her head in twain.

79. Sweet Willie   1933

This is our favorite ballad from the Southern Appalachians. Known in scholarly
circles as "The Douglas Tragedy" (Sir Walter Scott's *Minstrelsy of the Scottish Bor-*

der), and as "Earl Brand" (Child No. 7), the ballad in the mountains is usually called "Sweet Willie," or sometimes "Seven Brothers," or "Sir William and Fair Ellender," or "He Rode Up to the Old Man's Gate."

The ballad is ancient, going back to Scandinavian legend and the Nordic bards, to the Danish "Riborg and Guldberg," mentioned in Child. Scott claimed to have identified the ruins of a castle in southern Scotland as the site of the tragedy. He says, "There are the remains of a very ancient tower . . . in a wild and solitary glen, upon a torrent named Douglas burn which joins the Yarrow after passing a craggy rock called the Douglas crag."

Greig in *Folk-Songs of the North-East* reported finding the ballad in Scotland, and it is in Ord's *Bothy Songs and Ballads,* but it has been found much more frequently on this side of the Atlantic—in Newfoundland, Nova Scotia, and in Maine and at least eight southern states (see Brown). Brown prints three versions and reports the collection of another four.

As in most old ballads, the opening puts the hearer into the middle of the action—as if a play were opening with the third act. The listener's imagination supplies the setting and the background—one source of the ballad's mystery and charm.

It is not clear in the mountain version, but the crisis in the story occurs when the lady cries out the name of her lover, imploring him to slack his hand for "your wounds are deep and sore," and also "father I can have no more." There was an ancient superstition, explained clearly in the Scandinavian legends, that calling a warrior by name in the midst of the fighting would cause his death. A verse from the Grundtvig versions of "Riborg and Guldberg" reads (in translation):

> Though thou see me bleed,
> Name me not to death.
> Though thou see me fall,
> Name me not at all.

Whether disobeying this rule caused Sweet Willie's death in this instance we do not know, but die he did. American versions of ancient English and Scottish ballads invariably have lost the original supernatural element.

Frank Proffitt had a theory that the old, violent, tragic ballads shaped people and life in the mountains and that many mountain tragedies and family feuds were a result of their influence.

Of all the ballads and songs in our collection, this is the only one whose source we do not know. Frank Warner learned it, I think, during the summer of 1933 which he spent at home, in Durham, North Carolina. Perhaps he learned it from Dr. Brown's then unpublished collection, although this exact version is not included in the Brown printed text.

Frank Warner included this ballad in most of his programs for forty years. He sings it on his Minstrel recording, JD 204, "Come All You Good People," published in 1977.

Only recently we have found that version #30 of "Earl Brand" in Bronson's *The Traditional Tunes of the Child Ballads* (Vol. 1, p. 122), is called "Sweet Willie," and that it was collected from Mrs. Lloyd Bare Bragg, Elk Park, North Carolina, on August 7, 1933, and was published in *Beech Mountain Ballads and Folksongs,* by Mellinger Henry and Maurice Matteson (p. 10) in 1936. The fact that this version, collected in the summer of 1933, is identical in words and tune to the version Frank learned in North Carolina in the summer of 1933 only adds to our mystery. We did not meet Maurice Matteson until the winter of 1937 (it was he who put us in touch with Nathan Hicks on Beech Mountain), and by that time Frank had been singing "Sweet Willie" for some four years.

See: Brown, Vol. 2, 27; Child No. 7 11 ("Earl Brand"); Coffin and Renwick, 29, 213; Henry and Matteson, 10; Scott, *Minstrelsy of the Scottish Border,* Vol. 3, 246; Sharp, *English Folksongs of the Southern Appalachians,* Vol. 1, 21

SWEET WILLIE

He rode up to the old man's gate, And loud-ly he did say,
"You keep your old-est daugh-ter at home, The young-est one I will take a-way."

He got up on his milk white steed,
And she on her dapple grey.
He flang his bugle-horn around his neck,
And they went riding away.

They had not gone more 'n a mile and a half,
Untwil they both looked back,
And they see her father and seven of her brothers
Come a-trippling over the slack.

"Get right down," Sweet Willie he cried,
"And hold my milk white steed,"
While I fight your father and seven of your brothers
Or go dying in my own heart's blood."

She got right down without one word,
And helt his milk white steed,
Till she see her father and seven of her brothers
Go dying in their own hearts' blood.

"Sweet Willie"
Collected, Adapted and Arranged by Frank Warner
TRO – © 1976 and 1984 Devon Music, Inc., New York, N.Y. Used by Permission

"O slack your hand, Sweet Willie," she cried,
"Your wounds are deep and sore."
"O slack your hand, Sweet Willie," she cried,
"For father I can have no more."

"If you don't like what I have done,
You can love some other one.
And I wish you were home in your mother's
    chamberee
And me in some house or room."

They rode on to his father's gate
And tapped against the ring.
"O Father, O Mother, asleep or awake,
Arise and let me in."

Sweet Willie died like it was today,
Fair Ellen died tomorrow.
Sweet Willie died of the wounds that he
    received,
Fair Ellen she died of sorrow.

ROBY MONROE HICKS

Roby Hicks was born in 1882, the son of Samuel and Rebecca Hicks. Roby used to tell us that his parents were raised "in this country," but that their parents "come from Cherokee." Cherokee Indian territory was in the Great Smokies of what is now Tennessee until "The March of Tears" in 1838 when the United States government forced all the Cherokees to leave and relocate on the western plains. Though not far away, by Roby's reckoning "Cherokee" was another country. He told us how they still counted Cherokee fashion in his youth—one to ten:

    Saki
    Tally
    Choway
    Nikki
    Whiskey
    Su-tally
    Carl-cokey
    Sook-nail
    Sink-nail
    Squay

Dorothy Hartley, in her recently published book, *Lost Country Life,* about medieval English agriculture, says that our language is full of phrases from medieval agriculture. Americanization, she adds, has produced some oddities. For instance, medieval farm people, without formal education, used finger counts and tallies in place of arithmetic. "Many rural counts," Miss Hartley says, "went to America, were picked up by the Indians, and then in the nineteenth century were called 'Indian counts.'" Roby's Indian counting may well be an example of this.

One of Roby's brothers was Ben, the father of Nathan, our first friend on Beech Mountain, and another was Andy, the father of Rena, Nathan's wife. Marrying cousins or other close relatives was common in the mountains. In the days of isolation and nonexistent transportation the choices for a marital partner were few.

Roby's mother, Grandma Becky, was a remarkable woman. When still a girl she lost one arm in an accident in a cane mill. She was feeding cane into the mill to make molasses, and it caught her arm. But she married and raised a large family and managed to care for them all. Once when he was just a baby, Roby told us, he was playing on the ground outside their cabin door and an eagle was about to carry him off when his mother ran out and saved him. Roby said he learned most of his songs from his mother, and stories—Jack Tales, Indian tales, bear stories. They had a big fireplace, he said, "six-foot long," and on a winter's night his mother would sit inside the fireplace at one end and he would sit at the other, with the fire between them, and she would tell tales until midnight. He said, "She told me many a one. She learned 'em from her daddy. If he'd lived to now [1951] he would be about 125 years old."

Roby came down the mountain to see us the first afternoon we visited Nathan and Rena. He was a true mountain man, with no real outside influences. He could neither read nor write. Once I asked him if he had any idea how to spell a certain word (I was taking down the words to a song he was singing and couldn't understand one of them) and he said, "Honey, I always been so nearsighted I never did learn to read or write." But he possessed a phenomenal memory and innumerable skills. He made his own tools, and with them he made chairs, tables, churns, barrels, wagon wheels, sacks full of wooden forks and spoons, and, of course, banjos, dulcimers, and fiddles. We have one of Roby's fiddles, of his own design. The bottom and sides are one piece of wood, hollowed like a dug-out canoe, with the top nailed on. It is beautiful craftsmanship, and it plays with a tone rather like a hoarse viola. He and Buna, his wife, played all three instruments interchangeably, holding the fiddle in the crook of the elbow, the mountain way, rather than under the chin.

Roby and Buna raised eleven children. He did hardscrabble farming; they pulled galax leaves and herbs to sell; and he sold the things he made when he could find a market for them.

After we had a tape recorder, Frank taped a long conversation with Roby in 1951 in which he tells in great detail about mountain life in the early days when a hundred acres of land could be bought for a rifle (land then was selling for 75¢ an acre); when the nearest town or hamlet was fourteen miles away and it took four days and nights to make the journey by wagon and ox team. They bought only what they could not make: salt, "sody," cotton to spin and weave into cloth for clothes, an axe head, or a gun. They didn't make the trip often. For the most part, Roby said, "We made what we used, and we used what we made."

These are excerpts from the 1951 interview:

In the old days people would go to church and take all the children too, and they had fine meetings. If they had 'em like that now I would like to go to 'em. They would all shake hands afterwards with one another, and sometimes would go home with one of the others, and they would have a rejoicing time among one another, saying what the Lord had done for 'em. And if anyone was taken down sick the rest was ready to he'p, tend the crops and ever'thang and never ask for a penny. I can remember that. Now you can't get anybody to help you with anythin'. . . . Now there are cars and roads and all that. I am not so old—I am sixty-nine—and I can remember when there was no roads, and when these old roads was put through here. It would take twelve men and they would lay a road the easiest way—up hill and down—you couldn't hardly ride a horse up some of these steep hills.

We had as good stuff to eat as we do now. If you had a brute to kill you would eat the meat and can the rest and make shoes out of the hide. Daddy would make our shoes —or sometimes he would hire a special man to make shoes for 50¢ a pair. We never had no money. We would jist give him some chickens or something. A hen would sell for a shillin'—12½¢—but you didn't get the money. You would take something else that was worth the same thing. . . .

We still valued things by shillin's and pence. We raised beans and turnips and cabbages and punkins. And we had eggs. There was no market for anythin'—eggs or nothin'. We et eggs three times a day, and we'd throw 'em at trees and ever'thin else. We'd suck raw eggs too. You get so you like 'em. Even now I can take a plate of hot cornbread and just break raw eggs on it and eat it. We had big heavy plates then. One would make two or three now. We bought our plates and tin cups. Maybe a whole family would have only two plates in the house—jist two could eat at a time.

I guess the biggest thing happened around here lately is when they built up the 'lectricity and most ever'body got lights. I didn't care anything fer it when it come in—didn't want it at all. They mighty near forced it on me. I never signed up fer it, but first thing I know they had the wires in here, and they come and wired the house. I was in debt, and I didn't want to fool with it. . . . now I wouldn't do without it, as long as I can keep it. It is so handy, you see.

Roby knew many an Indian tale from his parents and other older relatives. "Some of 'em are hard to believe, but they're the gospel truth." It was common for the men in an area to chop down enough trees to build a log fort for protection against marauding Indians. Once, Roby's mother told him, all the settlers around had been staying in the fort for some time because they'd heard there were Indians about.

But one day one of the women went out to pick sallet greens—mostly branch lettuce, grows along the branch [creek]. She went too far and some Indians got her and scalped her with what they called a tomahawk. We call it a hatchet. She crawled into an old house, where the people had all been killed by Indians before. There was a tub of feathers in there, and she got some gum from where a tree had been cut down and she put that on her head and then covered it with feathers. After three days she crawled out and managed to get on an old nag that was wandering nearby, and she rode to the fort. They yelled "Indians!" when they saw the feathers on her head, but they got her in and she lived.

Then there was the man who dreamt that the Indians had stolen his horses. He went out to see and found his horses was gone and when he got back to the house the Indians had burnt it and kilt ever'body but one little boy. They'd scalped him, and he was cryin', "O Daddy, O Daddy!" He took him to a neighbor's house and got him doctored up and then he got him a gun and started out after Indians. The first one he saw he knocked

Roby and Buna Hicks and three of their children: Linzy at left with young Dewey in front, holding the microphone; Rosa at right, 1939.

him in the head and shot him and hollered, "Hooray for Old Slooshia!" That's what he called his gun. He said he'd kill Indians with it as long as he lived. He killed a lot of 'em. When the Indians found out the name of the gun, all he had to do was holler "Hooray for Old Slooshia!" and they'd break and run!

Roby could sing many a song, though he complained that he couldn't sing the way he used to. "People used to come from all around to hear me sing, but now my voice is shattered." But he did sing—in the oid-time way we found so moving. Some of Roby's songs were garbled from the better-known versions, but of great interest because they had stayed in Roby's memory from boyhood, with no help from the printed word.

80. Way Up in Sofield (or, The Sheffield Apprentice)   Roby Monroe Hicks, 1951

This is an interesting version of "The Sheffield Apprentice," which was printed frequently as a stall ballad or broadside and in songsters of the nineteenth century, but which also has been found often as a traditional song both in Great Britain and the United States. It is the unusual story of a rejected woman's revenge, and a hero who dies because of loyalty to his love.

The notes in the Brown collection say, "Our texts all derive from the printed ballad, sometimes with curious evidence of mishearing." The mishearing is evidenced in Roby's version.

Laws quotes numerous sources for ballad texts in this country. He also mentions Greig and Ord for two Scottish sources, and the *Journal of the Folk-Song Society* for fragments found in England.

We collected a clearer and more complete version of this ballad—called "The Sheffield 'Prentice"—from Martha (Mrs. Albert) Etheridge, Mrs. Tillett's sister, in Wanchese, North Carolina, on the Outer Banks, No. 152.

See: Belden, 131; Brown, Vol. 2, 353; Cazden II, 209; Creighton and Senior, 203; Laws, *ABBB*, O-39, 245; Sharp, *English Folksongs of the Southern Appalachians*, Vol. 2, 66

WAY UP IN SOFIELD (or, THE SHEFFIELD APPRENTICE)

Way up in So - field, in such a low de - gree, My

par - ents they dot - ed on no—— child but me.

*1st verse sung
    way up in So - field,

**this bar is often expanded to two, when words require it   for example: verse 2
    - lu - tion   not

208

It rolled [I roamed?] in such pleasure till a fancy me
    misled,
I soon was bound apprentice, and all my joys was
    dead.

I formed a resolution not long with him to dwell,
I did not like my master for he did not treat me well.
Unbeknownst to my poor parents, so I did run away,
Steered my course for London, oh, cursed be that
    day.

I had not been in London just weeks two or three,
Before a young lady from Holland, over she did
    come.
She offered me great wages to go and live with her,
To go and live in Holland and serve her for
    one year.

After long persuading me, I told her I would agree,
I would go and live in Holland and serve her for
    one year.
I had not been in Holland just months two or three
Before my young mistress grew very fond of me.

Her gold and her silver, her house and her lands,
If I'd consent to marry her would be at my command.
Oh no, dear honored lady, I cannot wed you both
None but pretty Polly, and bound it with an oath.

But this lady's being so proflicted that she could not
    be my wife,
She formed a cruel project to take away my life.
One cool summer's evening I walked out in the
    garden green,
A gold ring off her finger, as she did pass me by.

She slipped this ring into my pocket, and for this ring
    I must die.
Come all ye freeholders, both distant, near, and
    friends,
Do not glory in my downfall
For I am a ruined man.

81. Young Johnnie   Roby Monroe Hicks, 1940

This is the sad story of a girl who was planning to run away with her true love
Johnny. Through a maid, the girl's mother discovers the plan and forces her to marry
"young Samuel Moore." When the broken-hearted girl becomes deathly ill, her mother
relents and offers to send for Johnny, but her daughter says it is too late. With a farewell to everyone, she dies.

Brown says that this ballad, known generally as "Johnny Doyle," is Irish, but that
it is "also known in Scotland and England," and that it is found with some frequency
in America. Laws gives many sources and says that it may be found on a number of
broadsides and in early songsters.

Brown notes that the texts, wherever found in oral tradition, "are likely to be
somewhat defective or confused," and that is surely the case with this version from
Roby Hicks. Roby told us that he learned the song from his mother.

Buna Hicks sings this version, learned from her husband, on a Folk-Legacy record, FSA 22, Vol. 1.

Folk Songs of the Catskills (Cazden II) has a very good (and ungarbled) version of this ballad, and interesting notes.

See: Brown, Vol. 2, 265; Cazden II, 207; Eddy, 187; Flanders-Barry, *NGMS,* 248; Gardner, 69; Laws, *ABBB,* M-2, 180; Mackenzie, 106; Randolph, Vol. 1, 350

YOUNG JOHNNIE

One — thing — is — cer - tain, the truth I must con -
fess, When I go to meet - ing my true love goes to rest.
One Fri - day eve - ning, it hap - pened but — late, When
me and young John - nie was out to take a flight.

My father's maid was standing by, a few words
    heared she,
She run to my mommy and told upon me.
She bundled up his clothes and bid him to be gone.
How slowly, how slowly he moved along.

Then also they forced me to ride by young Samuel
    Moore,
Six double horsemen to ride by my side.
When they a-missed (?) me, I entered the door,
My earbobs they bursted and fell onto the floor.

Into sixty-five pieces my stay laces flew,
I thought in my soul my poor heart was broke in two.
Then also they forced me to stand by young Samuel
    Moore,
Then also they forced me to give him my right hand.

What to speak, I scarce-lie did design,
The thought of young Johnnie run so in my mind.
Up behind my oldest brother he carried me safe-lie home,
Through my mother's chamber and into my own room.
I threw myself down on my own bed,
So sick and so wounded my body I found.
I called to my old father to pray shut the door,
"By this time tomorrow you can let in Samuel Moore."

"He never shall rejoice me nor call me his wife,
By this time tomorrow, death shall end all strife."
My old mother standing by, with the tears all in her eye,
Said, "It's no better, we'll send for Johnnie Dile."
"You would not send for Johnnie, and now it is too late.
My journey is forward, and death is my fate.
Farewell my cruel parents, likewise brothers and sisters too."
The last words she spoke, she bid young Johnnie adieu.

BUNA VISTA (PRESNELL) HICKS

Roby brought his wife Buna to meet us on our second visit to their mountain in 1939. Slender, bright-eyed, beautiful in a way that has nothing to do with youth or age, Buna had a sense of fun and an interest in life and in music. She was born in 1888, the daughter of Andrew Jackson Presnell and Sarah Jane Eggers Presnell who was known as "Old Wash Eggers's girl." Wash "scouted"—hid out in the woods—for the four years of the War between the States to keep away from the Home Guard and involuntary enlistment in the Confederate Army. When Buna was thirteen she married Roby Hicks and moved down the mountain (from Egg Knob) to Spice Creek where her eleven children were born. The ones we know personally are Hattie, Captain (his given name), Stanley,[3] Linzy (married to Nathan's and Rena's daughter Mae), Rosa, and Dewey. One of their nine sons was lost in World War II. Linzy spent two years in Britain as a member of the Air Force ground crew. It was his wife Mae who visited us in New York (see p. 23). Some years ago he was ordained as a preacher in the Missionary Baptist Church there on the mountain. He will sing only sacred songs, and may drift quietly from the room when the music turns from hymns to "Fly Around, My Pretty Little Miss," or "A Rude and Rambling Boy."

Buna is always ready to play a tune or sing a song. She sings in the old-time way, with a full-throated sound that excites something deep within us. To hear Buna and her daughters harmonize on "A Voice from the Tombs" or "River of Life" is an experience not to be forgotten.

Buna and Hattie joined us for the American Folk Festival in Asheville in 1963. It was Buna's first trip away from home, and she enjoyed it immensely, though Hattie said she sat upright in bed all night because of the noise outside the hotel, where three

3. There is an article on Stanley and his banjo and dulcimer making on p. 139 of *FOXFIRE* 3, edited by Eliot Wigginton (Garden City, N.Y.: Anchor Press/Doubleday, 1975).

or four trucks and a few cars may have passed by. She loved playing for the audiences at the festival, and everyone loved her.

Buna knew many Civil War stories from her mother. "They had hard times in that war," she said. "If I could ever recollect all my mother told me, it would be a sight."

"What was the name of that old war?" she once asked us, "The one between the Republicans and the Democrats?" Her mother was a little girl during the war and her mother's father, Grandpa Eggers, was "scouting" the whole four years. Being without a man made life hard, and all the children had to help with the work. One evening about dusk Buna's mother was wandering through the woods gathering wood—just any trashy old wood she could pick up. She heard a noise and looked up and saw something standing against a tree—all black, with white teeth and wild rolling eyes. She didn't know what it was, and she was scared half to death. Years later, Buna said, her mother happened to see a picture in a book and she said, "That's hit! Hit was a yape!" (a remnant of a dialect from Somerset, perhaps). "Do you know about them yapes?" Buna asked us. We think it must have been a black man, perhaps a runaway slave. There were no blacks in the mountains then, so Buna's mother had never seen any.

Anyway, Buna said her mother just dropped the wood she had gathered and ran till she about dropped (on retelling the story recently to our son, Jeff, Buna said she "made her legs save her body"), and when she got home she just fell in the door. Her mother—Buna's grandmother—had had a hard day. "Whatever it is," she said to her frightened out-of-breath daughter, "tell me about it in the mornin'. . . . I cain't stand any more tonight."

These are other Civil War stories Buna told us:

My Grandpa Eggers, he tried to keep away all he could, you know, an' scouted and stayed out a long time . . . an' at last he come in one night an' he'd fotch his blanket in with 'im and he rolled up in front of the fireplace an' he was layin' thar. The other fellers come—the Home Guards come in—a-huntin' fer 'im, an' he said, "I ain't able to go tonight with you, but if you'll wait, I'll go with you in the mornin'. Come back an' I'll go wi' you in the mornin'." So he laid there till they got out an' was gone, and then he just tuck his blanket an' struck out again, scoutin' about here an' yonder. When they come back next mornin' he was gone . . . an' it made 'em very ill [ill-tempered or angry]. The Home Guards got ill about that—because he was gone and wasn't there.

One mornin' my Grandma was outside a-washin' clothes. She had her a pretty onion patch set out. She raised what she could, but it was hard with Grandpa away. Well, along come some fellers [soldiers] that wanted some onions to eat. . . . This story's got one o' them bad words in it. . . . Well, they stood and talked to her awhile while she was washin' and then they said, "Is there any onions around here? We'd like to buy some." She said, "No, there ain't. I don't know what they are." So the fellers went on, and she went on a-washin'. After awhile she said to my mother, "You know, I bet them damn fools meant ingons!"

Buna learned songs from her parents, from her Uncle Monroe Presnell, from her husband Roby. She has forgotten the sources of some songs, which is not too surprising. Two songs she has given us she learned from Roby's mother, Grandma Becky, whom she held in love and respect: "A Rude and Rambling Boy," and "Fathers, Now Our Meeting is Over."

82. Drunkard's Doom   Buna Vista (Presnell) Hicks, 1941
83. A Drunkard's Warning   Ida Cornett, 1960

Buna has sung this song to us on innumerable occasions, and we are always delighted to hear it, particularly the first line. Somehow "It was on a dark and starlish night" calls up an emotion, a feeling, that we don't try to analyze. We just enjoy it. Like Monroe Presnell's "The Drunkard's Dream" (of which this is a variant), this song has a happy ending, in spite of its title.

Frank Proffitt's half-sister (his mother's daughter by a previous marriage), Ida Cornett, wrote out a much longer version of this song for us on the one time we met her which she called "The Drunkard's Warning." We include it as a matter of interest. Mrs. Cornett did not give us a tune, but Buna's tune fits it.

Laws says this is one of the "Melodramatic and sentimental pieces, usually of professional origin." Belden includes a song of this title from Missouri—the same song basically, but with very different words.

We collected additional variants of the song from Frank Proffitt and from Rebecca King Jones, both in North Carolina, and from John Galusha in New York State.

See: Belden, 468; Brown, Vol. 3, 42; Burton and Manning, 104; Laws, *NAB,* Appendix 3, 277; Randolph, Vol. 2, 392

DRUNKARD'S DOOM

I started off to the drunkards' band,
They took me in with a welcome hand.
I dashed it out and left the place,
And sought to find redeeming grace.

The very hour that grace begun,
Ten thousand thoughts within me sprung.
I felt like Paul who once did pray,
I felt my sins was washed away.

On one dark and starless night,
I saw and heard an awful sight.
The lightnings flashed, loud thunder roared,
Across my dark denided soul.

I heard a voice say loud and long,
Far down beneath the drunkards throng,
"Come in young man, I'll make you room,
Because your road is pruin to ruin."

I bowed my head and saw below
Where all the dying drunkards go.
My thoughts thereof no tongue could tell.
Is this my home, a drunkard's hell?

I started on, got there at last,
I thought I'd take one social glass.
I poured it out and stirred it well
Until I thought of a drunkard's hell.

I dashed it out and left the place,
And sought to find redeeming grace.
The very hour the grace begun
Ten thousand joys within me sprung.

I started off to the Christian band,
They took me in with a welcome hand.
I started off to find my wife,
To find my long-neglected wife.

I found her weeping near the bed,
Because her little babe was dead.
I layed her down and breathed a prayer,
That God might bless and save her there.

A DRUNKARD'S WARNING

I boughed [bowed] my head to Jesus there,
And prayed to him an humble prayer.
I felt like Paul who once did pray,
I felt my sins was washed away.

I went a Christian home to change my life,
To see my long-neglected wife.
I found her weeping on the bed
Because her little babe was dead.

I told her not to weep no more,
For her little babe was just asleep.
Its little soul had fled away
To reign with Christ through endless day.

I took her by her pale white hand,
She was so weak she could not stand.
We both knelt down and breathed a prayer
That God might bless and save her there.

Now I live a happy life,
With a good home and a loving wife.

84. Fathers, Now Our Meeting Is Over
Buna Vista (Presnell) Hicks, 1959, 1974

This mountain gospel hymn is one Buna learned from her husband's mother, Rebecca Harman, who married Sam Hicks. In her later years everyone called her "Grandma Becky." It was she who lost an arm in a cane mill accident when she was just a girl. She taught her son Roby most of his songs and stories.

Buna told us that Grandma Becky always liked to hear this song when she went to church. "She only had one arm and she looked so pitiful . . . she'd go around among the crowd and tell 'em to sing this song when the meetin' broke up."

Buna sings this song on Folk-Legacy Records, FSA 22, Vol. 1. She also contributed it to Thomas G. Burton and Ambrose N. Manning's *Folksongs II*. The editors say that the song "was used to close camp meetings, accompanied by emotional exclamations and shouts."

George Pullen Jackson's version, he notes, was "recorded by L. L. McDowell, Smithville, Tennessee, and published in his *Songs of the Old Camp Ground*."

Buna first sang the song for us in 1959 when we visited Beech Mountain. Then in 1974 she and her daughter, Hattie Hicks Presnell, sent us a small tape which they had made. In addition to some conversation and other songs it included this one—sung fifteen years later but sounding much the same.

See: Burton and Manning, 49; Jackson, *Another Sheaf of White Spirituals*, 10; Lomax *ABF*, 571

FATHERS, NOW OUR MEETING IS OVER

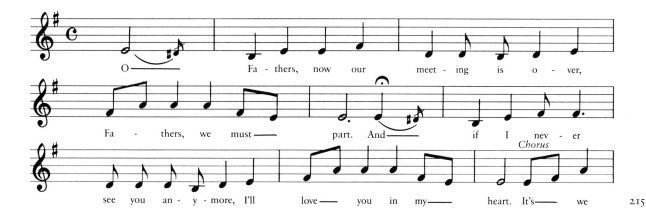

O— Fathers, now our meeting is over, Fa - thers, we must — part. And— if I nev - er see you an - y - more, I'll love — you in my — heart. It's — we

land on shore,——— Yes, we land on the shore, Yes,—— we

land on shore,——— And—— be saved for - ev - er - more.

O Mothers, now our meeting is over,
Mothers, we must part.
And if I never see you anymore,
I'll love you in my heart.
Chorus

O Brothers, now our meeting is over,
Brothers, we must part.
And if I never see you anymore,
I'll love you in my heart.
Chorus

O Sisters, now our meeting is over,
Sisters, we must part.
And if I never see you anymore,
I'll love you in my heart.
Chorus

85. River of Life   Buna Vista (Presnell) Hicks, with her daughters, Hattie Hicks Presnell and Rosa Hicks Presnell, 1951

I have found no other sources for this mountain hymn.
Buna and her daughters sing in harmony, in the open-throated traditional mountain style that makes the hair rise on the back of the listener's neck.

RIVER OF LIFE

1. Soon we'll come to the end of life's jour - ney, And per -

Tune:

haps we'll nev - er meet an - y - more, Till we get to

hea - ven's bright ci - ty Far a - way on the beau - ti - ful

Chorus

shore. If we nev - er meet a - gain this side of hea - ven,

As we strug - gle through this world and its strife, There's an -

oth. - er meet - ing place o - ver in hea - ven By the

side of that River of Life.

2. Where the charmin' roses
3. Oh, they say that we will

bloom for ev - er, And suf - fer - ing shall come no
meet by the riv - er, Where no storm clouds ev - er dark - en the

more, If we nev - er meet a - gain this side of
sky, And they say we'll be hap - py in

hea - ven, I'll meet you on that beau - ti - ful shore.
hea - ven, In that won - der - ful sweet by - and - by.

86. A Rude and Rambling Boy   Buna Vista (Presnell) Hicks, 1941

This is a truncated version of the well-known "The Butcher Boy," about a girl
who hanged herself for love—usually because of being jilted by her lover. As Buna sings

it, it is a ballad of family opposition to young lovers, with the tragic ending, a popular theme in traditional music.

Whenever we have shared a time of music with Buna, she usually has begun her contribution with this song, which must be one of her favorites. The last two and a half stanzas are almost identical to those found in most versions of "The Butcher Boy," though Buna's song does not include the stanzas from "There is a tavern in the town" which usually are included in the commonly known version. Buna does not sing of unrequited love, only of parental opposition.

Laws gives almost a page of sources for "The Butcher Boy," including broadsides and songsters. For a discussion of the ballad in England and America, see Belden and Emrich.

Lee Monroe Presnell sang a song with this title which is an entirely different song (No. 101).

See: Belden, 201–203; Emrich, *Folklore on the American Land,* 526; Laws, *ABBB,* P-24, 260 ("The Butcher Boy"); Library of Congress field recording AFS I 226; Linscott, 179; Randolph, Vol. 1, 229

A RUDE AND RAMBLING BOY

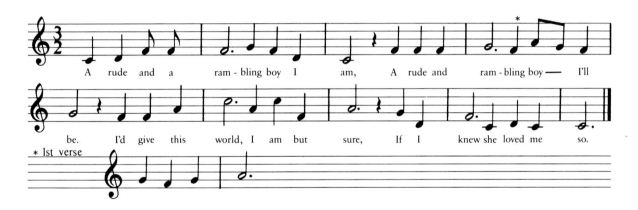

A rude and a ram-bling boy I am, A rude and ram-bling boy—— I'll
be. I'd give this world, I am but sure, If I knew she loved me so.

* 1st verse

Her old father came this to know,
That his daughter loved me so.
He cursed, he swore among them all,
He swore he'd use the cannon ball.

He come home so late in the night,
Inquirin' for his heart's delight.
Upstairs he run, the door he broke,
He found her hung by her own bed rope.

Out with his knife, and he cut her down,
All in her bosom a letter he found,
Said, "Dig my grave both deep and wide,
And bury sweet William by my side."

"All on my breast a snowy white dove
To show to the world I died for love."

87. Voice from the Tombs   Buna Vista (Presnell) Hicks, with her daughters, Hattie Hicks Presnell and Rosa Hicks Presnell, 1951

This song, or hymn, expresses somewhat the same thought as the well-known "Hark From the Tombs," which, entitled "Plenary," is in the *Original Sacred Harp*, p. 162. The words are credited to Isaac Watt, 1707, and the composer is given as A. Clark or A. C. Clark. This same song is in George Pullen Jackson's *Spiritual Folksongs of Early America*, p. 147, and in *Southern Harmony* by William Walker, p. 262. In both of the latter books the tune for the song is the same as "Auld Lang Syne," which is not our tune at all.

Buna's song, judging from the words, seems to be a more recent composition than "Plenary," perhaps dating to before the turn of the century. We have not succeeded in finding it in any available sources.

VOICE FROM THE TOMBS

Then a voice from those tombs seemed to whisper and say,
"Living man you must soon follow me."
I will go and I'll look on those cold marble slabs,
What a dark lonely place this must be.

Chorus

Then I came to the place where my mother was laid,
And in silence I stood by her tomb.
And her voice seemed to say in a low gentle tone,
"I am safe with my Saviour at home."

Chorus

88. Where the Sun Don't Never Go Down   Buna Vista (Presnell) Hicks, 1974

In August of 1974 Buna and her daughter Hattie Hicks Presnell (she married Uncle Monroe's son, Dewey) sent us a small reel-to-reel tape filled with conversation and with some songs. It is a delightful document, and we have transcribed it for our own archives. It starts out:

Well, this here is Buna Hicks . . . I know you remember me. I am goin' to try to put on a little tape, Mr. Frank and Mis' Anne. I remember you, and I thank you a lot for what you have helped me and all you have sent me. I have got 'em all. I jist never did get the writin' done to send back to you, but I thank you for all you have done for me and for the cakes and sweaters and all.

I thought I would put you on a little tape. I am gettin' deef, can't hear good, but I'll try to do the best I can. . . . I am looking for you to come to see me, too . . .

This white gospel song is one of the pieces on the tape. Of it Buna says, "Now my girl Hattie is goin' to try to help me with a song, 'Where the Sun Don't Never Go Down.' We will sing it the best we can."

Buna and her daughter sing this song on Folk-Legacy Record FSA 22, "Beech Mountain, North Carolina, Vol. I," and it is included in Thomas G. Burton and Ambrose N. Manning's *Folksongs II*. It is one of the old "camp-meeting" hymns so popular in the nineteenth century. Of them George Pullen Jackson in his *Another Sheaf of White Spirituals* says, "By 1870 the singing area [for camp-meeting songs] had come to include Western Pennsylvania and the whole upland Southeast" (p. xii).

WHERE THE SUN DON'T NEVER GO DOWN

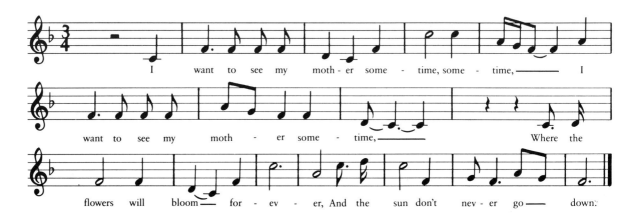

I want to see my moth-er some-time, some-time,——— I want to see my moth-er some-time,——— Where the flowers will bloom— for-ev-er, And the sun don't nev-er go— down.

Chorus
Where the sun don't never go down, go down,
Where the sun don't never go down,
Where the flowers will bloom forever,
And the sun don't never go down.

I want to see my father sometime, sometime,
I want to see my father sometime,
Where the flowers will bloom forever,
And the sun don't never go down.
 Chorus

I want to see my brother sometime, sometime,
I want to see my brother sometime,
Where the flowers will bloom forever,
And the sun don't never go down.
 Chorus

I want to see my sister sometime, sometime,
I want to see my sister sometime,
Where the flowers will bloom forever,
And the sun don't never go down.
 Chorus

I want to see my Saviour sometime, sometime,
I want to see my Saviour sometime,
Where the flowers will bloom forever,
And the sun don't never go down.
 Chorus

HATTIE HICKS PRESNELL

Hattie Hicks Presnell was born in 1907, the daughter of Buna and Roby Monroe Hicks, and married Dewey Presnell, the son of Lee Monroe Presnell (her great uncle), when she was nineteen. Dewey had spent part of his childhood with his family in Arkansas, where he learned many songs which Hattie, in turn, learned from him. She has learned songs, too, from her parents, from her father-in-law, and—through him—from the legendary Lie-hew (John Calvin Yonce).[4]

We do not remember meeting Hattie until 1951, but since then we have come to know her well and to appreciate her memory for songs and her many skills. Some of our most rewarding times in the mountains have been spent listening to Buna singing with her two girls—Hattie and Rosa.

Hattie has traveled with her husband to Arkansas, Canada, New York, Oklahoma, South Carolina, and Tennessee, but now she lives alone, by choice, in a cabin in the woods about half a mile from her mother.[5]

89. The Devil and the Farmer's Wife Hattie Hicks Presnell, 1951

Hattie's version of Child's "The Farmer's Curst Wife" (Child No. 278) does not include the "chorus of whistlers" mentioned by Child. The whistling refrain is found in many versions still—notably the one from Jean Ritchie's family in Kentucky.

4. For information about Lie-hew, see the profile of Lee Monroe Presnell, p. 238.
5. Interviews with Buna Hicks and her daughter Hattie Hicks Presnell are included in two other books: *Folksongs II* by Thomas G. Burton and Ambrose N. Manning, and *Some Ballad Folk* by Thomas G. Burton.

Child says, "A curst wife who was a terror to demons is a feature in a widely spread and highly humorous tale, Oriental and European." Belden says that "the song is something of a favorite in this country . . . most of the English texts noted since Child, and also one from Nova Scotia, one from Tennessee, and four recovered in Virginia, also have a whistling chorus." Belden also says, "The devils or imps in hell appear dancing in chains or dragging chains; but only in Nova Scotia and Missouri do the little devils come 'dancing on a wire'— an expression that suggests memories of the mystery plays." (See Chambers, Vol. 2, 142.)

See: Belden, 94; Brown, Vol. 2, 188; Burton and Manning, 72; Cazden II, 505; Child No. 278, 605 ("The Farmer's Curst Wife"); Coffin and Renwick, 148, 275; Sharp, *English Folksongs of the Southern Appalachians,* Vol. 1, 275

THE DEVIL AND THE FARMER'S WIFE

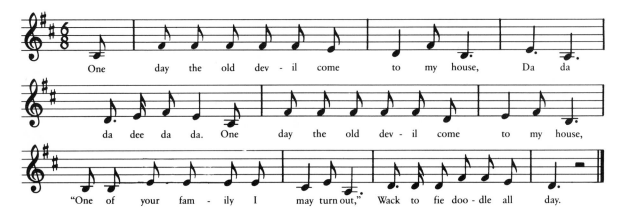

One day the old dev-il come to my house, Da da da dee da da. One day the old dev-il come to my house, "One of your fam-ily I may turn out," Wack to fie doo-dle all day.

"Old Mr. Devil, you surely in fun,"
Da, da, da dee da da.
"Old Mr. Devil, you surely in fun,
How can you spare my oldest son?"
Wack to fie doodle all day.

"Hit's not your oldest son I crave,"
Da, da, da dee da da.
"Hit's not your oldest son I crave,
Hit's your old scoldin' wife I'll take today."
Wack to fie doodle all day.

"Old Mr. Devil, with all of my heart,"
Da, da, da dee da da.
"Old Mr. Devil, with all of my heart,
I'll go to the house and help you start."
Wack to fie doodle all day.

He got her up on his back,
Da, da, da dee da da.
He got her up on his back,
Like a traveler a-waggin' his pack.
Wack to fie doodle all day.

He carried her down three steps of hell,
Da, da, da dee da da.
He carried her down three steps of hell,
She picked up a stick, and she lathered him well.
Wack to fie doodle all day.

Three little devils peeped over the wall,
Da, da, da dee da da.
Three little devils peeped over the wall,
Said, "Take her back, Pap, 'fore she kills us all!"
Wack to fie doodle all day.

Old Mr. Devil got her on his back,
Da, da, da dee da da.
Old Mr. Devil got her on his back,
Like a fool now he take a back track.
Wack to fie doodle all day.

He carried the old woman to the fork of the road,
Da, da, da dee da da.
He carried the old woman to the fork of the road,
He said, "Old woman, you're a hell of a load."
Wack to fie doodle all day.

The old woman went whistlin' across the hill,
Da, da, da dee da da.
The old woman went whistlin' across the hill,
"If the devil won't have me, I know who will."
Wack to fie doodle all day.

90. Pretty Crowin' Chickens   Hattie Hicks Presnell, 1951

Hattie Presnell sang this ballad to us in 1951. Child calls it "The Gray Cock" or
"Saw You My Father?"—but the story is the same. The lady's father and mother are away
(or sleeping), and she is entertaining her lover, John. She bids the cock to crow when
it is day, but he proves false and crows an hour too soon, so she sends her lover away.

Hattie sings this ballad on Folk-Legacy FSA 22, Vol. I. It may also be found in
Thomas G. Burton and Ambrose N. Manning's *Folksongs II*. She says she learned it
from Lie-hew Yonce,—probably through Monroe Presnell.

See: Chappell, *Popular Music of The Olden Time*, Vol. 2, 731; Child No. 248, 551
("The Gray Cock" or "Saw You My Father?"); Coffin and Renwick, 139, 267;
Herd, 324; Sharp, *English Folksongs of the Southern Appalachians*, Vol. 1, 259

PRETTY CROWIN' CHICKENS

The moon it shines bright, and the stars they give light, While this

225

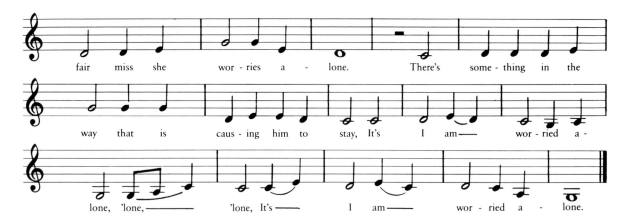

fair miss she wor-ries a-lone. There's some-thing in the way that is caus-ing him to stay, It's I am— wor-ried a-lone, 'lone,——— 'lone, It's——— I am——— wor-ried a-lone.

Her true love come at last, and he come very fast,
Come tripplin' through the plain.
This fair miss she rose, and she threw on her
    clothes,
For to let her old true lover in, in, in,
For to let her old true lover in.

"My pretty little chicken, my pretty crowin' chicken,
Say, don't you crow before day.
I'll make your wings of a yeller beading gold,
And your comb of the silver so gay, gay, gay,
And your comb of the silver so gay."

This chicken proved false-hearted to her,
And crowed one hour too soon.
She sent her love away, before it was day,

And he traveled by the light of the moon, moon,
    moon,
And he traveled by the light of the moon.

She saddled up her milk white horse,
And also her dapple grey.
She rode through the dark wilderness,
At the length of a long summer day, day, day,
At the length of a long summer day.

"My old true love, my sweet turtledove,
Oh, when shall I see you again?"
"When the moon and the stars enters in yonders
    green,
And the sky, it shall shed no more rain, rain, rain,
And the sky, it shall shed no more rain."

91. Talking with the Social Union   Rosa Hicks Presnell, 1941, and
Hattie Hicks Presnell, 1951

Rosa Hicks (later Mrs. Carl Presnell), the daughter of Buna and Roby Hicks, gave us the words to this song in 1941 when she was quite a young girl. She said she did not know the tune. In 1951 she and her sister Hattie Hicks Presnell sang it for us— this time on tape. They told us that it was the legendary "Lie-hew" who first taught it to people on the Beech. Lena Armstrong, Monroe Presnell's daughter, sings it, minus the third verse, on Folk-Legacy.

Professor Samuel Bayard of Pennsylvania State University, the authority on folk tunes, told us that the tune is probably a hymn tune and that the song seems to be based on, or modeled after, the words of the hymn, "This Heavenly Union."

Arthur Schrader has sent me a copy of pages 60 and 61 from a song book entitled *Revival Melodies* or *Songs of Zion*, published in Boston in 1842, which contain the words (five verses) and the tune of "Heavenly Union." He says its tune is the same basic melody found in *Christian Harmony* by Jeremiah Ingalls, printed in Exeter, New Hampshire, in 1805. The tune from Beech Mountain is similar. Here is the first verse from the song book:

Attend ye saints, and hear me tell,
The wonders of Immanuel,
Who saved me from a burning hell,
And brought my soul with him to dwell,
And feel this blessed union.

Annabel Morris Buchanan, in her *Folk Hymns of America,* p. 70, prints ten verses of "Heavenly Union" from *Wyeth's Repository,* Part II, 1813.

Some years ago we came across a file in the East Hampton, Long Island, Library which held a sheaf of songs written down in longhand (words only) by Lew Jones, a seaman who sailed out of Sag Harbor on a whaler in the 1870s. One of the songs was the hymn, which he called "The Union Hymn."

See: Folk-Legacy Records, FSA 23, Vol. 2, "Tobacco Union";
Randolph, Vol. 3, 274; *SING OUT!* Vol. 14, no. 2

TALKING WITH THE SOCIAL UNION

Come young and old and hear me tell How strong to-bac-co smok-ers smell, Who love to smoke the pipe so well. For to-bac-co they will sell, To burn and smoke in un-ion.

* 2nd and 3rd verses

They take the money from the poor,
Carry it away to their neighbor's door.
Hasten it away to some man's store
To buy and sell tobacco more,
To burn and smoke in union.

Then you can see from two to three
Standing in one company.
Then all bring all good leaf,
We can have a smoking spree,
Talking with the social union.

There's some church that you will view,
Where the men will smoke and chew.
They will spit on the carpet floor.
It will spread a foot or more,
Talking with the social union.

The twist so large within their mouth,
The juice run down their chin.
At this I always have to grin,
To think there is no little sin
In this tobacco union.

LINZY HICKS

Linzy Hicks, one of the nine sons of Buna and Roby Hicks, married Mae Hicks, the daughter of Rena and Nathan. It was Mae who visited us in New York City in 1944 while Linzy was overseas with the United States Air Force. Linzy takes his religion very seriously and is deeply sincere. In 1959, after preaching in small mountain churches for several years, he was ordained as a Missionary Baptist preacher. Frank Warner taped an interview with him that year and asked him about his preaching. Here are some excerpts from that interview:

F.W.: I hear you have just been ordained. We are proud of you. Tell us about it.

Linzy: I been preaching a long time . . . and I decided I would go and try to do the best I could, so I united with the church up here at Matney. . . . A year and a half ago they asked me to preach, and I have been asked to preach at revivals and prayer meetings . . . about three weeks ago the church ordained me and a church called for me, and I said if I could be of any help that's where I would be. . . .

F.W.: What was the last sermon you preached?

Linzy: The last subject I preached on was: Take up your cross and follow Me daily. If you gain the world and lose your soul, then what will it profit?

F.W.: Could you develop it a little bit for us?

Linzy: It is hard to get started, but I based it on the words of the Lord as He told me to do. You know He said take up your cross and follow me daily. . . . Some people want to take all the things of the world, but in the Bible He said what would it profit you . . . if you lost your soul in the end. . . . The way I see it and the way I have been taught by the Bible . . . we should not have too much of the worldly things . . . in our mind that would lead us off from the Lord . . . the Lord should come first in anything we have. . . . We must have the Lord before everything if He is to lead us out from here and on to life eternal. . . . If we try to get along with people we can lead them to the Lord and get them to see that the need of Him is great.

Linzy is a fine traditional singer, but will sing only religious songs. If he is in a group and someone begins to sing something of another kind, he may slip quietly out of the room—not bothering anyone, but not wanting to be a part of it.

92. Palms of Victory   Linzy Hicks, 1966

Linzy Hicks sang this song to us in 1966, the year after Frank Proffitt's death. We were visiting the Proffitt family, and as many of the Hicks family as could come were gathered around. Bessie Proffitt's mother, Rena Hicks, was there, and Bessie's sister, Mae (Linzy's wife), and their brother, Ray, and his wife, Rosa, and another sister, Anna, and her husband, Vance Presnell, and all the Proffitt children except Oliver who was still in the Air Force, and Ronald who was at the University of Kentucky. We were particularly moved by this song, which Linzy sang with great feeling and in a beautiful traditional style.

Professor Alan Buechner of Queens College, who is an authority on early American religious music, found the song for us in Moody and Sanky's *Gospel Hymns Consolidated, 1, 2, 3, and 4,* published in 1883, where it is called "Deliverance Will Come." Both words and tune are attributed to the Reverend John B. Matthias and are dated 1836.

Randolph has only one verse, collected in Pineville, Missouri, in 1929. He has no notes. Jackson includes a version and notes that *The Social Harp* attributes the song to Henry F. Chandler, with the date 1854.

In Linzy's words there are some interesting evidences of the folk process. For instance, in the third verse his first line, "He sauntered by the harbor that stood beside the way," is, in the original, "The songsters in the arbor that stood beside the way."

In looking through some family papers recently I came across a wallet carried by my father, William H. Locher, in 1887 when he was eighteen years old and had just come from Decatur, Illinois, to make his way in the city of St. Louis. In it, among other mementoes (one of them a contribution envelope from the First M.E. [Methodist Episcopal] Church in Decatur) was a piece of paper which, when unfolded, turned out to have the words, in my father's early handwriting, of "Deliverance Will Come." It is Linzy's song, with a few minor word changes, and with two additional verses:

> While gazing on that city, just o'er the narrow flood,
> A band of holy angels came from the throne of God.
> They bore him on their pinions safe o'er the dashing foam,
> And joined him in his triumph, Deliverance has come!
>> Then, Palms of Victory, Crowns of Glory—
>> Palms of victory, I shall wear.

I heard the song of triumph they sang upon that shore,
Saying, Jesus has redeemed us to suffer never more.
Then, casting his eyes backward on the race which he had run,
He shouted loud Hosanna, Deliverance has come!
    Then, Palms of Victory, Crowns of Glory
    Palms of victory, I shall wear.

See: Jackson, *Down East Spirituals,* 278; Randolph, Vol. 4, 64

PALMS OF VICTORY

I saw a way-ward trav-'ler in gar-ments tat-tered clad, And trav-'ling up the moun-ting,——— it seemed that he was sad. His back was lad-en hea-vy, his strength was al-most gone,——— He shout-ed as he jour-neyed,——— "De-liv-er-ance will——— come!" "Then——— palms of vic-to-ry, crowns——— of glo-ry,——— Palms of vic-to-ry I shall——— wear."

The summer sun was shining, the sweat was on his
    brow,
His garments worn and dusty, his steps seemed very
    slow.

But he kept pressing onward for he was wending
    home,
Still shouting as he journeyed, "Deliverance will
    come!"
    Chorus

He sauntered by the harbor that stood beside the way,
Attracted his attention, invited his delay.
His watchword being Onwards, he stopped his ears and ran,
And shouted as he journeyed, "Deliverance will come!"
Chorus

I saw him in the evening, the sun was bending low,
He had overtopped the mounting and reached the vale below.
He saw the golden city, his everlasting home,
And shouted, "Hoseanna, deliverance will come!"
Chorus

93. A Poor Wayfaring Pilgrim   Linzy Hicks, 1966

This is another of the songs Linzy Hicks recorded for us in 1966 when we had a gathering at the Proffitts' house, the year after Frank Proffitt died.

This song is well known, though we do not find it in many collections. It is a variant of Burl Ives's theme song, "I'm Just a Poor Wayfaring Stranger." Ben Botkin prints a version identical to the Ives's version from Smithville, Tennessee, where his informant said it was sung "by the old settlers of De Kalb County." George Pullen Jackson says that the tune of the "Wayfaring Stranger" is almost identical to that of "Parting Friends," learned by J. G. McCurry, editor of *The Social Harp,* from Mrs. Catherine Penn in 1829.

Annabel Morris Buchanan collected her version in Kentucky in 1935. Her notes are interesting:

This appealing spiritual, doubtless of campmeeting origin, is widely sung . . . throughout the southern highlands, and appears in various Negro versions. . . . The tune is probably a variant of some ancient Celtic strain. I have recorded, in addition to white and Negro sacred forms, numerous secular variants, generally to "The Dear Companion" . . . which melody Cecil Sharp considered a descendant of the old-world "Dowie Dens of Yarrow." . . . I have traced the spiritual through oral tradition to the 1780s or earlier. . . . The spiritual offers a typical example of the "family" or relative sequence, in which father, mother, and various relatives or friends appear in successive verses.

Although we have been familiar with this song for many years, we were particularly struck by the symbolism in the third line of Linzy's third verse: "I'll drop the cross of self-denial," which we had never heard before. Recently, however, we came across the same line in a version included in Duncan Emrich's *American Folk Poetry.* There are a number of word differences in the two versions, but that line is the same. The Emrich version, he says, was "collected by the W.P.A. Federal Music Project in Floyd County, Kentucky, ca. 1937."

See: Botkin, *A Treasury of American Folklore,* 880; Buchanan, 66; Emrich, *American Folk Poetry,* 380; Jackson, *White Spirituals in the Southern Uplands,* 271

I am a poor way-far-ing—— pil-grim, While trav-eling

through———— this world be - low. There is no

sick - ness, toil, or—— dan - ger, In that bright

world——— to which I go. I'm go-ing there——— to see my

fath - er, I'm go - ing there——— no more to——— roam, I'm just

go - ing o - ver Jor - dan, I am just go - ing o - ver home.

I know the clouds will gather o'er me,	I'll soon be free from every trial,
I know my pathway's rough and steep.	This form will rest beneath the sod.
But golden fields lie there before me,	I'll drop the cross of self-denial
Where weary eyes no more will weep.	And enter in my home with God.
I am going there to meet my mother,	I am going there to see my Saviour,
She said she'd meet me when I come,	Who shed for me his precious blood,
I am just going over Jordan,	I am just going over Jordan,
I am just going over home.	I am just going over home.

94. When Sorrows Encompass Me 'Round   Linzy Hicks, 1966

This is one of the three sacred songs that Linzy Hicks gave us in 1966. At that
time he sang just three verses. I did not write the words down when he sang them as

I usually did, because so many people were at the Proffitt house and so much was going on, and when I tried to transcribe them from the tape I found some of them difficult to understand. Recently I wrote to Linzy to see if he could help me, and in replying he sent two additional verses—the second and third verses shown here. The words are lugubrious, if ultimately triumphant, and haunting, and the tune is glorious. It is the tune of "Idumea." For information about "Idumea" see George Pullen Jackson's *Spiritual Folksongs of Early America,* p. 155, and *The Sacred Harp,* the shape note[6] hymnal.

Linzy told us in 1966 that he learned the song from his father, Roby Hicks, but in his recent letter he says also that "We sang this song at the church . . . it was in an old him [hymn] book that the primitiv Baptists brought."

Professor Alan Buechner found the song in an obscure Free Will Baptist hymnal called *Zion's Harp,* published in Dover, New Hampshire, in 1844. In the book the song is entitled "Meditation" and has a tune, attributed to H. Baker, which is quite different from Linzy's and much less distinguished. It has eight verses. The first three are almost exactly like Linzy's. Linzy's fourth verse is not in the longer version although it is one we particularly like. Linzy's fifth verse is number six in the printed song. The eighth, climactic verse, reads:

Our slumbering bodies obey
And quicker than thought will arise
Renewed in a moment and go shouting away
To mansions above in the skies.

Duncan Emrich calls the song "Death-Bed Song." His version too has eight verses and is identical to those in *Zion's Harp* except that instead of the verse four given there it has Linzy's fourth verse.

The Library of Congress recording was made by Alan Lomax from the singing of Mr. and Mrs. I. D. Cantrell, Sr., and others in August of 1942 in Smithville, Tennessee.

See: Emrich, *American Folk Poetry,* 382 (words only); Fuson, 217 (words only);
Library of Congress field recording AFS, 6675 B 1

6. Shape note singing is still widely practiced in many rural communities, particularly in the South, and it is a fascinating sound. The early shape note hymnals are historically invaluable since they record tunes that would otherwise have been lost. Many of these are folk tunes, since from very early times religious songs have been sung to secular tunes.

John Powell explains in his preface to George Pullen Jackson's *Spiritual Folksongs of Early America:*

Shape notes . . . indicate their pitch by their shapes, independently of the lines and spaces of the staff. They were invented to simplify the reading of music. There are two principal systems, the Four Shape and the Seven Shape. In the Four Shape, the first and fourth degrees of the scale are called *fa* and are represented by a right triangle; the second and fifth are called *sol,* represented by a round shape; the third and sixth, *la,* by a square head and the seventh, *mi,* by a diamond. The Seven Shape system has a different form of note for each degree of the scale and the nomenclature accords with our general practice. The nomenclature of the Four Shape system is of especial interest because it was known and practised by Shakespeare. Numerous references to it occur in his plays. In *King Lear* . . . Edmund . . . says: "My due is villanous melancholy" and then sings: "Fa, sol, la mi."

When sor-rows en-com-pass me 'round, And man-y dis-tress-es I see, As-ton-ished, I cry, "Can a mor-tal be found Sur-round-ed with trou-ble like me?"

Few seasons of peace I enjoy,
And they are succeeded by pain.
If e'er a few moments of praise I employ,
I have hours and days to complain.

Oh, when will my sorrows subside?
Oh, when shall my sufferings cease?
Oh, when to the bosom of Christ be conveyed,
In the mansions of glory and bliss?

May I be prepared for that day
When Jesus shall bid me remove,
That I may in rapture go shouting away
To the arms of my heavenly love.

My spirit to glory convey,
My body lie low in the ground,
I wish not a tear at my grave to be shed,
Let all join in praising around.

HOMER CORNETT

95. Wild Stormy Deep   Homer Cornett, 1959

One day in July 1959, when we were visiting the Proffitts in Mountain Dale (the name had been changed officially from Pick Britches Valley), a couple of neighbors stopped by to see what was going on. One of them was a shy young man named Homer Cornett. His brother, Burlie, was married to Frank Proffitt's sister, Ida. Frank said Homer knew some good songs, but it was quite a while before he could be persuaded to sing for us. At last he gave us two songs, in a high, haunting tenor voice. This white gospel song, probably dating from the turn of the century, is one of them. He didn't tell us where he learned it, and we have never heard it, or found it, anywhere else.

WILD STORMY DEEP

On the wild storm-y deep With Je-sus I'll—— sleep, And—— hold to His lov - ing hand. In a home —— a - bove I'll be there with God,—— And re - joice in a hap - py land.

Chorus
My soul was sad,
My heart was sore,
Out on this stormy sea.
I spoke to God
In humble ways,
And there He appeared to me.

I kneel myself
To His tender call,
And He took my sins away.
He prepared a home
Up there for me,
And there I'll forever stay.
    Chorus

There's a song of my soul,
Says, "Lord make me whole,
May happiness there ever be.
May I live a clean life
In this sinful old world,
For the Lord has set me free."
    Chorus

LEE MONROE PRESNELL

We met Lee Monroe Presnell, Uncle Monroe, for the first time in 1951 at Beech Creek, at the home of Roby and Buna Hicks. He endeared himself to us immediately. He was handsome, with white hair and a drooping moustache. He had a gentle, courteous voice and manner and, as we later discovered, a magnificent singing style. He was loved and admired by all who knew him. We were moved when he said at the end of an afternoon's fellowship, "I never seen folks I liked better to be with. You seem like my own folks. And I ain't tellin' you that because I'm in your presence."

Jeff and Gerret were drawn to him too. They were eight and five that summer. Monroe said to Gerret, "I've nary a boy, and I live all alone in a little house up tha'r. . . . Why don't you come and stay with me? Would you do it?"

Gerret rose to the occasion. "I will," he said, "if my mother will let me."

Uncle Monroe and Roby Monroe Hicks were related. We are not sure just how, though Monroe was Buna's uncle. "Roby was named for me," Monroe said, "since I'm older than he is." Buna Hicks's father, Andrew Jackson Presnell, and Uncle Monroe were brothers. We wonder if anyone knows all the ramifications of family lines and relationships on Beech Mountain!

We did a great deal of singing and recording during that 1951 visit. It was the first time we had had a tape machine in the mountains. Our machine, indeed, may have been one of the first tape recorders in the mountains. Frank asked Uncle Monroe if he would talk a bit and perhaps sing for us, and he graciously consented. First we got him to tell us a bit about himself:

> I was born on the Wataugy [Watauga] River, and my daddy was Eli Murphy Presnell, come from middle Tennessee, and my mother was raised on the waters of Wataugy—Harmon was her name. [She was the daughter of Council Harmon, old-time singer and storyteller. Much Beech Mountain lore is traced back to him.] There was twelve in family. I won't undertake to tell the names of all of 'em, but I am the youngest one. I was seventy-five on the fifteenth of last May. I tried to represent the old Primitive Baptist for about forty-two years, and I don't know whether I ever have preached or not, but the Lord knows I have tried. [Rena Hicks once said of Uncle Monroe, "He used to be the finest preacher

Lee Monroe Presnell, Beech Mountain, 1951.

you ever heard. He preached at my father's funeral—it was his request."] I am getting feeble and I am getting old, but at the same time I have got a hope. I stay on the spurs of the Beech Mounting, whar the a'r is fresh and healthy and the waters is cool. My wife died about seven years ago, and left me by myself. I am glad that the good Lord has blessed me and kept me to this present time. For what purpose I do not know why I am here, but for some purpose—some good purpose.

After singing several songs for us he took up a banjo, and we hear him tuning it. "People used to make fiddles out of gourds," he said, "they made good fiddles. They used thread strings—put beeswax on 'em. They made bows too, with a pin to hold the horse hair."

J. C. Presnell, son of Rosa Hicks and grandson of Buna and Roby Hicks, with Gerret Warner, 1951.

We used to call a dance a breakdown. They would hit the tune with their feet—they could hit that tune. I can see one of those parties now in my 'magination. We would call 'em in, the older ones, when I was a boy, and they would dance and play the fiddle and banjo nearly all night. Everything was so peaceful. There was no drinking, all lovely. Now, with a crowd like that there will be confusion before it is done. Then everybody loved each other. The change came as the pace increased and with more things to lead 'em astray. They's cars come in and then moving pictures and all such as that come in and other things followed 'em. In a sense, it is worth a lot and in a sense it leads off. It brought the good and the bad.

Uncle Monroe learned many of his songs from his mother, he told us, and "Pap would sing songs too." Some he learned during the years he spent in "Ar*kan*sas." Many others he learned from "Lie-hew," an almost legendary figure in that part of the world who traveled all over the southern Appalachians, staying with anyone who would offer him hospitality, planting songs and tales like a musical Johnny Appleseed. He earned the name by which he is always known by invariably confusing fact with fancy. We heard of him through Frank Proffitt and others, and Uncle Monroe gave us a firsthand account:

238

About "Lie-hew"—he was born in Washington County in Tennessee. He was a man who in some respects was useful, and in others he was funny. He stayed with me many a night and day. Sometimes he was awfully rough, and seemingly he was not exactly just right in mind. But he was a man who could take care of himself—he took care of his clothes and all his stuff mighty nice. He would use expressions that was funny. He said he owned a cow that never did go dry and, he said, she never did bring a *cafe,* and her mother never had a cafe in her life. . . . His name was John Calvin Yonce, but the poor feller never did tell the truth. Perhaps he never did know better—but the people called him 'Lie-hew' because of his lyin'. . . . That's what give him the name Lie-hew. He sang a lot of songs. He was a great singer, brother—one of the sweetest singers I ever heard in my life. I learned a lot of songs from him. . . . He sang low and sweet. There is no doubt about that. He died in the poor house . . . he is now in a happier world.

We have just two short letters from Uncle Monroe:

September 14, 1951

Mr and Mrs frank M Warner Your letter at hand also the picturs thank you for the Picturs I have thought of you all many times some how I had love for you all I hope to see you before so long I am getting old But I Will do my Best to sing some more for you I am as well as comond [common] I do hop this will find you all well and inJoying life May the good Lord Bless you all

Lee Monroe Presnell

January 3 1952

Mr and Mrs frank Warner Yessir got the christmas gifts you sent me and also the Picturs you all do look so sweet it did me good to know that I had frands many miles away that was thanking of me I hope to see you all agane in this worl But if not I hope to see you all in that happy world yes I thank you thank you thank you and Pray the Blessings of God upond you all

Lee Monroe Presnell

We did see him again, several times—the last time not long before he died.

96. George Collins   Lee Monroe Presnell, 1951

This version of Child's "Lady Alice," (Child No. 85) which Monroe Presnell learned from his mother, is not very close to any of the Child texts but is similar to those found elsewhere in North Carolina and other parts of the South. As in many old ballads, the listener is precipitated into the midst of the action: George Collins rides home one cold winter night and falls sick and dies—all in the first stanza. Mary (the girl is variously called Alice, Annice, or Mary) is sewing her silks so fine but lays them aside when she hears the news and follows the funeral procession, volubly expressing her grief and woe, at last demanding:

> Set down the coffin, push back the lid,
> Lay back the linen so fine.
> "Oh, may I kiss them pale clay lips?
> I'm sure they'll never kiss mine."

When assured by her mother that "there's more young men than George," she replies that it is George who has got her heart. The final verse about the lonesome dove turns up in many love songs.

Child says that "this ballad . . . is a sort of counterpart to 'Lord Lovel,'" and it seems to have been nearly as popular in this country—in the southern states at least. Brown mentions fourteen versions collected in North Carolina, and the song has been found throughout Virginia, West Virginia, the Carolinas, Tennessee, Mississippi, and as far west as Arkansas.

Nathan Hicks sang a shorter version of "George Collins" (omitting the verse about the coffin) to a different tune. It was printed in *Beech Mountain Ballads and Folksongs,* collected and edited by Mellinger Henry and Maurice Matteson. He also sang it for us.

See: Brown, Vol. 2, 131; Child No. 85, 181 ("Lady Alice"); Coffin and Renwick, 86, 241; Folk-Legacy Records, FSA 22, Vol. 1; Henry and Matteson, 2

GEORGE COLLINS

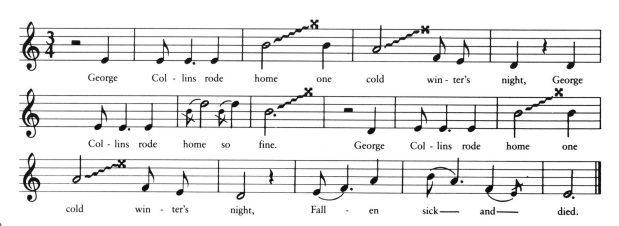

Mary was setting in yonders town,
A-sewing her silks so fine.
Oh, when she heard of George being dead,
She laid her silks aside.

She followed him up, she followed him down,
She followed him to his grave.
Down on her bended knees she fell,
She screamed, she cried, and prayed.

"O Daughter, O Daughter, what makes you weep so?
There's more young men than George.
"Mother, O Mother, George. is got my heart,
And now he's dead and gone."

"Set down the coffin, push back the lid,
Lay back the linen so fine.
Oh, may I kiss them pale clay lips?
I'm sure they'll never kiss mine."

"Oh, don't you see that lonesome dove
A-sailing through the pines?
She's mourning for the loss of her own true love,
Just like I mourn for mine."

97. Red Rosy Bush   Lee Monroe Presnell, 1951

This is a version, if a distant one, of "The Lass of Roch Royal," No. 76 in Child's *The English and Scottish Popular Ballads.* A complete and very good version of Child "D," "Fair Anny," was collected by Cox in West Virginia, who says of it, "Though derived by the contributor from an oral source, probably goes back to print. It seems to be formed from Jamieson's text (*Popular Ballads,* 1806, I, 37) and from Scott's *Minstrelsy,* 1802, II, 49" (p. 83). This ballad seems to be the original source of the well-known verses beginning, "Oh who will shoe my bonny feet," which, as Cox says, "easily become associated with any song on the theme of lovers' parting." He then lists ten or more unrelated songs or ballads in which they occur (see p. 87).

Belden calls the version he prints from Rucker, Missouri, "The False True-Lover." It is not unlike Lee Monroe Presnell's version, and it includes the verse about the red rosy bush and the willow tree. Of the verses mentioned above he says "the shoe-glove-band-father dialog that constitutes so striking a part of that ballad [Child No. 76] has wide currency, in various combinations, as an element of the floating love-lyric of American ballad singers (see Kittredge's note, JAFL XXX 304–5)." Then he gives his own list of the places where the verses appear.

Brown prints two versions, both contributed by Maude Minish Sutton from the North Carolina mountains. The first was called "The Storms Are on the Ocean" from the second stanza:

The storms are on the ocean,
The sea begins to roll—
The earth may lose its motion,
Ere I prove false to thee.

See: Belden, 480; Brown, Vol. 2, 88; Child No. 76, 161 ("The Lass of Roch Royal");
Coffin and Renwick, 78, 234; Cox, 83; Scott, *Minstrelsy of the Scottish Border,* Vol. 2, 49

RED ROSY BUSH

Go — dig — up that red ros-y bush, Stands by the
wil-low — tree, And — it will show — to the
wide — world 'round That she's for-sak-en — me.

* last few verses

Go show me the crow that is so black,
It surely will turn white.
If I forsake the darling girl I love,
The day will turn to night.

Oh, it's hard to love and can't be loved,
It's hard to change your mind.
You broken up the heart of many a poor boy,
But you never will break up mine.

I'll take my knapsack on my back,
And a parasol [parcel] in my hand.
I will travel this wide world over,
Until I find some better a land.

Till I find some better a land, my little love,
Till I find some better a land.
I will travel this wide world, my love,
Till I find some better a land.

Oh, it's who will shoe your pretty little foot,
And who will glove your hand?
Or who will kiss those red rosy cheeks
When I'm in a foreign land?

When I'm in a foreign[t] land, my little love,
When I'm in a foreignt land,
Oh, who will kiss those red rosy cheeks
When I'm in a foreignt land?

My papa will shoe my little foot,
My mama will glove my hand,
And you may kiss my red rosy cheeks
When you return from the foreignt land.

When you return from the foreignt land, my little love,
When you return from the foreignt land,

Oh, you may kiss my red rosy cheeks
When you 'turn from the foreignt land.

Oh, I wish I'd died when I were young,
Or never had been born,
Before I seen those red rosy cheeks,
And heard that flattering tongue.

98. The Two Sisters That Loved One Man   Lee Monroe Presnell, 1951

This ballad is Child No. 10, "The Twa Sisters." Child's notes say, "This is one of the very few old ballads which are not extinct as tradition in the British Isles. . . . It has been found in England, Scotland, Wales, and Ireland, and was very early in print." The Frank C. Brown notes say that the ballad is Scandinavian in origin, starting in Norway sometime before the seventeenth century and spreading to Sweden, Denmark, the Faeroes (and so to Iceland), Scotland, England, and America; and that the corresponding folk tale tradition is Slavic, probably Polish.

The "singing bones"—the revelation of the crime by a fiddle made from the dead girl's body—have almost entirely vanished from American texts, but a trace of them occasionally occurs.

The refrain in Uncle Monroe's version is unusual, and moving. I wonder if "jury" could be a corruption of "dew."

Mr. Presnell sings this ballad on Folk-Legacy Records, FSA 22, Vol. 1.

See: Brown, Vol. 2, 32; Child No. 10, 18 ("The Twa Sisters"); Coffin and Renwick, 32, 213

THE TWO SISTERS THAT LOVED ONE MAN

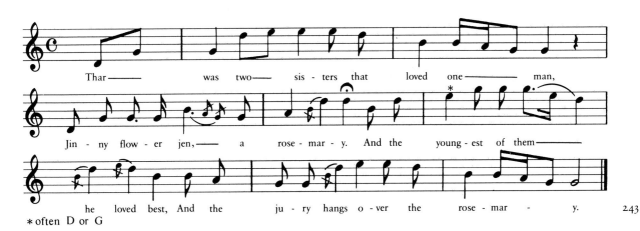

Thar was two sisters that loved one man,

Jin-ny flow-er jen, a rose-mar-y. And the young-est of them

he loved best, And the ju-ry hangs o-ver the rose-mar-y.

*often D or G

O Sister, Sister, walk with me,
Jinny flower jen, a rosemary.
Walk with me to the miller's pond,
And the jury hangs over the rosemary.

Oh, the oldest pushed the youngest in,
Jinny flower jen, a rosemary.
And they all perceived that the water was clear,
And the jury hangs over the rosemary.

O Sister, Sister, reach me your hand,
Jinny flower jen, a rosemary.
You may have half of all the land,
And the jury hangs over the rosemary.

O Sister, Sister, I won't reach my hand,
Jinny flower jen, a rosemary.
I will have all of the lands,
And the jury hangs over the rosemary.

O Sister, Sister, reach me your glove,
Jinny flower jen, a rosemary.
You may have sweet William for your own true love,
And the jury hangs over the rosemary.

O Sister, Sister, I won't reach my glove,
Jinny flower jen, a rosemary.
I will have sweet William for my own true love,
And the jury hangs over the rosemary.

Oh, she floated around and she floated down,
Jinny flower jen, a rosemary.
She floated down to the miller's pond,
And the jury hangs over the rosemary.

O miller, miller, come and see,
Jinny flower jen, a rosemary.
There is something here a-floating by me,
And the jury hangs over the rosemary.

Oh, it isn't a fish or it isn't a swan,
Jinny flower jen, a rosemary.
It is sweet William's own true love,
And the jury hangs over the rosemary.

99. Farewell to Old Bedford   Lee Monroe Presnell, 1951

"This is an old old song," Uncle Monroe told us. "I heard my parents sing it."
This leaves it something of a mystery, since we cannot find a reference to it in any other collection. We find it intriguing—especially the last verse, which uses the symbolism of a fiddler and his fiddle to suggest discouragement with life.

The "Old Bedford" must refer to the city in England, where there is a county
and town named Bedford on the River Ouse, northwest of London.

FAREWELL TO OLD BEDFORD

Well might I have enjoyed it,
All in pleasure,
If my cruel parents
Had left me alone.
I will drown away sorrow
In a full-flowing bumper.
I will drown away sorrow
In a bottle of wine.

Eight drams a bottle is,
And I don't care for folly.
Now never let trouble
Come into your mind.
I will drown her away
In a full-flowing bumper.
I will drown her away
In a bottle of wine.

Eight drams a bottle is,
And I don't care for folly.
I play on my fiddle
And dance all the time.
My fingers are frozen,
My bow it needs rosin,
My soundpost is down,
And my bridge it won't stand.

245

100. My Grandmother's Chair   Lee Monroe Presnell, 1951

Uncle Monroe delighted in the humor of this narrative song about a grandson, slighted in his grandmother's will, who did all right in the end. Before singing it he explained the story line:

> There was an old lady, you see, and she lived to be eighty-three years old, and she was wealthy. She had two grandsons. She called one Jim and one John. She made her will before she died, and she gave Jim all her property such as stock, and she give John the old arm chair. She put all the money she had in the bottom of that old arm chair, and Jim didn't know it, or John, or none of the neighborhood didn't know it. And now I will sing the song.

The only reference to this song we have found in other collections is in Randolph, Vol. 3, pp. 224–27. Randolph calls it "Granny's Old Arm Chair" and prints two almost identical versions from Missouri (each with four stanzas and chorus), one from Springfield and one from Clinton, where the singer said her copy was written down in the 1880s by her grandmother. Randolph says that "Three stanzas and a chorus were printed by Lucile Morris in the Springfield, Mo., *News and Leader,* Oct. 21, 1934. She says the song was popular in the 90's. Brewster (*Southern Folklore Quarterly* 4, 1940, pp. 199–200) gives an Indiana version."

The "two thousand pounds or more" mentioned in the last verse in all of the versions (including the one from Uncle Monroe) indicate an English origin. As further evidence: a few years ago at a theatre in New York City we attended a reconstruction of an evening in a turn-of-the-century English Music Hall (created and produced by Tony Barrand and John Roberts), and one of the stars (David Jones) sang "Granny's Old Arm Chair." Uncle Monroe would have been pleased.

In the Archives of the Library of Congress we have found two sets of sheet music for this song, both published in 1880 — one called "Grandmother's Chair," "As sung with great applause by Tony Pastor, words and music by John Read, arranged by Dr. W. J. Wetmore." This is published by S. T. Gordon & Son, 18 East 14th Street, New York, New York.

The other copy was entitled "Grandma's Old Arm Chair . . . known as Granny's Old Arm Chair." On this sheet music the song is said to have been "composed and sung by Frank B. Carr, America's Motto Vocalist," and it was published by White, Smith & Company, 516 Washington Street, Boston.

We don't know if a decision was ever reached as to who actually did write the song.

In 1941 we collected this song in an almost identical version from Mrs. Lena Bourne Fish in East Jaffrey, New Hampshire. Mr. Presnell's version shows a little more of the folk process.

My grand-moth-er, she, at the age of eigh-ty three, One day in May she tak-en ill and died. And af-ter she was dead,— the will of course was read By a law-yer as we stood by his side. To my broth-er it were found she had left two hun-dred pound, And the same un-to my sis-ter I de-clare. But when it came to me— the law-yer said, "I see Gran-ny has on-ly left to you her old arm-chair."

Chorus
How— they tit-tered,— how— they chaffed, How my broth-er and my sis-ter did laugh, Oh, when— they heard— the law-yer de-clare, "Gran-ny has on-ly left to you her old arm-chair."

* this bar varies with the the basic scheme is
number of syllables

247

I thought it hardly fair, but still I did not care,
And in the evening I taken the chair away.
How my neighbors at me chaffed, how my brother
     at me laughed,
Saying, "It will be useful, John, some day.
When you settle down for life and find yourself
     a wife,
It will be very handy, I declare.
And on a cold and frosty night, when the fire is
     burning bright,
You can be seated in your old arm chair."
     Chorus

What my brother said was true, for in a year
     or two,
Strange to say, I settled down in married life.
Oh, the girl I first did court, and then the ring
     I bought,
We went to church, and she became my wife.
And the old girl and me was happy as could be,
And when my work were over I declare,
On a cold and frosty night, when the fire was
     burning bright,
I'd be seated in my old arm chair.
     Chorus

One night the chair fell down, as I picked it up
     I found
A lot of notes, two thousand pounds or more!
When my brother of this heard
He run nearly mad with rage and tore his hair,
But I only laughed at him and said unto him, Jim
"Don't you wish you had the old arm chair?"
     Chorus

101. The Rambling Boy   Lee Monroe Presnell, 1951

"I learned this," Uncle Monroe told us, "from old Lie-hew. As I've said, he was
a great singer, one of the sweetest singers I ever heard in my life." We were excited when
we heard it, for it sounded to us like a forerunner of "The Unfortunate Rake," and
indeed it may be. It is certainly Irish, and the funeral directions are similar, and the
story in both instances is about a young man brought down in his prime—one to an
untimely death that stemmed from his riotous living, and one, in this case, brought
to the gallows by his career of robbing on the king's highway.

In writing of "The Work of Maude Minish Sutton" in "*Long Journey Home: Folk
Life in the South*" *Southern Exposure* (Summer–Fall 1977), Dr. Daniel Patterson includes a version of this song collected by Mrs. Sutton from Mrs. Ann Coffey. Mrs.
Sutton simply calls it "an eighteenth century highwayman ballad." (This same version
from Mrs. Coffey through Mrs. Sutton is published in the Brown collection.) The version differs in many ways from Uncle Monroe's, mentioning London city rather than
Dublin, and ending with a warning not to marry a demanding wife.

Laws mentions many sources for the song and quotes part of a version very like

Mrs. Coffey's. He notes that the song is found on a number of broadsides and that it has been reported from Somerset, Sussex, and Dorset.

Peter Kennedy's notes are interesting:

> This is one of the most popular of the highwaymen ballads, and it has been widely noted in England. It is interesting historically in that there is mention of the first London "policemen," the Bow Street Runners, who were established in 1751. [In the verse given below] they are called Ned Fielding's gang, referring to Henry Fielding (novelist and playwright) who was appointed a justice of the peace of Westminster in 1748 and started operations from the Bow Street Magistrates Court. . . . the Runners . . . were armed and patrolled the streets in order to raid gambling houses and pursue robbers and highwaymen.

The verse given by Kennedy reads:

> To Covent Gardens we went straight away
> Me and my wife went to the Play
> Ned Fielding's gang there did me pursue
> Taken I was by that curs-ed crew.

Uncle Monroe's version has a line: "But soon was mobbed by the follant (valiant?) crew."

See: Belden, 136; Brown, Vol. 2, 355; Henry, *Folksongs from the Southern Highlands,* 327; Kennedy, 712 ("Newlyn Town"), 730; Laws, *ABBB,* L-12, 172; Randolph, Vol. 2, 84; Thos. Coll. II, 120 ("The Irish Robber")

THE RAMBLING BOY

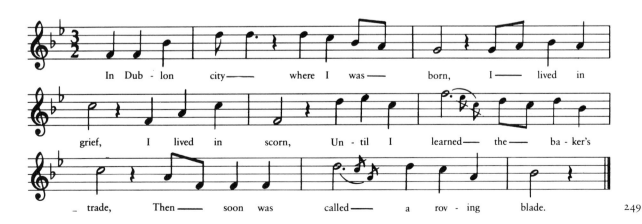

In Dub-lon city — where I was — born, I — lived in grief, I lived in scorn, Un-til I learned — the — ba-ker's _ trade, Then — soon was called — a rov-ing blade.

In Dublon City where I did stay,
I spent my money at balls and play,
Until at length my cash grew low,
Then forced to robbing I must go.

I took to me a handsome wife,
I loved her as I loved my life.
To keep her dressed both neat and gay,
Then I was forced to robbing on the old highway.

I robbed King William, I do declare.
I left him sleeping in his napkins square,
Bid him goodnight, stepped into my chair,
And in great haste rode home to my dear.

To green bright fields I did pursue,
But soon was mobbed by the follant [valiant?] crew.
My father will distracted run,
My mother cries, "O darling son!"

Just one thing that I do crave,
That's six young ladies to dig my grave,
And six young ladies to sink my pall,
All dressed in white, pink ribbings all.

And six young men to guard them home,
Give them swords and pistols all,
That they may fire a salute for joy:
Here lies a poor wise and a rambling boy!

5

Watauga County, North Carolina

FRANK PROFFITT

WHEN FRANK PROFFITT DIED in 1965, the *New York Times* carried a six-inch double-column story, and stories about him appeared in leading papers across the country—remarkable tributes to a shy mountain man, as he called himself.

Frank was born on June 1, 1913, in Laurel Bloomery, Tennessee, the son of Wiley and Rebecca Alice Creed Proffitt. His grandparents were John and Adeline Perdue Proffitt, who moved to the Cracker Neck section of the eastern Tennessee mountains from Wilkes County, North Carolina, shortly after the Civil War. Frank's grandfather, John Proffitt, went across the state line to join the boys in blue (as Frank sings in "Goin' 'Cross the Mountains"), and was a member of the 13th Tennessee Cavalry, U.S.A. His grandfather's brother fought with the Confederates. When Frank was a young boy the family moved back to North Carolina to the Beaver Dam section of Watauga County, just a few miles below the Tennessee border. Frank said that in his boyhood his life was like that of the pioneers—the earliest mountain settlers. He was sixteen when he walked barefoot across the mountains to see his first town—Mountain City, Tennessee. He moved in his relatively short life from a colonial pattern to the sophistication of the mid-twentieth century—talking and singing to college audiences, making LP recordings, and corresponding with people around the world.

After sixth grade at a mountain schoolhouse Frank left school to work full time on his father's farm, but throughout his life, he told us, he read whatever books and papers he could lay his hands on. He spent much time thinking and pondering, on rainy days, or during long winter evenings. And he learned songs: from his father, Wiley, from his aunt, Nancy Prather, and her husband Noah, from other kinfolk, from neighbors, from men who worked in the lumber camp at Shull's Mills (a local logging camp),

Frank Proffitt, Pick Britches Valley, Watauga County, North Carolina, 1941.

and from anybody he met who knew songs. He had a greater interest in these songs, and where they might have come from, than any of the other folk thereabout. They found his interest a bit hard to understand. "Why do you want to hold on to all that old stuff?" they would ask. He just did. In the years we knew him Frank recorded more than a hundred songs for us.

Frank spoke, and wrote, in a style reminiscent of early eighteenth-century America, or, sometimes, in an earlier idiom. He kept many of the phrases of the first-comers: "I feel beholden to all," "This caused me much inward misery," and "I might ought not to say it." His letters (we still have more than two hundred of them) were unusually revealing. His grasp of ideas, his rare perception of the world around him, his amused and compassionate understanding of people, his fun and humor, his integrity, were a source of constant satisfaction to us.

In 1941 he wrote:

It is beginning to get cool here now. It won't be long I know until frost nips the green growing things and turns them brown. Its been very dry here and the stream flowing by my house is getting so low that it dont turn the water wheel so fast any more but fast enough to keep my radio battery charged (I have a radio now) to keep playing. I've been a-squirrel hunting twice this fall. They are cutting hickory nuts now up on the Horse Ridge. I seen six in one tree. The nuts was sure hitting the ground. Browned squirrel and squirrel gravy and biscuits, coffee, and a little more gravy is not so bad thease chilly mornings. I wish you was here. We'd show the wimmin how to eat. I haven't been out to Nathan's since you all were here but Bessie has been there canning plums. . . . She stayed a week. I didn't like to be left that way but didn't see much I could do about it. . . . My beans done fairly well. We sold six thousand lbs. My back got mighty tired before we got done. They brought us from 3½¢ to 5¢ per lb. I sold my calves the other day. They was 3 months old and brought me $50 for the two. . . . I hope you can come again and we'll have a good old time and sang and sang, on and on til we get tired. . . .

Frank had a pride in his mountain heritage and people. He didn't like talk of hillbillies, for instance. But he liked to tell jokes about the mountains, like the day he found an old man by the side of a mountain road just a-cryin'. "What's the matter, old man?" "I'm jist disheartened," the man said. "That's the fourth time this mornin' I fell out'n my cornfield!" Some of the fields there in the mountains are that steep. Frank said he'd plowed a field so steep the dirt kept falling down his collar.

During the war years (World War II) Frank worked first on the TVA project and then for a time at Oak Ridge, Tennessee, as a carpenter, without any knowledge of what work was being done there. Later he worked in Toledo, Ohio, in a spark plug factory. In Toledo, he told us, he stayed with some other mountain people who had gone there to work, and he saw little of the city or its ways. Many times, when money ran out, he left home to take temporary jobs at carpentry or road building. Earlier, during the Depression, he worked for the Works Progress Administration, doing whatever job was offered.

George's Gap, on the way to the Proffitts' house.

Frank and Bessie had six children: Oliver, Ronald, Frank Jr., Phyllis, Eddie, and Gerald. They welcomed each one, but there were many mouths to feed and living was hard. As the song ("Beaver Dam Road," No. 119) says:

I've worked like a dog and what have I got?
No corn in the crib, no beans in the pot.
It's hard times on the Beaver Dam Road,
It's hard times, poor boy.

When we got to the mountains in 1951—the first time we had managed to make the trip since the war's end—we had a good visit on Beech Mountain with the Hickses,

The cabin Frank Proffitt built when he and Bessie Hicks were married, 1941.

but when we got to Pick Britches Valley we found only Bessie and the children. That is, the younger children. Oliver by that time had graduated from high school and joined the Air Force. Frank was away. He had taken a job working on the road somewhere, and, Bessie said, he had sold his guitar and wasn't singing any more. That was sad news. We knew it was the terrible struggle to make a living that had forced him to give up his music, and we knew too that giving up his music was a proof of his despair.

We have a letter from Frank dated December 30, 1951:

> We recived the nice box of presents and what a time the kids are having. . . . Oliver was home for the holidays and he's put on several pounds. He's training for Air Force Police and he is big enough to handle his job looks like. . . . We hope you can come down next summer and we will arrange to have you spend a few days with us. The boys can climb some of the hills and see what's on the other side. . . .

Still no mention of music.

The first song Frank Proffitt ever sang for us—"Hang Down Your Head, Tom Dooley"—turned out to be of great significance.

"Tom Dooley" was one of the three songs Frank gave us the first afternoon we met him in 1938. It was the first song he remembered hearing his father pick on a banjo. Frank's grandmother, Adeline Perdue, lived in Wilkes County and knew both Tom Dula and Laura Foster, for the song is about real people and a real tragedy. Many songs were written about the murder, but the song that came down in Frank's family is the one that went around the world. "Tom Dooley" became one of our favorite songs, and Frank Warner used it in every lecture and program from 1939 to 1959, telling the story of Tom and of Frank Proffitt. He taught it to Alan Lomax, who included it, minus the third stanza, in *Folk Song U.S.A,* in 1947. Frank included it on his first Elektra album in 1952, with credit to Frank Proffitt in the jacket notes. Then, in 1958, the Kingston Trio used the *Folk Song U.S.A.* version in a recording for Capitol Records—both on an album and as a single which sold more than three million copies. The song made the top of the hit parade, and is, as I have said, generally credited with starting the world-wide wave of interest in and enthusiasm for American folk music. We have evidence that it has been sung, and is still being sung, in almost every country of the world.

The only existing copyright on "Tom Dooley" was the one covered by *Folk Song U.S.A.* Copyright laws were, and are, confusing, but at long length, in 1962, there was an out-of-court compromise—after the time of the song's greatest popularity—which divides any subsequent royalties among the three people involved: Frank Proffitt, Frank Warner, and Alan Lomax.

Royalties from "Tom Dooley," while not approaching the pre-1962 scale, did make a substantial difference to Frank Proffitt and his family. In 1959 Frank wrote us:

> There was a few things I wanted to say that I might not have time or think of when we meet. . . . There was the usual gang around the store when you called me so I didn't talk

A group of Proffitt kinfolks on the steps of the house built by Frank's father. Frank is on the left in back; Bessie and Oliver are in the middle. In front of Frank is his Aunt Nancy Prather who taught him many songs. Pick Britches Valley, 1941.

much . . . but I did understand that they was some possibility of money for us. I wouldnt bore you with telling what getting something will mean to us, for frankly we are in pretty desperate condition. Anything that helps will seem like a divine gift.

Frank, Jr., told us later, after his father's death, that he remembered "just before the folk music started" that often the family had nothing to eat but potatoes three times a day, and not enough of that.

Beyond the money, "Tom Dooley" completely changed Frank Proffitt's life. For one thing, it brought him back his music.

Word got around that Frank was the source of the song. In 1960 J. C. Brown, then editor of the *Carolina Farmer* (now *Carolina Country*), a magazine which reaches nearly all rural folk in North Carolina, wrote a warm enthusiastic story about Frank in two issues of the magazine. This gave Frank a new status with his neighbors. Suddenly there were many newspaper interviews, letters from across the country, visits from strangers, and orders for the home-made fretless banjos Frank had begun to make to his father's pattern. Before the settlement with Capitol Records Frank had written us: "The Tom Dooley case sounds a little bad, but don't feel badly on my part if we don't win, for I have got more out of it than you realize. . . . I got to see you again . . . and to know that what we love millions of others do also. . . ."

In 1961 Frank was invited to participate in the first University of Chicago Folk Festival, along with Horton Barker, Roscoe Holcomb, Elizabeth Cotton, Memphis Slim, Willie Dixon, the Stanley Brothers, the New Lost City Ramblers, Alan Mills and Jean Carignan from Canada, Richard Chase, and Frank Warner. He had been reluctant to go, but he had been persuaded. The response to his singing was immediate. He could have no further doubt of his acceptance as a true mountain singer.

Writing of the festival in the May 1961 issue of WFMT's "Chicago Fine Arts Guide," Studs Terkel, who was the festival's master of ceremonies, said that it was the *real* folk singers—Horton Barker, the blind singer from Virginia; Roscoe Holcomb, the well digger from Kentucky; and Frank Proffitt, the farmer and carpenter from North Carolina, who "told us more than we have grown accustomed to expect . . . since a great many of us have come to equate folk music with cuteness, cleverness, and pretty sounds. . . . Often folksinging is not pretty; sometimes it is harsh, as life itself is harsh. Always it is true. . . . There was a singular reaction at the three-day festival. . . . the audience, consisting primarily of college students, acclaimed the Appalachian men rather than the slick pros. . . ."

After this Frank was invited to a number of colleges and universities and festivals. He spent a week in 1961 and another in 1962 at the Pinewoods Folk Music Camp of the Country Dance and Song Society near Plymouth, Massachusetts; he sang at the Newport Folk Festival in 1963; and he represented the state of North Carolina at the New York World's Fair in 1964. He made three recordings of his songs—one for Folkways, and two for Folk-Legacy. We were proud to be asked to write the notes for the Folkways record. Frank wrote us that he liked what we had said: "I am so proud you spoke of my kind of people, their ways and struggles. . . . I so much desire to only

Frank Proffitt in front of the second home he built, with his tobacco crop in the background, 1959.

be a representitive of my kind of people, neaver to just exault myself . . . just to bring to this generation a little bit of the past and my own attitudes toward life. So I would not want a word changed, not even my own quotes, which if not of correctness all is of sincerity."

From time to time during the more than twenty-five years that we knew him, Frank would send us a notebook in which he had written down the words of remembered songs. He sent us the last of these notebooks in 1964, and on the first page he had written:

Ray Hicks clogging while Frank Proffitt and Aunt Buna Hicks play a dance tune, 1959. Ray's mother Rena and a couple of grandchildren are in the background.

To all of those who's mind reaches above the hard facts of life does a Ballad have its meanings. With thease songs did our Forebears cheer their weary hearts in the New Ground clearings. Life to them was not dull for in their amagination they had a world of their own. This world they built is not for thouse who see only the dull drab facts of their surrondings, but only for folk of kindred minds seeking to preserve and exault a people of undaunted spirit who excepted [accepted] Life in a singing spirit, reaching in their hearts for things to brighten the days and years. I may neaver see the Lochs or Braes of my people. But in my amagination I have this world of old castles, of high Lord Chieftans, of those who used the sword. . . . To thouse who sleep in the soil far from the Bonnie Braes, my hope is they have not lived for nothing.

Frank Proffitt died suddenly, in his sleep, on November 22, 1965, and he was buried in the small private Milsap burying ground on a hillside about a mile from his home.

In 1967, with the help of many friends of Frank's, enough money was raised to put up a headstone at Frank's grave. It is a simple granite marker, and it says:

FRANK NOAH PROFFITT
1913–1965
GOING ACROSS THE MOUNTAIN–
O, FARE YOU WELL

Frank would be gratified and proud to know that Frank, Jr., is carrying on the family's singing tradition—in festivals and schools and colleges across the Southeast. He too sang at Newport and has been to Pinewoods, and for several years has been a visiting artist in North Carolina communities under the aegis of the North Carolina Council on the Arts.

102. Bolamkin   Frank Proffitt, 1959

This ballad, Child No. 93, full of blood and violence, has been collected widely in this country as well as in England and Scotland. (See citations.) Brown says that "Lamkin" is a Flemish version of the name Lambert, since many fine masons were of Flemish blood and were often brought to England as builders. The "Bo" is no doubt an abbreviation of "bold" since some versions of the ballad are titled "Bold Lamkin." Brown's version "B" was collected from Frank Proffitt the year before we met him, but Brown prints only two verses of Proffitt's version. Frank had some interesting comments on this ballad:

> I want to say that I never gave much thought to Bo Lamkin's feelings until I too got to building. It seems he got angry because "pay he got none." I have had a occasion or two of this kind, not much I am glad to say. I don't claim that I had murderous intent, but how I would have liked to take a big stone hammer and undone the work that pay I got none for. Old Bo, if he had only done this to his work would have had my admiration very much. Perhaps we would not have heard of him, then, which perhaps would have been just as well. I like to think of just where the place is now where he built the fine castle. For I believe it really happened as all the old ballad things. The older folks wanted a fact, then they went all out in building a legend around it, but never to destroy the fact that planted the seed. They kept it intact and thank God for it.

It is interesting that in the fourth and fifth verses Frank substitutes "landlord" for the old world title of "lord."

In the *Journal of American Folklore* 90, no. 355 (January–March 1977): pp. 49–67, Professor John DeWitt Niles of the University of California at Berkeley writes of "Lamkin: the Motivation of Horror." His first paragraph is interesting (as is the entire article):

> Everyone loves a good killing. The more bloody and cruel the killing, the more interesting it is likely to be, especially when the victims are helpless: a woman home alone, an infant child. But the most fascinating murder of all, to the popular mind, is a bloody killing of helpless persons *with no plausible motive.* Here we have the materials of tabloid journalism; here we have the Sharon Tate murders; and here we have the singularly unpleasant ballad of "Lamkin."

He goes on to say that the ballad "first came to light just over two hundred years ago" when Bishop Percy was sent a Kentish version in 1775, and that in 1776 Thomas Herd printed a text for the first time. The article is a detailed study of the ballad, and its findings cannot be condensed into a few lines; but we have been particularly interested in Professor Niles's conclusion that there is a much deeper motivation on the part of the mason than revenge for the nonpayment of his wages.

He discusses various theories advanced by other scholars, including that of Ninon Leader in his *Classical Hungarian Ballads and Their Folklore* (Cambridge University Press, 1967), where he cites a number of documents bearing on the European superstition that the blood, bones, or ashes of a human being are required if an important edifice is to stand firm. But then Professor Niles presents the idea that "Lamkin" or "Lambkin" is an ironic nickname for the devil, based on another ancient European belief that "the building of a great bridge, castle or church is a dangerous enterprise . . . which may require the assistance of . . . the devil" himself. And he must usually be paid not in money, but in lives. Professor Niles's theory is well documented and bolstered by numerous Scandinavian tales and legends. He agrees that most singers of the ballad would find such an interpretation hard to believe, but he believes the ballad expresses, really, the logic of a former age; and that "in its own peculiar way" it even presents a moral—"if you strike a bargain with the devil, give him his due, or there will be the devil to pay."

We appreciate Professor Niles's concluding paragraph: "And just as ballad singing is an ongoing process, the collecting and publishing of ballad tunes and texts should never stop, regardless of how many tunes and texts are already in print. . . . even the slightest fragment of a ballad collected in North America in the twentieth century may provide a clue to the song's prehistory."

On one of our visits to Frank Proffitt's (we think it was in 1959) he began—at Frank Warner's urging—to sing the old ballads, such as this one, unaccompanied. Until then he had sung all his songs to the chords he knew on the guitar or banjo and the old modal tunes had suffered. He himself was surprised and pleased at the way the music of the ballads came back to life. In 1963, when he had returned home from

singing at a college, he wrote us, "I sang the old songs without instrument and they
went over wonderful."

See: Brown, Vol. 2, 140; Child No. 93 196 ("Lamkin"); Coffin and Renwick, 89, 242;
JAF 90, No. 355, 49–67; Linscott, 303; Randolph, Vol. 1, 141;
Sharp, *English Folksongs of the Southern Appalachians*, Vol. 1, 27

BOLAMKIN

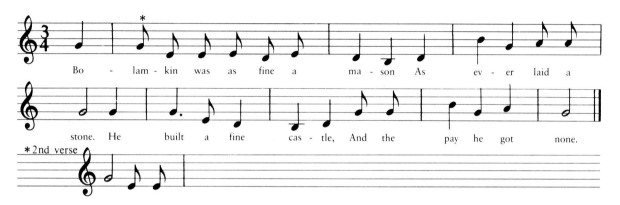

He swore by his Maker
He would kill them unknown.
Beware of Bolamkin,
When he'd come from home.
    Refrain (repeat last two lines of verse)

Bolamkin came to the castle door,
He knocked until it rung.
There's no one as ready as the faltress [false nurse].
She arose and let him in.
    Refrain

"Oh, where is the landlord,
Or is he at home?"
"No, he is gone to merry England
To visit his son."
    Refrain

"Where is the landlord's lady,
Did she go with him?"
"Oh, no," said the faltress,
"She's upstairs a-sleeping."
    Refrain

"How will we get her downstairs
Such a dark night as this?"
Stick pins and needles
In the little baby."
    Refrain

Bolamkin rocked the cradle,
And the faltress she sung,
While the tears and the red blood
From the cradle did run.
    Refrain

263

The lady coming down the stairs,
Not thinking any harm,
Bolamkin stood ready
And got her in his arms.
Refrain

"Bolamkin, Bolamkin,
Spare my life one day,
You can have all the gay gold
Your horse can take away."
Refrain

"Bolamkin, Bolamkin,
Spare my life one hour,
You can have my daughter, Betsy,
My own blooming flower."
Refrain

"Keep your daughter Betsy
To go through the flood,
To scour out the silver basin
That catches your heart's blood."
Refrain

Daughter Betsy a-sitting
In the parlor so high,
She saw her dear father
Coming riding hard by.
Refrain

"Dear Father, dear Father,
Don't blame me for what's done.
Bolamkin has been here
And killed your darling son.
Refrain

"Bolamkin has been here
And killed your baby.
Bolamkin has been here
And killed your lady."
Refrain

Bolamkin was hung
To the scaffold so high,
And the faltress was burned
To the stake standing by.
Refrain

103. Dan Doo   Frank Proffitt, 1938

This Child ballad No. 277 in its various—and sometimes very different—versions has been found in all parts of the British Isles and throughout the United States.

The "wether" in the ballad's original title, "The Wife Wrapt in Wetherskin," is the bellwether of the flock of sheep—the leader. A common way to tan sheep's hide in early days was beating it with hickory switches.

This is one of the three songs sung to us by Frank Proffitt in 1938 on our first trip to Beech Mountain. We collected a very different version (with the original title) from Mrs. Lena Bourne Fish in New Hampshire in 1941, No. 44.

Cazden II includes a fragment of the "Dan Do" version of this ballad, with the refrain, "Tinna Clinnama Clinchama Clingo." The notes include interesting information but say, surprisingly, "Most American examples of this ballad are as fragmentary as #136" (the one they include), since both the examples we collected are complete.

See: Belden, 92; Brown, Vol. 2, 185; Cazden II, 503; Child No. 277, 603 ("The Wife Wrapt in Wether's Skin"); Coffin and Renwick, 146, 274; Flanders, *VFSB*, 224; Randolph, Vol. 1, 187

DAN DOO

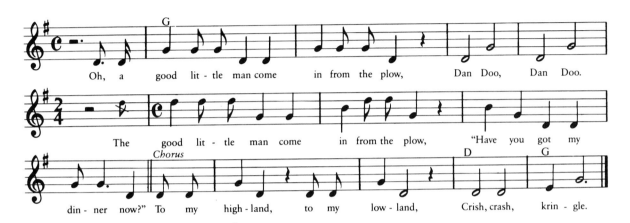

Oh, a good lit-tle man come in from the plow, Dan Doo, Dan Doo. The good lit-tle man come in from the plow, "Have you got my din-ner now?" To my high-land, to my low-land, Crish, crash, krin-gle.

"There's a little piece of bread a-layin' on the shelf,"
Dan Doo, Dan Doo.
"There's a little piece of bread a-layin' on the shelf,
If you want hit, you can get hit yourself."
    Chorus

Little man went out to his sheep pen,
Dan Doo, Dan Doo.
Little man went out to his sheep pen,
Down with the wether and off with his skin.
    Chorus

Little man went out behind the barn,
Dan Doo, Dan Doo.

Little man went out behind the barn,
Cut a hickory stick as long as his arm.
    Chorus

He laid the hide all on her back,
Dan Doo, Dan Doo.
He laid the hide all on her back,
The way he made the hickory crack. [or: He made
    that stick go whickety-whack.]
    Chorus

"I'll tell my father and all my kin,"
Dan Doo, Dan Doo.
"I'll tell my father and all my kin,
How you dress your muttonskin!"
    Chorus

"You can tell your father and your brothers too,"
Dan Doo, Dan Doo.
"You can tell your father and your brothers too
What a whuppin' I give you."
  Chorus

Next day little man come in from plow,
Dan Doo, Dan Doo.
Next day little man come in from plow,
She met him at the door, says, "Your dinner's ready
  now."
  Chorus

104. Lowland Low (or, The *Golden Willow Tree*) Frank Proffitt, 1959

  This well-known and popular ballad is No. 286 in the Child collection, where
it is called "The Sweet Trinity (The Golden Vanity)." The ballad goes by many names:
"The Golden Vallady," "The Merry Golden Tree," "The Turkey Shivaree," etc. Child's
version "A" is from Pepys *Ballads,* Vol. 4, 196, and is from a broadside dated 1682. It
begins:

  Sir Walter Rawleigh has built a ship
    In the Neatherlands,
  Sir Walter Rawleigh has built a ship
    In the Neatherlands,
  And it is called the Sweet Trinity,
  And was taken by the false gallaly—
    Sailing in the Low-lands.

Here the story has an ambiguous ending. After the cabin boy has fulfilled his mission
of sinking "the false gallaly," the captain offers him gold but not his daughter, and
the offer is spurned. No mention is made of what became of the cabin boy. Many versions end, as Frank's does, with the drowning of the boy—thus enabling sailors in the
fo'cs'le to sing with impunity about a mean and treacherous captain. But in some versions the boy's mates prevail—he is rescued, and the captain is forced to keep his word.
As Lomax says, this ending turns the story into a Jack Tale, with the weak underdog
outsmarting his stronger adversary.
  Frank Proffitt did not give us this song until 1959. At that time he said, "I am
happy to recall as much of this ballad as I have—out of memory dulled by years. There
could be some incorrect parts. It is surprising that this ballad would live inland so
long, sung by those who like me never saw the sea. But I catch the roll and movement
of the billowing waves in singing." The interesting lines in Frank's seventh verse: "He
took a little instrument just for the use / And cut him nine gashes in the salt water
juice," appear also in Brown's version "A," with the suggestion that "juice" was prob-

ably a corruption of "sluice." This makes more sense, perhaps, but we would find it hard to give up the phrase "salt water juice."

See: Belden, 97; Brown, Vol. 2, 191; Cazden II, 246; Child No. 286, 611 ("The Sweet Trinity [The Golden Vanity]"); Coffin and Renwick, 153, 277; Colcord, 158; Hugill, 62; Lomax, *FSNA*, 191; Sharp, *English Folksongs of the Southern Appalachians*, Vol. 1, 282

LOWLAND LOW (or, The *Golden Willow Tree*)

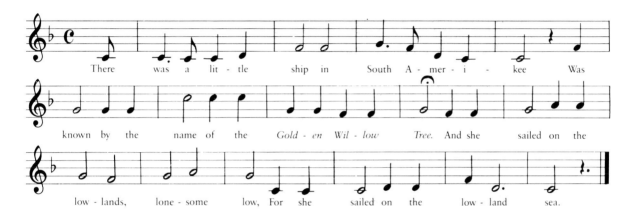

Now she had not been a-sailing, not very long,
In weeks not more than three,
Until they spied a ship all sailing high,
And it was the *Turkish Robberee.*

"Oh, what shall I do! Oh, what shall I do!"
Our jolly well captain, cried he,
"I a-feared we all will be took by the *Turkish Robberee*
And be sunk in the lowland sea."

Up steps a little man, "What will you give to me
For to sink her in the lowland, lonesome sea,
If I sink her in the lowlands, lonesome low,
If I sink her in the lowland sea?"

"I have at home houses and lands,
Also my youngest daughter will be at your command,
If you'll sink her in the lowlands, lonesome low,
If you'll sink her in the lowland sea."

All down in the briny deep swum he,
He swum beneath the *Turkish Robberee,*
All a-sailing high on the lowlands low,
Sailing so high on the lowland sea.

He took a little instrument just for the use,
And cut him nine gashes in the salt water juice,
And he sunk her in the lowlands, lonesome low,
He sunk her in the lowland sea.

267

Back he comes a-swimmin', back comes he,
Back to the side of the *Golden Willow Tree,*
As she sailed upon the lowlands, lonesome low,
As she sailed upon the lowland sea.

"Have you made the writ to your houses and
    lands,
And vowed for me to have your fair daughter's
    hand?
For I've sunk her in the lowlands, lonesome low,
I've sunk her in the lowland sea."

"A fool only gives of his houses and lands,
And his youngest daughter to be at your
    command.
You can go sink in the lowlands, lonesome low,
You can sink in the lowland sea."

Up he went and down went he until the count of
    three,
Then he sunk to the bottom of the lowland sea.
He sank in the lowlands, lonesome low,
He sank in the lowland sea.

105. Hang Man   Frank Proffitt, 1960

This version of "The Maid Freed from the Gallows" (Child No. 95) Frank Proffitt learned from his Aunt Nancy Prather, his father's sister. It has been collected very
widely in this country and abroad—on the Continent as well as in Great Britain. Brown
prints three texts and portions of nine others. See Coffin and Renwick for a complete
list of collections in which the ballad appears and also for a list of scholarly discus-
sions in print of the ballad as song, drama, etc.

In some texts the condemned singer is a man. Brown notes that this is true in
five North Carolina texts, for instance.

The ballad has been found in Maine and New Hampshire, but more often in
the South and West.

We were interested in the fact that in Frank's version the "crime" for which the
maid is to be hanged is stated—"For I have stole a silvery cup." Usually the reason for
the execution is not mentioned. Child's notes say that in European versions "a young
woman has fallen into the hands of corsairs; father, mother, brother, sister, refuse to
pay ransom, but her lover . . . stickles at no price which may be necessary to retrieve
her." Belden says that some British versions have the "prickly bush" refrain which seems
to connect this ballad with the "Seeds of Love," and that this prompted Miss Lucy Broadwood (*Journal of the Folk-Song Society* 5, pp. 233–5) "to interpret the golden ball [ap-
pearing in some versions, even occasionally in the U.S.] (silver cup, comb) as a symbol
of virginity."

See: Belden, 66; Brown, Vol. 2, 143; Child No. 95, 200 ("The Maid Freed from the Gallows");
Coffin and Renwick, 91, 243; Flanders-Barry, *NGMS,* 117

"Hold up your hand, Old Josh-u-way," she said, "Wait a while and see. I thought I saw my dear old fa-ther come Cross-ing o-ver the sea."

"Do you have any money for me,
Gold for to pay my fee?
For I have stole a silvery cup
And hangeth I am goin' to be."

"I don't have any money for you,
Gold for to pay your fee.
I have just come for to see you hang
On yonders gallows tree."

"Hold up your hand, Old Joshuway," she said,
"Wait awhile and see.
I thought I saw my dear old mother come
Crossing over the sea."

"Do you have any money for me,
Or gold for to pay my fee?
For I have stole a silvery cup
And hangeth I'm a-goin' to be."

"I don't have no money for you,
Or gold for to pay your fee.
I have just come for to see you hang
On yonders gallows tree."

"Hold up your hand, Old Joshuway," she said,
"Wait awhile and see.
I thought I saw my own true love come
Crossing over the sea."

"Do you have any money for me
Or gold for to pay my fee?
For I have stole a silvery cup
And hangeth I am goin' to be."

"Yes, I have some money for you,
And gold for to pay your fee.
I have just come for to save your neck
From yonders gallows tree."

106. James Campbell   Frank Proffitt, 1960

   This ballad is Child's "Bonnie James Campbell" (No. 210). It is a brief, beautiful, sad, and poetic ballad, rarely found in tradition. Child prints four texts, all from Scottish sources. The longest, "C," has six verses. The only unique lines in Frank's version (that don't appear in Child) are two from his fifth stanza: "The house is a-leakin', and the baby's unborn."

Motherwell (1846) calls the ballad "Bonnie George Campbell" and says "This is probably a lament for one of the adherents of the house of Argyle, who fell in the battle of Glenlivat . . . on the third day of October, 1594."

Frank Proffitt told us that he always considered this "in part a Proffitt family ballad. It was 'James Camill,' and we thought of it as an old riding song, with a swing. . . . The tune would be called a fiddle tune, and that's how we thought of it. The words weren't sung much." That makes it even more interesting—that the Scottish words and phrases and the name of the River Tay came down intact in oral tradition. He said he learned the song from his father and from his father's sister, Nancy Prather.

Evelyn Wells heard Frank Proffitt sing this ballad at Pinewoods Camp and wrote to us on September 8, 1961, that she had told Bertrand Bronson about it and that he was interested. She said "James Campbell" is rarely found. Sharp didn't find it. Nor, for that matter, did Frank C. Brown.

See: Bronson, Vol. 3, 291; Child No. 210, 497 ("Bonnie James Campbell");
Coffin and Renwick, 126, 258; Combs, 126; Davis, *More Traditional Ballads of Virginia*, 267;
Flanders, *Ancient Ballads Traditionally Sung in New England*, Vol. 3, 237; Motherwell, 195

JAMES CAMPBELL

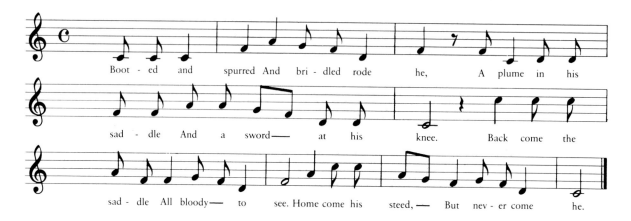

Boot - ed and spurred And bri - dled rode he, A plume in his sad - dle And a sword at his knee. Back come the sad - dle All bloody to see. Home come his steed, But nev - er come he.

Riding on the highlands,
Steep was the way,
Riding in the lowlands,
Hard by the Tay.

Out come his old mother
With feet all so bare.
Out come his bonnie bride
Riving [tearing] of her hair.

The meadows all a-falling
And the sheep all unshorn.
The house is a-leaking,
And the baby's unborn.

But Bonnie James Campbell
Nowhere can you see,
With a plume in his saddle
And a sword at his knee.

For to home come his saddle
All bloody to see.
Home come the steed,
But never come he.

107, 108. Lord Randall and **Jimmy Ransome**   Frank Proffitt, 1959

This ballad (No. 12) is not as old as many Child ballads. In the English tradition it goes back only to the end of the eighteenth century, although Belden says that an Italian text exists from the 1600s. It is widely known and collected both in Europe and America, always, as Belden mentions, "in substantially the same dialogue form, with repetition." Gerould, in *The Ballad of Tradition,* notes that it has been found "as far east as Czecho-Slovakia and Hungary, as far north as Scotland and Sweden, and as far south as Calabria." For its widespread recoveries in North America see Coffin and Renwick. Belden has extended notes and mentions the places where the ballad has been found in Britain and Ireland.

Brown prints four texts from North Carolina, none of them complete. We have been most interested in the fact that Frank Proffitt knew this very fine and complete version—even including the verse about the death of the dogs, which is missing from many variants. Frank also knew and recorded for us a more modern, somewhat Americanized version of this ballad which he called "Jimmy Ransome." Frank said to us:

These two songs was sung to me very early, and for that reason, I guess, the melody and words was very hard to separate, one from the other. Maybe I have not done so completely. "Jimmy Ransome" is a later song than "Lord Randall." It was sung on my mother's side of the family, and "Lord Randall" on my father's. I wonder if "Jimmy Ransome" come in along the line as a poison case, maybe. Maybe somebody took the name "Ransome" to rhyme with "handsome." The melody of the older ballad is almost not musical but has the feeling of all the other ballads of olden days. It has a broken time which only the very best of authentic balladeers may be able to grasp.

See: Belden, 24; Brown, Vol. 2, 39; Child No. 12, 22 ("Lord Randal"); Coffin and Renwick, 36, 216

LORD RANDALL

"Oh, it's   where have you   been, Lord   Rand-all   my   son,

Where have you been, my hand-some young one?" I've been a-
hunt-ing and a-ram-bling, Mo-ther, make my bed soon, I'm a-
tuck-ered and a-wea-ried, and I fain would lie doon."

* often ** often

"What did you spy while a-hunting, Lord Randall
my son?
What did you spy while a-hunting, my handsome
young one?"
"My bonnie, so true, Mother, make my bed soon,
I'm a-tuckered and a-wearied, and I fain would lie
doon."

"What did you eat for your supper, Lord Randall
my son,
What did you eat for your supper, my handsome
young one?"
"Fried eels and fried onions, Mother, make my bed
soon,
I'm sick unto death, and I fain would lie doon."

"Was there scraps from the table, Lord Randall
my son,
Was there scraps from the table, my handsome
young one?"
"My dogs eat them all, Mother, make my bed soon,
I am sick to the heart, and I fain would lie doon."

"Where might be your dogs, Lord Randall my son,
Where might be your dogs, my handsome young
one?"

"They ups and they died, Mother, make my bed
soon,
I am sick unto death, and I fain would lie doon."

"I'm a-feared you are pizened, Lord Randall
my son,
I'm a-feared you are pizened, my handsome young
one."
"I'm a-feared I am pizened, Mother, make my bed
soon,
For I'm sick unto death, and I fain would lie doon."

"What are you leaving to your Mother, Lord
Randall my son,
What are you leaving to your Mother, my hand-
some young one?"
"My cattle and oxen, Mother, make my bed
soon,
For I'm sick unto death, and I fain would lie doon."

"What are you leaving to your sister, Lord Randall
my son,
What are you leaving to your sister, my handsome
young one?"
"My gold and my silver, Mother, make my bed soon,
I'm sick unto death, and I fain would lie doon."

"What are you leaving to your brother, Lord
    Randall my son?
What are you leaving to your brother, my handsome
    young one?"
"My houses and lands, Mother, make my bed
    soon,
For I'm sick unto death, and I fain would lie doon."

"What are you leaving to your bonnie love, Lord
    Randall my son,
What are you leaving to your bonnie love, my hand-
    some young one?"
"Hell fire and damnation, Mother, make my bed
    soon,
For I'm sick unto death, and I fain would lie doon."

JIMMY RANSOME

"Oh, where have you been, my son Jimmy
    Ransome,
Oh, where have you been, my son all so
    handsome?"
"I've been a-rambling and a-gambling, Mama, make
    my bed down,
I'm sick at the heart, and I beg to lie down."

"Who did you meet in your ramblings, my son
    Jimmy Ransome,
Who did you meet in your ramblings, my son all so
    handsome?"
"My bride for to be, Mama, make my bed down,
I'm sick at the heart and beg to lie down."

"What did she fix for your supper, my son Jimmy
    Ransome?
What did she fix for your supper, my son all so
    handsome?"
"Fried eels and fried onions, Mama, make my bed
    down,
I am sick at the heart and beg to lie down."

"I'm afeared you are pizened, my son Jimmy
    Ransome,
I'm afeared you are pizened, my son all so
    handsome."
"Yes, I am pizened, Mama, make my bed down,
I'm sick at the heart and beg to lie down."

"What do you leave to your Mama, my son Jimmy
    Ransome?
What do you leave to your Mama, my son all so
    handsome?"
"My milk cow and oxen, Mama, make my bed
    down,
I'm sick at the heart and beg to lie down."

"What do you leave to your bride to be, my son
    Jimmy Ransome?
What do you leave to your bride to be, my son all
    so handsome?"
"All hell and damnation, Mama, make my bed
    down,
I'm sick at the heart and beg to lie down."

109. A Song of a Lost Hunter (or, My Love Heneree)   Frank Proffitt, 1959

This variant of Child's "Young Hunting" (No. 68) Frank Proffitt gave us in 1959.
His Aunt Nancy Prather had sung it when Frank was a boy, and when he first told
us about it he had been trying for sometime to piece together his memories of it. This
is what he said about the ballad before he sang it:

I wonder if this should be a ballad that would be known anywhere. In trying to recall the way the song went, it is possible I use a rhyming word of my own here and there. It was sung to me at an early age. As with many other ballads, a tale went with it, but only as I grew up I learned the tale, which gave me more insight into its meaning. It seems the hunter, Heneree, was lost, and he come upon this evil woman's castle. She had had the paths filled up to make young hunters lose their way except for the path leading to her lands. She was not a beauty—therefore her demands for bed sharing. As I remember, she had a hole dug where each time she would dispose of her unwilling lovers. However gruesome it may sound, she took Heneree to her bed to make love after stabbing him. This part may have been in the song too, but it was not of the kind to be sung to me in my early years. Only in the tale did these facts come out. I seem to remember there was a part of the song where she too was put in the deep hole, but this part I do not have words for.

"Young Hunting," under various titles, has been found in many parts of the United States, but more commonly in the South than the North. Coffin (*The British Traditional Ballad in North America*, p. 67) says it is extremely rare in the northern states, but it has been found in Maine (Barry-Smith), Vermont (*Journal of American Folklore* [1905] p. 295, tune only), and in Nova Scotia (Creighton and Senior). Its recovery in the South is widespread. See Coffin and Renwick, Belden (with extensive notes), and Brown. Versions of the ballad show many story changes, but those in the American South are so similar that Belden surmises they must stem from a stall ballad or a broadside, though none has been found. The various changes are discussed in detail in Coffin and Renwick. In some variants the parrot stanzas from "Lady Isabel and the Elf Knight" have attached themselves to this ballad and have been found both here and in Great Britain—even in Child, version "I."

We feel Frank Proffitt's version has the quality of an ancient fairy tale—a haunting, ghostly quality that is disturbing but beautiful.

See: Barry-Eckstorm, 122; Belden, 34; Brown, Vol. 2, 67; Cazden II, 239; Child No. 68, 139 ("Young Hunting"); Coffin and Renwick, 66, 230; Creighton and Senior, 36

A SONG OF A LOST HUNTER (or, MY LOVE HENEREE)

Pitch black was the night, as black as could be, Lost from his hunt-ing was

poor He-ne-ree. His true love is wait-ing a - tear-ing her hair, A-

274

"Who rides on my land at such a hour?
Who is it?" did cry she.
"Only I ride at such an hour,"
So said my love Heneree,
So said my love Heneree.

"Come down, come down my love Heneree,
And stay this night with me.
My bed is made all soft and warm,
And just for you and me,
And just for you and me."

"I cannot come down, I will not come down,
Your words beguile me sore.
I have a true love in old Scotland,
I wish to see once more,
I wish to see once more."

"I will not let you leave my lands,
From me you'll never part."
Out of her bosom she took her pen knife,
And stabs him to the heart,
And stabs him to the heart.

"Come to me, my servant man,
Come unto me I pray.
A dead man is in my bed,
Let's hide him well away,
Let's hide him well away."

"What is the hour, my servant man?"
"It is the hour of three."
The chickens are crowing for the middle of the night,
And the blood of pore Heneree,
And the blood of pore Heneree.

She tuck him by his yeller hair,
He tuck him by his feet,
They throwed him down beneath the ground,
In a hole so dark and deep,
In a hole so dark and deep.

"Come to my bed, my servant man,
Come sleep this night with me.
My bed is made of the softest fleece
And it awaits for thee,
And it awaits for thee."

"I will not lay upon your bed,
For this can never be.
For I'm afraid my blood will run
Like the blood of pore Heneree,
Like the blood of pore Heneree.

This song, which our mountain friends used to tell us was great "for pickin' on the banjer," is also known as "Down in the Willow Garden." It is found in Laws, in Lomax (*Folk Song U.S.A.*), also in his *The Folk Songs of North America*, in Cox, Davis, and Brown. The notes in Brown say: "The story here is akin to that of 'The Lexington Murder' and 'On the Banks of the Ohio.' One supposes that it is an Irish stall ballad, but I have found it reported only from the United States." Brown prints two texts, his "A" version being from Frank Proffitt, collected in 1939, about the same time he gave it to us. Frank and his father-in-law, Nathan Hicks, sang it together—Nathan playing his "dulcimore" in his own very loud inimitable style, and Frank playing the guitar. We suppose the "burglar's" wine was burgundy.

In the April–June 1979 issue of the *Journal of American Folklore,* Professor D. K. Wilgus of the University of California at Los Angeles has an article called "'Rose Connoley,' an Irish Ballad," in which he gives an in-depth discussion of the ballad in all its various versions and the places where it has been found, including a text found recently in the Irish Folklore Collection of University College, Dublin. The article includes a four-and-a-half page alphabetical listing of all American performances of the ballad. Professor Wilgus believes that "Rose Connoley" has an Irish origin, although he says he finds scant proof for his conclusion. He says, "It is as if an Irish local song never popularized on broadsides was spread by a single Irish peddler on his travels through Appalachia," and in a footnote he even suggests our old friend John Calvin "Lie-hew" Younce (see Monroe Presnell's description of "Lie-hew," page 238) as one who could fit this role. It is an interesting conjecture.

See: Brown, Vol. 2, 248; Cox, 314; Davis, *Folk-Songs of Virginia,* 273; Laws, *NAB,* F-6, 194; Lomax, *FSNA,* 267; Lomax, *FSUSA,* 302; Wilgus, *JAF* 92, no. 364 (April–June 1979): 172–95

ROSE CONNALLY

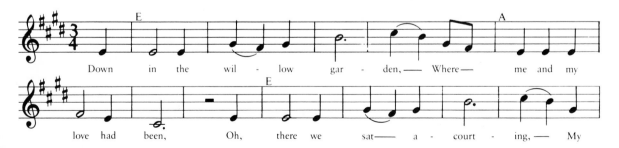

Down in the wil - low gar - den, ── Where ── me and my
love had been, Oh, there we sat ── a - court - ing, ── My

love dropped off to sleep. I had a bot - tle of the
bur - glar's wine, My true love did not know, And there I
poi - soned my own true love, — Un - der the banks be - low.

I drew my sabry through her, which was a bloody knife,
I threw her in the river, which was a dreadful sight.
My father always told me that money would set me free,
If I would murder that pretty little miss whose name was Rose Connally.

He sat before his old cottage door, a-wiping his weeping eyes,
A-looking at his own dear son upon the scaffold high.
My race is run beneath the sun, though hell's now waiting for me,
For I did murder that pretty little miss whose name was Rose Connally.

111. Court House   Frank Proffitt, 1941

This jailhouse song of Frank's is mentioned in Laws's *Native American Ballads* in Appendix 2, p. 266, "Native Ballads of Doubtful Currency in Tradition," and appears there, apparently, only because it is found in Randolph (Vol. 2, p. 151). There it is called "Saint Louis, Bright City." It was sung to Randolph by Mr. Wythe Bishop of Fayetteville, Arkansas, on December 9, 1941, who said he had learned it "in the late 80's or early 90's." Except for the name of the city, the first verse is the same in Frank Proffitt's version and in Mr. Bishop's, and the story is the same. The Randolph version, however, is fragmentary, having only three and a half stanzas. Randolph has no notes on the song. Apparently the Proffitt version is the only complete one that has been found.

In New York City—— I first seen the light, Brought up by good par-ents in the path-way of right. I be-came an or-phan at the age of ten years, On Mo-ther's grave—— I shed ma-ny tears.

I had scarcely reached manhood when I left my old home,
With a few of the fellows to the west we would roam,
Seeking employment, we scarcely could find,
The pay was so poor and the people unkind.

In St. Louis city we first met our fate,
We were arrested while walking the street.
The charges were burglary, the theft it was small.
They said, "We will place you behind a stone wall."

We were marched next morning to the courthouse for trial.
My pal was downhearted, so I gave him a smile.
We pleaded for mercy, but were shown none at all,
They gave us twenty years behind a stone wall.

We were handcuffed next morning and marched to the pen.
We arrived at midnight with a few other men.
The door was thrown open, and we marched in the hall
To learn to be convicts behind a stone wall.

While lying at night on a pallet of straw,
I swore I would never again break the law.
There's none but your mother to bear your downfall
When you are a convict behind the stone wall.

Come all you young fellows and listen to me,
When you lose life's pleasure you have lost liberty.
I've tasted life's pleasure, it's bitterer than gall,
It will give you a cell behind the stone wall.

112. Don Kelly's Girl   Frank Proffitt, 1941

Frank gave us this song early in our acquaintance. It was in the first notebook he sent us of the words of songs as they came to his mind. Later, when we paid our next visit, we recorded the tune. It is the only song about feuding that he gave us, and we did not hear anything about any local feuds in all the years we have been associated with mountain people.

Laws calls the song "Zeb Tourney's Girl," which would be an equally apt title for Frank's song. It all depends on whether one is referring to the girl (who is nameless in the song) as Don Kelly's sweetheart or her father's daughter. We never find out what the girl thinks of any of it.

The song appears in Hudson (p. 247), in the *Southern Folklore Quarterly* 3 (1939) and is on Library of Congress field recording 1345 B 1.

Laws says, "This melodramatic and almost satiric ballad sounds suspiciously unlike a mountaineer's conception of a feud. Although it is sung in the mountains, its cleverness of phraseology and its emphasis upon local color in lines like 'the moon shining down on the still' suggests that its composer was an outsider. The singer of the SFQ variant, however, 'said the ballad originated in the mountains and concerned an actual feud, but when or where it was first sung he did not know.'"

We find that "Zeb Turney's Gal," or at least a song by that title was copyrighted in 1925 by Carson Robison, Shapiro, Bernstein & Co., NY, using the composer's name(s) (pseud.) of Marjorie Lamkin and Maggie Andrews.

See: Hudson, 247; Laws, *NAB*, E-18, 185

DON KELLY'S GIRL

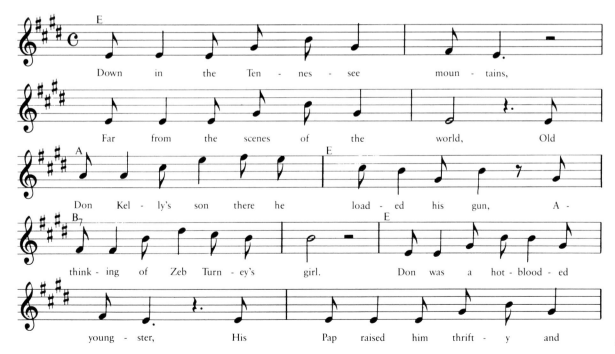

Down in the Tennessee mountains,
Far from the scenes of the world,
Old Don Kelly's son there he loaded his gun,
A-thinking of Zeb Turney's girl.
Don was a hot-blooded youngster,
His Pap raised him thrifty and

279

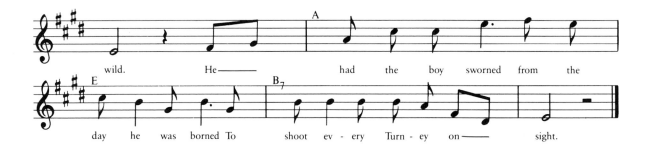

"Powder and shot for the Turneys,
Don't save a hair on their head,"
Old Don Kelly cried, as he layed down and died,
With young Don there by his bed.

Don made a vow to his Pappy,
He swore he would kill every one.
His heart in a whirl with his love for the girl,
He loaded his double barrel gun.

The moon shining down on the mountain,
The moon shining down on the still,
Young Don took a sip, swung his gun to his hip,
And set out to slaughter and kill.

Over the mountains he wandered,
The son of a Tennessee man,
With fire in his eye, and gun by his side,
A-looking for Zeb Turney's clan.

Shots ringing out through the mountains,
Shots ringing out through the trees,
Old Don Kelly's son, with the smoke of his gun,
Put the Turneys all down on their knees.

The story of Don Kelly's deeds
Has spread far and wide through the world,
How Don killed the clan, shot them down to a man,
And brought back old Zeb Turney's girl.

113. Hillsville, Virginia   Frank Proffitt, 1941

The song Frank called "Hillsville, Virginia" (which is, obviously, an adaptation of "Casey Jones") is about Sidney Allen who, with his brother Claude and other members of his family, took part in the "courthouse massacre" on a Saturday night in 1912. The song (under the title "Sidney Allen") is discussed in Laws and is found also in Hudson, Henry, and Thomas's *Ballad Makin' in the Mountains of Kentucky.* A different song about Claude Allen, Sidney's brother, is also in Laws (p. 179), Brown (Vol. 2, p. 567), Henry (p. 316), and on Library of Congress recording AFS L 7, which has a headnote by Alan Lomax.

Arthur Palmer Hudson's notes on "Sidney Allen" are informative: He quotes from *Literary Digest* 44 (March 30, 1912): 627–28:

When Judge Thornton L. Massie sentenced Floyd Allen to a year in the penitentiary . . . the sentence was received with a volley of pistol shots from the sentenced man and from twenty of his relatives and retainers in the court room. In less than a minute 200 shots had been fired, the judge, the sheriff, the prosecuting attorney lay dead, the clerk of the court and several of the jurors were suffering from bullet wounds, and the murderers had swung onto their horses and headed into the mountains.

According to the notes in Brown, Floyd and Claude Allen were later captured, tried, and executed. See *New York Times,* March 29, 1913, for a report of the execution and a history of the family.

When Frank Proffitt gave us the song he told us that Sidney Allen, then, was still living, that he made inlaid furniture and sold it at the county fair. Frank also said that Sidney had written a book, but we have found no mention of that elsewhere. Frank said that the bullet holes are still in the courthouse in Hillsville.

See: Henry, *Folksongs from the Southern Highlands,* 319; Hudson, 242; Laws, *NAB,* E-5, 178;
Thomas, *Ballad Makin' in the Mountains of Kentucky,* 155

HILLSVILLE, VIRGINIA

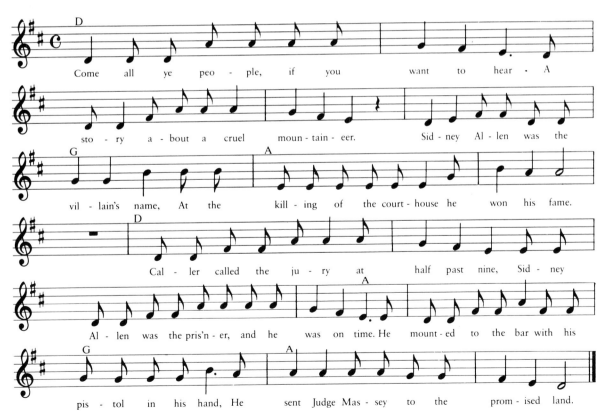

Come all ye peo - ple, if you want to hear - A sto - ry a - bout a cruel moun - tain - eer. Sid - ney Al - len was the vil - lain's name, At the kill - ing of the court - house he won his fame. Cal - ler called the ju - ry at half past nine, Sid - ney Al - len was the pris'n - er, and he was on time. He mount - ed to the bar with his pis - tol in his hand, He sent Judge Mas - sey to the prom - ised land.

Just a moment later and the place was in a roar,
The dead and dying were a-lying on the floor.
With a thirty-eight special and a thirty-eight ball
Sidney backed the sheriff up against the wall.

The sheriff saw that he was in a mighty bad place,
The mountaineer was staring him right in
    the face.
He turned to the window, and then he said,
"A moment more boys, and they'll all be dead."

Sidney mounted to his pony and away he did ride,
His friends and neighbors were a-riding by his side.
They all shook hands and swore they would hang
Before they'd give up to the ball and chain.

Sidney Allen traveled, and he traveled all around,
Until he was captured in a western town.
He is taken to the station with a ball and chain,
And they put poor Sidney on the east-bound train.

They arrived at Sidney's home at 11:41,
He kissed his wife and daughter and his two little
    sons.
They all shook hands and knelt down to pray
And they cried, "O Lord, don't take Papa away."

People all gathered from far and near
To see poor Sidney sentenced to the electric chair.
But to their great surprise, the judge he said,
"He is going to the penitentiary instead."

114. The Lawson Family Murder   Frank Proffitt, 1959

Frank Proffitt said of this song, "The tragedy happened in December of nineteen and twenty-nine, somewhere in North Carolina. I learned it from a friend of mine. The man killed his wife and six children and himself."

A very similar version appears in Brown (Vol. 2, p. 688) which mentions two additional texts and quotes from the *New York Times* of December 26, 1929: "Walnut Cove, N.C., Dec. 25 (AP)—Becoming suddenly insane, a Stokes county farmer today slew his wife and six children, and, after having laid them out for burial, went into a patch of woods near his home and killed himself. The body of C. D. Lawson, the 43-year-old father and husband, was found about half a mile from the home with a shotgun wound in his chest."

Laws (*NAB*, F-35, 209) says that according to D. K. Wilgus this song was copyrighted by Wiley Morris and that it appears on a Bluebird record.

THE LAWSON FAMILY MURDER

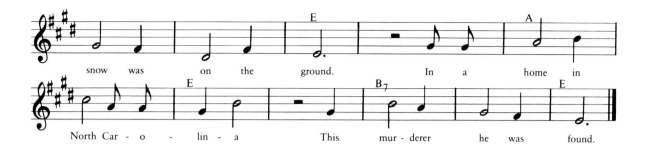

snow was on the ground. In a home in
North Car - o - lin - a This mur - derer he was found.

His name was Charles D. Lawson,
He had a loving wife.
But they never knew what caused him
To take his family's life.

They said he killed his wife at first,
And the little ones did cry,
Saying, "Papa, please spare us our life,
For we're not prepared to die."

But the raging man could not be stopped,
He did not heed their call.
He kept on firing fatal shots
Until he killed them all.

He picked them up so gently
And laid them on the bed,

And gently closed their eyes
When he seen that they was dead.

Then to some wood nearby he run
As fast as he could go.
Between the trees he made his way
Amid the falling snow.

And there upon the ground he stood
With the gun against his heart.
"Farewell, farewell, to all my cares,
From this world I will depart."

They buried them all in a single grave,
While the angels watched above.
And may God bless each one of them
With His great peace and love.

115. The Pretty Fair Widow (or, Lillie Shaw)   Frank Proffitt, 1959

This murder ballad about "the pretty fair widow" was one that Frank Proffitt remembered easily in all of its eighteen stanzas. He said of it, "this happened around in the 1880s. An account of it can be obtained from the Mountain City records. Also *True Detective Magazine* of September, 1952. The Sheriff was Charles Potter, and the deputies were Ham Parker and Rod Morefield."

Mountain City, Tennessee, is just over the line from North Carolina so this, really, was a local event.

Brown (Vol. 2, p. 721) prints a song of ten stanzas called "Lillie Shaw," but it is a lament by the murderer for his deed and for the fact that he is going to be hanged.

It is not this song at all. The Brown notes say that Mellinger Henry, in his *Songs Sung in Southern Appalachia* (p. 55), printed a ballad called "Lillie Shull"—collected in 1933 in Elk Park, North Carolina—which is substantially the same as the one in the Brown collection.

We don't know where Frank got his version of the ballad, but it seems to be unique.

On the Library of Congress field recording AFS 2871 A 1 there is a version of this song (almost the same as the Brown version) recorded by Herbert Halpert on April 1939 from the singing of Sabra Bare Hampton from Morganton, North Carolina. She said she learned it around 1915.

THE PRETTY FAIR WIDOW (or, LILLIE SHAW)

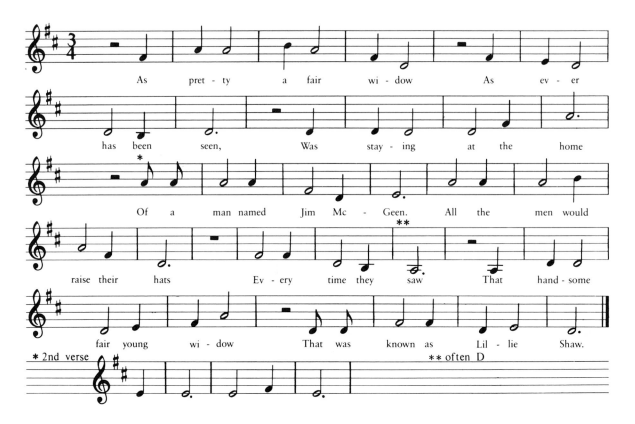

She left the house one morning
On the path out by the barn,
And had a little red pocketbook
A-swinging on her arm.

No one would ever thought
This was the last they'd saw
Of the happy smiling face
Of poor little Lillie Shaw.

The folks become alarmed
When she did not return.
They called for Sheriff Potter
To see what he could learn.

He formed a searching party
And searchèd all around,
But not a sign of Lillie
Could ever be found.

One day Grant Arnold
Was out hunting with his dog.
He stopped to rest hisself
Upon a hollow log.

He noticed there was blood
That was scattered all around,
And footprints leading off
In the miry ground.

He followed up the footprints
To the Preston place,
But of poor Lillie Shaw
He couldn't find a trace.

A man from North Carolina
Was traveling in the night
And far off in the woods
Melton saw a light.

He thought he'd go to the fire
And rest awhile and warm,
For it was very cold
And he didn't think no harm.

He saw no one around the fire,
This dark and chilly night.
He thought he'd chunk it up a bit
To make it burn more bright.

But when he moved a chunk of wood,
This is what he saw
In the flickering flame that burned,
The face of Lillie Shaw.

They searched the Preston house,
And what do you suppose?
Up in the attic loft
They found poor Lillie's clothes.

They took E. B. Preston
And put him in the jail.
They asked all about it,
But nothing would he tell.

The judge he passed the sentence
And this is what he said,
"You must swing from yonder scaffold
Until they call you dead."

To Mountain City the people came
On the hanging day,
They gathered around the courthouse yard
To hear what he would say.

"I am a innocent man," he said,
"And never broke the law."
But he's gone to a better world
For the murder of Lillie Shaw.

116. The Ballad of Naomi Wise   Frank Proffitt, 1941

Frank Warner grew up in North Carolina, and after his graduation from Duke
he became Boys Secretary of the Greensboro, North Carolina, YMCA. During the

course of his five years in that post he built and directed a summer camp in Randolph County, the scene of this ballad. It was a pretty wild and lawless county even in the late twenties. During the building of the camp some moonshiners or rum-runners—who did not favor having the establishment move into their territory—dynamited the small dam that had been built across Polecat Creek to make a swimming hole. There were other harassments, and eventually Frank was sworn in as a deputy sheriff, to give him some authority in the area. We have a snapshot of him carrying a shotgun and wearing his badge.

The notes about this ballad in the Brown Collection start out: "Judged by the breadth of its diffusion, 'Poor Naomi' ('Omie Wise') is North Carolina's principal single contribution to American folk song. . . . It appears to be a North Carolina product, based upon an actual occurrence." The notes then give a complete, though circumstantial, story of an event which took place in 1808, written in 1874 by Braxton Craven, president of Trinity College (which became Duke University in 1925), which then was located in Randolph County. This story was published in 1874 in the Greensboro *Patriot*; included in the story was a song very like this song given us by Frank Proffitt. Of it the Reverend Braxton Craven said, "The following is the song so well known in Randolph County as 'Poor Naomi.'"

For additional notes see Randolph's "Poor Oma Wise" and Belden's "Oma Wise."

In the early 1920s this song was copyrighted by Carson Robison—as were many other songs in public domain.

Colonel Tom Smith of West Virginia also gave us a complete version of this ballad which he called "Omie Wise." It tells the same story but with interesting variations in wording. Here are the last two of his eleven verses:

John Lewis included
To tell no more lies.
John Lewis acknowledged
He'd killed poor Omie Wise.

They took pore Omie
And laid her in the tomb.
They took John Lewis a prisoner
And put him in the rooms of jail.

Colonel Tom said: "There is a song that . . . I suppose is known wherever there are mountains, but I have a version different from any I have ever heard. . . . I learned it from a very beautiful young mountain girl by the name of Dorothy Porter when I was only ten or twelve years old. I used to hang around her and beg her to sing it until I succeeded in memorizing it."

See: Belden, 322; Brown, Vol. 2, 690; Laws, *NAB*, F-4, 193; Randolph, Vol. 2, 144

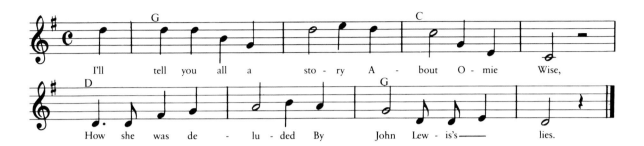

I'll tell you all a sto-ry A-bout O-mie Wise, / How she was de-lu-ded By John Lew-is's lies.

He promised to meet her
At Adams's spring,
To bring her some money
And some other fine things,

He brought her no money
And no other fine things.
"Get up behind me, Omie,
To Squire Ellis's we will go."

She got up behind him,
"So carefully we will go."
They rode till they come
Where deep waters did flow.

"John Lewis, John Lewis,
Please spare me my life,
And I will go a-begging
And never be your wife."

"No mercy, no mercy,
I will not spare your life.
You will not go a-begging,
And you won't be my wife."

He hugged her, he kissed her,
He threw her all around.
He threw her in deep water
Where he knew she would drown.

Her brother was fishing
Down below the old mill dam.
He saw a lonesome body
Come floating along.

He threw his net around her
And brought her to the shore.
Poor little Naomi
Will never smile no more.

They took John Lewis
And put him in the jail.
Laid her pale face on the pillow
For John Lewis to see.

Have mercy, have mercy
On a wild and reckless man.
The Bible says no murderer
Can reach the promised land.

117. Poor Man   Frank Proffitt, 1964

This is a song Frank Proffitt put together himself, remembering, he told us, the
bitterly hard times his people had experienced during the Depression and particularly

287

during the drought of 1932—which was followed by a devastating storm. Frank was just nineteen years old in 1932—old enough, in the mountains, to feel a man's responsibility for bringing himself and his family through whatever fate might present. This song speaks with Frank's own voice. It is a bitter outcry against all the unwarranted frustrations he was experiencing, yet there is a bit of optimism ("Things are gonna get better / By and by"). As we said in the final paragraph of our article on Frank in *Appalachian Journal* 1, no. 3 (Autumn 1973):

> Frank was strong, in character and in body. The kind of farming and hard work he had to do all his life make a man strong, if he doesn't give in. Frank didn't give in. He had faults, as he always insisted on stating. He was proud, and he took offense if he felt he was being treated unfairly. But usually, on second thought, his compassion and humor came to his rescue. If he was proud, it was of his mountains and his forebears who came from across the water, settled the land, felled the trees, broke the new ground, kept their songs and traditions, helped build the country. We can all be proud.

See: Folk-Legacy Records, *FSA* 36

POOR MAN

I worked all the win-ter-time,—— I worked through the spring, —— I plant-ed my corn and 'ta-ters—— Then it would-n't rain. There ain't a thing for a poor man In this world.——

I stood on the hillside,
I looked at the sky,
"Lord," I said,
"What makes you let it get so dry?"
    There's not a thing for a poor man
    In this world.

I got down on my knees,
For rain I thought I'd pray,
Along came a great big flood
Washed everything away.
    There's not a thing for a poor man
    In this world.

Hush up, Honey,
Now, don't you cry,
Things are gonna get better
By and by.
> There ain't a thing for a poor man
> In this world.
> Lord, have mercy.

I worked all that summer,
I worked all that fall,
Lord, I spent my Christmas
In a pair of overalls.
> There ain't a thing for a poor man
> In this world.

118. Tom Dooley   Frank Proffitt, 1938

This was one of the songs Frank Proffitt sang to us the first day we met him in June 1938. It was the first song he remembered hearing his father pick on a banjo. Frank's grandmother, Adeline Perdue, lived in Wilkes County and knew both Tom and Laura Foster, for Tom Dooley—really Tom Dula—did live. Tom was a native of Wilkes County and was known to be a wild one. He rode hard and drank hard and had a way with the ladies, especially Laura Foster. When the Civil War came he joined the Confederates and fought until he was taken prisoner and put in a stockade at Kinston, North Carolina. After the war he made his way home on foot, and took up his old ways. He renewed his relationship with Laura but also was involved with Ann Melton, though she had a husband and two children. One day, at Ann's instigation, many believed, Tom lured Laura Foster into riding off with him. On the hillside he stabbed Laura and buried her in a shallow grave. It is a sordid tale, well covered even by the New York papers who sent correspondents to cover the two trials, which lasted two years. Tom, to the end, refused to implicate Ann, though she had been arrested too, so eventually she was freed. Tom was convicted and hanged in 1868.

Many songs were written about Tom Dooley, but it is the one that came down in Frank's family that eventually went around the world and is believed to have sparked the world-wide interest in American folk music.

In August 1963 Frank Proffitt wrote us:

> Enclosed you will find some pictures taken last Sunday in Happy Valley. We was invited to go down with some friends who previously had been there. The valley is very pretty with behind the times look, and in going up the valley I was impressed that we passed three Dula mailboxes and a Dula graveyard. . . . We went from there to Ridge country . . . 4 or 5 miles wandering off on narrow roads. At last, driving out on a meadow knoll at a big oak in the meadow which was fresh mowed was Tom's grave. We spent some time there under the oak, eating lunch also. One could not think of murder or sordidness amid the quiet peaceful solatude. The views of low lying hills, the distant mountains and valley below would not allow this for me. There is a dignity to a grave, and while I knew Tom reprisinted the instability of emotions of mtn. folk, one knows this also brought reconition of much degree to the mountain ballad singers all over. . . . One can understand why

a song could come from such a happening. The hills, the valley, and all combined gives one a desire to sing or tell something thats neaver been told before. It was good to think of Tom roaming as a boy hereabouts in youthful innocents and of Laura following the path to the spring house for the milk crock. . . . I somehow think Tom will appricate my thoughts of him. I sit as no judge by a man's grave. But allow him to exsplain the why to a merciful God.

The strange mysterious workings which has made Tom Dooly live is a lot to think about. Other like affairs have been forgotten. I feel sure you know and I dont have to exsplain that I dont ignore the lack of morals in this matter of long ago. My preference is to believe the old tale, that Tom was meek and repentant, rather than the sensational writers of that day with fiendish brazen braggart pictures. Tom was a personality I feel, weak, easily led. The best that could be said is he didnt conform to rules.

I have my picture, others can have theirs. For he was one of the mountain folk, and did cridit to himself singing among the homesick North Carolina Rebels during the war.

An in-depth account of the facts behind the Tom Dula case has been written by John Foster West in his book *The Ballad of Tom Dula*.

See: Brown, Vol. 2, 711; Folk-Legacy Records, *FSA* 1; Laws, *NAB*, Appendix 3, 278; *New Lost City Ramblers' Song Book*, 153; West, *The Ballad of Tom Dula*

TOM DOOLEY

Chorus
Hang your head, Tom Dooley,
Hang your head and cry.
Hang your head, Tom Dooley,
Poor boy, you're bound to die.

I met her on the mountain,
And there I took her life.
I met her on the mountain,
And stobbed her with my knife.
Chorus

Hand me down my banjo,
I'll pick it on my knee.
This time tomorrow
It'll be no use to me.
Chorus

This time tomorrow,
Reckon where I'll be.
If it hadn't been for Grayson,
I'd have been in Tennessee.
Chorus

This time tomorrow,
Reckon where I'll be.
Down in some lonesome valley,
Hanging on a white oak tree.
Chorus

119. Beaver Dam Road   Frank Proffitt, 1941

This local song borrows the refrain "Hard times, poor boy" (used in many a jail-house song and other laments), but nothing else. Frank said the sheriff caught a fellow making a little whiskey and took him over to the Boone jail. While he was there he made up some of the verses of the song, and he and other inmates sang it to pass the time. Since then it has traveled the countryside and others have added more verses. They are still doing it, maybe.

Frank lived in the Beaver Dam section of Watauga County, where the product of small mountain stills was "put up" in fruit jars, like any other home product.

BEAVER DAM ROAD

I've worked like a dog and what have I got? No corn in the crib, no beans in the pot. It's hard times on the Bea - ver Dam Road, —— It's hard times, —— poor boy.

Since I didn't have no hog for to kill,
I set me up a purty little still.
Oh, it's hard times on the Beaver Dam Road,
It's hard times, poor boy.

Yonder come Ray Wilson in a Chevrolet car,
A-looking for the man with the old fruit jar.
He watched my house all the live-long night,
He catched me just about daylight.

He said, "Old boy, you're in to it now,
If you ever get out it will cost you a cow."
He took me by the arm, and he led me to the car,
I bid farewell to the old fruit jar.

He took me to Boone and put me in jail,
Had nobody for to go my bail.
I told that judge that my corn wasn't hoed,
Still he give me ninety days on the Beaver Dam Road.

Well, my wife sent a letter, said she's farring mighty
    good,
Got a man a-hoeing taters and a-chopping all the
    wood.
It's a low down man riding 'round in a car,
Picking on a man with the old fruit jar.

All my friends, I'm a-warning wherever you are,
Don't keep your liquor in a old fruit jar.

120. Cluck Old Hen   Frank Proffitt, 1941

Frank told us he had known this fiddle and banjo tune all his life and that everyone in his area knew it. The fact that it was so well known may be a reason it doesn't
appear in any of the collections. Perhaps collectors thought it unimportant. Frank made
a wonderful thing of it with his fretless banjo accompaniment—which may be heard
on Folk-Legacy recording FSA 1, 1962.

We can't keep from adding here a verse given us by our good friend Tom P. Smith
from West Virginia:

The old hen she cackled
She cackled in the morn
She cackled for the rooster
To come get his pecker warm.

CLUCK OLD HEN

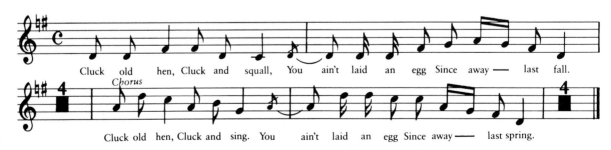

Cluck old hen, Cluck and squall, You ain't laid an egg Since away — last fall.

Chorus

Cluck old hen, Cluck and sing. You ain't laid an egg Since away — last spring.

I have got
A good old hen.
She lays eggs
For railroad men.
Chorus

My old hen,
She won't do.
She lays eggs
and 'taters too.
Chorus

The old hen cackled,
Cackled in the lot.
Next time she cackled,
She cackled in the pot.
Chorus

121. Goin' 'Cross the Mountain   Frank Proffitt, 1959

This song, which Frank Proffitt said was a banjo tune and also a play-party song, he learned from the playing of his father, Wiley Proffitt. The words identify it as a song of the Civil War—from the point of view of one of those Southern Yankees. "Goin' 'cross the mountain / If I have to crawl / To give Jeff's men a little taste / Of my rifle ball."

The first line of this song is carved on the simple granite stone marking Frank's grave in the private Milsap burying ground about a mile from his home.

Frank also gave us two verses of another, play-party version, of this song, sung on Beech Mountain:

Rise up, my true love,
And give me your hand.
I want a wife,
And I know you want a man.

We'll travel on together,
For soon we must part.
Soon we must part
With a sad and aching heart.

GOIN' 'CROSS THE MOUNTAIN

Go - in' 'cross the moun - tain, Oh, fare thee well.

Go - in' 'cross the moun - tain, Hear my ban - jo tell.

*variant   **variant

Got my rations on my back,
My powder it is dry.
Goin' 'cross the mountain,
Chrissy, don't you cry.

Goin' 'cross the mountain
To jine the boys in blue.
When it's all well and done,
Then I'll come back to you.

Goin' 'cross the mountain,
If I have to crawl,
To give Jeff's men a little taste
Of my rifle ball.

Way 'fore it's good daylight,
[If] nothing happens to me,
I'll be way down
In old Tennessee.

I 'spect you'll miss me when I'm gone,
But I'm going through.
When this fighting's over,
Then I'll come back to you.

122. Gonna Keep My Skillet Greasy   Frank Proffitt, 1959

This song Frank sang us seems definitely to have a black or minstrel origin, but
it was a favorite in the mountains. It is too optimistic in tone to be a blues. Let's just
say it is another one of those good banjo tunes that don't need any other excuse for
their appeal.

There is a version of this song in John W. Work's *American Negro Songs and
Spirituals* (p. 244). The words are different enough to quote:

O de times is very hard,
I'm goin' get me a dime's worth o' lard—
I'm goin' keep my skillet greasy if I can,
    (Refrain)
    If I can, can, can, if I can, can, can,
    I'm goin' keep my skillet greasy if I can.

I will go to ol' man Gene's,
Get myself a sack o' beans.
I'm goin' keep my skillet greasy if I can.

O de rabbit's in de log,
I ain't got no rabbit dog—
Goin' to keep my baby eatin' if I can.

The song has special meaning for us, because sometime in the early sixties Frank sent us a particularly fine country ham as a gift. In thanking him Frank Warner wrote a parody of this song he had given us. These are a few of the verses:

Well, I got me a ham of meat,
It's the best I ever eat!
I'm gonna keep my skillet greasy all the time, time, time,
Gonna keep my skillet greasy all the time.

I'll be singing 'Blackjack Davy'
When I get my grits and gravy.
Gonna keep my skillet greasy all the time . . .

Meat for folks, bone for dog,
Warners living high on the hog.
Gonna keep my skillet greasy all the time . . .

Every time I taste that ham,
I think of good old Beaver Dam.
Gonna keep my skillet greasy all the time . . .

And here are some excerpts from Frank Proffitt's reply:

News is good of Frank and Anne,
Huddled 'round the fryin' pan,
Keepin' the skillet greasy all the time . . .

As we sing of hams and grits,
We might start a batch of hits,
Just to keep our skillet greasy all the time . . .

Any time you want a ham,
Drop a line to Beaver Dam,
And keep that skillet good and greasy all the time . . .

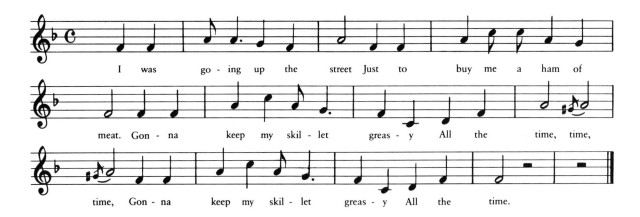

I was go-ing up the street Just to buy me a ham of meat. Gon - na keep my skil - let greas - y All the time, time, time, Gon - na keep my skil - let greas - y All the time.

I'm going to buy me a quart of brandy
Just to give to my little Mandy,
And keep her good and boozy
All the time, time, time,
And keep her good and boozy
All the time.

If I could hang around your door,
I would never work no more.
I'd just hang around your shanty
All the time, time, time,
I would hang around your shanty
All the time.

123. Groundhog Frank Proffitt, 1941

This is a nursery and fun song—as well as a favorite banjo tune—that grew up in the Appalachian mountains and is indigenous to that part of the country. Its humor is pioneer American, as the groundhog, or whistlepig (known in northern states as the woodchuck), is an American animal. The notes in the Brown collection say that "Although the habitat of the creature . . . reaches from Canada well towards the Gulf of Mexico, he is the subject of popular song only in the southern Appalachians; the song is known in Virginia, West Virginia. . . . Its appearance in the Ozarks is doubtless due to immigration from Kentucky. It [the song] has not been found in the northern states, nor is it a Negro song." Brown prints three texts and mentions two additional recordings. For additional sources see Sharp and Lomax.

Groundhogs, Frank Proffitt said when he sang us the song in 1941, were "as thick as fleas" in the mountains. He said of the tune, "I heard my father pick it years ago when I was a little boy—about the first song I ever heard him play." We have never been able to figure out why "The hide's in the churn," and Frank Proffitt couldn't either. Lately, however, I have learned of an old country custom of soaking meat in milk to make it more tender. Perhaps that explains this line, although apparently Frank Proffitt was not familiar with the practice.

Frank Proffitt sings this song on Folkways record FA 2360.

See: Brown, Vol. 3, 253; Cox, 498; Davis, *Folk-Songs of Virginia*, 246; Lomax *ABF*, 271; Randolph, Vol. 3, 150; Sharp, *English Folksongs from the Southern Appalachians*, Vol. 2, 340

GROUNDHOG

Shoul-der up my gun, whis-tle up my dog, Shoul-der up my gun, whis-tle up my dog, Goin' ———— to the moun-tains to catch a ground-hog, Ground-hog!

Two in a stump and one in a log,
Two in a stump and one in a log,
Don't I wish I had a dog.
Groundhog!

Yonder comes Sal with a great long pole,
Yonder comes Sal with a great long pole,
To punch that groundhog out of his hole.
Groundhog!

Joe, go tell Ma to get the gun and come,
Joe, go tell Ma to get the gun and come,
'Cause that groundhog got me by the thumb!
Groundhog!

Yonder comes Sal with a snigger and a grin,
Yonder comes Sal with a snigger and a grin,
With groundhog gravy all over her chin!
Groundhog!

Eat the meat and tan the hide,
Eat the meat and tan the hide,
Made the best shoe strings ever was tied!
Groundhog!

Meat's in the cupboard, and the hide's in the churn.
Meat's in the cupboard, and the hide's in the churn.
If that ain't great groundhog I'll be durned!
Groundhog!

124. I'm Goin' Back to North Carolina   Frank Proffitt, 1959

This is a song that came to be identified with Frank Proffitt. As he sang it, it was peculiarly haunting and poignant. All he said of it was that it was a well-known banjo tune and that he used to play and sing it when he was part of a local group that played for dances and parties in people's houses in his area.

There are two texts of a similar song in Brown (Vol. 3, p. 326). The first, with four verses, is called "My Home's Across the Smoky Mountains," and the other, with two verses and untitled, begins "I am going over Rocky Mountain." Pete Seeger, in his Folkways album called "Nonesuch," with Frank Hamilton (FA 2439), combines the two texts from Brown. Clarence Ashley and the Carolina Tar Heels recorded a similar version for Victor (40100) in 1928.

In a song with such a simple folk lyric it is easy, and even appropriate, to change words and insert verses to suit the singer's mood and location. That has no doubt happened to this song—to good effect.

I'M GOIN' BACK TO NORTH CAROLINA

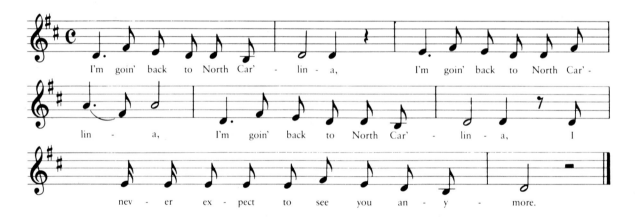

I'm going to leave here Monday morning,
I'm going to leave here Monday morning,
I'm going to leave here Monday morning,
I never expect to see you any more.

How can I ever keep from crying,
How can I ever keep from crying,
How can I ever keep from crying,
I never expect to see you any more.

I'm going across the Blue Ridge Mountains,
I'm going across the Blue Ridge Mountains,
I'm going across the Blue Ridge Mountains,
I never expect to see you any more.

125. I'm Goin' to Pick My Banjo (or, Old Woman in the Garden)
Frank Proffitt, 1959

Frank Proffitt told us that this credo for five-string banjo pickers was an old-time favorite in the mountains. That is all we know about it.

I'M GOIN' TO PICK MY BANJO (or, OLD WOMAN IN THE GARDEN)

Old woman in the garden, Scratch-in' a-way with the hoe. I'm set-tin' on the door-step, Mak-ing my fin-gers go. I'm goin' to pick my ban-jo, I'm goin' to pick my ban-jo, I'm goin' to pick my ban-jo, I'll pick it while I can. Pick it in the morn-in', Pick it in the eve-nin', I'm goin' to pick my ban-jo Right to the prom-ised land.

Old hound, he's jist a-restin',
Too lazy to hunt the coon.
I 'spects he's jist like I are,
He'd druther hear a tune.
Chorus

Old woman, she's so ragged,
She can't run around.
So she has to stay to home
And bake my hoe cake [or "biscuit"] brown.
Chorus

Preacher says I'll never
Reach the promised land.
So I guess I'll stay right here
With my banjo in my hand.
Chorus

126. I Wish I Was a Single Girl Again   Frank Proffitt, 1941

Frank Proffitt sang us three songs about the troubles of married life. This first one had a poignant meaning to us, who had seen during our first visits to the mountains what housekeeping and child-rearing were like in a bleak mountain cabin. In some versions (see Brown, for instance) the woman's plight is based on the fact that she married a drunkard. This is the same song except that there is no reference to a drinking husband. The wife's complaint seems to be about the quality of life itself.

See: Belden, 437; Brown, Vol. 3, 54; Folk-Legacy Records, FSA 36; Lomax, *FSNA*, 166; Lomax, *FSUSA*, 48

I WISH I WAS A SINGLE GIRL AGAIN

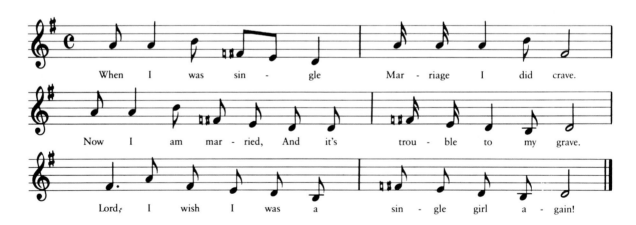

Dishes to wash,
And the spring to go to,
I've no one to help me,
Lord, I have it all to do!
Lord, I wish I was a single girl again!

When I was single
I had plenty to eat.
Now I am married,
It's old turnips without the meat.
Lord, I wish I was a single girl again!

When I was single
I went dressed so fine.
Now I am married,
I wear rags all the time.
Lord, I wish I was a single girl again!

Three little children
A-lying in the bed.
All of them so hungry
They can't raise up their head.
Lord, I wish I was a single girl again!

I took in some washing,
Made a dollar or two.
My husband went and stole it,
Now I don't know what to do.
Lord, I wish I was a single girl again!

127. When I Was Single   Frank Proffitt, 1941

The second song is a humorous complaint from the man's point of view and could occur in any society, not just in the mountains. Not satisfied with the horrors offered by his first wife, the man takes on another immediately after her death — and finds things worse than ever. The notes in Brown say that "There is a sort of antecedent to it in the *Westminster Drollery* of 1672. . . . The song is known in England and very widely in America, though not, so far as I can find, in New England." However, the song was also sung to us by Lena Bourne Fish in New Hampshire. Belden says that it is "quite possibly a printed stall ballad or a music-hall piece originally, but I have found it only as a collector's item."

See: Belden, 438; Brown, Vol. 3, 37; Eddy, 181; Kennedy, 461

WHEN I WAS SINGLE

mon - ey would jin - gle, Oh, I wish I was sin - gle a - gain.

*2nd verse

I married me a wife, oh, then,
I married me a wife, oh, then,
I married me a wife,
She's the plague of my life,
And I want to be single again.

She got her a rope, oh, then,
She got her a rope, oh, then,
She got her a rope,
My poor neck she would choke,
Oh, I wish I was single again.

She beat and she banged me, oh, then,
She beat and she banged me, oh, then,
She beat and she banged me,
She swore she would hang me,
And I want to be single again.

My wife she died, oh, then,
My wife she died, oh, then,
My wife she died,
And I laughed till I cried,
Because I was single again.

But I married me another, oh, then,
I married me another, oh, then,
I married me another,
She's the devil's grandmother!
And I want to be single again.

128. Single Girl, Married Girl   Frank Proffitt, 1941

The third song about the troubles of married life has a theme very much like "I Wish I Was a Single Girl Again"—but it is a different song with a different tune, and one which we have not found anywhere but in Frank's singing of it, although we have found a reference to a Carter Family version on Victor Album Vi 20937, sung at their first recording session on August 1, 1927.

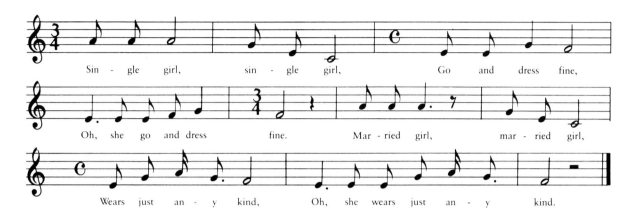

Single girl, single girl,
Going where she please,
Oh, going where she please.
Married girl, married girl,
With a baby on her knees,
Oh, a baby on her knees.

Single girl, single girl,
Goes to the store and buys,
Oh, she goes to the store and buys.
Married girl, married girl,
Rocks the cradle and cries,
Oh, she rocks the cradle and cries.

129. Johnson Boys   Frank Proffitt, 1941

    This is a dance tune for fiddle and banjo — one of the oldest in the mountains. The words are incidental. Frank Proffitt learned the tune from his father's picking and picked up verses from people on Beech Mountain, friends from Virginia, and others here and there — even three from Frank Warner who had learned two of them from Dr. Brown at Duke University in the twenties. These are the fifth and sixth verses in Proffitt's version. The seventh verse is one Frank Warner made up himself in the early thirties.

See: Brown, Vol. 3, 395; Lomax, *FSNA,* 223

JOHNSON BOYS

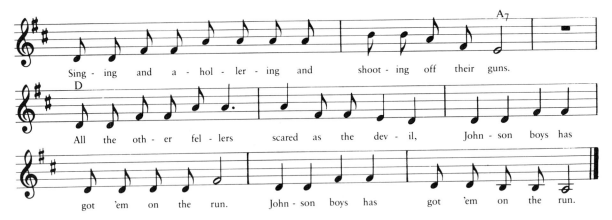

Sing - ing and a - hol - ler - ing and shoot - ing off their guns.

All the oth - er fel - lers scared as the dev - il, John - son boys has

got 'em on the run. John - son boys has got 'em on the run.

Johnson boys, won't do to mess with,
They stick together just like glue.
If you start any kind of trouble,
They'll beat the hell out of you.
They'll beat the hell out of you.

Johnson boys went to the mountain,
They didn't reckon long to stay,
Met up with some high-borned ladies,
Didn't get back till the break of day.
Didn't get back till the break of day.

Johnson boys, getting mighty sassy,
Johnson boys, thinks they're men,
Comb their hair and wash their faces,
Look pretty good for the shape they're in.
Look pretty good for the shape they're in.

Johnson boys, they went a-courtin',
Johnson boys, they didn't stay.
Reason why they went no further,
Had no money fur to pay their way.
Had no money fur to pay their way.

Johnson boys, brave and hearty,
They knows how to court old maids.
Kiss and hug and call 'em honey,
Rush up pretty girls, don't be afraid.
Rush up pretty girls, don't be afraid.

Johnson boys, play your fiddle,
Johnson boys, sing your song,
Johnson boys, hug in the middle,
Hug in the middle and you can't go wrong.
Hug in the middle and you can't go wrong.

Johnson boys, mowing in the meadow,
Big black snake bit one on the toe.
He commenced a-yelling and a-hollering,
It's a sight to see them Johnson boys go!
It's a sight to see them Johnson boys go!

130. Marching On   Frank Proffitt, 1959

In spite of all our years of singing together, we never thought to ask Frank Proffitt if he knew any Civil War songs until 1959 when there was beginning to be a lot of talk about the coming centennial of the war. He remembered this one immediately. These verses (Frank said it had many more but these were all he remembered) he learned from his father, Wiley, and his father's brother, Noah. Their father, as we have said, was a "Southern Yankee." Mountain people felt they had little at stake in the Civil War. They owned no slaves and states' rights meant little to them. Many mountain men "scouted" during the four years of the war—took to the woods to avoid being conscripted by the Home Guard who constantly were seeking recruits for the Confederate army. Others felt some kinship with the idea of preserving the Union and so joined the northern army. Frank told us that his grandfather's brother was conscripted by the Confederates and so fought for them, although his sympathies were more with the North. The tales handed down to Frank from those unhappy days are fascinating indeed, and so is this song.

Civil War songs from the northern side tended to be sentimental reminiscences about home and mother, or crusading songs about saving the Union. This is neither one. It strikes a more modern note—the proverbial gripe of a G.I. who can take it but doesn't have to pretend to like it. We don't known another song from this period which so gibes at its own leaders—unless it be "Life on the Vicksburg Bluff" on the Confederate side.

The tune—originally used for a Sunday School song—is "John Brown's Body," or "The Battle Hymn of the Republic."

MARCHING ON

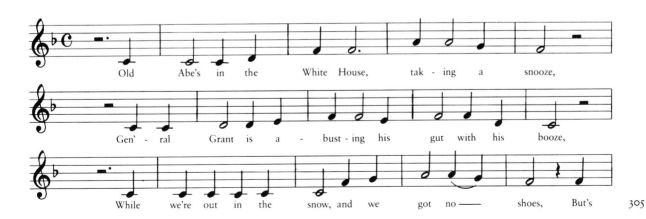

Old Abe's in the White House, tak-ing a snooze,

Gen'-ral Grant is a-bust-ing his gut with his booze,

While we're out in the snow, and we got no —— shoes, But's

305

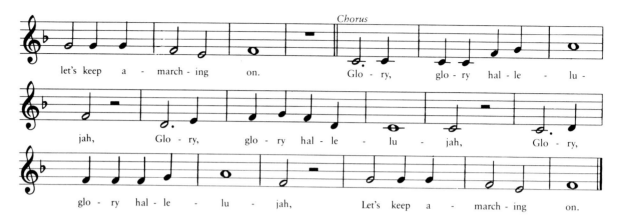

*let's keep a - march - ing on. Glo - ry, glo - ry hal - le - lu -
jah, Glo - ry, glo - ry hal - le - lu - jah, Glo - ry,
glo - ry hal - le - lu - jah, Let's keep a - march - ing on.*

Every time you shoot a Rebel, there is one thing
    for shore,
Every time you shoot a Rebel, there is one thing
    for shore,
For every one you shoot there will be a dozen more,
But let's keep a-marching on.
Chorus

Old Abe he freed the colored folks, glory hallelue,
Old Abe he freed the colored folks, glory hallelue!
I wish to the Lord that he would free me too,
And I'd go a-marching home.
Chorus

They say that we are winning, but I can't hardly
    tell,
They say that we are winning, but I can't hardly
    tell,
For down at Chickamaugie they surely give us hell!
But we go marching on.
Chorus

Winter is a-coming, it's a-getting mighty cold,
Winter is a-coming, it's a-getting mighty cold,
Soon all the generals will be a-crawling in their holes,
While we go a-marching on.
Chorus

"Marching On"
Adapted and Arranged by Frank Warner
TRO—© Copyright 1961 and 1984 Melody Trails, Inc., New York, N.Y. Used by Permission

131. Moonshine   Frank Proffitt, 1938

Moonshine and illegal stills have long been celebrated, or deplored, in mountain songs and literature. There are an abundance of mountain laments for the evils of drink: "The Drunkard's Doom," or "The Drunkard's Warning," for instance. This song is something else, for it is in praise of the potency of the mountain stills' product, and it is full of verve and imagination. We believe it is a local song, and we don't know anything more about it. An almost identical version is to be found in the *Frank C. Brown Collection*, collected in 1940 in Crossnore, North Carolina.

"Moonshine," like "Tom Dooley," was sung to us by Frank Proffitt on our first visit to Beech Mountain in 1938.

See: Brown, Vol. 3, 73

MOONSHINE

Come all you booze fight-ers, if you want to hear 'Bout the kind of li-quor that they sell a-round here. It's made way back in the lone-some hills, Where there's plen-ty of moon-shine stills.

One drop'll make a rabbit lick a hound dog,
Hit'll make a rat whup a wild hog,
Make a mouse bite off a tom cat's tail,
Make a tadpole raise a fuss with a whale.

Then you take just another little bit,
And get ready to have a fit.
First thing you know you're feeling mighty tight,
Out on the street, trying to raise a fight.

Make a fice dog bite off a elephant's snout,
Make a poodle dog put a tiger to rout,
Make a toad frog spit in a black snake's face,
Make a hard-shell preacher fall from grace.

Then you begin to get awfully sick,
And you feel worse than the very old nick.
You say that you never will drink it any more,
But you've said that a hundred times before.

Hit'll make a lamb lie down with a lion,
After drinking that old moonshine,
Just throw back your head and take a little drink,
And for a week you won't be able to think.

The bootleggers is a-getting mighty thick,
And the blockaders is a-getting mighty slick.
If they keep on, badges they'll have to wear,
To keep from selling to each other, I declare.

This was another song Frank Proffitt learned from his Aunt Nancy Prather. It is a Civil War song, of course, and seems to have been a local one. Aunt Nancy's father (Frank's grandfather) fought with the Union army. Frank told us that she sang this song with great feeling.

POOR SOLDIER

It's well I recollect when he bid me farewell,
He went with head held high,
Away to fight for the Stars and Stripes,
Perhaps away to die.
Poor soldier, hungry and cold,
Poor soldier, hungry and cold.

I know not where he is tonight,
God alone only knows.
Keep him safe and sound from all harm,
Protect him from all foes.
Poor soldier, hungry and cold,
Poor soldier, hungry and cold.

133. Reuben's Train   Frank Proffitt, 1959

When Frank Proffitt sang this song he said, "This is one of the oldest simple banjo tunes. Any mountain boy was excited when he learned to pick 'Old Reuben.' It was generally the first tune learned, by playing two strings. There are about fifty different verses to this, as everybody added them all along." He also said that "a tune somewhat like this was recorded by a man named Grayson called 'Train 45' on Victor about 1930."

Brown prints two texts, one (with this title) has three verses and a chorus: "A hundred miles / A hundred miles / You could hear the whistle blow / A hundred miles." The other text is a Negro version with seven stanzas called "Old Reuben," which tells about Reuben's getting drunk and going off to Mexico. In Lomax *The Folk Songs of North America* the song is called simply "Reuben." Its first verse is quite different:

> When old Reuben left home,
> He wasn't but nine days old.
> When he come back he was a full grown man, O Lordy,
> When he come back he was a full grown man.

But it goes on to tell about old Reuben's train and that you could hear the whistle blow a hundred miles, ending with "Nine Hundred miles from his home."

Lomax gathered his eight stanzas from here and there "along the song-hunting trail." He says the song "is a harmonica blower's tune and a favorite piece among country banjo-pickers and fiddlers in the South."

In *Folk Song U.S.A.* Lomax relates the well-known song "Nine Hundred Miles" to this song about Reuben (which he calls a Tidewater, Virginia, version of the better-known song), and also to the song we collected from Frank Proffitt called "Gonna Keep My Skillet Greasy."

See also Benjamin A. Botkin and Alvin F. Harlow's *A Treasury of Railroad Folklore.*

See: Botkin, *A Treasury of Railroad Folklore,* 464; Brown, Vol. 3, 264;
Lomax, *FSNA,* 565; Lomax, *FSUSA,* 244, 254

REUBEN'S TRAIN

back, The rails are a-car-ry-in' me from home.

* later verses begin

If the b'iler don't bust
'Cause it's eat up with rust,
I'll soon be a long ways from home.

If you don't believe I'm gone,
Just look at the train I'm on,
You can hear the whistle blow a thousand miles.

I'm a-goin' down the track,
I ain't never coming back,
And I'll never get no letter from my home.

Well, the train run so fast,
Till I knowed it couldn't last,
For the wheels was a burning up the rails.

Old Reuben had a wreck,
And it broke old Reuben's neck,
But it never hurt a hair on my head.

Now I'm walking up the track,
Hoping now that I'll get back,
I'm a thousand miles away from home.

If I ever get back to you,
You can beat me black and blue,
But I'll never leave my little shanty home.

134. Shulls Mills   Frank Proffitt, 1960

Frank Proffitt sang "Shulls Mills" to us in 1959, and then in 1960 he gave us more verses that had come to mind. He said it was a local song and that various men had added verses to it. We have put the verses together in what seems a logical order.

Frank said, "In the early 1920s Whiting's Lumber Company cut the timber on Grandfather Mountain. They brought the logs down to a valley called Shulls Mills, where the mill set. Old timber cutters has told me they cut one winter when it snowed and froze every night and day. When it thawed in the spring, the stumps of the trees was ten feet high.

"Around this job gathered many women who was seeking a easy dollar. They rented a house on a knob—which is to this day known as Whores' Knob.

"I remember the Beaver Dam boys who went working on this job, and they sung a song of the following. I have heard it many a night as they went by on the road by home—a wonderful sad melody."

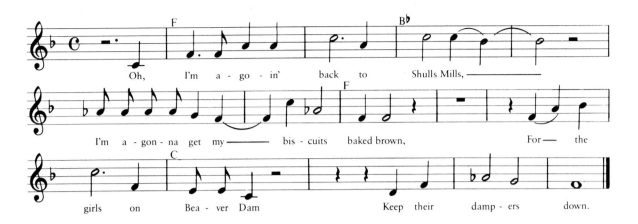

Oh, I'm a-goin' back to Shulls Mills, —— I'm a-gonna get my —— bis-cuits baked brown, For—— the girls on Bea-ver Dam Keep their damp-ers down.

I'm long and I'm tall, Lord,
I'm skinny and I'm mean.
When the women sees me coming,
You can hear them scream.

The girls on Beaver Dam,
They think they're so fine,
But I'll take the women on Whores' Knob
Every doggone time.

My old double bit,
It's filed good and keen,
It's the choppin'est axe
That's ever been seen.

My axe makes my money,
I keep it mighty keen.
The girls on Beaver Dam
Thinks I'm purty damn mean.

Got to keep the skidway
Filled up all the time.
Got to keep the train a-runnin'
Or you can't make a dime.

I hear that log train a-coming,
Sounds like it's running away.
I hope it don't wreck
Till I gets my pay.

Goin' by the commissary,
Only way to get my pay.
I won't have a nickel
When it comes pay day.

The girls at Shulls Mills
Got loving on their minds,
But the girls on Beaver Dam
Wants money all the time.

Goin' to leave Monday,
Make the big trees fall.
Goin' to where I can hear
Old Whiting's log train squall.

Away up on Grandpappy Mountain,
Makin' the big trees fall.
When I gets my pay
Hain't gonna work a-tall.

311

135. This World Is Not My Home   Frank Proffitt, 1941

Thanks to the knowledge of our friend Professor Alan Buechner, an authority on early American religious music, we find that this song of Frank Proffitt's is a variant of the song, by the same title, in a book called *Old Time Camp Meetin' Songs,* edited and published by Albert E. Brumley of Camdenton, Missouri, in 1971. The music in the book is in shape notes but with modern harmonies, quite unlike, and less interesting than, the older shape-note hymnals. Mr. Brumley was an enthusiast for religious songs of this kind and published a number of collections of white gospel songs. The dedication in this volume is interesting:

> We, the publishers, dedicate this book of olde-time camp meetin' songs to the memory of those stalwart pioneers of a by-gone era who were dedicated to the advancement of Christianity through the medium of "Brush Arbor" revivals and camp meetings. . . . Many of the songs found in this book were "born" in such meetings, and some are still popular in church services and singings.

In George Pullen Jackson's *Another Sheaf of White Spirituals* there is a song taken from William Walker's *Southern Harmony* (1854, p. 293) called "Heaven is My Home," with this chorus:

> This world is not my home,
> This world is not my home.
> This world's a wilderness of woe,
> But heaven is my home.

And with a much more exalted first verse than anything in Frank's song:

> When I can read my title clear
> To mansions in the skies,
> I'll bid farewell to every fear,
> And wipe my weeping eyes.

See: Brumley, 25; Jackson, *Another Sheaf of White Spirituals,* 54; Walker, 293

THIS WORLD IS NOT MY HOME

312   This world is not — my home, I'm just a - pass - ing through. My

plea - sure and my hopes Done passed be - yond the view.

Man - y friends and —— kin - dred have gone on be - fore, And I

can't feel at home in this world —— an - y - more.

Chorus
It's O Lord, you know,
I have no friend like you.
If Heaven's not my home,
O Lord, what will I do?
Angels beckons me to heaven's open door,
And I can't feel at home in this world anymore.

I've got a loving mother,
Over in the glory land.
I never expect to stop
Until I grab her hand.
She has gone to live and rest forevermore,
And I can't feel at home in this world anymore.
        Chorus

Heaven's expecting me,
That's one thing I know.
I fixed it up with Jesus
A long time ago.
He will aid me through though I'm weak and poor,
And I can't feel at home in this world anymore.
        Chorus

136. Trifling Woman   Frank Proffitt, 1959

Frank Proffitt recorded this song for us in 1959. He said, "Several years ago they had a big timber job very close to home, and some of the fellows was a-singin' songs. I heard some of this song then but didn't catch much of it. Several years later I heard the son of one of those men a-pickin' the song on the banjo, and I asked him about it. He said his dad had made up some of the verses, and he give 'em to me. He said verses were added by different ones but he didn't know all of 'em. Anyway it's a old sawmill hands song."

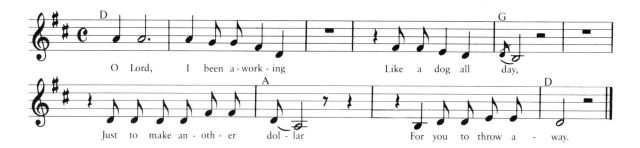

O Lord, I been a-work-ing   Like a dog all day,

Just to make an-oth-er dol-lar   For you to throw a-way.

You spend all my money
And go dressed so fine,
While I wear old clothes
And don't have a dime.

I'd be better off
Just to go on away,
And let you do what you want to
All the livelong day.

You won't bake my biscuits,
You won't cook my beans,
You want to stand by the log road
So you can be seen.

I'd rather be a-hanging
On a old grape vine,
Than to know I have to spend my days
With you all the time.

137. 'Way Down in Columbus, Georgia   Frank Proffitt, 1959

Frank Proffitt said this was "a road gang song of the thirties, sung by Negro convicts who were wonderful singers. We worked right along side of 'em. I was working for the state, but I wasn't part of the gang! But I was working just as hard, I believe, or maybe harder, because I wasn't singing quite so loud." (If Frank had been writing that sentence in a letter, he would have interjected "Ha!" at that point.)

There are two Library of Congress field recordings of this song: AFS 2831 B 1, recorded by Herbert Halpert from the singing of Mrs. Esco Kilgore, Wise, Virginia, in April of 1939; and AFS 9744 B 3 from Mrs. Nonnie Shanklin of Hopkinsville, Kentucky, in April of 1948, also by Herbert Halpert.

'Way down in Columbus, Georgia,
Just a-feeling mighty low.
I'm just a-counting minutes
Till it's time for me to go.
    Chorus

Ten long years is what they give me,
Ten long years and a day.
Here I swing that twelve-pound hammer
Wasting my best years away.
    Chorus

138. W. P. and A.   Frank Proffitt, 1959

Frank Proffitt was a mine of good local songs, and this has long been one of our favorites. We will let him explain it in his own words:

Of all the things that have ever happened in the mountains, nothing has ever equalled the coming of the "work" program that Franklin D. Roosevelt put in effect that was known as the Works Progress Administration. Out of the hollers, out of the ridges, the roads was filled with signers . . . who wanted to get on the 30¢ an hour, $9 a week bonanza. Of course everyone couldn't get on, and out of it was much bitterness and hatred. But those who "got on" had a wonderful feeling of eating high on the hog.

Some of the men got started singing a little rhyming song while they worked through the day, rolling the wheelbarrows and digging on the banks. These verses just come on spur of the moment singing.

W. P. AND A.

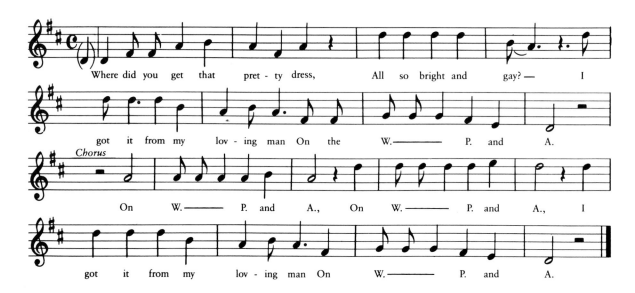

Where did you get that pret-ty dress, All so bright and gay? — I got it from my lov-ing man On the W.——— P. and A.

Chorus

On W.——— P. and A., On W.——— P. and A., I got it from my lov-ing man On W.——— P. and A.

I axed for credit at the store,
The man he said OK.
He know'd darn well I had a job
On W. P. and A.

    Chorus

I said hello to my best friend,
But nothing would he say.
I seen right then he'd tried to get
On W. P. and A.

    Chorus

I asked a man if he would help
Me stack a little hay.
He said, "You go and hang yourself
On W. P. and A."
    Chorus

Don't plant no corn, don't raise no crop,
I tell you it don't pay.
Come join our happy, merry crew
On W. P. and A.
    Chorus

Farewell to hoeing in the corn,
Goodbye cutting hay.
I'd rather go and make my dough
On W. P. and A.
    Chorus

When I die just dig a hole
Way down beneath the clay.
And tell them all I killed myself
On W. P. and A.
    Chorus

139. Wild Bill Jones   Frank Proffitt, 1959

Frank Proffitt told us that this song was brought back to North Carolina by "fellows who had gone to West Virginia a-minin' and a-cuttin' timber."

Laws, in his NAB, says, "The history of this piece has not been traced." Versions have been found, however, by a number of collectors, including Hudson, Lomax, Randolph, Sharp, and Chappell, but not by Brown.

Lomax (*FSNA,* p. 266), says the confrontation and shooting described in the song is just "the sort of incident that sparked the longest and bloodiest of mountain feuds"— the Baker-White feud in Clay County, Kentucky.

> See: Chappell, *Folksongs of Roanoke and the Albemarle,* 193; Hudson 239;
> Laws, *NAB,* E-10, 180; Lomax, *FSNA,* 270; Randolph, Vol. 2, 105;
> Sharp, *English Folksongs from the Southern Appalachians, Vol. 2,* 74

WILD BILL JONES

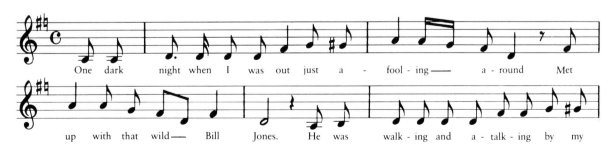

One dark night when I was out just a-fool-ing a-round Met up with that wild Bill Jones. He was walk-ing and a-talk-ing by my

317

true love's—— side, And I bid him for to leave—— her a - lone.

But he looked at me and said that he'd like to see me dead,
But he would not leave my true love alone.
Oh, it's tell me if you can, who's gonna be your man,
Is it me or the wild Bill Jones?

But she only turned away and nothing would she say,
Put her arms around that wild Bill Jones,
Put her arms around that wild Bill Jones.

Well, I'm a hard-working man, and I do the best I can,
But you won't leave my true love alone.
So I fired three shots right in his side,
And he gave one dying groan.

She begged me to spare her life and she would be my wife
For she had never loved that wild Bill Jones.
But I only turned away for nothing could I say,
For I'd killed that wild Bill Jones.

So I started down the track never aiming to come back,
But the law went and grabbed me right away.
So in jail I am today for my crime I have to pay,
For I shot and killed that wild Bill Jones.

Now please take my advice, don't go walking out at night,
You might meet up with that wild Bill Jones.
If you draw your revolver from your side,
He will give that awful dying groan.

North Carolina Outer Banks

6

THAT PART OF NORTH CAROLINA known as the Outer Banks consists of a long line of low, narrow, sandy islands stretching some 175 miles along the state's coastline from the southern border of Virginia to below Cape Lookout. They are separated from the mainland by broad sounds—Albemarle, Currituck, Croatan, Roanoke, Pamlico. Pamlico Sound is a shallow inland sea more than three times the size of Puget Sound in the state of Washington. It extends from Roanoke Island, where the first English colony in the new world was established by Sir Walter Raleigh in 1585, to below Ocracoke Inlet. From it runs a network of sounds, bays, rivers, creeks, lakes, and ponds which comprise the greater part of northeastern North Carolina, so that large sections are marsh and swampland and still are sparsely settled or not settled at all.

The Outer Banks have long been known as "the graveyard of the Atlantic," for here the heavy seas and dangerous shoals of Cape Hatteras have claimed many hundreds of ships. Legend says that Nag's Head got its name from the nefarious activity of certain inhabitants of the region who would hang lanterns on the necks of wild beach ponies. As the ponies cropped the beach grass on dark evenings the bobbing lights would look to mariners, struggling to keep afloat in a storm, like ships riding at anchor. They would put in, and would be wrecked on the shoals. The loot from wrecked vessels augmented many a meager living made by fishing.

Legend, and history too, has many tales of heroism and of rescues, to balance the other legends. The story of the United States Coast Guard on the Banks is a proud one.

In the old days the native residents were called bankers, because they lived among the sand banks. The dunes, especially around Nag's Head, are huge and are filled even now, perhaps, with Indian arrowheads, pieces of flint (used to fire the old muskets), ancient coins, or pieces of Croatan pottery. The bankers had a way of speaking that intrigued the ear and the imagination.[1] There was an "oi" sound: "Oim goin' over on the Sound soid, but Oi'll be back by hoi toid." And winning phrases: "Come roight in, take a cheer and set into 'er." Our friend Cliff Tillett was in the Coast Guard in the 1920s and was in New York for a short period. "Oi was in Toimes Square once," he said. "You'd think ever'body there was fifteen minutes late." At another time he was ill and briefly in the hospital on Staten Island. "Ever'body," he said, "thought Oi was Oirish, said they could see it roight into me." He told us recently that in his early days people living ten miles apart on the banks talked differently from each other. "You could tell where they was from."

Before bridges connected the Outer Banks to the mainland, rescued seamen, finding themselves alive and on land, often would settle down and stay, marrying and raising a family. Cliff Tillett tells many a story of this kind. The first Gallop on the banks (his mother was a Gallop) came from Ireland and settled there as the result of a shipwreck.

Important Civil War battles were fought at Hatteras Inlet and on Roanoke Island. The USS *Monitor,* the first federal ironclad, lies at the bottom of the sea off Hatteras—finally located after 117 years. The pirate Blackbeard was killed at Ocracoke in 1718. In 1903 the Wright brothers made the world's first airplane flight from Kill Devil Hill at Kitty Hawk, just north of Nag's Head.

Vast changes have taken place in the Outer Banks region in recent years. Until the early twentieth century all traveling was by boat—under sail. Fishing was the main occupation and source of income. The bankers, then, were as isolated as the people in the Appalachians, and they kept their songs and their way of speaking as the mountain people did until the tide of progress and development swept them away.

There are bridges and causeways and many developments now, as well as highways and free ferries and, we are grateful to say, a National Seashore Park—the first national seashore recreational area. It includes the southern part of Bodie Island and all of Hatteras and Ocracoke islands except for the villages themselves. A stretch of ocean beach more than seventy miles in length has thus been preserved, one hopes, forever.

CHARLES K. (TINK), ELEAZAR, AND DICK TILLETT, AND CAPTAIN ALBERT AND MARTHA ETHERIDGE

We remember Charles K. Tillett—always known as "Tink"—as a dear friend, although we spent only a few hours with him one afternoon in 1940 at his house in Wanchese.

---

1. It is similar to the speech still heard in Cornwall, as we found when we were in southwest England a few years ago.

Since Frank had known Tink's nephew, P. D. Midgette, at Duke[2] and knew that Dr. Frank Brown had recorded his singing, we started out as friends. We were sad, and frustrated, because we had to leave him so soon after discovering his whereabouts, but we had high hopes of spending a week with him the following summer.

We sent the Tilletts a Christmas greeting, and we have a note Tink wrote us, dated December 31, 1940:

Mr. and Mrs. Frank Warner
Just a word of thanks for the nice present we reseved from you Xmas we certely injoy them. We hope you will get here nex summer to see us again from hope you a hapy new years
C.K. Tillett & family
Wanchese, N C

In May of 1941 we wrote to ask if June would be a good time for our visit. We have a postcard dated May 18:

Mr. Warner,
It is with regret that I have to inform you of my husband's death last April 6th.
Would be glad to offer you board but I have rented my home to another family all except two rooms. However I would be glad to have you visit us. And if I can assist you in your work I assure you it will be a pleasure.
Sincerely,
Mrs. C. K. Tillett

We went back, of course, and have been going back ever since. Mrs. Tillett, as well as her husband, was a fine singer. Over the years we came to know her very well, until her death in the sixties. Mrs. Tillett's father kept Bodie Island Light, and she was born in the lighthouse there. The Tilletts' son, Cliff, and his wife, Marie, and the next two generations still are our friends. We visit them whenever we can. Cliff and Marie still talk in the old way: "How you farring?" or, "Oi loike beans cooked with meat into it." Cliff won't sing now, though when he was a boy, he tells us, he and his friends built a tree house, and they would all sit up there by the hour singing Cliff's song. "I thunked it up," he says; but, alas, he can't now remember what it was.

Tink was a fisherman and a fishing guide and a jack-of-all trades, and Cliff has followed the same life. Cliff and Marie's son, Ron, started fishing, then ran a crab factory, and now owns a fleet of deep sea troll boats and is a county commissioner.

Cliff says everybody in Wanchese has a nickname—like his father, "Tink." Mrs.

---

2. When Frank and I were first married I once overheard Frank say, "I went to school with a Midgette," and I had a mental picture of a very small friend before learning that all the Outer Banks Midgettes were six-footers and members of the Coast Guard.

Mr. and Mrs. Charles K. Tillett, with their son, Cliff, and a nephew, Hub Tillett, Wanchese, North Carolina, 1940

Tillett's name was Eleazar, but she was called "Lease" or Aunt Lease—and was always called "Phyllis" by her husband. Cliff is Charles K. Tillett, Jr., but when he was little he walked like an old man named Clifton Hills, and he has been "Cliff" ever since. Cliff's brother, Dick, is called Bo, since Cliff called him "Chorobo." Uncle Crowder is "Plussy," Sophia is "Chofe," and Dick's son is Frog. Marie's brother, Amos, is called "Tart," and his son is "Little Tart," even though he is now an officer in the Coast Guard, stationed on Long Island. Mary Tillett is Mary Bink, since she is the wife of Bink Tillett, and Charlie Daniels is Charlie Bailey, the son of Bailey Daniels, because there are so many Tilletts and so many Daniels.

Marie is a Daniels, kin to Josephus Daniels, secretary of the navy under Wilson, and to his son, Jonathan Daniels, the newspaper editor from Raleigh, who used to come every year to the Daniels Day family reunion on Roanoke. An uncle, Charlie Daniels (whom we met in our early visits), used to say, "You live hard and die hard and then go to hell—and that's too damn hard!"

Dick Tillett has kept an interest in his father's songs and remembers many of them. In 1971 he recorded for us those he remembered well. This is his introduction on the cassette of his father's songs:

Dear friends, this is the voice of Dick Tillett bringing you a collection of old songs and ballads that my dad, the late C. K. Tillett, used to sing. If some of them are not like you have heard them, think nothing of it, because no two versions are the same. Don't expect too much from my singing. But to you who can sing, those who are talented with that priceless gift of song, why not memorize some of these oldie goldies and keep them going just for old times' sake—for they hold something sacred and beautiful of another day. Thank you.

Martha Etheridge was Mrs. Tillett's sister. She and her husband, Captain Albert Etheridge, also lived in Wanchese.

140. Lord Thomas   Eleazar Tillett and Martha Etheridge, 1941

Eleazar (Mrs. C. K.) Tillett and her sister, Martha (Mrs. Albert) Etheridge, sang us this most complete version of "Lord Thomas" or "The Brown Girl" (Child No. 73, "Lord Thomas and Fair Annet") in 1941.[3] It has twenty stanzas, so that it tells the whole story, and is, in fact, very close to the standard versions of the ballad. (One of

3. Although Mrs. Tillett and Mrs. Etheridge sang this ballad for us in 1941, we apparently did not record it—or the small disk on which it was recorded has been lost. In 1979 Mrs. Tillett's son, Dick Tillett, recorded the tune for us from another Wanchese lady—Mrs. Ivey Evans—who remembered the song but not all the verses. We are most grateful to Mrs. Evans and to Dick Tillett, and delighted to have a tune from a close neighbor of Mrs. Tillett's.

A visit to Wanchese in 1951. Mrs. C. K. (Eleazar) Tillett is at the left and her sister, Mrs. Albert (Martha) Etheridge is at the right. Sally Daniels, a cousin, is in the middle, and Cliff Tillett at the back. Many people, like Mrs. Etheridge, go barefoot on the banks because of the sand.

the sisters said as they finished singing, "Some of them old songs seem kind of silly.) One difference is that in the sixteenth stanza Ellen says:

> I'm blind, I'm blind, fair Ellen cried
> I think I scarce can see
> I think I feel my own heart's blood
> Come trickling down my knee.

Usually it is "Are you blind, Lord Thomas, she said / Are you blind or can't you see? / Can't you see my own heart's blood / Come trickling down my knee?"

Belden says, "Child has nine versions of this ballad (which has parallels in Scandinavian and Romance balladry), all but one of which are Scotch. This one, D, is an English broadside of the seventeenth century, frequently printed since and current also in oral tradition . . . from it have come all the American versions as well as most of those gathered from oral tradition in Great Britain since Child's time." Belden mentions twelve texts collected in Missouri and prints five of them. Brown notes the collection of fourteen versions in North Carolina and prints four complete texts and fragments of several others. See also Sharp and Coffin and Renwick.

We collected two other versions of this ballad: one called "Lord Thomas" from Rebecca King Jones in Crab Tree Creek, North Carolina, which has only seven verses and so an incomplete story. The second one was given to us by Frank Proffitt. He called it "Fair Ellender." Of it he said:

> The killing of Laura Foster [see "Tom Dooley"] was looked upon as a Fair Ellender type by the . . . folks of that day. The legend of Tom Dooley is built around this song. . . . Whether it agrees with facts does not take away the wonderful pastime of the mountain folk who arose above their invairment [environment] in song and tale and thereby lived in a world of make believe that is now beginning to be apprec[i]ated outside of the hills.

Here is Frank Proffitt's tune and one verse of his version of the ballad (1959).

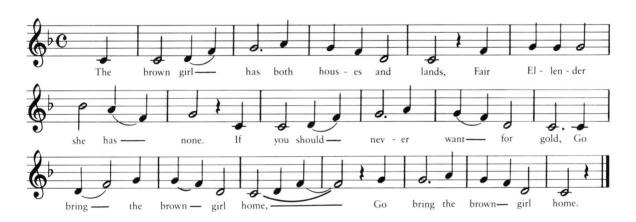

See: Belden, 37; Brown, Vol. 2, 69; Child No. 73, 152 ("Lord Thomas and Fair Annet");
Coffin and Renwick, 68, 231; Sharp, *English Folksongs from the Southern Appalachians*, Vol. 1, 115

LORD THOMAS

love of ma - ny had gained. Fair El - len she was a

ve - ry poor girl, Lord Thom - as he loved her —— well.

* or see transcriber's notes

"Mother, O Mother, come riddle my riddle,
Come riddle both in one.
Shall I marry fair Eleanor,
Or bring the brown girl home?"

"The brown girl she has houses and lands,
Fair Ellen she has none.
I will advise you a very good blessing
To bring the brown girl home."

He dressed himself in very red,
In very red and green,
And every city that he rode through
They taken him to be the king.

He rode up to fair Ellen's hall,
And lightly tapped on the ring.
Who should be ready but fair Ellen herself
To arise and let him come in.

"What's the matter, Lord Thomas?" she cried,
"What's the matter?" said she.
"I have come to ask you to my wedding."
"And that's bad news," said she.

"Mother, O Mother, come riddle my riddle
Come riddle it both in one.
Shall I go to Lord Thomas's wedding,
Or stay with you at home?"

"You know that few will be your friends,
But many will be your foes.
I will advise you as a very good blessing
To Lord Thomas's wedding don't go."

"I know that few will be my friends,
And many will be my foes.
But what cares I for all of that?
To Lord Thomas's wedding I'll go."

She dressed herself in very red,
In very red and green,
And every city that she rode through
They took her to be the queen.

She rode till she came to Lord Thomas's hall,
And lightly she tapped on the ring.
None so ready as Lord Thomas himself
To rise and let her come in.

He took her by her lily white hand,
And led her through the hall,
And sat her down at the head of the table
Among the ladies all.

"Is that your bride?" fair Ellen cried,
"I think she looks wonderful brown,
When you might have married as fair a young girl
As ever the sun shone on."

"Despise her not," Lord Thomas cried,
"Despise her not," cried he.
"For I love the end of your little finger
Better than her whole body."

The brown girl having a little pen knife,
The blade was keen and sharp,
Right between fair Ellen's ribs
She pierced her to the heart.

"I'm blind, I'm blind," fair Ellen cried,
"I think I scarce can see.
I think I feel my own heart's blood
Come trickling down my knee."

He took the brown girl by the hand,
And led her through the hall,
Took out his sword, cut off her head,
And threw it against the wall.

He put the point against his heart,
The handle against his chest.
"This is the end of three long lives.
Lord, take our souls to rest."

"Father, O Father, go dig my grave,
Go dig it both wide and deep.
Bury fair Ellen in my arms
And the brown girl at my feet."

"Bury fair Ellen in my arms
And the brown girl at my feet.
And when the final trumpet sounds
We'll all be sound asleep."

141. The Banks of Newfoundland   Captain Albert Etheridge, 1941

Captain Albert Etheridge said of this song, "I learned this as a youngster when I was aboard a dredge boat." Depicting the horrors of the icy storms of the North Atlantic passage, it has been sung with feeling by British and American sailors. Stan Hugill says, "An old friend of mine . . . who never shipped in steam in all his long sea career, told me that he heard it when young sung at the capstan with all the twiddles and quavers seamen of the old school would adorn this type of song with." His version has a chorus which was used only as a last stanza by Captain Etheridge, and it begins:

Ye ramblin' boys o' Liverpool, ye sailormen beware,
When yiz go in a Yankee packet ship, no dungaree jumpers wear,
But have a monkey jacket all up to your command
For there blows some cold nor'westers on the Banks of New-f'n-land.
    Chorus
    We'll wash her an' we'll scrub 'er down, wid holystone an' sand,
    An' we'll bid adieu to the Virgin Rocks an' the Banks o' Newf'n'land.

In Hugill's, and in most versions, there is a romance between the sailor singing the song and an Irish girl who is a passenger on the packet ship, and who tears up her red flannel petticoats to make mittens for the sailors' hands. She doesn't appear in the Etheridge version. Another difference in this North Carolina version—perhaps due to the more temperate climate?—is that the significance of "no dungaree jacket wear" is lost, and the lines read:

> If ever you go sailing, a dungaree jacket wear,
> Likewise a stout monkey jacket always at your command
> To face the cold nor'wester on the Banks of Newfoundland.

I believe this is the only time this song has been found in oral tradition south of the Mason-Dixon line.

See: Colcord, 173; Doerflinger, 123; Hugill, 411; Laws, *ABBB*, K-25, 153; MacKenzie, 385; also found on broadsides

THE BANKS OF NEWFOUNDLAND

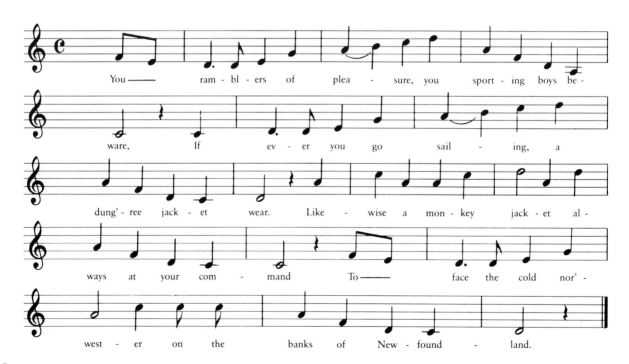

You — ram - bl - ers of plea - sure, you sport - ing boys be -
ware, If ev - er you go sail - ing, a
dung' - ree jack - et wear. Like - wise a mon - key jack - et al -
ways at your com - mand To — face the cold nor' -
west - er on the banks of New - found - land.

There was two sailors shipped on board, Mike Sweeney and Jim Moore,

'Twas in the winter of fifty-six those sailors suffered sore.

They pawned their clothes in Liverpool and cashed the notes in hand,

Not thinking of the cold nor'wester on the banks of Newfoundland.

Last night as I lay in my bunk a-dreaming all alone,

I dreamed I was in Liverpool, away down in Malboon (Mary-le-Bone],

With my true love all by my side and a jug of ale in the hand,

But when I awoke my heart was broke on the banks of Newfoundland.

Now we have a fair wind and to New York we will go,

With tug boats ahead of us and the hills all covered with snow.

We'll wash her down and scrub around with holy stone and sand.

We'll bid adieu to the virgin rocks on the banks of Newfoundland.

142. Barbaree   C. K. (Tink) Tillett, 1940

This ballad of Tink Tillett's which has long been a favorite of ours has not been collected extensively from oral tradition though it is in a number of collections and may be found on old broadsides and in a number of early American songsters including *The Forget Me Not Songster.* The Lomaxes print a version from Bermuda—similar to this but without the last verse—in *Our Singing Country.* The version in Chappell is also from Mr. Tillett but is entitled "The Queen of Russia and the Prince of Wales."

In his notes for the version in *A Pioneer Songster,* Harold Thompson says that the song is a version of Child No. 285, "The George Aloe and the Sweepstake." Laws, on the other hand, says, "A relationship between ("Barbaree"] and . . . Child 285 has been observed by Cecil Sharp and others. . . . Though the two pieces have points of similarity, they are quite different in phraseology and content. . . . The author [of "Barbaree"] was probably inspired by the other ballad." However, see Bronson, Vol. 4, p. 308, and Coffin and Renwick, pp. 153, 277, for an opposing point of view.

Sharp, in his *One Hundred English Folksongs,* (p. 32), says that the ballad is related to an "old broadside sea song reproduced in Ashton's *Real Sailor Songs,* and that Ashton thinks 'the ballad was probably written in the latter part of the 16th century.'" He points out that it is quoted in a play, "The Two Noble Kinsmen," written by "the memorable worthies, Mr. John Fletcher and Mr. William Shakespeare."

In connection with the two versions which he includes in *Shanties from the Seven Seas,* Stan Hugill says that the song "takes us to the once savage Riff Coast of North Africa, lair of the Corsairs, with the romantic name of High Barbaree." For years after the American Revolution the young United States was forced to pay annual tribute to the Barbary corsairs or "pirates" to protect her shipping and merchantmen in the Mediterranean. It was not until 1815 that Commodore Stephen Decatur conquered the corsairs and put an end to this shameful practice.

See: Barry-Eckstorm, 413; Brown, Vol. 2, 352; Chappell, *Folksongs of Roanoke and the Albemarle,* 50; Colcord, 153; Laws, *ABBB,* K-33, 157; Lomax, *Our Singing Country,* 212

BARBAREE

There were two ships from old En-gland came, Blow high, blow — low, and so sail we. One she was the *Queen of Rus - sia* and the oth - er *Prince of Wales, —* Cruis - in' down on the coast of Bar - ba - ree.

"Step aloft, step aloft," our jolly bos'n cried,
Blow high, blow low, and so sail we.
"Look ahead, look astern, look aweather'd , and alee,
Then look down on the coast of Barbaree."

"There is no ship ahead, there is no ship astern,"
Blow high, blow low, and so sail we.
"But there's a lofty ship awind'ard and a lofty ship is she,
Cruisin' down on the coast of Barbaree."

"Hail, hail, that lofty tall ship,"
Blow high, blow low, and so sail we.
"Are you a man-o-war's-man or a privateer?" said he,
"Cruisin' down on the coast of Barbaree."

"I'm no man-o-war's-man or privateer," said he,
Blow high, blow low, and so sail we.
"But I'm a jolly pirate a-seekin' for my fee,
Cruisin' down on the coast of Barbaree."

Broadside, broadside along them we did lay,
Blow high, blow low, and so sail we.
Till at length the *Queen of Russia* shot the pirate's mast away,
Cruisin' down on the coast of Barbaree.

"Oh, quarters, quarters," this jolly pirate cried,
Blow high, blow low, and so sail we.
"The quarters I will give you I will sink you in the tide!
Cruisin' down on the coast of Barbaree."

So we tied them one by one, and we tied them two
 by two,
Blow high, blow low, and so sail we.
We tied them three by three, and we chucked 'em in
 the sea!
Cruisin' down on the coast of Barbaree.

143. Bony on the Isle of St. Helena C. K. (Tink) Tillett, 1940

It was interesting to find a song about Napoleon on the Outer Banks of North Carolina, learned, as Tink said he learned this song, through oral tradition (though those were not the words he used). Tink was not sure from whom he learned it—perhaps from a shipwrecked sailor. In any case, he sang it as he learned it, which accounts for the phrase in the next-to-last line of the last stanza, "Be'est it best in time," the meaning of which he did not know. In oral tradition one sings what one hears, and does not worry overmuch about its meaning. It was several years before we came across a version in Belden's Missouri collection, where it is called "The Isle of St. Helena," that translated the line for us: "Be ye steadfast in time."

Versions of the song may be found also in Sharp, Brown, Chappell, the *Forget Me Not Songster,* and other early nineteenth-century songsters.

Belden's notes say: "For the occurrence of this lament for fallen greatness in broadside and songbook print see Kittredge's note JAFL XXXV 359. It has been recorded from tradition in Ireland (JFSS II 88), Sussex (JFSS II 89), and in Newfoundland (BSSN 198-9)" as well as in the U.S.

Mr. Tillett knew two verses of another song about Napoleon:

Oh, one night sad and lonely he lied on his bed
And his head had declined on his pillow
Oh, a vision surprising came into his head
He thought he was crossing the billows.

He dreamed as his vessel dashed over the deep
He beheld that rude rock so craggy and steep
The place where the willows do now seem to weep
O'er the grave of that once-famed Napoleon.

These verses are part of a complete song in Huntington (p. 215) called "One Night Sad and Languid." Huntington also has a version of "The Isle of St. Helena" (p. 205).

A version of the ballad may be heard on Rounder Record #0094, "Songs from *The Social Harp*," performed by traditional singers with notes by Daniel W. Patterson.

See: Belden, 146; Brown, Vol. 2, 385; Chappell, *Folksongs of Roanoke and the Albemarle*, 156; Huntington, 205; Rounder Record #0094, "Songs from *The Social Harp*"; Sharp, *English Folksongs of the Southern Appalachians*, Vol. 2, 245; *The Social Harp*, 159

BONY ON THE ISLE OF ST. HELENA

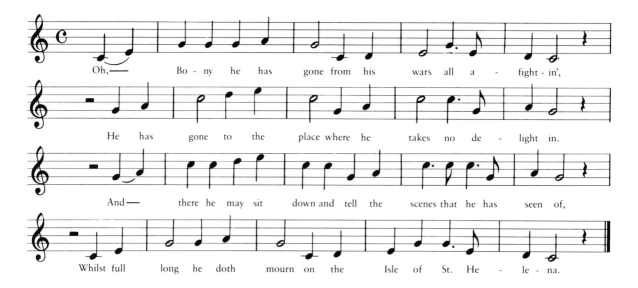

Oh,— Bo-ny he has gone from his wars all a-fight-in',
He has gone to the place where he takes no de-light in.
And— there he may sit down and tell the scenes that he has seen of,
Whilst full long he doth mourn on the Isle of St. He-le-na.

Oh, Louisy she weeps for her husband's departin',
She dreams when she sleeps and she wakes broken-hearted.
Not a friend to console her, even those who might be with her,
For she mourns when she thinks on the Isle of St. Helena.

Oh, the rude rushin' waves all around the shores a-washin',
And the great billows heaves on the wild rocks are dashin'.
He may look to the moon o'er the great Mount Diana,
With his eyes o'er the waves roll around St. Helena.

332

No more in St. Cloud he'll be seen in such splendor,
Or go on with his wars like the great Alexander.
For the young king of Rome and the prince of
   Gehenna,
They have caused him to die on the Isle of St.
   Helena.

O you Parliaments of England and you Holy
   Alliance,
To a prisoner of war you may now bid defiance.
For his base intrudin' and his base mis-
   demeanors
Have caused him to die on the Isle of St. Helena.

Come all you's got wealth, pray beware of ambition,
For it's a degree of fate that may change your
   condition.
Be'est it best in time, for what's to come you know
   not,
For fear you may be changed like he on the Isle of
   St. Helena.

144. The Fisherman's Girl   Eleazar Tillett and Martha Etheridge, 1951

In 1951 Mrs. Tillett and her sister, Mrs. Etheridge, both of Wanchese, North Carolina, sang us this interesting ballad with its inner-line rhyming and its sentimental assault
on the tender emotions. It is another of the sentimental ballads—like "The Blind Child's
Prayer" and "The Two Orphans"—which have been such an important part of American song. This differs in that it has a happy ending, with cruel fate outdone, for once.
The structure and rhyming are clever enough for it to have been a stage song, but we
have found no references to prove this.

The only other place we have found the song is in Mary O. Eddy's *Ballads and
Songs from Ohio.* There are some changes, indicating the song's travel. Our version
is in the third person while the Ohio version in the lament at the end of each stanza
has the girl herself saying, "With my friends all dead and gone." And there are changed
phrases: "So fast falls the snow" instead of "So cold blows the wind." But these do not
affect the story.

Miss Eddy's only note says that her version of the song and of the song which
follows it in her book, on page 178, "The Fisherman's Boy," (there is no music for either
song) "were written in an album belonging to my father, Rev. Franklin Eddy, bearing
the date, 'Ashtabula, 1852.' Both songs are in his handwriting."

Laws includes "The Fisherman's Boy" (the story is similar to "The Fisherman's
Girl," but the song is very different) on page 287 of his *American Balladry from British Broadsides* and mentions that it is to be found on broadsides and in songsters, in
Eddy (see above) and in Greenleaf, p. 200, as well as in Scotland and Sussex. In mentioning "related ballads" he includes "The Fisherman's Girl" and says it is to be found
in *Journal of American Folklore* 35, p. 367.

See: Eddy, 177; *JAF* 35, p. 367; Laws, *ABBB*, 287

Down in—— this coun - try a poor girl was a - weep - ing, All——
down in—— this coun - try poor Ma - ry Ann did mourn, She's——
come in - to this na - tion, she's lost her dear re - la - tion, Cried the
poor lit - tle fish - er - man's girl with her friends all dead and gone.

"I once enjoyed my friends, oh, they rendered me
so tender,
My past with my brother was happy night and morn.
But death has made a slaughter, poor father's in
the water,"
Cried the poor little fisherman's girl with her friends
all dead and gone.

"So cold blows the wind, and I cannot find no
shelter,
So fast blows the snow and how dreadful is the
storm.
I have got no father or mother, but I have a tender
brother,"
Cried the poor little fisherman's girl with her friends
all dead and gone.

"So cold blows the wind, and I cannot find no
shelter,
Fast falls the snow and I must hasten to my thorn.
My bed it is the bushes, my cover green rushes,"
Cried the poor little fisherman's girl with her friends
all dead and gone.

It happened as she passed by a very noble
cottage,
A gentleman's breast for her did burn.
He said, "You poor little lonely creature, and he
viewed each tearful feature
Of the poor little fisherman's girl with her friends
all dead and gone.

He took her to the fire, he warmed and he
fed her,
The tears begin to fall, and they fell to the floor.
Saying, "Live with me forever, we'll part again oh
never,
You are my dearest sister with her friends all dead
and gone."

Now she's got a home, and she lives with her brother,
Now she's got a home and she need ne'er to scorn.
For God was her protector, likewise her kind
conductor,
The poor little fisherman's girl with her friends all
dead and gone.

145. The Golden Glove (or, The Dog and the Gun)   Dick Tillett, 1971

Mr. C. K. (Tink) Tillett died in 1941 and Mrs. Tillett some twenty-five years later. Now that they are gone, only their son Dick Tillett remembers any of their songs. Indeed, traditional singers on the Outer Banks have all but disappeared. We feel very fortunate to have obtained from our friend Dick some of the important songs his father knew but did not have a chance to sing for us because of our brief time together.

This song, known both as "The Golden Glove" and "The Dog and the Gun" (and sometimes, in England, as "The Squire of Tamworth"), is one of the songs that Dick gave us in 1971.[4] Both his father and his mother knew it. It has been collected in some eight states of the Union and very widely in England. Belden refers to Kittredge's note in *Journal of American Folklore* 29, pp. 171–72, for information on the frequency of this ballad in print and in tradition. He adds, "Bell, *Ancient Poems, Ballads, and Songs of the Peasantry of England,* p. 70, says that it is sung 'in every part of England'" and notes that it has long been a favorite in Aberdeenshire.

See also Brown for a list of the collections in this country which include the song, as well as Laws. It is also found in Harold Thompson's *A Pioneer Songster* which was published in 1958. Thompson tells us, "According to Scarborough, a copy of the ballad was entered at Stationers' Hall about 1782. The song was printed in this country as a broadside in the early nineteenth century."

In most versions of the ballad the lady hands the young farmer a "glove flowered with gold" which she says she has found. In the Tillett version, as in some others, having discovered that the farmer loves her, she loses her glove, depending on him to find it, as of course he does.

See: Belden, 229; Brown, Vol. 2, 474; Laws, *ABBB,* N-20, 212; Thompson, 71

THE GOLDEN GLOVE (or, THE DOG AND THE GUN)

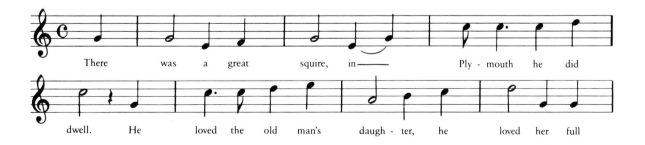

There was a great squire, in—— Ply-mouth he did dwell. He loved the old man's daugh-ter, he loved her full

4. Dick said of this song, "Here is an old English ballad that some say come over on the *Mayflower.*"

well. The day it was ap - point - ed —— the wed - ding was to

be, The squire was —— cho - sen to take her a - way.

Instead of going to the wedding the lady went
to bed.
Her thoughts of a farmer went swiftly through her
head.
Her best coat and breeches the lady did put on,
And then she went a-hunting with her dog and
her gun.

She hunted around where the farmer did dwell.
It ran through her mind that she loved him full well.
Often did she fire but nothing did she kill,
At length the brisk young farmer came out in the
field.

"Why aren't you to the wedding?" the lady she
replied,
"To wait on the squire and give to him his bride?"
"Oh, no," says the farmer, "the truth to you I'll tell.
I love that fair lady, I love her full well."

That pleased the young damsel to hear him speak
so bold.
She paid very good attention and lost her golden
glove,

Saying, "The one that will find it and bring it
unto me,
He is the one I'll marry, his bride I will be."

As the young farmer came to know the news,
Straight to the lady, straight to her he goes,
Saying, "Honor me fair lady, for I have found your
glove.
Now won't you be kind and grant me your love?"

"It is already granted," the lady she replied,
"I love the breath of the farmer as he goes
riding by.
I will be the mistress of my dairy and the milker
of my cows,
While Charles the brisk young farmer goes
whistling to his plow."

"It is now we are married, I will tell you all
the fun!
I hunted up my farmer with my dog and
my gun!
It is now I am married so safely in his care,
And never will depart until death does declare."

146. The Jolly Thresher   Eleazar Tillett, 1954

Mrs. Tillett told us she learned this song from her husband. It is obviously an
English song, speaking as it does of hedging and ditching—occupations unknown on
this side of the water.

Peter Kennedy includes the song in his *Folk Songs of Britain and Ireland,* listing a number of English sources, including the Copper family of Rottingdean in Sussex, whose title for the song is "The Honest Labourer." Peter Kennedy says that in England "thresher" is pronounced "thrasher"—as indeed it was by Mrs. Tillett and by Herbert (Hub) Tillett, son of Tink's brother Wood Tillett. Hub sang the song to us, to a somewhat different tune, in 1976.

In the English versions (but not in this) the huntsman, or gentleman, who meets the thresher on the road commends him for his industry and his cheerful mien and gives him "thirty acres of good land," to make his lot easier.

The late Duncan Emrich, in his book *American Folk Poetry,* includes as the last item in the collection the words to a version of this song which is called "The Jolly Thresherman." His notes say that it was collected by John Harrington Cox and published in "Traditional Ballads, Mostly from Virginia" as one of the *W.P.A. American Folksong Publications,* No. 3, n.d., 1939, p. 70. This version has seven verses—one more than the one found in England. The final, additional verse is an admonition from the nobleman:

Saying, "Now you may be happy all of the days of your life,
And now I do entreat you, be kind to your wife,
Be kind to your wife, your children all around,
There are few such noblemen here to be found."

See: Cazden II, 346; Emrich, 773; Kennedy, 562

THE JOLLY THRESHER

337

"Thresher, O thresher, come tell unto me how,
Can you maintain your family with only but one
    cow?
Your family it is large, your wages it is small,
And how you do maintain them I know not at all."

"Sometimes a-ditchin' or a-hedgin' I go,
Sometimes I reap, and other times I mow,
Sometimes I follow the harrow and the plough,
I earn all of my money by the sweat of my
    brow."

"When I go home at night just as tired as I can be,
I take my youngest child and dangle it on my knee,
While the others come around me, their rattling
    and their noise,
And this is all the comfort a poor man enjoys."

147. John Reilly   C. K. (Tink) Tillett, 1940

This song of Mr. Tillett's is another Irish ballad of parental, or at least paternal, opposition to young love. It is Irish not only by reason of its name, but the fourth verse mentions the town of Bray. The girl's father planned to shoot her lover, but her mother gave her a thousand pounds to help the young man sail for "Americay." While still on the high seas ("In two or three weeks after / While sailing o'er the sea") the lover turns about and comes back for his love. Their ship, however, is wrecked and both are drowned.

This same song, with one less stanza, appears in Chappell's *Folksongs of Roanoke and the Albemarle.* It was contributed to Chappell by Mr. Tillett a few years before he sang it for us. Chappell has no notes. Its story is entirely different from the story told by a song of the same name (sometimes with "George" substituted for John) that appears in many collections. See Laws, *ABBB,* N-36 and N-37, pages 221–22, and Brown, Vol. 2, p. 305. The notes in Brown begin, "Again a ballad of the returned lover; *not to be confused with another of the same name in which Johnny, returning from America to claim his bride, is shipwrecked and both are drowned.*" (The italics are ours.) Whether this refers to Mr. Tillett's song, and whether this means other versions of Mr. Tillett's song are known to the editors of the Brown collection, is not clear. The Brown notes then continue and include a seven-stanza version of the better-known "John Reilley" which is based on the mistaken identity and broken-token themes. Although the broken token appears in Tink's song, it does not seem to serve any purpose.

There is a version of "John Riley" in Huntington's *Songs the Whalemen Sang,* found in a manuscript book from the ship *Cortes* (New Bedford, 1847), which is very similar to Mr. Tillett's version.

Recently we came across a small booklet which has long been on our shelves. We picked it up one summer in the bookstore at Pinewoods Camp (see page 35), intrigued by the dialect word "yacre" because our Appalachian mountain friends occasionally pronounced words in this way. Buna Hicks, for instance, said "yape" for ape. The book is called *A Yacre of Land: Sixteen Folk-Songs from the Manuscript Collection of Ralph Vaughan Williams* (London: Oxford University Press, 1961). "A Yacre of Land" is the title of the first song in the book, contributed by a singer from Yorkshire.

The second song, sung to Vaughan Williams by Mr. and Mrs. Truell of Gravesend, Kent, on December 31, 1904, is "John Reilly," and it is Tink's song exactly. There are a few minor changes, which help to make certain points in the story clear. The mother gives the young couple ten thousand pounds, instead of one thousand; and it is nearly twelve months—instead of "two or three weeks"—after sailing for "Americay" before John Reilly returns to fetch his bride. The shorter time, in the days of sailing ships, has always bothered us.

See: Chappell, *Folksongs of Roanoke and the Albemarle*, 66; Greenleaf, 182; Huntington, 105; *JAF* 52, p. 31.

JOHN REILLY

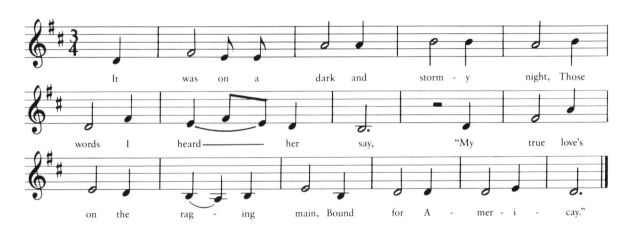

It was on a dark and storm-y night, Those words I heard—— her say, "My true love's on the rag-ing main, Bound for A-mer-i-cay."

"John Reilly was my true love's name,
His age was scarce eighteen.
And he's the finest youngest man
My eyes has ever seen."

"My father he has riches great,
While Reilly he is poor.
Because I loved a sailor lad,
He drove him from his door."

"John Reilly was my true love's name,
He lived near the town of Bray.
My mother took me by the hand,
To me these words did say,

'If you be fond of Reilly,
O shun his company.
Your father sought to take his life
And leave his country.'

339

'O Mother, dearest Mother,
Where shall I send my love?
His very heart lies in my breast
As constant as the dove.'

'Well daughter dear, I'm not severe,
For here's a thousand pounds.
Go send your love to Americay,
And purchase there some ground.'"

Soon as she got this money,
To Reilly she did run
Saying, "My father sought to take your life,
This night he charged his gun."

"But here's a thousand pounds in gold,
My mother sent to you
To sail for a country,
And I will follow too."

'Twas on the morning after,
When Reilly he did sail
And just before he got on board
Those words to her did say,

"Now let this be a token,
Come braken it in two.
You may have my heart and half this ring,
Until I meet with you."

In two or three weeks after,
While sailing o'er the sea,
Young Reilly he came back again
And took his love away.

The ship was wrecked, all hands got lost,
Her father grieved full sore.
He found Reilly in his true love's arms,
Lay drownded on the shore.

And on her breast a letter,
Was written there with blood,
Saying, "How cruel was my father,
Who sought to shoot my love."

Now let this be a token
To all fair maids so gay,
To never let the lad they love
Sail for Americay!

148. My Parents Raised Me Tenderly   C. K. (Tink) Tillett, 1940,
Eleazar Tillett, 1941

Mr. Tillett sang five verses of this version of "The Maid I Left Behind" during
our one afternoon with him in 1940. He said it was incomplete and that it was "a very
long song." The next summer, after his death, Mrs. Tillett sang four additional verses.
We have put them together to make a complete version.

Belden gives the song the title "Peggy Walker" from the versions in *Lonesome
Tunes* (1916) by Wyman and Brockway. "The Girl I Left Behind Me," he says, has been
"since the 18th century the favorite farewell song of British soldiers and sailors, frequently issued by the ballad press" and that "either the whole song or bits of it or merely
the refrain line is widely known in America." He does not include a tune, although
he prints three texts.

Brown prints six versions of the song (one of them from Mrs. Tillett) and mentions the text of a seventh. Brown's Volume 4 (the music of the texts) includes a tune from Mr. Tillett. See also Cazden II, p. 159.

The Tillett tune bears no resemblance to the fiddle tune known as "The Girl I Left Behind Me."

See: Belden, 198; Brown, Vol. 2, 378; Brown, Vol. 4, 213; Cazden II, 159; Cox, 300; Doerflinger, 305; Gardner, 98; Laws, *ABBB*, P-1A, 248

MY PARENTS RAISED ME TENDERLY

There was a wealthy gentleman who lived within this part.

He had a loving daughter fair, and I had gained her heart.

And she was noble-minded, too, most beautiful and fair.

And with Columbus's [Columbia's] daughter she surely would compare.

I sent unto my true love, I told her my sad tale.

With aching hearts and broken sighs we both did weep and wail.

I told her that my intention was quite soon to cross the main.

Says I, "Will you prove faithful, love, till I return again?"

Then drops of tears came in her eyes, her bosom
    hove a sigh.
"Dear you," said she, "fear not for me. My love can
    never die."
"Though," says the maid, "I had a dream which I
    cannot believe,
That distance breaks the link of love and leaves a
    maid to grieve."

I placed a kiss upon her cheek, saying, "Love, have
    no fear."
And swore by Him that rules the skies that I would
    prove sincere.
"Then go," says she, "My prayers shall be for health
    and prosperous winds.
May Heaven grant you a safe return to the maid you
    leave behind."

[additional verses]
According to the agreement then I went on board
    the ship,
And for the town of Gloucester first made a
    pleasant trip.
I found that gold was plenty there, the girls were free
    and kind.
My love began to cool a bit for the maid I left behind.

Then for Rumford town I next set sail to that
    hospitable land,
Where handsome Jenny came on board and took me
    by the hand,
Says, "I've gold a-plenty, fine houses, and rich
    land,
If you'll consent to marry me shall be at your
    command."

With her of course I soon agreed, I'll own it in my
    shame.
For what man is content at will when he knows
    himself to blame.
It's true I had gold a-plenty, my wife is somewhat
    kind.
My pillow is haunted every night with the maid I left
    behind.

My father's in his winding sheet, my mother too
    I fear.
The girl I love stands by their side a-kissing off
    the tears.
Of broken hearts they all have died, now to return
    I find
That God has seen my cruelty to the friends I left
    behind.

149. Indeed Pretty Polly   C. K. (Tink) Tillett, 1940

There are many ballads in oral tradition called "Pretty Polly." Some of them are versions of "Lady Isabel and the Elf Knight" (Child No. 4), some are versions of the murder ballad which contains the line "I dug on your grave the most of last night," some are about the lady who was shot by her lover who mistook her for a swan ("Polly Vaughn"). This is an altogether different song—with its story of the young man who wishes to avoid marriage until he finds his love has wed another and tries to recapture her interest when it is too late.

Only in Randolph have we found anything like it. It is just one verse, called "Polly and Willie," though the informant (Mr. Kelley of Cyclone, Missouri) says "some people call it 'Pretty Polly.'" He first heard it about 1889. This verse purports to be spoken from the lady's point of view, as though *she* spurned marriage in the first place; but it really is the last stanza of Mr. Tillett's song, where the lady is taunting her one-time lover with his own words:

> Pretty Polly, pretty Polly, come jump up behind me,
> Come jump up behind me an' leave him alone.
> O no, no, my dearest Willie, I once loved you dearly,
> An' in your sweet comp'ny I took a delight,
> When a woman is once wed, her joys are all fled,
> For freedom an' bravely she j'ines to all slavery,
> An' since we're both single I'll bid you goodnight.

Randolph's notes say: "This is a fragment of "The Tardy Wooer" as recorded by Ord (*Bothy Songs and Ballads,* 1930), who remarks that 'this is a real bothy song, and a matter of thirty years ago it was a great favorite in the North of Scotland.'"

See: Ord, 83; Randolph, Vol. 1, 415

INDEED PRETTY POLLY

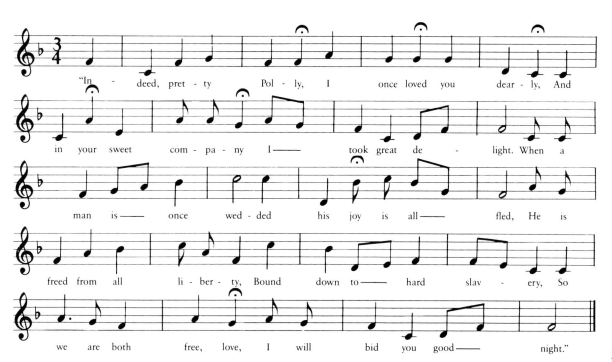

"In - deed, pret - ty Pol - ly, I once loved you dear - ly, And
in your sweet com - pa - ny I —— took great de - light. When a
man is —— once wed - ded his joy is all —— fled, He is
freed from all li - ber - ty, Bound down to —— hard slav - ery, So
we are both free, love, I will bid you good —— night."

"But indeed, pretty Polly, there is one thing I would
     tell you,
That is to ask me to your wedding, love, and I will
     do the same.
For you need never mind a husband you will find,
If there's any such a thing,
If there's any such a thing,
If there's any such a thing in the world to be had."

So she wrote him a letter to come to her wedding,
To come to her wedding on the ninth day of June.
This letter he reads and his poor heart did bleed,
Crying, "I have lost her,"
Crying, "I have lost her,"
Crying, "I have lost her, I have lost her indeed!"

With his bridle and saddle he rode to her station,
He rode to the place where pretty Polly did dwell.
And when he got there through his troubles and
     snares,
The bride and the bridegroom,
The bride and the bridegroom,
The bride and the bridegroom was out on the floor.

"O indeed, pretty Polly, if I only had of known it,
If I only had of known, love, that you'd be wedded
     so soon,
We would have married, no longer have tarried,
So step up beside me, love,
So step up beside me, love,
Step up beside me, love, and leave him alone."

"O indeed, pretty William, I once loved you dearly,
And in your sweet company I took great delight.
But remember you said when a man was once wed,
He was freed from all liberty,
Bound down to hard slavery,
So we are both free, love, and I'll bid you
     goodnight!"

150. The Prince Boys   C. K. (Tink) Tillett, 1940

This pirate song which Mr. Tillett called "The Prince Boys," is a version of "The
Bold Princess Royal"—the story of a ship, overtaken by a pirate, whose captain ignores
a request to heave to and manages to outrace the pirate ship, to everyone's delight.

Chappell prints this same version (with some interesting variations) which he got
from Mr. Tillett a few years before he recorded it for us. Chappell calls it "Buxter's
Bold Crew." Brown prints a fragment of three verses called "Lorena Bold Crew," also
from the Outer Banks.

According to Laws, Eckstorm prints a version from Maine, from manuscript, but
all other collected versions on this side of the Atlantic are from Newfoundland (Colcord, and Greenleaf, p. 78) or Nova Scotia (Creighton, and Doerflinger). He notes that
it has been found in England—in Yorkshire, Sussex, Essex, Norfolk, and Kent, and
also on broadsides.

See: Brown, Vol. 2, 353; Chappell, *Folksongs of Roanoke and the Albemarle,* 52; Colcord, 148; Creighton,
     Songs and Ballads from Nova Scotia, 107; Doerflinger, 142; Eckstorm, 256; Laws, *ABBB,* K-39, 155

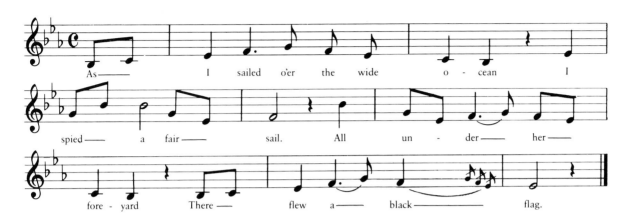

As——— I sailed o'er the wide o - cean I
spied——— a fair——— sail. All un - der——— her———
fore - yard There——— flew a——— black——————— flag.

"Lord, Lord," cried our captain,
"And what shall we do!
If they be bold pirates,
They'll be sure to heave us to."

Up steps our noble mate, boys,
Says, "That they can't do.
We'll h'ist our main tops'l,
Way from them we will go."

"We will turn our jackets
The linings be red.
If they be bold pirates,
They'll be under a great dread."

They come running down on us
And hailing us so,
"Where are you from, my noble prince boys?
And where do you go?"

Up steps our noble captain,
And answered them so,
"We are just from Newfoundland,
Bound down to Bordeaux."

"Pack your main tops'l,
And heave your ship to,
For I have got a letter
To send on by you."

"I'll pack my main tops'l,
And heave my ship to.
It will be in some harbor,
Not alongside of you."

We tried them to the windward,
But nothing could they do.
Now we'll try them to the leeward
For an hour or two.

Now we've got clear boys,
Here's cup and here's can.
Here's a drink of good brandy
For every man!

Drink a health to your sweethearts,
Drink a health to your wives,
Drink a health to the noble prince boys
For saving our lives.

345

Drink a health to your sweethearts,
And all pretty girls you know.
Drink a health and full remembrance
To Buckster's bold crew.

151. Scarborough Sand   C. K. (Tink) Tillett, 1940

This sad song, sometimes known as "The Drowned Sailor," may be found in Brown and in Chappell, also from Mr. Tillett, where it is called "In Robin Hood's Church Yard." The notes in Brown say that three stanzas of the song are in Sharp (*FSE,* Vol. 4, pp. 22–24) as collected in Oxfordshire, and that Ord (pp. 332–33) says that though of English origin the song is a favorite in northeastern Scotland. Brown also mentions receiving another copy of the song (which is not printed) called "Robin Hood Side." The first line of the fifth stanza of this version of Mr. Tillett's read "As she was walkin' around Robin Hood Side." In Ord, Brown's notes say, the phrase is "by Robin Hood's Bay," and that Robin Hood's Bay is a fishing village on the Yorkshire coast.

Laws mentions "The Drowned Lover" in Sharp and Marson, vol. 2, p. 12, as collected in Somerset, which, he says, is "apparently the ancestor of 'Scarborough Sand.' According to Baring-Gould (Part IV, p. xxxii), the earlier piece dates from a broadside of 1671, and the later . . . [probably] . . . was printed as a broadside by Catnach, Harkness, and others."

As in so many other instances, we regret not having asked Mr. Tillett to tell us where he learned the song and what he knew about it. The song, apparently, is a rarity in this country.

See: Brown, Vol. 2, 329; Chappell, *Folksongs of Roanoke and the Albemarle,* 70; Laws, *ABBB,* K-18, 149

SCARBOROUGH SAND

There was a young la-dy—— in Scar-b'rough did
dwell. She was court-ed by a sail-or whom she loved —— him full

*2nd verse

When he was a-sailing all on the salt sea,
A storm there did arise and to their great
surprise,
A storm there did arise and the billows did roar,
Which's driven many a poor seaman upon a lee
shore.

As soon as she heard that her true love was
dead,
She run raving distracted quite out of her head.
"A kind adieu to all my pleasure since my joys has
fled,
My grave shall be instead of a new marriage bed."

As she was a-walking on Scarborough sands,
A-cryin' and lamentin' and wringin' her hands,
She cried, "O you cruel billows wash my true love
on shore,
So that I may behold his sweet face once more."

As she was walkin' around Robin Hood Side,
She spied a young sailor washed up by the tide.
As she drew nearer to him in a maze she did
stand,
For she knew 'twas her true love by the mark on his
hand.

A-cryin', "I have found you my own dearest love!"
She hugged and she kissed him a thousand times
o'er.
She says, "Now I'm quite willing to lie by your
side,"
And in a few minutes after this fair maid did die.

In Robin Hood Churchyard this couple was laid,
And a large double tombstone placed over their
head,
Saying, "Ye tender-hearted lovers as you do pass by,
You can weep and lament where this couple does
lie."

152. The Sheffield 'Prentice   Martha Etheridge, 1941

This is a clearer and more complete version of the ballad Roby Monroe Hicks
in the North Carolina mountains called "Way Up in Sofield," about the apprentice who
runs away from his master in London and becomes a servant to a lady in Holland.
His mistress proposes marriage, and because of his loyalty and love for her chamber-

347

maid he refuses—only to have the lady accuse him as a thief. For this he is condemned to die and bids a sad farewell to the girl he loves. For Roby's song, see No. 80.

See: Belden, 131; Brown, Vol. 2, 354; Cazden II, 209; Cox, 294;
Creighton and Senior, 203; Huntington, 192; Laws, *ABBB*, O-39, 245;
Sharp, *English Folksongs of the Southern Appalachians*, Vol. 2, 66

THE SHEFFIELD 'PRENTICE

I did not like my master,
He did not use me well.
I formed a resolution
Not long with him to dwell.
Unknown to my dear parents,
I from him ran away,
I steered my course for London,
Oh, cursed be that day.

A handsome young lady
From Holland was there.
She offered me great wages
To serve with her one year.
And with her persuasion,
So soon I did agree
To go and live in Holland,
Which proved my destiny.

I had not been in Holland
For months two or three,
Before my young mistress
Grew very fond of me.
She says, "I've gold and silver,
And houses and rich land,
If you'll consent to marry
Shall be at your command."

"O dearly honored lady,
I cannot wed you both.
I have lately made a promise,
Likewise a solemn oath,
To wed with none but Polly,
Your prettiest chamber maid.
Excuse me, my dear mistress,
You have my heart betrayed."

All in an angry humor,
Away from me she run,
Resolved to have revenge
And that before it was long.

She being so perplexed
That she could not be my wife,
She swore she'd seek some vengeance
To take away my life.

One day as I was walking
Along the garden gate,
Flowers there were springing
So delightful and gay.
A gold ring from her finger,
As I was passing by,
She slipped it in my pocket,
And for it I must die.

Come all who stands around me
My destiny to see.
Don't glory in my downfall,
But pray come pity me.
Believe that I'm quite innocent!
I bid this world adieu.
Farewell to pretty Polly,
I die for the love of you.

153. Paul Jones   C. K. (Tink) Tillett, 1940

Tink Tillett knew many songs which he had learned as a young man from people whose memories stretched back to the 1840s. He sang his songs with the distinctive Outer Banks speech pattern which is so interesting and, now, so rare. He showed great spirit in singing the rousing chorus of this ballad, which, incidentally, isn't a part of any of the other versions we have seen, except the one in D. P. Horton's *Naval Songs* (New York, 1889), which adds it after the first and last verses.

John Paul Jones is perhaps still our most renowned naval hero. This ballad about him was widely sung in Revolutionary days and later, as our young country was learning to be proud. It was printed on broadsides and in songsters during the first half of the nineteenth century and was popular in England as well as in America.[5] Brown prints two versions and notes that Mackenzie gives a detailed history of the ballad,

5. It is included in the Isaiah Thomas Collection of early American broadsides in the American Antiquarian Society in Worcester, Mass.

"showing that Paul Jones was the subject of British as well as American ballads . . . citing numerous collections and songsters containing pieces about him, both British and American." See also Thompson's *A Pioneer Songster* (p. 111, from ms.), Cazden I, Chappell, Creighton and Senior, and Neeser's *American Naval Songs and Ballads* (pp. 26–27).

The battle commemorated by the song took place on September 23, 1779, off Flamborough Head, Yorkshire. Commodore Jones, on the *Bonhomme Richard,* with a small squadron of ships, was cruising around the British Isles when he sighted a convoy of merchant ships under the protection of the forty-four-gun ship HMS *Serapis,* Captain Richard Pearson, and the *Countess of Scarborough,* twenty guns. The *Bonhomme Richard* attacked the *Serapis* single-handedly and won the battle by grappling and boarding her, even though the *Richard* sank. The "glasses" in the fifth stanza refer to hour glasses (or perhaps half hour), indicating the duration of the battle. Captain Pearson was knighted for his part in this battle which the British lost—probably because the convoy was saved. There is a plaque honoring him in Westminster Abbey. There are evidences of the folk process in this version of the song. Pearson has become "Pierce." The ships "laid in store" are perhaps "laden with store," as "We'll toss off our cannons" may have been "toss off our cans" (of grog) to celebrate the victory. The ship *Alliance,* an American ship which in the confusion of the battle attacked the *Richard,* has become the "*Reliance.*"

Mr. Tillett sang us five stanzas of this ballad during the one afternoon we had with him. The other verses were given us the next year, after Tink's death, by his brother-in-law, Captain Albert Etheridge, who told us that he learned the song when he was a boy from "Uncle George Charles Daniels. . . . I was coming right along in the road out there when he stopped me and said 'You don't know that song'—and he learned it to me right then."

The first two lines of the fourth stanza were supplied from *The Forget Me Not Songster.*[6] Neither Mr. Tillett nor Captain Etheridge could remember those lines, although they did remember the last two lines of the stanza.

See: Brown, Vol. 2, 523; Cazden I, 16; Cazden II, 65; Chappell, *Folksongs of Roanoke and the Albemarle,* 48; Creighton and Senior, 226; Laws, *NAB,* A-4, 120; Mackenzie, 205; Thos. Coll. I, 107

PAUL JONES

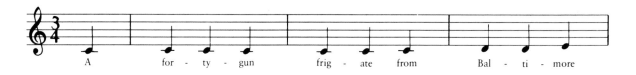

A   for - ty - gun   frig - ate   from   Bal - ti - more

6. According to Joseph Hickerson, Head of the Folk Archive at the Library of Congress, the original *Forget Me Not Songster* goes back to the 1820s. Later editions were reprints, sometimes with additional songs.

came, Her guns mount - ed for - ty, the *Rich - ard* by name, Went

cruis - ing the chan - nel of old Eng - land land, With a *Refrain*

no - ble com - man - der, Paul Jones was the man. Hur -

rah! Our coun - try for - ev - er, hur - rah!

We had not sailed long before we did spy
A large forty-four and a twenty close by.
Both noble vessels were laid in the store,
Our captain pursued for the bold York shore.
    Refrain

At the hour of twelve, Pierce he come alongside,
With a loud-speaking trumpet, "Whence came you!"
    he cried.
"Pray give me an answer, I've hailed you before,
Or this very instant a broadside I'll pour."
    Refrain

Paul Jones he exclaimed, "My brave boys, we'll not
    run.
Let every brave seaman stand close to his gun."
When the broadside was sent by those brave
    Englishmen,
Like bold buckskin heroes we returned it again.
    Refrain

We fought them five glasses, five glasses so hot,
Till sixty bold seamen lay dead on the spot.
Seventy more lay bleeding in gore,
How Pierce's loud cannons on the *Richard* did
    roar.
    Refrain

Then our gunner got frightened, to Paul Jones he
    came,
"Our ship is a-sinking, likewise in a flame!"
Then Paul Jones exclaimed in the height of his
    pride,
Saying, "This day I'll conquer or sink alongside!"
    Refrain

The shot flew so fast that they could not stand,
The flag of proud Britain was forced to come down.
The *Richard* bore down, the *Reliance* did rake,
Which caused the heart of poor *Richard* to ache.
    Refrain

"Paul Jones"
Words and Music Collected, Adapted and Arranged by Frank Warner
TRO—© Copyright 1971 and 1984 Melody Trails, Inc., New York, N.Y. Used by Permission

351

Now my brave buckskins, you've taken the prize,
A large forty-four and a twenty likewise.
Both noble vessels were laid in the store,
We'll toss off our cannon to our country once
more!
Refrain

God bless the widows that shortly must weep
For the loss of their husbands now sunk in the deep.
Here's a health to brave Paul Jones, a sword in
the hand,
Who still stood in action and gave his command.

154. A Poor Little Sailor Boy   Eleazar Tillett, 1941

Mrs. Tillett said she learned this song when she was six years old and that it was the first song she ever learned.

The song is known as "The Poor Little Soldier Boy" in all versions we have seen except Mrs. Tillett's. It is so called in Belden, where the notes say "Perhaps made to be sung by beggar boys at street corners, perhaps merely a piece of parlor sentiment." We are sure Mrs. Tillett did not think of it in this light. Belden says also that broadsides of the song were printed both here and in England, but that he has not found it in British collections of traditional song. Cox says that it is a version of "The Soldier's Homeless Boy," a song "ascribed in a Philadelphia broadside to Charles Bender." Cox suggests that it may be an imitation of "The Poor Fisherman's Boy" (see Eddy's *Ballads and Songs from Ohio,* p. 178). The stories are indeed very similar.

According to Belden and to Brown, "The Poor Little Soldier Boy" has been recorded from tradition in Newfoundland, Pennsylvania, West Virginia, North Carolina, Arkansas, and five other states.

See: Belden, 273; Brown, Vol. 2, 396; Cox, 275

A POOR LITTLE SAILOR BOY

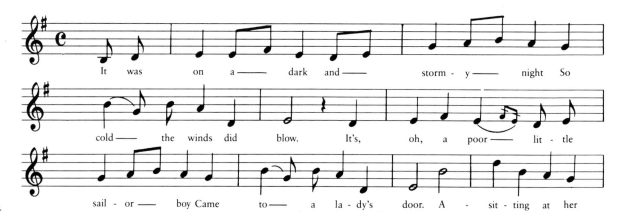

It was on a dark and storm-y night So cold the winds did blow. It's, oh, a poor lit-tle sail-or boy Came to a la-dy's door. A-sit-ting at her

win - dow, He lift - ed his eyes with joy, Say - ing,

"For the Lord's sake some —— pi - ty —— take On this

poor — lit - tle sail - or boy!" Say - ing, "For the Lord's sake some —

pi - ty —— take On this poor — lit - tle sail - or boy."

"The rain it is descending down,
And the night is drawing on,
And if you don't some pity take,
I shall die before it is morn.
My mother died when I was young,
My father went to the war.
The next news came that he was slain
And died with wounds and scars.
The next news came that he was slain
And died with wounds and scars.

Many a day all in his arms,
He toted me with joy,
But now I'm left quite friendless
A poor little sailor boy.
But now I am left quite friendless

I will sit me down and cry,
The children can run to their parents at home,
No home or friends have I.
The children can run to their parents at home,
No home or friends have I.

The lady rose from her chair
And opened the ancient door,
Says, "Come you in little sailor boy,
You never shall want for more.
For on the seas my son was lost,
He was my only joy,
As long as I live I freely will give
To the poor little sailor boy.
As long as I live I freely will give
To the poor little sailor boy.

155. A Sailor's Grave Eleazar Tillett, 1941

Mrs. Tillett told us that she learned this song when she was a child. Spending her life, as she did, on North Carolina's Outer Banks, close to what is known as "the graveyard of the Atlantic," songs of the sea had a special meaning for her, and for all of her kin and neighbors. She told us that one of her cousins told her that "once when he was sick at sea he had his canvas bag all ready and the round shot, but he got well. Then another sailor died, and they used the bag for him."

The only other place we have found this song is in William Doerflinger's *Shanty Men and Shanty Boys* (renamed *Songs of the Sailor and Lumberman* in later editions), where he says that the author of "The Sailor's Grave" was Eliza Cook, mid-Victorian poet. "Set to music by John C. Baker of New Hampshire, the song was published at Boston in 1847." Doerflinger recorded the song from the singing of William Laurie of Sailors' Snug Harbor, and he adds, "'I picked it up,' Laurie said, 'from an old sailor who used to sing it for money on the street in Greenock.' No sentimentalist, Laurie could never sing this song without a catch in his voice." Mrs. Tillett would have understood how he felt.

There are some interesting evidences of the folk process in Mrs. Tillett's version of the song, since some of the author's phrases were too literary for oral tradition. We have indicated them by words in brackets in the text of the song.

See: Doerflinger, 160

A SAILOR'S GRAVE

Our bark was far, oh, far from land When the fair-est
We had watched him through long hours of pain, Our hopes were

of our gal-lant band Grew dead-ly pale and whined [pined] a-
great, our cares in vain. Death struck, he gave no coward's a-

way Like a twi-light of an au-tumn day.
larm, But smiled and died in his mess-mates' arms.

Death struck, he gave no coward's a-larm, But smiled and died in his mess-mates' arms.

We had no costly winding sheets,
We placed two round shots at his feet.
He lies in his hammock as snug and
    sound,
As a king in his long shroud marble band.
We proudly decked his funeral best
With a starry flag upon his breast.
We gave him this as a badge of the brave,
And then he was fit for a sailor's grave.
We gave him this as a badge of the brave,
And then he was fit for a sailor's grave.

Our voices broke, our hearts turned weak,
And tears were seen on the brownest cheek.
And the quiver played on the lips of the pride [proud]
As we lowered him down the ship's dark side.
Then a plash and a plunge, our task was o'er,
And the billows roared as they roared [rolled?]
    before.
And many wild prayers hallowed the waves
As he sank beneath in a sailor's grave.
And many wild prayers hallowed the waves
As he sank beneath in a sailor's grave.

156. The Southern Girl's Reply   Mrs. C. K. (Eleazar) Tillett, 1941

Mrs. Tillett sang this song to the tune (with interesting variations) of "The Bonnie Blue Flag," one of the most stirring and popular songs on the Confederate side in the Civil War. The name of its original Irish tune was "The Jaunting Car."

The song is the reply of a southern girl to her northern lover. She is firmly loyal to the Lost Cause, sad with the sense of irreparable loss, yet noble and generous in sentiment—a fine example of southern womanhood.

The song has many similarities to "The Homespun Dress" (which is found in Belden, p. 360, and Brown, Vol. 2, p. 435), but Mrs. Tillett's song, so far as we know, has not been found elsewhere in oral tradition.

Our friends Arthur and Penn Elizabeth Schrader found, in the American Antiquarian Society in Worcester, Massachusetts, a printed version, without music, in a small book called *Songs and Ballads of the Southern People, 1861–1865,* edited by Frank Moore and published by Appleton in 1886. There the song, or poem, is entitled "True to the Gray," and Pearl Rivers is given as its author. Arthur Schrader has found the same poem, by Pearl Rivers, in *Allan's Lone Star Ballads: A Collection of Southern Patriotic Songs, made during Confederate Times,* p. 200. It seems logical to assume that Allan was Moore's source for the poem. The folk process of change is evident, and has improved the original text, which is as follows:

TRUE TO THE GRAY (by Pearl Rivers)
I can not listen to your words, the land is long and wide;
Go seek some happy Northern girl to be your loving bride.
My brothers they were soldiers—the youngest of the three
Was slain while fighting by the side of gallant Fitzhugh Lee!

They left his body on the field (your side the day had won),
A soldier spurn'd him with his foot—you might have been the one.
My lover was a soldier—he belonged to Gordon's band;
A saber pierced his gallant heart—yours might have been the hand.

He reel'd and fell, but was not dead, a horseman spurred his steed,
And trampled on the dying brain—you may have done the deed.
I hold no hatred in my heart, no cold, unrighteous pride,
For many a gallant soldier fought upon the other side.

But still I can not kiss the hand that smote my country sore,
Nor love the foes who trampled down the colors that she bore;
Between my heart and yours there rolls a deep and crimson tide—
My brother's and my lover's blood forbid me be your bride.

The girls who loved the boys in gray—the girls to country true—
May ne'er in wedlock give their hands to those who wore the blue.

THE SOUTHERN GIRL'S REPLY

"The Southern Girl's Reply"
Collected and Adapted by Frank Warner
356   TRO—© Copyright 1962 and 1984 Ludlow Music, Inc., New York, N.Y. Used by Permission

My lover was a soldier too,
He fought at God's command.
A sabre pierced his galliant heart,
You might have been the man.
He reeled and fell but was not dead,
A horseman spurred his steed,
And trampled on his dying brain,
You might have done the deed.
Chorus

They left his body on the field
Who the fight this day had won.
A horseman spurred him with his heel,
You might have been the one.
I hold no hatred in my heart,
Nor cold nor righteous pride,
For many a galliant soldier fought
Upon the other side.
Chorus

But still I cannot take the hand
That smote my country sore,
Or love the foe that trampled down
The colors that she bore.
Between my heart and yours there rose
A deep and crimson tide.
My lover's and my brother's blood
Forbids me be your bride.
Chorus

157. Her Bright Smile Haunts Me Still   Eleazar Tillett and Martha Etheridge, 1951

This song was given to us by the Gallop sisters—Mrs. Tillett and Mrs. Etheridge. Is is something of the same genre as "The Snow Is on the Ground." We find it is included in both *Heart Songs Dear to the American People*, edited by Joe Mitchell Chapple, p. 380, as composed by W. T. Wrighton with words by J. E. Carpenter, and in *Love Songs the Whole World Sings*, edited by Albert E. Wier, p. 28.

The song is literary and poetic, full of flights of fancy, images, and allusions, but Mrs. Tillett said her husband Tink sang it. As far as we have been able to discover, all of Tink's songs were learned through oral tradition.

These are the words from the songster version.

It's been a year since last we met,
We may never meet again.
I have struggled to forget
But the struggle was in vain.

357

For her voice lives on the breeze,
And her spirit comes at will,
In the midnight on the seas,
Her bright smile haunts me still.
Refrain
For her voice lives on the breeze,
And her spirit comes at will.
In the midnight on the seas
Her bright smile haunts me still.

At the first sweet dawn of light,
When I gaze upon the deep,
Her form still greets my sight
While the stars their vigils keep.
When I close my aching eyes,
Sweet dreams my senses fill,
And from sleep when I arise
Her bright smile haunts me still.
Refrain

I have sailed 'neath alien skies,
I have trod the desert path,
I have seen the storm arise
Like a giant in his wrath.
Every danger I have known
That a reckless life can fill,
Yet her presence is not flown,
Her bright smile haunts me still.
Refrain

The Weir version does not include the final verse.

HER BRIGHT SMILE HAUNTS ME STILL

It's been a year since last we met, We may nev - er meet — a -

gain. I have strug-gled to for - get, But the strug-gle was in —
vain. For her voice lives on the breeze, Her spir - it comes at
will. In the mid - night on the seas Her bright smile haunts me
still, In the mid - night on the seas — Her bright smile haunts me still.

I have sailed a falling sky,
And I've charted hazard's paths.
I have seen the storm arise
Like a giant in his wrath.
Every danger I have known
That a reckless life can fill,
Though her presence is now flown,
Her bright smiles haunts me still.
Though her presence is now flown,
Her bright smiles haunts me still.

At the first sweet dawn of light
When I gaze upon the deep,
Her form still greets my sight,
While the stars their vigor [vigil] keep.
When I close my aching eyes
Sweet dreams my memory fill.
And from sleep when I arise
Her bright smiles haunts me still.
And from sleep when I arise
Her bright smiles haunts me still.

158. Seventy-Two Today   C. K. (Tink) Tillett, 1940

This, we seem to remember, is the first song Mr. C. K. Tillett sang for us. His son, Dick Tillett, told us years later that he thought "some of the time" it was his father's favorite song. That is a little hard for us to believe, since he knew so many songs, most of them far more noteworthy than this. But who can tell why a song is someone's favorite?

We have not come across the song anywhere else, but it sounds like a music hall or stage song. Many songs of that genre have moved into tradition.

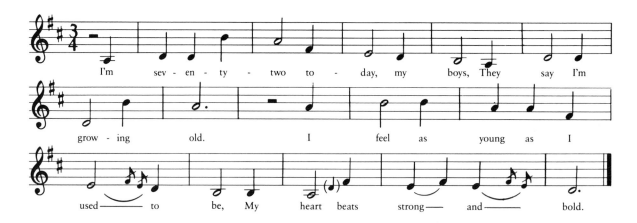

I'm sev-en-ty-two to-day, my boys, They say I'm grow-ing old. I feel as young as I used to be, My heart beats strong and bold.

No ache or pain my limbs astale [assail],
Though I am old it's true.
So walk your horse while you are young,
If you'd trot him at seventy-two.

You see young men when they go out
To spend their night in glee,
Drink whiskey, wine, and beer, get tight,
Oh, none of that for me.

When I was young I used to sit
All in some shady grove,
With some pretty girl all on my knee,
I'd tell her of my love.

I'd place my arms about her waist,
I would hug and kiss her too.
I think I could enjoy it all over again,
Although I am seventy-two!

With a laugh and a smile and a ha ha ha
I will keep this end in view.
I will praise ye all both great and small,
Although I am seventy-two.

159. Old Rosin the Beau   Dick Tillett, 1972, 1978

This is one of the songs given us by Dick Tillett. Its title is widely known, perhaps because the tune has been used for so many other songs. Spaeth (*Read 'Em and Weep,* p. 41) says the tune was used for a number of political songs between 1840 and 1875. S. Foster Damon, in the Brown University facsimile "Series of Old American Songs," includes a Ditson print of the song, without date, in which it is called "a favorite Southern ballad," and notes that "Mr. Martyn sang it in New York in the late thirties," but says its origin is "lost in the mists of antiquity."

Belden prints two versions of "Old Rosin"—without music. His notes are most interesting: "One does not know whether to write 'beau' or 'bow.' Most texts do not show the subject to be a fiddler but rather a toper who was something of a gay dog with the ladies. . . . It was printed as a stall ballad by Ryles of Seven Dials, and Joyce has a tune so called (OIFMS No. 352) from Limerick but without words. . . . All agree that it is old but do not know whether it is English, Scotch, or Irish in origin. Just possibly it goes back to a refrain quoted by Moros in Wager's *The Longer Thou Livest the More Fool Thou Art,* which is dated by Furnivall 'ca. 1658':

Robin lende to me thy Bowe, thy Bowe,
Robin the bow, Robin lende to me thy bowa.

If so, 'bow' is the original form, and the use of resin on fiddle bows has transformed Robin into Rosin."

According to Belden and to Brown, the song has been reported from tradition in Pennsylvania, Mississippi, Montana, Virginia, North Carolina, and Missouri.

The words of the Tillett version differ from those seen in other collections except the one in Chappell, which is similar but has no music.

See: Belden, 255; Brown, Vol. 3, 61; Chappell, *Folksongs of Roanoke and the Albemarle,* 97; Damon, "Series of Old American Songs," Harris Collection, Brown University; Randolph, Vol. 4, 371

OLD ROSIN THE BEAU

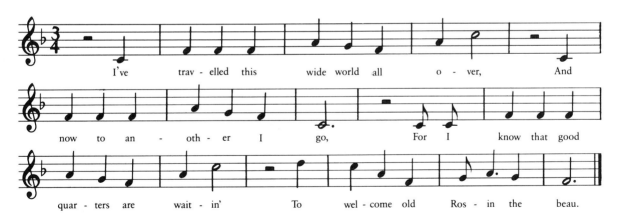

I've trav-elled this wide world all o-ver, And now to an-oth-er I go, For I know that good quar-ters are wait-in' To wel-come old Ros-in the beau.

A good round of delight I have traveled,
Nor will I behind leave a foe,
But while my companions are jovial,
They will drink to old Rosin the beau.

When I'm dead and laid out on the counter,
The people all anxious to know
Will raise up the lid of my coffin
And peep at old Rosin the beau.

361

When through the streets my friends bear me
The ladies will squeal with deep woe,
And come to the doors and the windows
To peep at old Rosin the beau.

Then get me some fine jovial fellows,
And let them stagger and go,

And dig a deep hole in the meadow,
And in it toss old Rosin the beau.

Then let these same jovial fellows
Surround my grave in a row,
Where they drink from my favorite bottle
To the health of old Rosin the beau.

160. Somebody's Waiting for Me   C. K. (Tink) Tillett, 1940,
Dick Tillett, 1972

During our one memorable afternoon with Mr. Tillett in 1940 he brought out what he called his "accordeen" and played this tune for us. He did not sing it, so we did not get the words—just the title. Many years later, in 1972, long after Tink's death, we were visiting his son, Cliff, and Cliff's wife, Marie, in Wanchese, and Cliff took us across the road to pay a visit to his brother Dick. Dick had become interested in remembering his father's songs and had sung some of them on to a cassette which he shared with us. One of them gave us the words to "Somebody's Waitin' for Me." Dick said they always called it "the shanty song." It certainly is not a sea shanty, so "shanty" must refer to the cabin in the chorus. The only way we can explain the last line of the first verse is that it was the tune they sang as they sailed away! The "didn't have a bob" in the first verse indicates that the song is English, probably music hall in origin.

On the afternoon in question, while we were talking about Tink's music, Dick remembered that his father's accordion was in the attic, and he said to us "you ought to have that." Cliff agreed, so Dick went upstairs and retrieved it and they presented it to us, an act which we found very moving. We consider it a treasured possession. An older friend who once worked with Sears Roebuck recognized it as a model that was advertised in the Sears Roebuck catalog at the turn of the century. That is no doubt how Tink acquired it.

SOMEBODY'S WAITING FOR ME

362   Once   on   a   time,   it   was   a   ve - ry   long   time,   A——

year, or it may be three, I was out of a
job, and I did-n't have a bob, When an old tar said to
me, "Would you like to come and — have some fun While you're
young and stout and strong?" So the ve-ry next day we —
sailed a-way To the dear old shan-ty — song. There is —
some-bod-y wait-ing for me At an old cab-in
down by the sea. — In the land where I wish I could
be There is — some-bod-y wait-ing for me.

I know a face, it is a very sweet face,
It's the face of my very best girl.
I've seen all sorts in the different ports
While I sailed around the world.
On my last trip east I had a very rare feast,
The taste of cake is still on my tongue.
But then I sailed west to my very very best
Little girl, again, and home.

Chorus
There is somebody waiting for me
In an old cabin down by the sea.
With a smile and a wee cup of tea
There is somebody waiting for me.

363

161. The Snow Is on the Ground   Eleazar Tillett, 1951

It was in 1951 that Mrs. Tillett sang this song for us. She said it was her husband's song and that "he would sing that every time there was snow on the ground. . . . he would get up and look out and see the snow, and sing 'The hills and the dales is all covered in white!' . . . every time—he would wake everybody up with it!" She said too, "I believe that's the oldest song I know. Tink learned it from his father, Tommy Tillett. . . . and Aunt Sally Jackson would sing it. She was older than Tink's father." Tink himself must have been born in the early 1870s.

The only place we have found the song is in *The Forget Me Not Songster,* where it is called "Remember the Poor" and is described "As sung by Mr. T. Bryan, with unbounded applause." There is no music in the songster, so we have nothing with which to compare Tink's tune. But his version is such an interesting example of the folk process that we are including here (from the *Songster*) what must have been the original literary composition.

Cold winter is come with his keen cutting breath
   And the verdure all fall from the trees;
All nature seems touch'd at the finger of Death,
   And the streams are beginning to freeze.
When the wanton young lads o'er the river do slide,
   And Flora attends us no more;
When you are enjoying a good fire-side,
   Can you grumble to think on the poor.

When the cold feather'd snow doth in plenty descend
   And whiten the prospect all round;
When the keen cutting winds from the North shall attend,
   Hard chilling and freezing the ground.
When the hills and the dales are all cover'd with white,
   And the rivers congeal with the shore;
When a bright twinkling star shall proclaim a cold night,
   That's the time to remember the poor.

When the poor harmless hare shall be traced to the woods,
   By the footsteps indented in snow;
When your lips and your fingers are started with blood,
   And the marksmen a game shooting go.
When the poor Robin Red-Breast approaches your cot,
   And the icicles hang at your door,
When your bowl smokes with something reviving and hot
   Can you grumble to think on the Poor.

Soon a thaw will ensue and the waters increase,
    And the rivers vehemently flow;
When the fish from their prison shall gain a release,
    And in danger the travellers go.
When the fields are o'erflown by the proud swelling flood,
    And the bridges are useful no more;
While in health you're enjoying every thing that is good,
    That's the time to remember the poor.

Moral

Soon a day will be here, when a Saviour will come
    All nations shall join in one voice;
All the world shall unite to salute the sweet morn,
    All the ends of the earth shall rejoice,
When grim Death is depriv'd of his all-killing sting
    And the grave is triumphant no more;
Saints, angels and men, hallelujah shall sing,
    And the rich shall remember the Poor.

THE SNOW IS ON THE GROUND

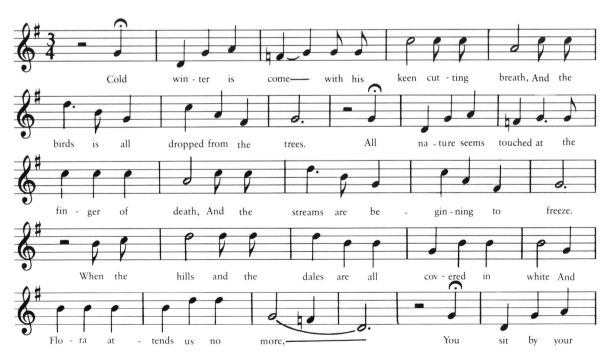

Cold win-ter is come—— with his keen cut-ting breath, And the birds is all dropped from the trees. All na-ture seems touched at the fin-ger of death, And the streams are be-gin-ning to freeze. When the hills and the dales are all cov-ered in white And Flo-ra at-tends us no more,—— You sit by your

365

fire - side, re - viv - ing and hot, Will you grum-ble to think on the poor?

When the north wind's ascending and chilling the ground
And the sportsmen again shooting go,
And the happy young lads o'er the rivers can slide
And the bridges are useful no more.

When the lakes are all froze with winter's cold breath,
And the rivers congeals to the shore,
You sit by your fireside, reviving and hot,
It is time to remember the poor.

When the poor harmless hare is tracked to the woods
With his footsteps all dandied in snow,
And the robin red breast he approaches your cot,
And icicles hang at the door,

The time it will come when our Saviour we'll see,
All nations shall join in one war,
When the saints and the angels hallelujah shall sing,
And the rich will remember the poor.

CURT MANN

In the summer of 1941 we decided, instead of going to Nag's Head by way of Elizabeth City and the causeway, to come from farther south and take the ferry from Mann's Harbor directly to Roanoke Island. Now, of course, there is a bridge and the ferry is only a memory. It was late afternoon when we reached Mann's Harbor, and when we saw a sign saying "Tourists" on a large pleasant-looking frame house set far back from the road, we decided we might stop, and take the ferry in the morning. The house belonged to Mr. C. W. Mann and was by far the most imposing of the handful of houses then comprising Mann's Harbor. We had a large comfortable room and a "down-home" dinner with the family, grace before the meal and all.

We met the grown-up son of the family, Curt—a raunchy type who slipped Frank a couple of unprintable songs during the course of the evening. We would have included them if they had had anything to recommend them, but they were as new and raw and unpalatable as the famous East Lake booze from the same county. A lot of neighbors came in after supper and we had some music. Surprisingly, Curt led the whole congregation in singing the following song, which we have been singing ever since.

Home of Mr. C. W. Mann, Mann's Harbor, North Carolina, 1940.

162. Lonesome Valley   Curt Mann, 1941

There are many songs something like this in the revivalist tradition, but the only other place we have found this song is in Alan Lomax's *Folk Song U.S.A.* The first verse (which, in our version, doubles as a chorus) is the same. The others are somewhat different, but it is the sort of song that an individual singer can feel free to change or add to as he goes.

The Lomax notes are interesting: "The same people who once were 'bound for the promised land,' now find themselves in 'a lonesome valley.' The descendants of the self-reliant pioneers . . . go to town to take the lowest-paid jobs in textile mills and auto plants and hear themselves called 'hillbillies.' . . . These are the people who are creating with their 'string bands' a fast-stepping . . . religious music, based on the resources of both Negro and white spirituals." The "music symbolizes the essential unity of the two races. . . . No one knows whether 'Lonesome Valley' is of Negro or white origin. Certainly its origin is of no account compared to the fact that it is sung by the Okies in California" [and] "by a Negro Holiness congregation in Memphis or Chicago" and by our isolated friends in Mann's Harbor.

George Pullen Jackson, in his *Spiritual Folksongs of Early America,* includes one stanza of this song and its tune which he recorded in 1933 at the Highlander Folk School in Monteagle, Tennessee. He says, "The source of this spiritual song is very likely 'In Seaport Town.' See Sharp I, 310, in which there is the recurring phrase: "'Till at last they came to a lonesome valley,' and where considerable melodic similarity is to be found. . . . The 'lonesome valley' symbolized, among both negroes and whites, the mourning period which was a necessary forerunner of religious conversion."

See: Jackson, *Spiritual Folksongs of Early America,* 215; Lomax, *FSUSA,* 352

LONESOME VALLEY

369

Mother would like
To go there with you.
Mother would help you
If she could.
Mother would take
That journey for you, but
You got to go there
By yourself.
Chorus

Some folks say
That John was a Baptist.
Others say
He was a Jew.
But the Holy Bible
Plainly tells you
That he was
A preacher too.
Chorus

There is one
Who'll go there with you.
He will be
Your friend tonight.
If you'll change
Your way of living,
And you'll choose
The road that's right.
Chorus

MARTHA ANN MIDGETTE

One of the neighbors who dropped by Mr. Mann's house during the evening we were there was a twelve-year-old girl named Martha Ann Midgette. She had a sweet voice and she loved to sing. One of the songs she gave us was this one.

163. Tommy   Martha Ann Midgette, 1941

We think "Tommy" must be a local product. We haven't found it anywhere else, and the first line of the last verse: "Tommy owns a speed boat," could be a clue. Mann's Harbor is right on the water and much of the traveling is done by boat.

TOMMY

Tom - my came to see me, Tom - my came last night.

Tom - my asked me to mar - ry him, Of course I said — all right.

Tommy went asked mama,
Mama came out to see.
Mama went back with a tear in her eye,
Said Tommy had asked for me.

Tommy went asked my papa,
Papa came out to see.
Papa went back with a smile on his face,
Said he was glad to get rid of me.

Tommy owns a speed boat,
Tommy owns a store.
Tommy's going to carry me away,
And we'll live forevermore.

164. Wallabug   Martha Ann Midgette, 1941

This is a little nonsense song from Martha Ann Midgette. Its humor is of the pioneer, Arkansas-traveler type, but what could be more American traditional than that? We think it, like "Tommy," must be a local product.

371

Bought an old cow from Farm-er Jones,—— She weren't no-thing but

skin and bones. Fat-tened her up as fine as silk, She jumped the fence and

Chorus

skimmed her milk. Wal - la - bug wal - la - bug, you can't fool me.

I'll be as good as good can be. If you see a wal - la - bug

night or day, Make a noise like a wal - la - bug and roll a - way.

There was an old woman from Oisocket,
She put her false teeth in her pocket,
She put her pipe up on the shelf,
She sat right down and she bit herself.
     Chorus

SUE WESTCOTT

Manteo is the other town on Roanoke Island. Manteo and Wanchese get their names from two Indian braves who were taken from the Island to England in 1584 by two of Sir Walter Raleigh's officers and who lived to return to their native land. Sir Walter founded the first English colony on the North American continent on Roanoke Island in 1585,—now known as the Lost Colony, because when he was able to return two years later the original huts remained, but no people. Paul Green's pageant of "The Lost Colony" in song and story was first presented in a natural outdoor amphitheatre at

Mr. and Mrs. Colin Westcott and their family, Manteo, Roanoke Island, North Carolina, 1941. Mrs. Westcott (Sue) is the daughter of Mr. Mann.

Manteo in 1937 and, except for the years of World War II, has been repeated there every summer since.

While we were on Roanoke Island in 1941 we visited Sue (Mrs. Colin) Westcott and her family in Manteo. Mrs. Westcott was the daughter of Mr. Mann of Mann's Harbor. She recorded a number of songs for us. The one that follows is an interesting example.

165. Old Grey Beard   Sue Westcott, 1941

This song is more commonly known as "The Old Man's Courtship." Belden and Brown between them list all sources and references. Brown prints five versions, only one of them—"C"—with the refrain about the old grey beard. The other four all use "with his old shoeboots and leggins," or "his old boots a-leaking." The Belden version has it "with his old grey beard newly shaven."

Belden says that the theme (as well as the man) is old, going back "at least to 1730, when it was published in London in *The Musical Miscellany,* volume III, on page 110 of which it is found, in Scottish or northern dialect."

Sharp prints two versions under the title "My Mother Bid Me"—one from North Carolina and one from Virginia. It has been found in oral tradition in a number of other southern states and in Ohio, Indiana, and Michigan, as well as in several English counties.

Folk Songs of the Catskills (Cazden II) prints a version (without tune), and the notes mention a text from Delaware County in the western Catskills. Versions from the Northeast are not common.

See: Belden, 264; Brown, Vol. 3, 17; Cazden II, 488; Sharp, *English Folksongs of the Southern Appalachians,* Vol. 2, 93

OLD GREY BEARD

My ma-ma told me to meet him at the gate, I won't— have it! I met him at the gate and he swal-lered a plate, With his old grey beard a-flap-ping.

My mama told me to get him a chair,
I won't have it!
Gave him a chair and he growled like a bear,
With his old grey beard a-flapping.

Mama told me to give him some fish,
I won't have it!
Gave him some fish and he swallered the dish,
With his old grey beard a-flapping.

Mama told me to give him some pie,
I won't have it!
Gave him some pie and he swallered a fly,
With his old grey beard a-flapping.

Mama told me to take him to the door,
I won't have it!
Took him to the door and he fell on the floor,
With his old grey beard a-flapping.

The Culpeper house at Nag's Head, with the sand dunes in the background.

CAPTAIN JOHN AND ALWILDA CULPEPER

Captain John Culpeper and his wife, Alwilda, were natives of Nag's Head. They lived in a comfortable house set way back from the road against one of the high sand dunes. The house used to be nearer the one highway that runs along near the shore, but when one of the hurricanes that frequent that part of the coast brought the ocean almost to their door, they picked up the house and moved it back.

Captain John was a fisherman, of course—tall, and taciturn until one got to know him a bit, dark-skinned from the sun right up to the hat line on his forehead. Miss Alwildie (as they pronounced her name) was white haired, short and plump, and as voluble as her husband was reticent. They became, over the years, our good friends.

375

Captain John Culpeper and his wife, Alwilda, of Nag's Head, North Carolina, 1940.

166. Show Me the Man Who Never Done Wrong
(or, Rocking the Baby to Sleep)   Alwilda Culpeper, 1940

Mrs. Culpeper sang us this song—or fragment of a song—in 1940. We have become much more interested in it and more curious as to how she learned it since we have begun looking for references to it.

Randolph has a song called "Rock All Our Babies to Sleep" from a Mrs. Laura Wasson, Elm Springs, Arkansas, who learned it in the early nineties. It is the same song but with five verses and a number of variations. It begins:

Show me the lady that never will roam,
Away from her fireside at night,
Who never goes roaming out after the boys,
But would sit by her fireside so bright.

Frank Warner with Captain and Mrs. Culpeper on the porch of the Culpepers' house at Nag's Head, North Carolina, 1941.

Chorus
Hayly, highly, holy, hush bonny baby,
Hush bonny baby and do not cry.
Hayly, highly, holy, hush bonny baby,
Mamma will come to you by and by.

The only other American reference we have found is in the Library of Congress *Check list* (1942, p. 337) of the Archive of American Folk-Song, as sung by Nathan Judd with guitar at the Arvin, California, Farm Security Administration camp, for Todd and Sonkin in 1940.

Alan Lomax includes a song called "The Old Man's Lament" which has many similarities to this song but many differences: "I am weeping and weary with rocking this cradle, and nursing a baby that's none of my own." However, all Lomax says of the song is that it was "collected and arranged by Seamus Ennis, Dublin. Song is common in Northern and Western Ireland, frequently printed on broadsheets." So it is not an American version.

Peter Kennedy's *Folk Songs of Britain and Ireland* includes "Rocking the Cradle," a version almost exactly like the one in Lomax, which he obtained from John Doherty in Donegal, Ireland. Kennedy lists a number of other Irish sources, one in Wales, and one in Canada, but none in the United States. He adds: "There is a belief in Ireland that the tune of this song was the lullaby sung to the Christ child by the Virgin Mary."

See: Kennedy, 469; Lomax, *FSNA,* 375; Randolph, Vol. 3, 117

SHOW ME THE MAN WHO NEVER DONE WRONG
(or, ROCKING THE BABY TO SLEEP)

Oh, show me the man who nev - er done wrong, Nor ev - er went out on a spree, But stayed right home by his dear lit - tle wife And rocked the dear ba - by to sleep.

Chorus
Sing hi - ly, ho - ly, la - ly bi - ba - be, Rock - ing the ba - by and toss - ing him high, Sing hi - ly, ho - ly, la - ly bi - ba - be, Your ma - ma will come by and by.

I am just forty-four, my dear little wife,
She is ten years younger than I.
She's fond of her pleasure and drinks lager beer,
And often comes rolling in tight.
    Chorus

She says it's no harm, don't make no alarm,
While I am out on the street.
She tickles my chin, she says now go on in,
And rock the dear baby to sleep.
    Chorus

KACK AND SASS HATHAWAY

Two other Nag's Head friends were sisters—Kack and Sass Hathaway. They were contemporaries of ours. We knew them for years but never heard them called anything else. They, and their parents, were from Elizabeth City, but they had spent all the summers of their lives at the beach and were as near to natives as summer people can get. They introduced us to the Culpepers, for which we will always be grateful.

167. Careless Love   Kack and Sass Hathaway, 1933

Frank Warner learned this version of "Careless Love" in 1933 from Kack and Sass Hathaway at Nag's Head. They had learned the song from some of the bankers, and they used the local dialect, which is a conglomerate of dialects from a number of English counties. They always sang "Lerve, O lerve, O keerless lerve."

Versions of the song are found in many places and some of them are too well known to be remarkable, but this one is different from any we have seen or heard. We have always found it touching rather than funny.

Randolph prints three versions—"A" seems to be an entirely different song, though it has a "careless love" refrain. "B" is very like "A" but without the refrain, and "C" is almost identical to the versions found in Sandburg and Lomax. Lomax says that in metre and tune "Careless Love" resembles early blues sung by blacks in the Delta, but that mountain singers say it is an old song and that it "seems to be derived from such southern English fragments and couplets as:

> It was in the month of sweet July
> When I first listened to your lies
> And now my apron, it won't tie
> And I wish I'd never heard your lies.

He concludes that "the blues, like the Negro hoe-downs, spirituals, and ballads, used Anglo-American song-forms as their starting point." Sharp includes a song called "Every

Night When the Sun Goes In" which has two verses similar to this song—though it does not include the refrain:

It's once my apron hung down low (3 times)
He'd follow me through both sleet and snow
   True love, don't weep, true love, don't mourn (2 times)
   True love, don't weep nor mourn for me,
   I'm going away to Marble town.
It's now my apron's to my chin (3 times)
He'll face my door and won't come in.
     etc.

See: Laws, *NAB,* Appendix 3, 277; Lomax, *FSNA,* 585; Lomax, *FSUSA,* 64; Randolph, Vol. 4, 306; Sandburg, *The American Songbag,* 21; Sharp, *English Folksongs of the Southern Appalachians,* Vol. 2, 268

CARELESS LOVE

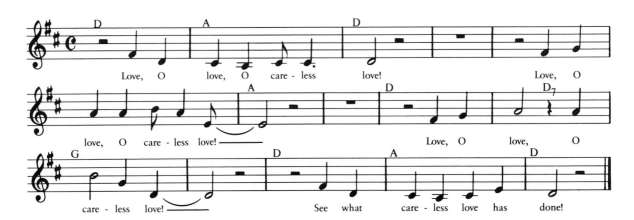

When I wore my apron low,
When I wore my apron low,
When I wore my apron low,
You was always a-hangin' 'round my door!

Now my apron strings won't pin,
Now my apron strings won't pin,
Now my apron strings won't pin.
380 You pass my door, but you won't come in!

I wonder what my mother will say,
I wonder what my mother will say,
I wonder what my mother will say,
When I come home in a family way.

She'll hang her head and bite her tongue,
She'll hang her head and bite her tongue,
She'll hang her head and bite her tongue,
'Cause she done the same when she was young!

Love, O love, O careless love!
Love, O love, O careless love!
Love, O love, O careless love!
See what careless love has done!

SUE THOMAS AND J. B. SUTTON

On our trips south we usually headed first for Nag's Head on North Carolina's Outer
Banks, where we wanted to see Sue Thomas, our wonderful black friend whom we'd
known since before we were married. She lived in Elizabeth City but spent her summers on the beach cooking at Mrs. Modlin's Arlington Cottage—in the early days a
fisherman's boardinghouse—not a hundred yards from the ocean. Frank had gone there
fishing when he was a student at Duke. Sue was a wonderful cook, a fine woman, and
a sweet singer. We won't forget her fried fish and cornbread, or the cake walk she did
one evening when we arrived unexpectedly, or Sue herself. After dinner she would join
us on the porch, and we would sing far into the night.

In the early years she had taught us "He's Got the Whole World in His Hand,"
and "Hold My Hand, Lord Jesus." Both these songs are on Frank's first Elektra recording (EKL-3, 1952)—although he had been singing them across the country since
the thirties.

After many visits with Sue at Nag's Head, we arrived at the Arlington one
summer—it was 1941—to find she was not there but at home in Elizabeth City. She
was cooking, we found, at Walgreen's Drug Store. But we had an afternoon with her
in her house at 405 Poplar Street, and met her husband Verdon, and her son too, who
happened to be visiting. He was a son by an earlier marriage, and his name was J. B.
Sutton. That was our only recording session with Sue, but it was a worthy one. Even
now, on the tapes made from those early disks, her voice is strong and clear. She used
the v/w interchange picked up on the beach,[7] and in her recording we hear her say
"How many werses shall I sing?" And in "Hold My Hand, Lord Jesus" she sang:

There's a race that we must run,
And a wictory to be von,
Every hover [hour], give me powver
To go through.

J. B. Sutton was a chauffeur for a man in Elizabeth City. He recorded a few songs
for us that day, too. We wish we had had more time with him and that our recording
of his singing could have been high fidelity. One snatch of a song he gave us was "O

---

7. See footnote 8 (below) in the notes for the song "Wictory Shall Be Mine," No. 176.

Frank Warner with Sue Thomas on the porch of the Arlington Cottage at Nag's Head, North Carolina, 1933. Photo by Anne Locher.

Bud" (see song No. 175). Frank knew it as a haunting memory of his young years in the deep South—whistled or sung by some young black on a lonely road or across a field late at night.

The war, and the lack of a car, stopped our travels for a number of years, but we kept in touch with Sue, as with our other friends. The last letter we have from her—the last, anyway, that we find in our files—is dated February 11, 1952:

> 405 Poplar St
> Elizabeth City, N.C.
> February 11, 1952

Dear Mrs. Warner,

Just a few lines to let you no I receved your letter a few days a go and you no I was sure glad to hear from you all. Glad to hear about your family I sure would be glad to see your boys if you all come down hear this summer to nags head please bring your boys to see me. I am old and cant work licke I ust to work but I want to see you all so bad. . . . I often think about you all and how we all ust to sing. . . .

I am looken to hear from you real soon give my love to all your family

> Your truly as ever
> Susie Thomas

In the early sixties we found ourselves in Elizabeth City and decided to find Poplar Street again and to try to find out what had happened to Sue. We found Poplar,

Anne Warner recording Sue Thomas in Elizabeth City, North Carolina, 1941. Standing are Sue's husband, Verdon Thomas, and her son, J. B. Sutton.

and #405, but no one was at home. We spoke to a man coming down the sidewalk who, unbelievably, turned out to be John Sutton. We had a great reunion. He said "Mama" had died some years before. He and his wife, Willie Mae, were living in her old house but expecting to move into a new housing development. We have a letter from him written in 1964:

405 Poplar St.
Eliz. City, N.C.
12-29-64

Dear Mr. and Mrs. Warner:

Thanks so much for the lovely card. We think you have a very fine family. We hope you had a Merry Christmas and will have a happy New Year.

As you no I love dogs your dog [included in our family picture on our Christmas card was our German Shepherd, Maggie] looks like a wonderful dog and if you ever see a chance Please send me one. We are still living at the same place but are looking to move about the 15 of January will write to you when we move. Give our love to the family. I will keep in touch with you.

From John and Willie Mae Sutton

We never heard from him again.

168. He's Got the Whole World in His Hand   Sue Thomas, 1933

Sue Thomas sang this song for Frank in the summer of 1933 — several years before we were married, before he had even thought of collecting songs. He learned it immediately and used it in every concert or program for years. It was a favorite with anyone who heard it. We believe Frank was the first singer to introduce the song.

Some years later Marian Anderson — who had learned it, she said, from a collector in Virginia — began using it in her programs of spirituals. Then Mahalia Jackson sang it, and Odetta. We delighted in hearing it from such fine singers. But then Lonny Donegan in London adopted it, and the skiffle boys, and they added a fast beat and hand-clapping at intervals, and interjected exclamations of "brother!" —

He's got you and me, brother,
Clap! clap!
In his hand . . .

Before one knew it, the lovely spiritual declaration of faith and trust that Sue sang so movingly had become a camp song, known throughout the land. When we began to sing it during a program the crowd would instantly join in, which would have been

384

fine, but they would insist on the new fast beat and the clapping. We stopped singing it, though we kept our appreciation of its message and its charm.

Here it is, then, as Sue sang it, with the verses she gave us. We have found a printed version of the song in the paperbound *Spirituals Triumphant, Old and New* (No. 68), edited and arranged by Edward Boatner, printed in both round and shaped notes. In the book the verses are somewhat different:

1. He's got the whole world in His hand
2. He's got my mother in His hand,
3. He's got my father in His hand,
4. He's got all power in His hand,
5. He's got the fishes of the sea in His hand,
6. He's got the whole church in His hand.

Improvisation adds joy and beauty to a song of this kind.

HE'S GOT THE WHOLE WORLD IN HIS HAND

He's got the trees and the flowers right in His hand,
He's got the trees and the flowers right in His hand,
He's got the trees and the flowers right in His hand,
He's got the whole world in His hand.

He's got that crap-shootin' man right in His hand,
He's got that crap-shootin' man right in His hand,

He's got that crap-shootin' man right in His hand,
He's got the whole world in His hand.

He's got that back-slidin' sister right in His hand,
He's got that back-slidin' sister right in His hand,
He's got that back-slidin' sister right in His hand,
He's got the whole world in His hand.

He's got the little bitty baby in His hand,
He's got the little bitty baby in His hand,
He's got the little bitty baby in His hand,
He's got the whole world in His hand.

He's got you and me right in His hand,
He's got you and me right in His hand,
He's got you and me right in His hand,
He's got the whole world in His hand.

169. Hold My Hand, Lord Jesus   Sue Thomas, 1933

This gospel song, with its message of confidence and hope, was sung to us by Sue Thomas on the porch of the Arlington Cottage at Nag's Head, North Carolina. It was in 1933 on my first visit to the Outer Banks, before Frank and I were married—in fact, on my first trip to the South.

For many years Frank sang "Hold My Hand" to close every program. It was the song most often requested by people who had heard him before. Many people have written us of the courage and inspiration it gave them in moments of crisis. One friend told us he sang it in a foxhole in the Battle of the Bulge. It was a favorite of Carl Sandburg's too. Listening to the radio broadcast of the festivities at Sandburg's seventy-fifth birthday dinner at the Blackstone Hotel in Chicago on January 10, 1953, we were delighted to hear Carl close his remarks by singing this song—mentioning both Sue Thomas and the Warners.

Someone once told us they had heard the song in the Bahamas, but we have never found it anywhere else.

HOLD MY HAND, LORD JESUS

386

race that we must run, And a vic - t'ry to be won, ——

Ev - ery ho - ur, —— give me pow - er —— To go —— through.

I'll go through, Lord Jesus, I'll go through,
I'll go through, Lord Jesus, I'll go through.
Refrain

I'll pray too, Lord Jesus, I'll pray too,
I'll pray too, Lord Jesus, I'll pray too.
Refrain

I'll bow low, Lord Jesus, I'll bow low,
I'll bow low, Lord Jesus, I'll bow low.
Refrain

I'm your child, Lord Jesus, I'm your child,
I'm your child, Lord Jesus, I'm your child.
Refrain

"Hold My Hand Lord Jesus"
Words and Music Collected, Adapted and Arranged by Frank Warner
TRO—© Copyright 1971 and 1984 Melody Trails, Inc., New York, N.Y. Used by Permission

170. Let Me Ride   Sue Thomas, 1933

Sue Thomas sang this song, but Frank learned it long before he knew Sue. It is one of the songs he absorbed in his childhood in the deep South—almost by osmosis. It is unequaled for group singing, and Frank used it over the years with all the groups with which he was associated—at YMCA conventions, at Y boys' camps, at the Seminars on American Culture at Cooperstown, with school and college audiences, at Pinewoods Folk Music Camp. Everyone responded to it. It is a song of triumph.

"Let Me Ride" is No. 26 in *Spirituals Triumphant,* edited by Dr. Edward Boatner. The "low' down" in the last line means, of course, lower down, or let down, as the chariot of the Lord was let down to take Elijah to heaven.

There are two Library of Congress field recordings of the song: AFS 3262 A 1, Negro choir from the Metropolitan Community Church, Chicago, recorded in May, 1937, by Sidney Robertson Cowle; and AFS 1315 B 1, Vera Ball and Dock Read, Livingston, Alabama, recorded July, 1937, by John Lomax.

See: Boatner, No. 26

I've been converted, let me ride.
I've been converted, let me ride.
I've been converted, let me ride.
Low' down your chariot and let me ride!

I've got my ticket, let me ride.
I've got my ticket, let me ride.
I've got my ticket, let me ride.
Low' down your chariot and let me ride!

I'm bound for Heaven, let me ride.
I'm bound for Heaven, let me ride.
I'm bound for Heaven, let me ride.
Low' down your chariot and let me ride!

In the Kingdom, let me ride.
In the Kingdom, let me ride.
In the Kingdom, let me ride.
Low' down your chariot and let me ride!

Troubles over, let me ride.
Troubles over, let me ride.
Troubles over, let me ride.
Low' down your chariot and let me ride!

171. Nobody Knows   Sue Thomas, 1939

Anyone at all familiar with Negro spirituals knows "Nobody knows the trouble I've seen / Nobody knows but Jesus." This is quite a different song and one we have not been able to find in print, although it is obviously a composed song. Sue gave it to us in 1939, and it has long been a favorite of ours. It is a cry of anguish and loneliness, yet it shows, at last, the resilience and hope that are characteristic of black religious songs.

No - bod - y knows how hea - vy my load, No - bod - y knows how
thron - y [thorny] my road. No - bod - y cares if I'm
trou - bled on the way, How dark the night, how— dark— the day.
*often

Chorus
Nobody knows, nobody cares,
My heavy burden nobody shares.
My only comfort, my only stay,
Jesus is walking by my side always.

Nobody knows how heavy my cross,
Nobody knows how bitter my dross.
Nobody cares if I am ill,
Life's hardships have broken my will.
Chorus

Nobody knows how hard I must toil,
Causing my heart sometime to recoil.
Nobody cares when I'm too tired to sleep,
I lay awake and bitterly weep.
Chorus

Nobody knows but Jesus my Lord,
No comfort found but in his sweet word.
He cares and numbers me with the blessed,
He promise me a home in heaven of rest.
Chorus

172. You Can't Hurry God   Sue Thomas, 1941

Sue Thomas gave us many fine songs, this among them. It is surely a church song,
but we have not found it in any of the hymn books we have collected over the years.
Sue had a beautiful voice, and her spiritual songs were filled with hope and meaning.
We especially like the rhythm and the timing in the chorus.

Though the path—— you tread may seem so dark and drear-y,——
Bur-dened with care, no light an-y-where; 'Neath your hea-vy
load you may be-come so wea-ry, But—— He will come and an-swer
prayer.

Chorus

You can't hur-ry God, why don't you wait, my broth-er?——
Just o-bey the word that you—— have heard. Keep on call—— ing
Him, for in some-day or 'noth-er, —— He will come and an-swer prayer.

Often you have felt you could endure no longer,
Burdened, you call, on your All-in-all.
Asking Him to make you just a little bit
    stronger,
He will come and answer prayer.
    Chorus

On your bed of sickness, what a terrible feeling,
Nerve-wracking pains, again and again.
Call on God, and tell Him that you need His
    healing,
He will come and answer prayer.
    Chorus

When all hope is gone, and you see no need of
    praying,
Trembling with fear, you shed many a tear.
Lift your head and wait, for His delaying,
He will come and answer prayer.
    Chorus

173, 174. **Mail Day** and **Thirty Days in Jail**   J. B. Sutton, 1941

These two songs from J. B. Sutton, Sue Thomas's son, are jailhouse blues—
expressing in a few lines all the pain, sorrow, and frustration of a man behind bars.
We don't think he was speaking from personal experience. J. B. was, when we met
him, acting as a chauffeur for a man in Elizabeth City, and was a respected citizen.
But something gave him the ability to sing these songs with feeling.

There are two Library of Congress field recordings of these songs: AFS 89 A 2,
by Pete Harris of Richmond, Texas, recorded by John Lomax, May 1934; and AFS 3988
A 3, by Finons (Flat Foot) Rockmore of Lufkin, Texas, recorded by John and Ruby
Lomax, October 1940.

MAIL DAY

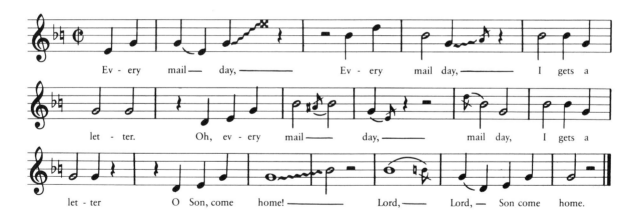

Ev - ery mail— day, —— Ev - ery mail day, —— I gets a
let - ter. Oh, ev - ery mail—— day, —— mail day, I gets a
let - ter O Son, come home! —— Lord, —— Lord, — Son come home.

I couldn't read it,
Read it,
To keep from cryin'.
I couldn't read it, read it,
To keep from cryin'
To save my soul.
Lord, Lord, to save my soul.

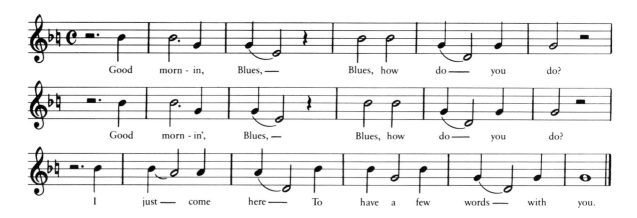

Good morn-in, Blues, — Blues, how do — you do?

Good morn-in', Blues, — Blues, how do — you do?

I just — come here — To have a few words — with you.

Thirty days in jail,
With my back turned to the wall.
Thirty days in jail,
With my back turned to the wall.
Look here, Mr. Jailkeeper,
Put another man in my stall.

I don't mind being in jail,
But I got to stay here so long.
I don't mind being in jail,
But I got to stay here so long.
When every friend I have
Has done shook hands and gone.

175. O Bud   J. B. Sutton, 1941

All we know of this song is that Frank, when he was a boy in the deep South, used to lie abed and hear the song hauntingly shouted or sung—particularly the last line which is a refrain—by young blacks going down the road or crossing a field late at night.

As John W. Work says in his chapter on the blues in *American Negro Songs and Spirituals,* "spirituals are choral and communal, the blues are solo and individual . . . the creations of nameless individuals who coined them out of experiences fraught with disillusionment, disappointment, and hopelessness." Each singer of the blues "always gives her or his own coloring to the song by modifying, omitting, and adding lines." We don't suppose the words to "O Bud" were ever the same, or that they mattered. It was the long, lonesome sound of the refrain that would ease the singer and would haunt his hearer.

I don't like No farm-er's rule, says, "Get up in the morn-ing With the dog-goned mule."— O Bud, Bud, —— Bud, — Bud, O Bud.

I'm going up the maple,
Coming down the pine,
Looking for the woman
Got a rambling mind.
O Bud, Bud, Bud, Bud, O Bud.

ANNIE _____

176. Wictory Shall Be Mine[8]   Annie _____, 1937

In 1937 (before we had been to the southern mountains or done any real collecting), we were visiting Frank's brother, Mel, and his wife, Mary Louise, in Elizabeth City. One morning after breakfast we went into the kitchen to talk to Annie,[9] their "daily" on the chance that she could give us a tune. Annie said she couldn't sing, never had much of a voice, but that she had one child who could. After a little urging she told us this story. These are her words, as nearly as we could remember them when we made our notes just after the visit:

I've got four children. Three of them were strong and right smart, but the youngest was weak and unsteady and couldn't do anything for herself. We were mighty worried

8. This is an example of the v-w interchange characteristic of the Outer Banks speech pattern when we first visited there in the thirties. It was picked up by the many blacks who worked on the beach in the summer and so was in fairly common use among blacks in Elizabeth City. The editors of the *North Carolina Folklore Journal,* in whose November 1977 issue our story about Annie's daughter first appeared, added this note: Joseph Wright records that initial v had become w in middle Buckinghamshire, Norfolk, Suffolk, Essex, Kent, and east Sussex (*The English Dialect Grammar* [1905; rpt. Oxford: Oxford University Press, 1968], pp. 227–28, sec. 281).
9. I can find no record of Annie's last name or of her daughter's name.

about her. The doctor said, "I can't do nothing for her, and all you can do is just take her home and look after her and be sweet to her. She's not going to be like the rest of your children."

So we did. She kept on growing but didn't show much improvement. Everybody had to look after her and do everything for her, and she was slow learning to talk and couldn't go to school.

Well, one day a man came over to the house with a gittar. He played mighty pretty, and we were all so happy when this little girl started showing some interest. She came over by him and stood there a long time listening. The next time he came she showed a lot of excitement and didn't leave him all the time he was there. After this had happened several times she started making like she was playing, and so the man took her on his lap and tried to show her how to pick the strings. Before long she could pick real good, and then she learned some chords. Now you *know* what that did to us. Everybody was mighty proud of her.

We bought a little gittar for her, and she just stayed with it all the time—had to have it by her bed at night. It wasn't long before she was playing *and* singing. Then the preacher heard about how good she was getting along and to encourage her he asked us to bring her over to the Wednesday night prayer meeting and let her sing a little song. That was fine. She did right well, and everybody told her how smart she was and how much they liked her song.

She just kept on getting better and better, till the folks all around and about came to hear her sing. By the time she got to be a big girl she was singing in the protracted meetings. She would sit up on the platform and listen to the preacher preach, and then she'd match him with a song. Now she's singing in revival meetings all up and down the coast of Virginia and North Carolina. I reckon she's made more of what you might call white folks' dollars than all the rest of my children.

One night she was singing in one of these meetings and all of a sudden this song was *give* to her. She calls it "Wictory." And no matter how low or how bad you feel, if you sing this song it will raise your spirits. Leastways that's what it does for me. I'll try to sing it for you. When I clap my hands, that's the gittar.

WICTORY SHALL BE MINE

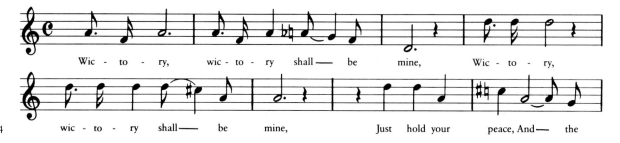

Wic - to - ry, wic - to - ry shall — be mine, Wic - to - ry, wic - to - ry shall — be mine, Just hold your peace, And — the

394

Lord will fight your bat - tles, —— Wic - to - ry, wic - to - ry shall — be mine!

> Wictory, wictory shall be mine,
> In the morning,*
> Wictory, wictory shall be mine,
> Just hold your peace,
> And the Lord will fight your battle,
> Wictory, wictory shall be mine!

"Victory" ("Wictory")
Collected, Adapted and Arranged by Frank Warner
TRO—© Copyright 1959 and 1984 Hollis Music, Inc., New York, N.Y. Used by Permission

STEVE MEEKINS

Kill Devil Hill at Kitty Hawk on North Carolina's Outer Banks is where the Wright brothers made the first airplane flight in December of 1903. The best of their four flights lasted just fifty-seven seconds, but it changed the world.

We had heard of a Steve Meekins at Kitty Hawk who "knows the old songs," and, fortunately, that summer morning in 1940, we found him at home. Unfortunately, he said he was getting old and couldn't remember much, but we did record nine of his fiddle tunes, played on a homemade fiddle (he said it was 185 years old), and one song—an old minstrel piece called "Walkin' in the Parlor."

Just "up the car road" in Colington we met Johnny Moore—the world's first airplane casualty, though not a serious one. As a boy in 1903 he was helping the Wright brothers, and as their plane took off he got an arm caught in some of the lines. Now he lives back in the swamp land, has a large family, and takes out fishing parties. When we met him he was about to go out, but he promised to be back in the evening and to do some singing. One of his daughters said, "Daddy can sure sing up a storm when he's a mind to. . . . He sings a lot to we young'uns." But when we went back that night he wasn't there. One of his boys (named Orville Stanley) told us, "He should be in by now, but maybe he's a-drinkin'." So we got no songs from Johnny Moore.

---

*Or, In the evening, or, In the noontime, or, In trouble, etc., as the spirit moves the singer.

177. Walkin' in the Parlor   Steve Meekins, 1940

The notes about this song in the Frank Brown collection concern a series of songs or fragments included under this general title: "The pieces here assembled under this title are all descendants of a highly popular song of the minstrel stage a hundred years ago. . . . In its fuller form it is a burlesque version of Bible stories." Version "A" which Brown prints (eight verses) is very well known as "The Sunday School Song," with its first verse:

> Young folks, old folks, everybody come,
> Come to our Sunday school and make yourselves at home.
> Please check your chewing gum and razors at the door,
> And you'll hear more Bible stories than you've ever heard before.

The verses go on through Adam, Noah, David, Salome, Daniel, Pharaoh, and Jonah, the stories all told in a flippant, tongue-in-cheek manner. See Cox, and Ford (*Traditional Music of America*). All versions, say the Brown notes, "go back to the minstrel song of the 1840s, [and] differ widely, even in the chorus. Bits of it are reported as sung by Negroes in Mississippi . . . and Alabama." One fragment in Brown resembles Steve Meekins's version—version "E" from Sampson County, North Carolina—and includes the verse:

> Walk in, walk in, walk in, I say,
> Walk in de parlor and hear de banjo play—
> Walk in de parlor and hear de banjo ring,
> Watch a nigger finger while he pick upon a string.

Mr. Meekins's version, though strongly rhythmic, was more a recitation than a song and had no real tune.

See: Brown, Vol. 3, 399; Cox, 503; Ford, *Traditional Music of America*, 278

WALKIN' IN THE PARLOR

I came from old Virginny,
With my head full of knowledge.
I never went to free school,
Nor any other college.

But one thing I will tell you,
For I am a solemn Jack,
I will tell you how the world was made
In the twinkling of a crack.

Walk in walk in, walk in I say,
Go in the parlor and hear the banjo play.
Go in the parlor to hear the banjo ring,
And watch this nigger singer as he picks upon
the strings.

The world was made in six days,
And then they made the sky,
And then he hung it overhead
And left it there to dry.
Then he made the stars
Out of nigger wenches eyes,
To give a little light
When the moon did not rise.
Chorus

Then he made the sea,
And in it put a whale.
Then he made the raccoon
With rings around his tail.
All the rest of the animals
Was finished one by one
And stuck against the fence to dry,
As fast as they was done.
Chorus

WARREN PAYNE

In 1951 Frank's Duke University friend P. D. Midgette, was living in Engelhard, North Carolina, in Hyde County, on the western side of Pamlico Sound. Much of Hyde County is marsh and swampland. P. D. thought he might find some interesting people for us to meet, so we went over and stayed at the Engelhard Hotel—a low rambling wooden structure run like a boarding house. Food was passed around in large serving dishes, and guests carried dishes to the kitchen after meals. Jeff and Gerret were with us, and we paid $5 a day for the four of us—room and board! We kept notes on two of the meals:

Breakfast: Fruit, sausages, eggs (have another hot egg?), buttered toast, apple sauce, coffee, and milk.

Dinner: Fried chicken, fried fish, peas, okra, tomatoes, lettuce, green peppers and onions, pickles, potatoes, corn bread, rolls, blueberry muffins, iced tea.

P. D. arranged on the spur of the moment for Frank to put on a free concert in the Engelhard high school one of the nights we were there. In order to get word of it around he got the Jolly brothers (who had a shop that serviced radio equipment on shrimp boats) to ride around in their sound truck, through the town and on the roads through the surrounding swamplands, broadcasting the following message over their loudspeaker:

Captain Billie Payne, Nebraska, Hyde County, North Carolina, 1951.

Tonight, Tuesday evening, August 14, at eight o'clock in the high school auditorium Mr. P. D. Midgette, Jr., will introduce Frank Warner and family. . . . Mr. Warner is a collector and singer of old-time songs. . . . the musical program has been arranged for our entertainment. . . . you should come and hear music that you will probably never hear again.

As a result we had a good crowd, and got a few leads to singers—although we are inclined to remember too the swamp mosquitoes that tried to outnumber the people! That night we heard about Captain Billie (C.W.) Payne, who lived not far away in a settlement called Nebraska, with his daughter Senia (called "Seeny"), Mrs. Tom Young. We went to see them the following afternoon in their picturebook cottage in the woods. Cap'n Billie was born in 1860, so he was ninety-one that year—an engaging old gentleman with white hair and drooping moustache. He had spent his working years sailing local boats back and forth to the mainland, carrying passengers and mail and doing shopping for people who lived on the Outer Banks or along the inland

The Payne cabin, Hyde County, North Carolina, 1951.

waterways, bringing back clothes, hardware, anything that could not be made or raised on the Banks.

Mrs. Young said her father used to sing a lot but that he didn't remember much any more. He wanted to sing for us, and tried very hard to give us a version of "William Taylor"—which we wanted very much to have—but he could not get through more than a line or two, and was so frustrated that he began to cry. For the rest of our visit we talked about his sailing days rather than songs, and heard some stories about his shopping expeditions and how he often used to bring back a dozen ladies' hats, which were quickly bought up by the ladies at home.

We met Warren Payne in Gull Rock nearby who gave us a few songs he had learned from his father, Millard Fillmore Payne, who had been raised at Fairfield, North Carolina, on the other side of Lake Mattamuskeet. Warren Payne was seventy-four years old that summer and had been running the mail for thirty years, taking over from his father who started the route. He has always used a horse and buggy but now, he said, they want to extend the run and put on a car. Last year (1950) was the first time a car could get through every day of the year because of the poor roads. Warren hasn't been able to get a driver's license because of lack of book learning. "When I went to school they didn't have no grades. I went as far as 'horseback' in the speller and as far as the fifth line in arithmetic."

Mr. Payne has had no teeth for thirty-three years, but he can eat most anything—apples and pears, for instance. Peanuts aren't so good, he says. He had to get glasses because of the eye test he took when applying for a driver's license, but "I'd just as soon be dead as wear both glasses and false teeth all the time, with all the trouble they is."

So many people in Hyde County have the same name, Warren Payne said, that—as on Roanoke Island—you have to have special names to tell 'em apart. Two of the Frank Gibbs are known as "Cuttin' Frank" and "Whistlin' Frank." There is "Burnt Sam Gibbs," and "Tobacco-mouth Sam Gibbs." Sam C. "Cat" Spencer, and Sam D. "Dog" Spencer, and Sam H. "Hog" Spencer. "If you go down to the crossroads there, you can call anybody you see Mr. Spencer or Mr. Gibbs. There ain't but two men there and one is named Spencer Gibbs and the other Gibbs Spencer."

178. Lather and Shave   Warren Payne, 1951

This is one of the songs Warren Payne sang for us—one which we found particularly interesting since Mr. Payne had lived all his life in rural Hyde County as his father had before him, yet he knew this version of "The Irish Barber," somewhat incomplete though it be.

Laws says the song appeared on several broadsides but gives no dates. Versions appear in Belden, Beck, and several other collections. Laws calls the song the "Love-of-God Shave," and explains that when Pat, or Paddy, asks for a shave on credit the barber uses an old rusty razor he keeps for just such a purpose. Pat then rushes out the door saying he's rather be shaved by a brick. A few days later he hears a jackass bray just as he is passing the barbershop and assumes that some other poor devil is being given a love-of-God shave.

In Peter Kennedy's *Folk Songs of Britain and Ireland* the song is called "The Irish Barber." It has eight verses and the final line is "But, be Japers, I'd sooner be shaved by Old Nick." It also has the refrain:

To me fol-the-diddle-air-o
Fol-the-diddle-air-um
Hi-diddly-air-um
Fol-the-diddle-andy

Kennedy cites sources in Wexford, Ireland, and also in England, in Somerset and Hampshire; as well as those in the United States and one in Australia.

Joseph Hickerson, Head of the Archive of Folk Culture, Music Division, Library of Congress, notes that Norman Cazden reports the appearance of this song "on an 1858 broadside," and that he "finds its earliest printing in a collection to be in *Tony Pastor's Comic and Eccentric Songster* (New York, 1862, pp. 71–72)."

See also "Music of the Catskills" in *New York Folklore Quarterly* 4, no. 1 (Spring 1948): 32–46.

Joe Hickerson recorded the song in 1971 for Folk-Legacy, FSI 39, "Joe Hickerson with a Gathering of Friends."

Folk Songs of the Catskills (Cazden II) has extensive notes on the song and prints two versions with two tunes.

See: Beck, *Songs of the Michigan Lumberjacks,* 225; Belden, 251; Cazden II, 453; Folk-Legacy Recording FSI 39; Henry, *Folksongs from the Southern Highlands,* 409; Kennedy, 510; Laws, *ABBB,* Q-15, 280; Shoemaker, 134

LATHER AND SHAVE

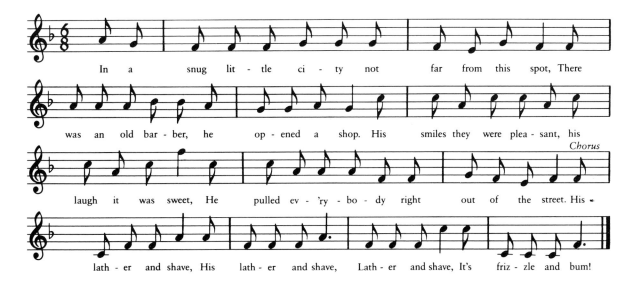

In a snug lit-tle ci-ty not far from this spot, There was an old bar-ber, he op-ened a shop. His smiles they were plea-sant, his laugh it was sweet, He pulled ev-'ry-bo-dy right out of the street. His *Chorus* lath-er and shave, His lath-er and shave, Lath-er and shave, It's friz-zle and bum!

One morning when Paddy was going that way,
His beard had been growing for many a day.
He looked at the barber and give him a nod,
He wanted a shave by the pure love of God.
Chorus

"Walk in," said the barber, "Put down in my chair.
I'll soon mow your beard off right down to a hair."
He spread his lather o'er Paddy's big chin,
And with a straight razor to shave did begin.
Chorus

"Sit still," said the barber, "And don't make a din,
While working your jaws I'll be cutting your chin."
"Not cutting but sawing, with the razor you've got.
It wouldn't cut butter if it was made hot."
    Chorus

"O Mother," says Paddy, "And what are you doin'?
Lay off all your tricks or my jaws you will ruin!
You can shave all your people and shave 'em all sick,
But, Christ, I had rather be shaved with a brick!"
    Chorus

"Lay off all your tricks and don't shave me no more,"
And Paddy he bolted right out of the door.
"You can shave all your people and shave 'em all sick,
But, Christ, I had rather be shaved with a brick."
    Chorus

One morning when Paddy was walking by the door,
The donkey he set up a considerable roar.
"O Mother," says Paddy, "Just listen to 'im rave,
He's singing the tune of love God and shave."
    Chorus

7

Other Places, Other Singers

TOM P. SMITH

SOMETIME IN THE LATE FORTIES in Greenwich Village we met a man named Tom P. Smith who became a close friend until his death in 1959. He lived with his daughter Betty on Christopher Street in the Village, but he was born and bred in West Virginia. Christened "Colonel Tom" by Frank on first acquaintance— perhaps because his tall spare frame and his courtly manners spoke of the old South—he was "Colonel Tom" or "The Colonel" forever after. Colonel Tom gave us a number of interesting songs from his native state. He was a natural storyteller too. His stories were precise and pointed and polished—and often long! But never too long. If one gave the Colonel the time and attention he required, one was never disappointed, or bored. I am sorry that we were too intent, then, on our song collecting to realize that we had a never-to-be-repeated chance to record his stories.

One of his stories we remember, however, because it became part of our own family folklore. I will try to tell it as the Colonel told it to us:

When I was a boy in the nineties we had a colored woman working for us whose name was Doon Coots. The colored community in Guyandotte had a church, but they couldn't support a full-time preacher so they shared one with other churches in nearby towns. He would come to the church in Guyandotte on the fourth Sunday of each month.

Preacher Merritt was impressive. No one could deny that. He was very tall—six feet, six inches. He wore a frock coat and gray-striped trousers and carried a gold-headed cane. His hair and beard were trimmed to look like the Sunday School pictures of the Saviour. He never wore shoes, winter or summer, but he never seemed to experience any discomfort from going barefoot, even with snow on the ground.

On the fourth Sunday all the women in the congregation would prepare dishes for

Anne Warner recording Tom P. Smith in Carl Carmer's living room, upstairs from the Warner apartment—probably to avoid the noise of the children, New York City, 1952.

the occasion. From the pulpit Preacher Merritt would announce his decision as to where he would bestow his favors. "Today, I will take dinner with Sister Tompkins—likewise supper." Then, after church, all the sisters would converge on Sister Tompkins' house with their fried chicken and Brunswick stew and hot biscuits and the rest.

One Sunday Doon Coots hurried home to say the preacher was having dinner at her aunt's and could she go and help out—and of course she could.

The next morning young Tom's mother asked Doon what the day had been like.

"Oh, Mis' Smith," she said, "we had a time. There was ever'thin' on the table— ham and chicken and turnip greens and cornbread—ever'thin' spread out. The preacher, he sat down and he seen a big bowl of somethin' in front of him, so he took a spoon and he reach over and taste it. 'What dis truck?' he say, and somebody say 'Hit's b'iled custard.' He took another bite and then another, and then he say, 'A-law, dis sure *is good*!

Some *ol'* sister fix dis truck. Ain't none o' these younguns could do it!' An' then he wave at the table and say, 'Put these knickknacks away—I'll be back for supper.' An' he pull the bowl over and he eat all of it!"

Ever since hearing that story, when one of the family finds some dish on the table particularly delectable he (or she) will say "Some *ol'* sister . . ." That is a compliment indeed.

Colonel Tom did record for us a few paragraphs about his early life:

> I was born in 1888 down on the south bank of the Ohio River near Kentucky in a little town at the mouth of what they call the Guyandotte Valley, in West Virginia. The river, and later the town, was named Guyandotte by George Washington when he made a survey through there and so it was called during my boyhood. Now it is a part of Huntington. It was the end of the James River and Kanawha Turnpike, before the Civil War, and it handled great hordes of people traveling to the West from Virginia and the Carolinas.
>
> Back of us, immediately up the hill, was the county where my father came from . . . Logan County, which was formerly part of Fincastle County, Virginia. My father's grandfather was the first member of the Virginia legislature from the newly formed county of Logan. He rode to Richmond on a mule and signed the roster with his mark.
>
> My father had a very retentive memory. When he was a child his mother would have an old mountain woman come in to do sewing. She was a singer, and he stuck close around her to learn songs. My mother, on the other hand, picked up a lot of songs which were traditional in her family and came from England through Virginia. . . . The songs she knew and the songs my father knew were of very different types and categories. Naturally I picked up a good deal from the colored people who lived in and around our town, as well as from the mountain people who came down and attended dances . . . and rode their rafts down the river . . . and were always shooting up the town on Saturday night.

After he had sung for us all the songs he could think of one July afternoon in 1949 he said, "I am reminded of the farmer who went out to milk his cow—and he milked, and milked, and milked, and milked—and then threw the hide over the fence!" But nothing gave Colonel Tom more pleasure than sharing his early memories and his songs.

179. The Wreck on the C & O   Tom P. Smith, 1949

Laws says that this ballad "is said to have been composed by a Negro who worked in the round house at Hinton, West Virginia." The story tells of the death of George Alley, engineer of a train wrecked by a landslide near Hinton on October 23, 1890.

Versions of the ballad appear in a number of American collections, and there are extensive notes about it in *A Treasury of Railroad Folklore* by Ben A. Botkin and Alvin F. Harlow, and also in the newly published *Long Steel Rail* by Norm Cohen. Cohen says that "upwards of seventy versions collected by folklorists or their commercial counterparts, the A & R men for the phonograph companies, attest to the widespread popularity of this train-wreck ballad."

Colonel Tom's notes follow:

When I was five years old (during the panic of 1893) one of the great adventures that I had was to go to the depot on Sunday with my father to watch the trains go by. Those first trains on the C & O were very beautiful . . . all painted yellow. The crack train was the F.F.V. . . . Those initials . . . do not denote "Fast Flying Virginian"—that meaning was tacked on to it later. That was the time when railroads were just switching to the first vestibule trains. Up to that time all the trains had open platforms—you had to go outdoors to get from one car to another. The crack train on the C & O, then, was the first one to have the vestibule train. It didn't stop in Guyandotte, and we came to associate the vestibule train with speed.

Sometime in the eighties there was a wreck on the C & O that was immortalized in a song by a colored man who was a cobbler in Montgomery, West Virginia, just east of Charleston. . . . For about thirty or forty years this colored man with a wooden leg would get on every local train that stopped in Montgomery and sell copies of this song . . . for ten cents—just words, no music. . . .

This version of "The Wreck on the C & O" which I am going to give you is creditable to Alec Twyman, a colored man who is still living in this year 1949 in Guyandotte. He then was in his late twenties, . . . worked for the C & O shops, and had an old guitar of which he was the master. He would sit on the Fire House fence at night—a long fence with a platform behind it . . . where the firemen were supposed to drain the hose. They usually forgot, so it froze in winter and rotted out in summer, and the houses always burned down. But Alec would sit there, and we boys would sit just as close as we could get. His voice wouldn't carry more than about ten feet. Alec said he "done et too much tobacca." He chewed "Mail Pouch," and we would beg a little chew from him now and then and sit there in an ecstasy of delight listening to him sing . . . fireflies all around us, and dog fennel fragrant in the town lot behind us.

It seems that crack train #4 on the C & O was going east in the night or early morning. Her engineer was a young man from Hinton named George Alley. With him was Jack Dickerson, his fireman, who later on, and until he was an old old man, was the pilot on the F.F.V. on the C & O. . . . Alec could play an accompaniment that sounded exactly like the railroad trains screaming through the narrow valleys, and you could hear that roar of the wheels and that lonesome die-away whistle that you hear in the mountains and that makes your heart go right down into your boots. And when the train ran into the station to take water, with Alec in charge of that guitar you could hear the injector of the engine take water. . . .

I have treasured this song that Alec Twyman sang so much and so long that I feel just a little bit of hesitancy about singing it. It is sort of a desecration of a work of art for me to do it. . . . But I just want to get it on some sort of record.

Carl Sandburg, in his *American Songbag* (p. 371), prints just the chorus of this song (with some variations), calling it "There's Many a Man Killed on the Railroad."

There's many a man killed on the railroad, railroad, railroad,
There's many a man killed on the railroad
An' cast in a lonely grave.

See: Botkin, *A Treasury of Railroad Folklore,* 451; Cohen, 183; Cox, 224; Laws, *NAB,* G-3, 218;
Lomax, *ABF,* 31; Randolph, Vol. 4, 124

THE WRECK ON THE C & O

Oh, down— comes old Num-ber Four,[1] the fast-est on the line, A-
(repeat 1st verse only)

run-ning o-ver the C & O road, twen-ty min-utes be-hind time. They
And his

run her in-to Hin-ton, her en-gi-neer was there. George
part-ner, Jack— Dick-er-son, was rid-in' by his side, *Chorus* A-

Al-ley was his name, with bright and gold-en hair. Oh,
wait-in' for their orders, in the cab-in they did ride.[2]

man-y a man's been mur-dered by the rail-road, By the

1. Although most versions of this ballad begin "Down comes the F.F.V., the fastest on the line," and although Colonel Tom discusses the F.F.V. in his story about the train, his version of the song refers to "old Number Four" instead.
2. Colonel Tom solved the problem of singing these two extra lines to the first verse by using once more the second half of the tune for that verse.

rail - road, by the rail - road. Oh, man-y a man's been mur - dered by the rail - road, And sleep - in' in his lone - some grave. —

George Alley's mother came to him with a bucket
    on her arm,
And begged her son to quit the road before he came
    to harm.
He said, "All right, now Mother dear, don't you
    worry about your son.
I'se a-comin' back here to live with you, but I'se
    a-goin' to make this one last run."

George Alley says to his partner Jack, "Now give me
    a little extra steam
For I'se a-goin' to run old Number Four the fastest
    ever was seen.
Oh, over this road I means to fly, with a speed
    unknown to all,
And when I whistle for Big Ben Tunnel, they are
    surely goin' to hear my call."

George Alley says to his partner Jack, "A rock ahead
    I see,
And none is here to save this train excepting you
    and me.
Now from this cabin you must jump, your own
    dear life to save.
I wants you to be an engineer when I'se a-sleepin' in
    my grave."

"Oh, no, Georgie, that won't do, I wants to die
    with you."
"No, no, Jack, don't talk that way, I want to die for
    me and you."
From that cabin he did jump, old New River was
    high,
And kissed his hand to Georgie, as old Number Four
    flew by.

George Alley's mother came to him, when she heard
    that he must die,
And bowed her head upon his bed, and softly she
    did cry.
But the preacher man says, "Miz' Alley, your boy did
    save that train.
And heaven did send him on that last run—he
    surely didn't die in vain."

180. Git Along, Josie   Tom P. Smith, 1949

The Brown University Harris Collection calls this song "Jim Along Josie" and
says that it "was another sweeping success in the burnt-cork tradition." S. Foster Da-

mon's notes go on to say that the song was written by Edward Harper, who sang it in his drama 'The Free Nigger of New York' about 1838 (E. L. Rice: *Monarchs of Minstrelsy,* p. 24).

Tom Smith said, "My mother learned this song from old Uncle Fred, my grandfather's personal man. He had almost nothing to do except have a good time and play his banjo and go in and out of the kitchen and torment the colored women in there. He was polite society, always dressed up in my grandfather's clothes. He could promote him out of them before they were worn much, and grandfather always said it made him mad because Fred looked better in his clothes than he did! This song was one of Uncle Fred's favorites. These are the words I remember."

Frank Warner found the tune approximately the same as one he heard in his childhood, with the words:

Run nigger, run, the patterol'll ketch you
Run nigger, run, it's almost day . . .

This referred to the "patrol" which saw to it, in slavery days, that all blacks were back on their respective plantations by sundown. For further reference to this song see Rounder Record #1005, a re-recording of "Gid Tanner and Skillet Lickers" (1927), "Run Nigger Run" or "The Pateroller Song."

GIT ALONG, JOSIE

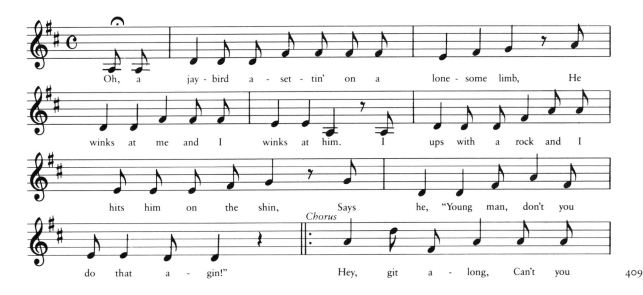

Oh, a jay-bird a-set-tin' on a lone-some limb, He
winks at me and I winks at him. I ups with a rock and I
hits him on the shin, Says he, "Young man, don't you
do that a-gin!" Hey, git a-long, Can't you

git a - long, Jo - sie?   Hey, git a - long, Can't you   git a - long, Joe?

Oh, de woodchucker laughed at de banjo song,
And he axed me to play old Hey Git Along.
And to please dese varmints style up a gum [in high
    style]
I plays up Jinny, git yo' hoe-cake done!
Chorus

181. Lynchburg Town   Tom P. Smith, 1949

Colonel Tom told us that he learned this song from his mother, who had learned it from "old Uncle Fred, her father's body servant." It is an example of the many early blackface minstrel songs which found their way into oral tradition. This is one of the type that gathers its verses as it goes and swaps with similar songs. Sandburg includes a version called "Goin' Down to Town" with the same last verse.

Frank Proffitt in North Carolina gave us an unusual variant which he called "Lebeck Town."

Goin' down to town,
Goin' down to town,
Goin' down to Lebeck town
To weigh my tobacco down.

Comin' in to town,
Goin' to buy my gal a gown.
If she don't hug my neck,
I'll stomp it in the ground.

Comin' home from town
With as much as I can bring,
Hearin' that peckerwood
A-peckin' on a string.

Goin' down to town,
Goin' down to town,
Goin' down to Lebeck town
To weigh my tobacco down.

See: Brown Vol. 3, 498; Lomax, *Our Singing Country*, 60; Sandburg, *The American Songbag*, 145

Oh, I wished I had a big black hoss, A sad-dle, and some corn, And a pret-ty lit-tle gal fer to stay at home And to feed him when I'm gone. *Chorus* Oh, I'se goin' down to town, I'se goin' down to town, I'se goin' down to Lynch-burg town, Fer to tote my to-bac-cer down.

Oh, if I had a scoldin' wife,
As sure as you air born,
I'd tote her down to New Orleans,
And trade her off for corn!
Chorus

I'm gonna get some sticks and stones
To make my chimbley higher,
To keep that doggone old tom cat
From puttin' out my fire.
Chorus

"Lynchburg Town"
Collected and Arranged by Frank Warner
TRO—© Copyright 1959 and 1984 Hollis Music, Inc., New York, N.Y. Used by Permission

182. The Old Geezer   Tom P. Smith, 1949

Colonel Tom, when he sang us this bit of nonsense, said, "I'm tired of hearing people sing this song to the tune of 'Turkey in the Straw.' I am going to give you the correct melody which has been lost in antiquity, of which I seem to be the only living representative!"

Carl Sandburg has a somewhat longer version in his *American Songbag* which he calls "There Was an Old Soldier." Of it he says: "A leading favorite of the Grand Old Army of the Republic, one of the healthiest survivors of the contest between the Blue and the Gray, and a widely-known piece of American folklore."

Folk Songs of the Catskills (Cazden II) has extensive notes tracing the probable origins of this nonsense ditty.

See: Cazden II, 533; Sandburg, *The American Songbag*, 432

Oh, there was an old gee-zer, and he had a wood-en leg, And he had no to-bac-co, but to-bac-co he would beg. An-oth-er old gee-zer—— he had a wood-en crutch; He al-ways had to-bac-co, but he nev-er had much.

Said geezer number one, "Won't you give me
a chew?"
Said geezer number two, "I'll be durned if I do!
If you'll always save your money and not throw away
your rocks,
You will always have tobacco in your old tobacco
box."

JOSEPH HENRY JOHNSON

It took more than a day, in 1940, to get from New York to North Carolina. On our trip south that year we made it as far as Suffolk, Virginia, after driving through miles of peanut fields north of the city limits. We decided to stop there so that we could drive through the Dismal Swamp by daylight rather than at night. As we drove in we saw a huge sign on top of the bank building: "Suffolk, Va., Peanut Capital of the World." It was true—Suffolk was and is the home of Planters Peanuts and any number of other processors of peanut butter, peanut brittle, peanut oil, fertilizer, and the home of the Virginia-Carolina Peanut Association.

We found a room for the night and went to the Elliott Café for dinner. A tall young black man waited on our table, and before ordering we asked him if he knew anybody thereabout who might know the old-time songs. Our waiter (his name was Bill Moss) studied[3] a bit and allowed that there *must* be somebody. "Let me call Jesse," he said. So the other waiter (a very short young man named Jesse McDonald) joined us. "These people," said Bill, "are looking for somebody around here who knows the old-time songs." Jesse pondered. "Well, let's see," he said, and then, "Well, there's Uncle Joe — *he* knows all those old songs." Bill objected. "But you know Uncle Joe is dead!" "No," said Jesse. "He's mighty low, but he ain't dead."

After some discussion, they agreed to meet us in the morning (it would be Sunday) and to take us to find Uncle Joe, which they did. He lived way out at the end of town, in a pretty cottage with hollyhocks growing up to the roof. His wife had died, and he was staying with a niece, Mamie Baker, and her family. As we drove through that part of town, through every open window we could hear that wonderful radio program which was so justifiably popular at that time, "Wings Over Jordan," an inspiring chorus of black voices that seemed a foretaste of heaven. We like, too, to remember passing a restaurant called "Deep Evening Café."

Bill went in the house to see how the land lay, and came out to say that although Uncle Joe had had a stroke and was bedridden, he would be glad to see us. So we all went in — through the house and the kitchen, greeting everyone getting ready for church or Sunday School, then out through the dogtrot to another cottage where we found Uncle Joe lying in a big double bed.

Frank talked to him for a few minutes, and then sang him a verse of a song he'd learned in his childhood in Alabama:

> Oh, the raccoon got a bushy tail,
> And the possum tail hit's bare,
> And the rabbit ain't got no tail a-tall
> 'Cep' a little bunch of hair.

Uncle Joe grinned. He said he "surely *did* know that song."

Joseph Henry Johnson was his name, but everyone in Suffolk called him Uncle Joe. He was an admired citizen as well as an uncommon salesman, for he sold peanuts on the streets of Suffolk to people uniformly engaged in raising or processing peanuts. He knew his product. He raised his own peanuts, picked, parched, and packaged them, and carried them up and down the streets in a big basket while shouting his own original vending cry, for which he was famous: "Fresh peanuts is the best of all." One line he often used, "Buy 'em and try 'em!" became the slogan of the peanut industry. When people heard Uncle Joe's cry in the mid-morning or afternoon they would leave their shops or offices or homes and go out to greet him, to buy a bag of peanuts, and to listen to his songs. But Uncle Joe's real profession, he told us, was preaching the love

3. Frank told this story many times over the intervening years on the concert and lecture stage and always, as was natural to him, slipped into the southern idiom. The story is told in Frank's words.

Bill Moss and Jesse McDonald in Suffolk, Virginia, 1940.

of God. So when he had gathered some people around him, he would sing them the old spirituals or the Bible A-B-C or his own songs, such as "Nothing Seems Better to Me" (No. 185).

Bill went out to the car for the recording machine, since Uncle Joe said he'd like to try it, and we recorded his "Fresh Peanuts" and as many songs as he had strength to sing. His voice was weak but his spirit was strong. That morning with Uncle Joe has been an influence in our lives ever since. When he died, not many months thereafter, the editor of the Suffolk newspaper (whom we had met during our stay there) sent us a double-page spread from the paper about Uncle Joe's story and the tributes to him from fellow townspeople.

To quote from an earlier Suffolk *News-Herald* story of January 27, 1941, before Uncle Joe's death:

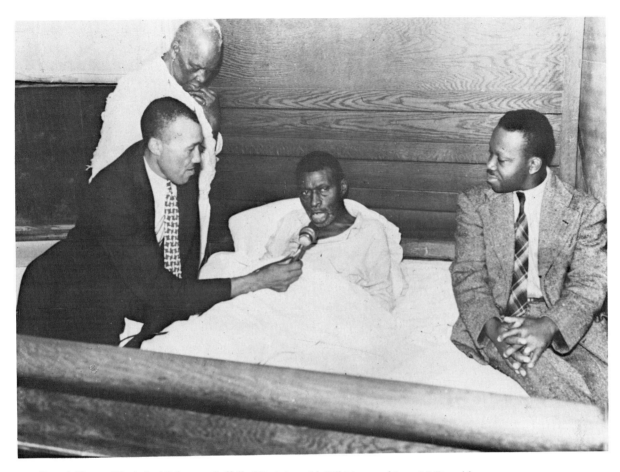

Joseph Henry (Uncle Joe) Johnson, Suffolk, Virginia, with Bill Moss and Jesse McDonald, 1940. Standing is Aunt Armise Spruille, who had been a slave in her childhood.

During National Peanut Week and the National Peanut Festival the goober will have many bi-phrases to catch the attention of the American public. The best of them all is "Buy 'em and try 'em," . . . the work of a 70-year-old Negro peanut salesman on the streets of Suffolk. . . .

Early in the morning Uncle Joe Henry Johnson . . . gets to the city market where he starts off on his selling turn. Everybody in ear-shot turns to at his opening "OO-Ow-o-o-o, I got FRESH PEANUTS this mawnin', one bag for a nickel, two for a dime." People stop their work . . . they smile and break out laughing. But laughing with him, not at him. . . . They seem to get a brief respite from their worldly worries as the old peanut peddler carries on with his homemade rhymes.

Joseph Henry Johnson was an important citizen in Suffolk, Virginia, and an important person in our lives.

183. The Bible A-B-C   Joseph Henry Johnson, 1940

This alphabet is quite different from the two other alphabet songs we collected—"The Woodsman's Alphabet" from John Galusha in New York's Adirondack Mountains, and "The Sailor's Alphabet" from Captain Etheridge on North Carolina's Outer Banks. This, to Uncle Joe, was a recitation. He said it very quickly, almost in a monotone, so that getting all the words down correctly was difficult.

Joseph Henry Johnson was a devout Christian and he really knew his Bible. Whether he put this together himself, we don't know; but he surely could have done so.

THE BIBLE A-B-C

A is for Adam who was the first man
B is for Bethlehem where Jesus was born
C is for Cain who slayed his brother
D is for Dan'l who was cast in the lions' den
E is for Elijah who was taken up to heaven
F is for the flood that drownded the world
G is for the giant Goliath who was slayed by David
H is for Hannah who gave her son Samuel to the Lord
I is for Isaac the son of Abraham
J is for Jacob who interpreted the dream
K is for Korah who was swallowed up by the earth
L is for Lazarus who Christ raised from the dead
M is for Methuselah who was the oldest man

N is for Nazareth the home of Jesus
O is for Olive the Mount where Jesus prayed
P is for Pharoah who was drowned in the Red Sea
Q is for the Queen of Sheba who visited Solomon
R is for Rome where Paul was put in prison
S is for Sodom the city destroyed by fire
T is for Tyre where Paul preached all night
U is for Uzzah who steered the Ark
V is for the vine, represents Christ
W is for the Watchman on the wall of Zion
X is for the Cross of Christ
Y is for the yoke of Christ
Z is for Zion the home of the blessed

184. Fresh Peanuts![4]   Joseph Henry Johnson, 1940

Street cries are a part of folklore, the earliest form of advertising. Most everyone knows the verse about "Sweet Molly Malone"—

4. See the article by Anne Warner, "Fresh Peanuts is the Best of All: A Street Cry from Suffolk, Virginia" in *Folklore and Folklife in Virginia* 1 (1979): 68–72.

She wheeled her wheelbarrow
Through streets wide and narrow
Crying Cockles! and Mussels!
Alive, alive-o.

But street cries were everywhere in the new world as well as in Dublin's fair city, and not just in the South—though one is apt to associate them with Charleston and New Orleans. In 1730, we have been told, there was a black man named Black Peg who used to peddle hot ears of corn on the streets of New York City[5] crying:

Hot corn, hot corn! I have to sell
Come buy my corn, I'll treat you well
My corn is good and that I know
For on Long Island it did grow.

We have picked up other interesting examples of the art. An old Negro in Salisbury, North Carolina, where trains used to stop to let passengers have lunch in the station restaurant, used to consider the passengers left on the train (those who didn't go to the restaurant) his customers. He would go through the train with a big basket on his arm, flinging open the door of each car in turn and announcing:

I got ham and chicken sandwiches,
Hard-boiled eggs and pie.
I'll be here—you'll be gone—
You'll be hongry!

We've been told he never failed to sell all his wares.

FRESH PEANUTS!

Fresh peanuts! Is the best of all,
They's raised in the summer and dug in the fall.
I got fresh peanuts! One bag for a nickle,
One bag for a nickle, and two for a dime,
Three fifteen, and all of 'em mine.

If you don't think they good, just buy 'em and try 'em!
Shelled by the hand, parched in the pan,
I has to sell every one if I can.
Please don't deny 'em, just step up and buy 'em,
I got fresh peanuts!

5. From the Fall 1943 issue of the *Nassau County Historical Journal.*

Joe *Henry* Johnson is my name!
Selling peanuts is my game.
I got fresh peanuts! One bag for a nickle,
One bag for a nickle, and two for a dime,
Three fifteen and all of 'em mine.

You don't think they good just buy 'em and try 'em!
Shelled by the hand, parched in the pan,
I has to sell every one if I can.
Please don't deny 'em, just step up and buy 'em!
I got fresh peanuts!

I'll sell a who-o-ole five cents worth for just one
        nickle,
I'll sell a who-o-ole ten cents worth for one little
        dime.
A who-o-ole twenty-five cents worth for a quarter
        of a dollar!
I got fresh peanuts!

185. Nothing Seems Better to Me   Joseph Henry Johnson, 1940

This is one of Uncle Joe's own songs. He put it together out of his deep feelings and his belief in the Almighty.

Uncle Joe's voice was so weak when he attempted to sing this song that, unfortunately, the tune cannot be determined. Even as a recitation it carries his spirit.

NOTHING SEEMS BETTER TO ME

There is a place where I must go,
This is the part interresses me so.
I'll go on fighting for mercy so free,
Nothing seems better to me.
    Chorus
    Nothing seems better to me,
    Nothing seems better to me,
    And now I am fighting for free liber*tee,*
    Nothing seems better to me.

Nothing, oh, nothing, no where I've been,
Since Jesus has promised he'd shelter me in.
Whilst I am shouting salvation so free,
Nothing seems better to me.
    Chorus

Nothing, oh, nothing, that I can *find,*
This is the thing interresses my mind.
Singing and shouting for eterni*tee,*
Nothing seems better to me.
    Chorus

418

Nothing, oh, nothing, that I con*test,* [can test?]
That seems to fill my sad heart's request.
Since Jesus have shook that 'Manuel tree,
Nothing seems better to me.
    Chorus

Nothing, oh, nothing, that I can *tell,*
Nothing seems to suit my conscience so well.
My voice will be shouting, "Oh, great jubilee!"
Nothing seems better to me.
    Chorus

ARMISE SPRUILLE ASKEW

Uncle Joe was living with his niece Mamie Baker, and also with her grandmother, Armise Spruille Askew, known as Aunt Armise. The next summer—1941—after Uncle Joe's death, we went back and had a visit with Aunt Armise. Here are some excerpts from my notes made at that time:

> You-all looks peart as a cricket. . . . Yassir, I caught your favor just as soon as you come in. [Meaning she recognized us from the year before.]
> [About Uncle Joe:] *Most every*body liked him. You know, I don' care *how* good you are, ever'body ain't goin' to like you. But *most* ever'body liked him.
> [When asked how old she was:] Lord, Lord, Lord. I *do* not know! I *do* not know. When I was young they never tol' chirren their ages nohow. . . .
> I didn't belong to *nobody* but my daddy, but my daddy belonged to a lawyer named Spruille so I was a Spruille. Mitty they called me, but my name was Armise. Ever'body on the plantation wanted to play with me. . . . They took me from my mammy before I was done nursin', and when I'd see my mammy I'd holler, "Titty mammy! Titty mammy!" till ever'body called me "Titty mammy." They called me "old 'oman" when I war little. . . . I was the pet.
> I was raised *way* down South, in Edenton. I was raised by a white woman who never struck me a lick. . . .
> I used to be mean . . . when the chirren would get me mad I wouldn't fight, I would go to kill. I killed a boy dead one day. My mother was washin' clothes, and she asked me to bring three buckets of water from the well. Some people could jist put a bucket on their head and tote steady-headed, but I would hol' onto it with one hand. On the way back the first time a boy chunked me . . . and he did it the second time, and the third time . . . with a half a bat between the shoulders. I didn't say nothin' . . . I jist put the bucket down and picked up the bat and let him have it . . . then picked up the bucket and went on . . . then I jist went in and sat by the fireplace. His mama came and said, "Your girl killed my boy!" My mammy was washin' . . . she took her arms out of the tub and shook 'em to get the suds off and wiped her hands on her apron and went over. The boy was lyin' there dead, with the blood runnin' out of his nose . . . but he got all right later. That night Uncle Mose called daddy, "Elder Spruille, your gal killed my boy today." Daddy said, "I tol' him about that gal . . . Cornshoe the eternal heart, I tol' him she would kill." That was a by-cuss. He said, "How come you killed that boy?" I said, "Daddy, I

toted the two buckets and put 'em in the tub and Bud chunked me, he hit me right between the shoulders, and I picked up the bat and sent it over the palings at him."

I cut a boy once and sent him from the beach. I was on the beach [Nag's Head] cutting fish, had a pinie [a knife] on my wrist sharp as a razor. I went down for a fortnight before they hung up the seines and Old Man Spruille was down there. He says, "Can you cut fish? Le' me show you how to cut fish." They give me the knife. . . . I'd never cut herring before, but I did jist as good as he did. I hadn't been there a week before a feller said, "That's a pretty gal, I'm goin' to hug her." I says, "You better not put yo' hands on me!" I went to the spring and when I come back, there he was and he started to put his hands on me . . . and I set down the buckets and made a cut and then crossed it. He was sure bleedin' and had to go from the beach. Tom Hunt Holley said, "God damn it, you should have cut his God damn guts out!" He was the keenest cussin' man I ever *did* see in my life. Nobody didn't ever bother me no more. . . .

You know you have a hard time in this worl', but if the Old Man gets you you'll have a worser one. . . . the Devil, he tries to dominize the Bible. . . .

The citizens on Roanoke Island after the Surrender tried to catch the black chirren to carry 'em to the old wheat thrashers, but the Yankee soldiers would save 'em. We thought they was the most beautiful men we ever saw, with gold buttons. But they looked like the sun never did shine on 'em because they never smiled. . . .

This is a little song Aunt Armise remembered:

Poor railroad man, he ain't got no home,
He's here today and tomorrow gone.
I wish to the Lord the train would blow
And take me back to the pantry do'.

ANONYMOUS

186. Raccoon

The first two verses of this song Frank learned in his childhood, before he realized that he was learning songs. Perhaps he learned them from the black children with whom he played in Selma, Alabama, before he left there at the age of six. He never sang with an old-time black man or woman who did not know this song. It always brought back memories of their childhood, how the "old man" would play the banjo while the "chillen" danced, and how every now and then he would stop and sing a verse.

The other two verses Frank added over the years—we are not sure from where.

In the late forties, when Frank's mother, Mabel Preston Warner, was living with us in New York City, after Frank's father's death, she remembered another three verses which she said she "heard Negroes singing in the cotton fields in Dallas County, Alabama," when she was a girl.

> I went down to that Hog-eye town
> And sot me down to the table,
> I et so much of that hog-eye grease
> Hit all run out my nable.

> I took my gal to the ball las' night
> And sat her down to supper,
> She fainted and fell from the big armchair
> And stuck her nose in the butter.

> Possum's in the holler tree,
> Turkey's in the straw,
> Don't dance after the cake is in
> You're sho' to make it raw [to make it fall].

Brown says that "The raccoon has a bushy tail" stanza "appeared early in blackface minstrel songs." Davis reports it from Virginia and Randolph from Missouri. Randolph's notes are interesting. He says the verse derives "from an ante-bellum minstrel bit entitled 'Old Sandy Boy,' (*Negro Singers' Own Book,* 1846, p. 309)" and he adds the refrain:

> Oh come a-long, oh Sandy boy,
> Oh come a-long, oh do,
> Oh what will Uncle Gabriel Say?
> Kitty cain't you come a-long too?

The verse is found also in Newman I. White's *American Negro Folk Songs,* as collected from Alabama Negroes, which takes us back to Frank's earliest memories of the song.

See: Brown, Vol. 3, 208; Davis, *Folk-Songs of Virginia,* 319; Randolph, Vol. 2, 334;
White, *American Negro Folk Songs,* 234

RACCOON

Oh, the rac - coon got a bush - y tail, And the

pos - sum tail hit's bare, And the rab - bit ain't got no

tail a - tall 'Cep' a lit - tle bunch of hair. ————

Love, hit is a killin' fit,
Beauty hit's a blossom,
Effen yo' want yo' finger bit,
Jes' stick it at a possum!

I tuck my gal to the barbecue,
And this is all she'd eat:
Was a pot and a half of Brunswick stew,
An' a side and a half of meat!

Love, hit is a funny thing,
Shaped jes' like a lizard,
Crawls right down your backbone,
And nibbles at yo' gizzard.

REBECCA KING JONES

Frank's mother took us first to see Rebecca King Jones in 1939. We are not sure how she knew of her. Rebecca lived off the Raleigh road—Route 70, between Durham and Raleigh—in the section known as Crab Tree Creek. She lived alone (as she said, "except for Jesus") in a small cabin in the woods. She wore, usually, a calico dress and apron, boots, and a sunbonnet. She was then in her seventies, but she carried her own water, milked her cow, and raised her own chickens and her own vegetables. She was a gay and loving spirit. "Here are my chirren!" she would say, greeting us with a hug. When we first played back one of her disks so she could hear how she sounded, she said, "Well! I didn't know my voice *was* so purty!" It was, too, high and clear and sweet. She said, "It was a plum gift from the Lord—to give me this voice. That's a talent the Lord gives you."

Perhaps because she was so eager to please, she would plunge into a song whether she fully remembered the words or not. Sometimes she would substitute words that came to her on the spur of the moment. But some of her songs were lovely and complete, her "Barbara Allen" for instance, for which she knew two tunes, or "Drowsy

Rebecca King Jones, Crab Tree Creek, North Carolina, 1940.

Sleeper," or "Pretty Polly." And even some that sound garbled are interesting variations.

One day, when we were spending some time in Durham, we went out to Crab Tree Creek and carried Rebecca home to have lunch with us and with Frank's mother. Rebecca dressed up for the occasion, in a gray satin dress with lace at the throat, and a white hat. We had a fine recording session which we all enjoyed enormously, and then lunch. Her manners were charming. She ate everything with a spoon, but arranged her knife and fork on her plate as the rest of us did.

On the way home she told us about the medicines and cures that were used when she was a girl:

> To cure dropsy, soak nine cut nails [hand made, or "cut"] in a pint of apple vinegar and a pint of black molasses.
> For open sores, evergreen roots and leaves boiled in hot lard.
> For a tonic, boil wild cherry bark, a handful of sarsaparilla, a pint of apple vinegar, rock candy, and a pint of good whiskey—take a spoonful before breakfast.
> Sprained ankle, put under waterfall.

Rebecca said, "I'm afraid to look for love root [ginseng?] because I am loving too good anyway!" And she said, "I've seen old wizards pass my home right often." We wonder what they looked like!

Rebecca recorded for us a few of her early memories:

> I was born the sixteenth of April in 1866—the year after the war's surrender—the spring after the Yankees come through. My father came home then. He fought at Gettysburg and he come home through Manassas Gap.
>
> I was raised a hard worker to the plow handle, the grubbin' hoe, axe, and workin' in the cotton gin, driving a steer cart. I went to Raleigh and drove a ox cart once when there was some young men come out driving of a nice little pony, and they says to me, "Let's have a race!" And I said, "All right, good old boy, let's go to it!" My father had sent me down to get plow points and such things as you need to work on the farm. He would trust me to go anywhere. He said he would trust me to take a thousand dollars—if I lived, he knew I would bring every penny back 'cep' what he tol' me to spend. . . . Anyway, this boy couldn't make a thing off me—I kept right up behind them with my ox. They thought I would just sit there and not say anythin', but I was ready fer 'em at that time. I said, "Tom, let's go!" and he did. He was one old cow I tell you. The boys said, "I don't want to race with you again—that's the travelin'est cow I ever see in all my life!"
>
> You know one Sunday, we were comin' home from Sunday School and there was several boys that wanted to come home with me, but I felt embarrassed, you know, me being bar-footed too. So I ran away from 'em and went home and my grandfather says to me, "Honey, why didn't you let the boys come home with you? You shouldn't have

run away from 'em like that." I said, "O Grandfather, I couldn't let them see the prints of my toes in the sand! . . . comin' home with young men! Let 'em court someone else that's got shoes on—grown wimmin. I don't claim myself to be grown till I have some shoes."

So my granddaddy said, "Al, you buy Becky some shoes. She's too old to be going bar-foot." My father say, "She never said anythin' about it." And granddaddy say, "She didn't want to put you to no expense." About five or six months after that my father got me some shoes. I was about fifteen then, I guess.

I have lots of friends, but the Lord is my best friend. He is my keeper.

Once she said to us: "My life has been wonderful to myself . . . and to others too . . . Mr. Warner. . . . A man might be the vilest sinner, but I would get down in the dust of the road to pray for him if it would save his soul. . . . There is no one can see God but the pure in heart . . . it must be undefiled."

This is one of several letters we have from Rebecca:

Cary, N C
November 11 1940

My Dear children I am sure sory I havnt riten you before now I had lost your areDress and couldent find it untill now. . . . I reseivied the picters and they weare just good and I shure thank you and Mr Frank it was just sweet of you both being so kind well Annie I have had cold and had it rite tuff. . . . I am still going and I truly hope this will find you both well and happy With much love to you both

Rebecca K Jones

We saw Rebecca again after the war, but a few years after that we found she was no longer living in her little house and we were never able to get in touch with her again. We don't know when she died.

187. Barbara Allen   Rebecca King Jones, 1941

Rebecca gave us this lovely and complete version of the ballad (Child No. 84) which she called "Barbrew Allen," and two uncommonly beautiful tunes.

Lena Bourne Fish, in New Hampshire, also gave us a complete text of "Barbara Allen," with a tune very different from Rebecca's and also very fine. Her version does not include the rose and briar ending which Belden says is almost unfailing in American copies although it does not appear in the Child versions. For Mrs. Fish's variant of the ballad, see song No. 40.

See: Child No. 84, 180 ("Bonny Barbara Allen"); Coffin and Renwick, 82, 239; Belden, 60

One morning in the month of May
When the red buds they were swelling,
Young William Green on his deathbed lay
For the love of Barbrew Allen.

He sent his servant to this town
To the place where she was dwellin',
Saying, "O my love, I will call for you
If your name be Barbrew Allen."

So she arose and went to him
To the place where he was lying,
And every word she could say to him,
"Young man I believe you are dying."

"Oh, yes, I am sick and I'm very sick,
And I'm on my deathbed lying,
But one sweet kiss from your rosy lips
Mought save me from dying."

He raised his hands from the cold clad sheets
Where his body was lying,
She drew herself away from him,
"Young William, I cannot have you."

So he turns his face against the wall,
She turns her back upon him,
Says he, "Say adieu to the ladies all
And adieu to Barbrew Allen."

So she arose and left the room
Where her true love was dying,
And all the friends there seems to say,
"Hard-hearted Barbrew Allen."

So she walks away across the fields
As if to drew herself from him,
And all the little birds singing seems to say,
"Hard-hearted Barbrew Allen."

So she did not get more than a half a mile
Before she heard those death bells ringing,
And they rang so clearly and seems to say,
"Hard-hearted Barbrew Allen."

So lay him down here upon the ground
And let me look upon him,
Then the more she looked the more she weeped,
And she broke down in crying.

Then she stooped and kissed his cold pale cheeks
That she had refused him dying,
Says, "Mother, O Mother, you are the cause of this,
You would not let me have him."

"Mother, O Mother, go make my bed,
Go make it soft and narrow,
For William Green has died for pure pure love,
But I will die for sorrow."

"Father, O Father, go and dig my grave,
Go dig it deep and narrow,
For William Green has died for me today,
I will die for him tomorrow."

"He will be buried in the old churchyard,
And I shall be buried by him."
And out of his grave springs a red rose vine,
And out of hers a sweet brier.

And they grew and grew to the old church top,
And they could not grow any higher,
And locked and tied in a true lovers' knot,
And the rose run around the brier.

188. Wake, O Wake, You Drowsy Sleeper   Rebecca King Jones, 1939

A number of people sang versions of this song to us, one of them which we liked very much was from Lee Monroe Presnell on Beech Mountain. We like Rebecca's best of all, perhaps because her way of singing it made it particularly appealing.

The song—about a lover at his lady's window begging her to go away with him in spite of her parents' opposition to the idea—has various endings. In some versions she agrees to go with him, in some she says she cannot and expects to die of sorrow, in others both lovers die from self-inflicted stabbings. The tragic ending results from the song having been mixed in many cases with another song (apparently of American origin) called "The Silver Dagger" which does end with a double suicide. We have not found any version except Rebecca's that ends with the charming verse:

"A pretty flower was made to bloom, love,
Pretty stars were made to shine,
And pretty girls was made for boys, love,
And maybe you was made for mine."

Uncle Monroe's version, which he called "Awake, Awake, My Own True Loveyer,"[6] has eight verses—two more than Rebecca's six—but it tells the same story. It ends:

Come back, come back, my own true love-yer
And stay a little while with me.
I will forsake my dear old mother
And go along by the side of thee.

The song is widespread on both sides of the Atlantic. For a study of the antiquity and range of its theme Belden suggests consulting C. R. Baskervill's paper in the *PMLA* 36: 565–614. Versions have been reported from Surrey, Sussex, Dorset, and Somerset, and on this side of the water from Virginia (Sharp), West Virginia (Cox), New York (Thompson), Mississippi (Hudson), etc. Many of the versions (as in two of Belden's Missouri texts) have the "Silver Dagger" tragic ending.
Laws refers to a broadside of the song published by H. J. Wehman.
Uncle Monroe said of the song, "That's an old old song, sung in the earliest times in this country."

See: Belden, 118; Cazden II, 197; Cox, 348; Hudson, 161; Laws, *ABBB*, M-4, 181;
Sharp, *English Folksongs of the Southern Appalachians,* Vol. 1, 361; Thompson, 390

WAKE, O WAKE, YOU DROWSY SLEEPER

"Wake, O wake,—— you —— drow-sy sleep-er, Wake, O wake,——

6. *The Oxford Universal Dictionary* gives this way of pronouncing "lover" as an obsolete form which dates to Middle English (1150–1450).

it is al - most day. How can you sleep, you —— cru - el

crea - ture, Since you have stol'n —— my heart a - way?"

"O hush, hush, hush, don't you wake my mother.
No songs of love will she let me hear.
If you sing songs, go court some other,
And whisper lowly in my ear."

"Come go with me, you will stop my pining,
And sit you down by the side of me,
And lay your loving arms around me,
And say you'll love no one but me."

"My father he lies in the next room simple,
A-taking of his natural rest,
And in his hand he holds a weapon,
He swears he will kill the one I love best."

"I'll go with you in some lonesome valley,
And I will spend my days with you,
Although my meat may be pretty berries,
And the water that I drink be the morning dew."

"A pretty flower was made to bloom, love,
Pretty stars were made to shine,
And pretty girls was made for boys, love,
And maybe you was made for mine."

189. Chimbley Sweeper   Rebecca King Jones, 1940

This is one of the two play-party songs Rebecca gave us which we assumed were
her own and not to be found elsewhere. To our astonished delight we have found this
one in Leah Jackson Wolford's *The Play-Party in Indiana* (p. 173), first issued in 1917,
edited and revised in 1959 by W. Edson Richmond and William Tillson and published
by the Indiana Historical Society *Publications* 20, no. 2 (Indianapolis, 1959). Bill Tillson was a good friend of ours, and he gave us our copy of the book in 1960. In it this
song is called "I'm a Poor Old Chimney Sweeper." The words are almost identical, and
there are the same number of verses. What is more, it gives directions for the dance,
which it says is a "circle dance for any number of players." We are including the directions at the end of these notes with the kind permission of the Indiana Historical Society.

The notes in the Indiana book (p. 282) say that the song "appears to be confined
to the Middle West," a statement which perhaps must be somewhat amended by our
having found it in North Carolina. The notes refer (re: the last stanza of the song)
to Thomas Talley's *Negro Folk Rhymes* (p. 143), "Slave Marriage Ceremony Supple-

ment." We remember that Alex Haley in *Roots* (Doubleday, 1976) speaks of the slave marriage ceremony of stepping over a broomstick.

These are the directions for the dance: All join hands to form a circle around one boy who stands in the center and sweeps the ground with a large broom. During 1 (I am a poor old chimbley sweeper / I have but one daughter, and now I can't keep her) those in the ring circle left. At 2 (So since she has resolved to marry /Go choose you one and do not tarry) the boy in the center circles right inside the ring, scanning the girl players for a partner. He carries the broom in his right arm as if it were a gun, and at 3 (Now you have one of your own choosing / You have no time for to be losing) places it on the ground between him and the girl chosen. At 4 (So join your right hand) / they join right hands, and at 5 (this broom step over / You can kiss the lips of your own true lover), each places his (and her) right foot over the broomstick, and the boy kisses his partner. He steps over the broomstick, taking his partner's former place in the ring. At the same time she steps over the broomstick, picks it up, and takes his place in the center. Repeat from the beginning with the girl inside the ring, and so on.

Rebecca's refrain, "Fa la la day," is missing in the Indiana song.

CHIMBLEY SWEEPER

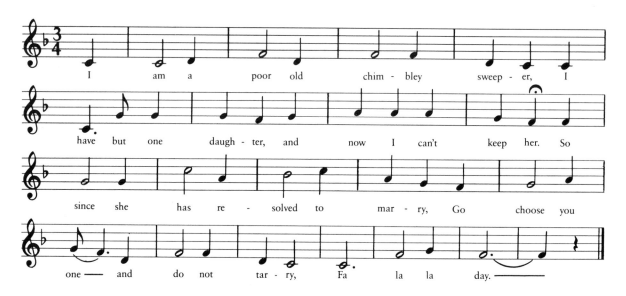

I am a poor old chim - bley sweep - er, I have but one daugh - ter, and now I can't keep her. So since she has re - solved to mar - ry, Go choose you one — and do not tar - ry, Fa la la day. —

Now you have one of your own choosing,
You have no time for to be losing,
So join your right hand, this broom step over,
You can kiss the lips of your own true lover.
Fa la la day.

190. Rocky By Baby, By-O   Rebecca King Jones, 1940

This lullaby, obviously, is a version of the well-known nursery rhyme:

Rockaby baby on the tree top,
When the wind blows the cradle will rock.
When the bough breaks the cradle will fall,
And down will come cradle, baby, and all.

Rebecca said to us as she finished singing, "Now I did not get that all just right, I am sure." Even so we find her words, and her tune, more engaging than the original.

ROCKY BY BABY, BY-O

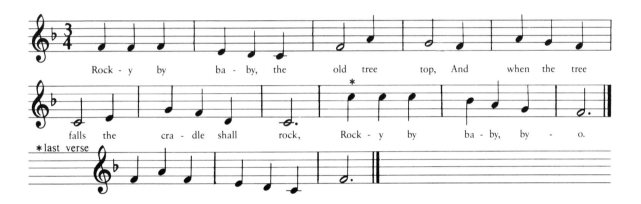

Father will come to pick up his gun,
Into the woods, he will bring some meat home,
Rocky by baby, by-o,

When the baby wakes from sleep he will have
All the good meat to choose there [from],
Rocky by baby, by-o.

PRISCILLA DYER ALLEN

In the summer of 1941, on our way to see our northern singers, we stopped in Cheshire, Massachusetts, to see a New York City friend, Joe Busti, who was visiting his family there in the Berkshires. Joe had long been interested in our search for songs, and on the second day of our visit he said he had heard that the postmistress in nearby Plain-field might know some. So that afternoon we went to call on Priscilla Dyer (later Mrs.

Hubbel Allen) who was, indeed, the young postmistress of that village. She sang us a number of interesting songs, most of them learned from her great aunt, Genevieve Ford, who was born in 1854, who had, in turn, learned them from her father, (Priscilla's great grandfather) born in 1811. The father's family had migrated from Connecticut in 1790. When her aunt was ten years old, Priscilla told us, she was sent to the store one day for a spool of thread. She told Priscilla that she found everything draped in black, and the storekeeper told her Lincoln had been assassinated. She went home and told her mother, who wept and threw her apron over head.

One of Priscilla's songs interested us particularly—she called it "Bold Dickie and Bold Archie." Priscilla's aunt, from whom she learned it, told her she thought there was a first verse to the song which she never could remember. Even so, the story is complete.

191. Bold Dickie and Bold Archie   Priscilla Dyer Allen, 1941

This is a version of Child ballad No. 188—"Archie O Cawfield"—about Scottish border raiders known to have been active in the mid-1500s. It is probably related also to Child No. 187, "Jock o'the Side." It is one of the rare survivals of the Scottish border raid ballads concerning events known to have happened in the sixteenth century. Evelyn K. Wells, in her book, *The Ballad Tree,* devotes a chapter to these songs. She recognized our tune as the one used for the love song, "A Brisk Young Sailor Courted Me," and traced it back through the many songs for which it has been used to a Scottish hymn of 1564. Miss Wells describes in impressive detail the world of the Scottish border:

> Some sixty of Child's 305 ballads tell their tales against this background. They reflect the isolation of the wild moorlands, and the mazes of the back-country routes that baffle the intruder, the rude economy, the lawless individualism with its barbaric codes and stalwart virtues, the speed and tenseness of life, the internal dissension, and the hatred of England.
>
> Interest centers largely upon feats of prowess and valor rather than victory in and for itself . . . and upon the vigor and zest with which the quarrels are pursued. . . . each ballad confines itself to one episode. . . . Plots depend upon wit and audacity, rather than on physical endurance, though that also is greatly admired. . . . Ruse and trickery are part of the game . . . [and] there is a sense of lusty enjoyment in every trick.

Miss Wells says that almost no border raid ballads "have stood transplanting to American soil, being too localized in time, place, and circumstance to maintain their hold elsewhere." The songs of our own Southwest, of course, reflect the same lawlessness and violence and lusty enjoyment. Indeed this ballad, with its continuous mounting and dismounting of horses reminds us of an early western movie.

Eloise Hubbard Linscott has a version of the ballad in *Folksongs of Old New England,* with a different tune. She doesn't mention its relation to "Archie o' Cawfield" but calls it the "story of a pirate" and says that the song "was *not* sung by women."

In the *Burl Ives Song Book* there are two verses of an American parody of this ballad called "The Escape of Old John Webb," concerning, Ives says, an incident in 1730.

See: Barry-Eckstorm, 393; Child No. 188, 461 ("Archie O Cawfield");
Coffin and Renwick, 117, 253; Ives, 30; Linscott, 172; Wells, 55

BOLD DICKIE AND BOLD ARCHIE

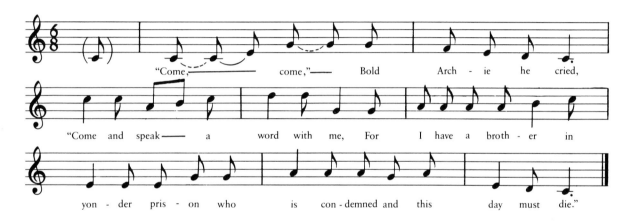

"Come, come," Bold Arch - ie he cried, "Come and speak a word with me, For I have a broth - er in yon - der pris - on who is con - demned and this day must die."

"Oh, no. Oh, no," the other he said,
"Oh, no, that never can be,
For I have ten men as good as myself,
We will go set the poor prisoner free."

So they mounted their horses, and away rode they,
Who but they, so merrily,
Until they came to the prison gate,
Where they all dismounted most sorrowfully.

"Bold Dickie, bold Dickie," bold Archie he cried,
"Come and speak a word with me,

For I have come with full forty men,
And I am determined to set thee free."

"Oh, no. Oh, no," bold Dickie he cried,
"Oh, no, that never can be,
For I've full forty-weight of good Spanish iron
Betwixt my ankle-bone and my knee."

But they broke bolts and they broke bars,
And they broke whate'er came in their way,
And they took the poor prisoner under his arms
And they marched him out courageously.

So they mounted their horses and away rode they,
Who but they, so merrily,
Until they came to the riverside,
Where they all dismounted most sorrowfully.

"Bold Archie, bold Archie," bold Dickie he cried,
"Come and speak a word with me.
My horse is lame and he cannot swim,
And oh, I fear this day I die."

"Oh, no. Oh, no," bold Archie he cried,
"Oh, no, that never can be.
My horse is strong and I know he swims,
He will take us both over most joyfully."

So they mounted their horses and away rode they,
Who but they, so merrily,
Until they came to the other side,
Where they all dismounted most sorrowfully.

"Bold Archie, bold Archie," the sheriff he cried,
"Come and speak a word with me,
If you'll bring back the iron that you carried off,
I am sure we will set the poor prisoner free."

"Oh, no. Oh, no," bold Archie he cried,
"Oh, no, that never can be,
For the iron will serve to shoe our horses,
And the blacksmith he rides in our company."

So they mounted their horses and away rode they,
Who but they, so merrily,
Until they came to the tavern gate,
Where they all dismounted most joyfully.

They hired a fiddle, they hired a room,
Who but they, so merrily,
And one of the best dancers there was in the room
Was this poor prisoner just set free.

ROY WALWORTH

Roy Walworth was an official of the New York Central Railroad whom Frank Warner saw frequently in his capacity as Traveling Secretary for the Railroad YMCA. One day (January 22, 1941) they were having lunch together in the Commodore Hotel when Roy said, "I love to hear those old-time songs you sing, Frank. They remind me of the songs my father used to sing when I was a boy in Selkirk in Oswego County, in upstate New York." He told Frank that his earliest memories were of his father building a fire in the big stove early in the morning and singing old-time songs. Roy's father's name was Fayette E. Walworth. He was born in 1848 and died in 1933. At one time he lived in Ashtabula, Ohio, where he was a captain in the U.S. Life Saving Corps—forerunner of the U.S. Coast Guard. Frank asked Roy if he couldn't remember at least one of his father's songs, and he did—singing it quietly there in the hotel dining room.

192. Doodle Dandy   Roy Walworth, 1941

Roy Walworth learned this song from his father who told him that it was sung by the Continental troops as they marched down the Hudson from Washington's headquarters in Newburgh to take over New York City as the British left to set sail for England. This was at the close of the Revolution, in 1783. An amusing anecdote has come down from that period. Some say that the British, as they left, ran the Union Jack to the top of the flagpole—and then greased the pole. In those days a man had to climb the pole to raise or lower the flag.

We haven't found the song anywhere else, though Miss Elsie Edsell of Ilion, New York, whom we met in Cooperstown, said she remembered her great grandfather, named William Clopsoddle, singing it.

Frank Warner, in singing it, always repeated the first four lines at the end.

John Langstaff included the song in his *Hi! Ho! The Rattlin' Bog.*

DOODLE DANDY

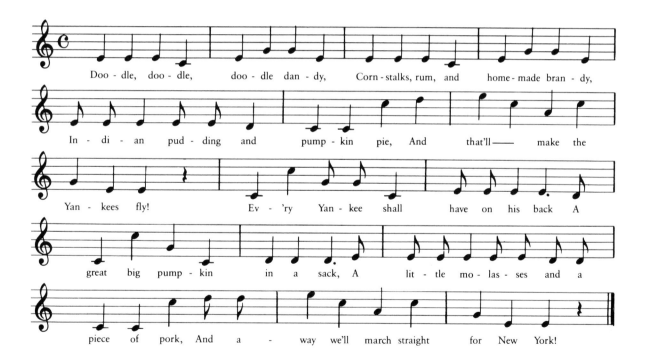

435

193. The Song of the Rebel Soldier   Clem Strudwick, 1934, and others

Although it is seldom thought of in those terms, this is a protest song, widely sung in the South during the desperate days of Reconstruction. It is the expression of the bitter, stubborn mood of a defeated people. Written as a poem by Major Innes Randolph, who served four years in the Confederate army as a member of General J. E. B. Stuart's staff, and who later was a newspaper man with the *Baltimore American,* the poem quickly became a song (to a tune close to "Villikins and his Dinah") and was taken to their hearts by a people who adapted it to fit their own memories and situation. We have collected perhaps a dozen versions, some of them with only slight variations from this one, some very different indeed. Frank learned this version from the late Clem Strudwick of Hillsborough, North Carolina. Frank sang it in 1957 in the RKO Civil War movie "Run of the Arrow" (starring Rod Steiger) in which he played a Rebel soldier, and has recorded it twice—for Elektra and Prestige, Int. The words are included in *Poems by Innes Randolph,* compiled by his son: Baltimore, 1898 (p. 30).

Manly Wade Wellman, in his biography of Wade Hampton of South Carolina, called *Giant in Gray* (Scribner's, 1949), says, "Here and there [in 1866], at picnics and parties, a baleful new folk song began to be heard—a pronouncement of stubborn enmity, not without a plain man's pride." He then gives a three-stanza version, learned "from a descendant of South Carolina Confederates."

Among the other versions we have collected, are:

1. From Dr. Julian M. Ruffin, School of Medicine, Duke University, February 13, 1953. This has a number of verbal changes, but is the same song.

2. From a Captain D. H. McDonald, USN, February 2, 1953. A bitter version, starting out, "Oh, I'm a good old Rebel, yes, by God, I am." The Captain says, "I've heard my uncles sing it many a time to the tune of fiddles, banjo, and guitar. They fought in the late unpleasantness. When I get three quarters way through the jug, I sing it too." Then he added, "Of course it's just a song, and it in no way reflects my state of mind. I am a loyal naval officer."

3. From Basil Duke Henning, Master of Saybrook College of Yale University, December 31, 1958, through our friend Marshall Bartholomew (for so many years the distinguished Director of the Yale Glee Club and an early collector of American folksongs), who wrote us:

> Our friend Mr. Henning found time during the holidays to recall and copy out his version of the "Unreconstructed Rebel." If ever there was a hymn of hate, here it is, blasphemous, profane, and everything that we would like to forget. It is, nevertheless, a vivid account of how thousands of Confederate veterans felt at the close of the War Between the States.

There are a number of changes in this version.

Stanza 2: I fit with Stonewall Jackson, of that there is no doubt,
Got wounded in the Wilderness, and starved at Camp Lookout.
I caught the rheumatism a-sleeping in the snow,
But I killed a score of Yankess, and I wisht it had been mo'.

Stanza 4: And when the war was over I jined the Ku Klux Klan,
And when it come to lynchin' I was the right-hand man.
I love to see a nigger a-hangin' to a tree,
But if it was a Yankee, it was all the same to me.

4. From an unknown source, since no name or date is attached. It is handwritten on Hotel Commodore stationery, and it has a few verbal changes but is substantially the same as the version from Hillsborough.

5. From Lieutenant John McCreary (through Frank's friend, Elias Abelson), who learned it from "a friend in Atlanta, Georgia." Sent to us on January 7, 1955, it is quite a different song:

Oh, now I am just a Rebel, suh, and that is all I am,
For this fair land of freedom, suh, I do not give a damn.
For me, I fought agin it, and I only wish we'd won,
And I don't want no pardon, suh, for anything I've done.

Oh, we routed Hooker's Army for the bold Confederacy,
And we rode beneath the Stars and Bars in Stuart's Cavalry.
We fought agin the Yankees and we whipped 'em where we could,
And if they would of turned us loose we might have beat 'em good.

Now, I hate your starry banner for it's gory with my blood,
As for your constitution, suh, to me that's same as mud.
We fought that out at Kennesaw amidst the stones and dust,
And we got ten thousand Yankees there before the rest got us.

Now I hate your Freedman's bureau and I hate your boys in blue,
That chicken-snaggin, scalawaggin, carpet-baggin' crew!
For I am jist a Rebel, suh, and that is all I am,
I won't be reconstructed, and I don't give a damn!
[Shout:] To hell with you and your federalized abolitionist army!

6. Perhaps the most interesting version of all is called "An Old Unreconstructed." It was given to Frank by Mr. Lloyd R. Bowman of Cleveland, Ohio, in April of 1948. It follows "The Song of the Rebel Soldier" as Song No. 194.

See: Cox, 281; Lomax, *ABF,* 535; Lomax, *Cowboy Songs,* 94

437

I'm a good old Reb-el sol-dier,—— and that's just what I am, And for this Yan-kee na-tion—— I do—— not give a damn! I hate the star-ry ban-ner — it's stained with south-ern blood,— And I hate the piz-en Yan-kees, and I fit 'em all I could.

*starts often

I followed old Marse Robert for four years near about,

Got wounded at Manassas and starved at Point Lookout.

I cotched the rheumatism from fightin' in the snow,

But I kilt a chanct of Yankees and I wisht I'd a-kilt some mo'.

Three hundred thousand Yankees are stiff in southern dust!

We got three hundred thousand before they conquered us.

They died of southern fever, and southern steel and shot;

And I wisht we'd a-got three million instead of what we got!

I hate the Yankee nation and the darkies dressed in blue,

I hate the Constitution of this great Republic too!

I hate the Freedman's Bureau, with all its mess and fuss,

Oh, the thievin', lyin' Yankess, I hate 'em wuss and wuss!

I can't take up my musket to fight 'em any more,

But I ain't gonna love 'em, and that is sartin shore.

And I don't want no pardon for what I've done or am,

And I won't be reconstructed, and I do not give a damn!

"The Rebel Soldier"
Adapted and Arranged by Frank Warner
TRO—© Copyright 1961 and 1984 Melody Trails, Inc., New York, N.Y. Used by Permission

438

Sometime in the winter of 1947–48 Frank Warner presented an evening of folk music for a men's club in Cleveland, Ohio, and included "The Song of the Rebel Soldier." A member of his audience was a Cleveland business man named Lloyd Bowman, who explained to Frank after the program why he obviously was so moved by that song. His grandfather had sung a similar song to him when he was a child, and it was a deep-rooted memory. Frank said he would very much like to have the story, and so Lloyd Bowman sent him in April of 1948 the following story about the song, "An Old Unreconstructed."

194. An Old Unreconstructed   Lloyd Bowman, 1948

My grandfather was born in the Netherlands in 1835 and his name—as discovered in his papers in 1920 after his death—was Arn Jans Borka van Zuyverden. He never told anyone his real name, but was known to his family and all his friends as Andrew Jackson Baker, or "A. J." About the time of the 1849 Gold Rush he shipped as a cabin boy to New York, where he jumped his ship and signed on another that was rounding the Horn, bound for California. Here he took his new name and worked with a freight wagon train into Texas where he opened a business as harness and saddle maker in Fort Worth. When the Civil War broke out he joined the Confederate army, serving under Jeb Stuart in the cavalry. He himself "didn't rightly know" how he got from Texas into a Virginia company, but he said "when another regiment was going where we wanted to go, we just went along for the fight. Every man owned his own horse and arms and was pretty much his own boss."

After the war he raised a family of four daughters and eventually, when his wife died, went to live with one of them in Fort Wayne, Indiana. They lived in a German community, and A. J. hated Germans. The part of Holland where he was born was near the German border, and the hatred was bred there. After the Franco-Prussian War, Germany annexed this part of Holland, which increased his bitterness. I expect the Germans among the Yankee troops didn't help this feeling. A. J. had a concertina or "squeeze box," and he loved to sit and play and to sing—songs of his boyhood, sea chanties, songs of the gold fields, the old West, and songs of the war. He sang the song he called "An Old Unreconstructed" with special feeling. Whenever he had a fuss with some of his German neighbors he'd take his squeeze box and sit on the front porch and sing it at the top of his voice! He used to say he wasn't "afeared of human or heathen or the Devil ahoss." And he used to tell me, "It ain't the winning or losing that counts, it's the will to fight and to keep on fighting, win or lose, as long as you've life in your body and you're right."

Of all the songs he sang and the stories he told, I feel that "An Old Unreconstructed" is his song, and its story of an unbroken spirit is his story. It just seemed to fit him so perfectly. As I can remember him sitting there stomping and singing in defiance, it isn't a memory of a man singing a song. It is the memory of a man making a declaration of his creed, his belief, his faith.

These are the verses of the many more sung by his grandfather, Andrew Jackson Baker, that Lloyd Bowman could remember. Not one of these verses is in the poem by Major Randolph, but they carry the same defiant and unconquered spirit. Frank Warner sings this version on Elektra's EKL 13, which is long out of print.

AN OLD UNRECONSTRUCTED

I rid with Old Jeb Stuart and his band of southern
    horse,
And there never were no Yankees who could meet
    us force to force.
No! They never did defeat us, but we never could
    evade
Their dirty furrin politics and their cowardly
    blockade.

Well, we hadn't any powder and we hadn't any
    shot,
And we hadn't any money to buy what we hadn't
    got.
So we rid our worn-out horses, and we et on plain
    cornmeal,
And we licked 'em where we kotched 'em, with
    southern guts and steel.

We sunk the ship at Sumpter; we broke her plumb
    in two.
And we showed the bully Yankees just what we
    aimed to do.
At a little crick called Bull Run, we took their
    starry rag
To wipe our hosses down with, and I ain't here
    to brag.

We whupped the best they sent us, and we whupped
    'em fair and true.
We whupped their German immigrants and the
    Eyetalians too.
We whupped Frogs and Square Heads and all their
    furrin might,
But when they went and got the Micks, we knew
    we'd got a fight.

There aren't many left of us who rode out at the start,
And them that are, are weary, weak in body, sad
    of heart.
But we fit a fight to tell about, and I am here to say,
I'll climb my hoss and folla Marse to hell come
    any day.

"Old Unreconstructed"
Words and Music Collected, Adapted and Arranged by Frank Warner
TRO—© Copyright 1971 and 1984 Melody Trails, Inc., New York, N.Y. Used by Permission

DEAC (C. T.) MARTIN

On one of Frank Warner's business trips to Cleveland, Ohio, he met Deac Martin who, with his wife Helen, became our good friends. Deac often visited us in our Greenwich

Village apartment, and we found we had many musical interests in common. Deac's special interest was barbershop harmony—the collection of such ballads and the singing of them. He was interested also in old-time hymns, and in folk music too. Eventually he compiled and published an enormous book called *Deac Martin's Musical Americana,* which tells more than one could hope to know about American popular music of all kinds from before the turn of the century. We are happy to include here a traditional song which Deac taught us.

195. **Away, Idaho** (or, We're Coming, Idaho)   Deac (C. T.) Martin, 1952

Deac Martin gave us this song in 1952. He learned it from his mother, Mary Virginia Gooch (Martin) who lived in Missouri and whose people came by way of Kentucky from Gooch's Landing in Virginia, near Jamestown.

The song, with Frank French listed as its author, was published by H. M. Higgins in Chicago in 1864. In the Lomaxes' *Our Singing Country* (p. 269) is a song called "Way Out in Idaho," but it is about railroading. In Alan Lomax's *The Folk Songs of North America* is a song with essentially the same tune and meter as Deac's, called "We're Coming Arkansas," that praises the healing properties of the hot springs there. Since Idaho is farther west than Arkansas, perhaps Frank French took a known song and rewrote it to fit a new interest—Idaho's gold.

Randolph prints three versions, the first two dealing with the healing waters of Eureka Springs, Arkansas. His third variant is a version of Deac Martin's song, *with no tune,* but with two additional verses:

We leave old Tennessee,
And through Arkansas we go—
Look back upon our dear old home,
Way out in Idaho.

Farewell old mother, home,
I'll never see thee more,
My treasures and life are in the West—
Way out in Idaho.

In 1958 Elektra Records published a Frank Warner album, "Our Singing Heritage," which included this song. Our good friend Holman J. (Jerry) Swinney was then Director of the Idaho Historical Society and Museum in Boise. There was an exhibition of state history just opening, and he immediately had this song (from the record) put on tape and arranged to have it played over loudspeakers at intervals during the exhibition. As a result it became something of a state song.

Norm Cohen, in *Long Steel Rail,* (p. 560) includes a song called "Way Out in

Idaho," which seems to have no connection with this song of Deac Martin's. It is a railroad song with the refrain:

Way out in Idaho, way out in Idaho,
A-working on the narrow gauge, way out in Idaho.

See: Lomax, *FSNA*, 309; Randolph, Vol. 3, 14

AWAY, IDAHO (WE'RE COMING, IDAHO)

They say there is — a land Where the crys-tal wa-ters flow O'er beds of ore of pur-est gold — Way out — in I-da-ho. A-way, I-da-ho, We're com-ing, I-da-ho, Our four-horse team will soon be seen Way out — in I-da-ho.

We'll need no sieve or spade,
No shovel, pan or hoe.
The largest chunks lay top of ground,
Way out in Idaho.
     Chorus

We'll face hard times no more,
And want we'll never know,
When we have filled our packs with gold
Way out in Idaho.
     Chorus

Additional Songs Collected by the Warners from the Singers Included in This Volume

There are a number of other singers and songs in the Warner Collection. Understandably, it was not possible to publish the whole collection in this volume.

Laws, *American Balladry from British Broadsides* — ABBB
Laws, *Native American Balladry* — NAB

Priscilla Dyer Allen
    Arthur O'Bower
    Babylon's Fallen
    Charlie Is My Darling
    Lord Lovel   Child No. 75
    My Pony
    Nicodemus
    When I was Young

Homer Cornett
    Poor Ellen Smith   *NAB*, 196

Captain John and Alwilda Culpeper
    The Boston Burglar
    The Dark-Eyed Sailor
    The Gypsy's Warning   *NAB*, 277
    Killy Clyde

Captain Albert Etheridge
    The Sailor's Alphabet

Lena Bourne Fish
    Along the Railway
    Away, Old Men, Away
    Barney McGee
    By Old Smoky Mountain   *NAB*, 278
    Captain Kidd   *ABBB*, 158
    The Charming Engineer
    Crazy Jane
    The Cuckoo
    The *Cumberland*'s Crew   *NAB*, 127
    Darby O'Leary
    The Darby Ram
    Down to the Club
    The Drummer Boy of Oxford Town
    The Faded Coat of Blue
    The Fellow That Looks Like Me
    The Grandfather Clock
    Grandmother's Old Arm Chair
    I Admire a Black-Eyed Man
    I'm Saddest When I Sing

444

446

Discography of Albums Which Include Songs and Stories Collected by Anne and Frank Warner

Frank Warner

SONGS OF THE HUDSON VALLEY, Disc Records, 1946

FRANK WARNER SINGS AMERICAN FOLK SONGS AND BALLADS,
    Elektra Records EKL 3, 1952

SONGS AND BALLADS OF AMERICA'S WARS, Elektra Records EKL 13, 1954

OUR SINGING HERITAGE, Elektra Records, EKL 153, 1958

SONGS OF THE CIVIL WAR, Prestige International 13012, 1961

THE CIVIL WAR, Heirloom Records, HL 503, 1962

COME ALL YOU GOOD PEOPLE, Minstrel Records, JD 204, 1976

*Frank Proffitt**

FRANK PROFFITT SINGS FOLK SONGS, Folkways Records, FA 2360, 1962

FRANK PROFFITT, REESE, NORTH CAROLINA, Folk-Legacy Records, FSA 1, 1962

FRANK PROFFITT, MEMORIAL ALBUM, Folk-Legacy Records, FSA 36, 1968

Other Albums

BEECH MOUNTAIN BALLADS,* Vols. I and II, Folk-Legacy Records, FSA 22 and 23, 1964

THE FOLK BOX, Elektra Records, EKL Box (in cooperation with Folkways Records), 1964

THE FOLK FESTIVAL AT NEWPORT, Vangard Records, VRS 9064, 1959

THE FOLK MUSIC OF THE NEWPORT FOLK FESTIVAL, Folkways Records
    FA 2432, 1959–60

SONGS AND SOUNDS OF THE SEA, National Geographic Records, 1973

DAYS OF '49: Jeff Warner and Jeff Davis, Minstrel Records, JD 206, 1977

STEADY AS SHE GOES, Collector Records 1928, 1977

*Material performed by traditional artists.

Cassettes

GRASS ROOTS:* An Oral History of the American People, Visual Educ. Corp., Princeton, N.J., 1976

SOME BALLAD FOLKS*—distributed with book of same title, Eastern Tennessee State University, 1978

*Material performed by traditional artists.

Music Transcriber's Notes

A NOTE ON THE MODAL SCALES

The nomenclature of the full seven-note scales that fall into the pattern of the Church modes is well standardized using the names of the ancient Greek scales, nomenclature which is used here. In a case of a full scale where the accidentals do not allow such classification (rare), I will simply describe the scale in each case. I do not feel there would be much value in describing an elaborate classification system for just a few items. I describe the hexatonic (six-note) scales generally by locating the gap or by stating how one of the pentatonic gaps was filled in: for example, "hexatonic, no sixth," or "hexatonic—major, no seventh." There are a great many pentatonic tunes in the collection; the nomenclature here is less standardized for these. I have followed Sharp in using as paradigm the five notes, C-D-F-G-A-C for the pentatonic scale. Those notes beginning on C give the structure for mode I, beginning on D for mode II, and so on. For more information, and for a particularly good exposition of the relation between the pentatonic and the more modern hexatonic and heptatonic scales, the reader should see the preface to Sharp, *English Folksongs of the Southern Appalachian,* pp. xxx–xxxiv.

JOHN GALUSHA

Yankee John was a most exciting singer, with a tremendous intensity and a remarkable sense of narrative. His pitch was not always very secure. This seems to be because of the limitations of his range—a limitation that probably was not present when he was a spry young man of, say, sixty-five. He would have been a truly extraordinary singer at an earlier age when he had his full vocal capabilities. The limitations of range would often cause him to change key in the middle of a song, sometimes several times. Nevertheless, his underlying sense of the correct tune was so strong that I was able to feel confident in the transcription (as was not always the case with the early Proffitt material, for example). Most of the songs he sang to the Warners are not highly ornamented, but I believe at an earlier age he would have sung in a much more ornamented style. There are several places where the decorations creep through. In the songs in 3/4 meter, Yankee John has a consistent stylistic idiosyncracy of holding the middle quarter note of the bar at high points of the tune. This device seems to be prompted by a melodic intention and is apparently unrelated to any particular word stress.

1. Cabin Boy
The F-natural in the third line gives a strong Mixolydian feel to this otherwise Ionian melody. The hold at the start of the third strain of music is consistent and undoubtedly intentional.

2. The *Flying Cloud*
The tune is very close to other versions of the same song. The mode is Ionian.

3. The Bonny Bunch of Roses-O
A certain amount of guesswork has been done here as Yankee John's tune is not at all consistent. It is even possible that he was mixing up two different versions. The problem is compounded by the fact that he began in an uncomfortable key, and he changed keys in a confusing way until settling down in the second verse. Three verses are recorded; the second and third are reasonably consistent, and it is these that have been primarily used in reconstructing the published tune. The first, while probably not correct in the general outline of the tune, is sung in a more interesting and more highly ornamental style (in keeping with the clear Irish ancestry of the song). This style is, in my opinion, a clue to what would have been Yankee John's way of singing in his younger years. The tune is Ionian mode.

4. Lass of Glenshee
The long holds at bars 6, 9, and 14 are a stylistic element and not intrinsic to the tune. It is these holds that produce the rather peculiar nineteen-bar length. The singer may wish to shorten each of these long notes by three beats to give the usual sixteen-bar structure. The mode is hexatonic—minor with no sixth.

5. Plains of Baltimore
Here again we find the crossing of two modes. The seventh scale degree is raised at cadence points (Ionian) and flat otherwise (Mixolydian).

6. The St. Albans Murder
This very strong tune is marked by the great upward sweep of the opening two bars. The tune covers an unusually wide range (octave and a fourth). The alternate shown for bars 9 and 10 has a different harmonic feel. I cannot tell which is correct as only two verses are recorded. The tune is Ionian mode.

7. The Waxford Girl
There is considerable ambiguity in the singing here as to the third degree of the scale (G or G-sharp) and hence ambiguity of the mode. For various structural reasons, it is my belief

that G-natural is correct throughout (and thus the tune is Dorian mode). Two verses are recorded; in both, the second note of bar 30 is sung as G-sharp (but not at the analogous place in bar 14).

8. The Ballad of Blue Mountain Lake

To the reader who is familiar with this tune, either from the singing of Frank Warner or from the well-known sea chantey with the same chorus, bar 8 will seem peculiar. This is as Yankee John sang it. The mode is Dorian.

9. The British-American Fight

A striking tune. It isn't until the fourth bar that the listener has a clear sense of the tonic, and the cadence at the halfway point is to four rather than the usual five. The mode is Mixolydian; the seven-one chord progression at the cadence that is characteristic of this mode is strongly implied by the ending of the tune.

10. The British Soldier

There was discussion as to whether the last note of bar 15 should be C or C-sharp, especially in view of the C-sharp in bar 10. I am convinced that the C-natural is correct in 15; the sharp in 10 is again due to the "leading tone feeling" moving upward to the D of bar 11. The tune is Dorian (ignoring the C-sharp).

11. The *Cumberland* and the *Merrimac*

Frank Warner sang this with raised seventh (C-sharp) at bars 6, 13, and 21. Yankee John sang flat seventh throughout—thus the tune is pure Mixolydian mode.

12. The Days of Forty-Nine

Here we see clearly Yankee John's use of the hold at an important melody point. The tune is Dorian mode.

13. General Scott and the Veteran

Two verses are recorded; in the first the opening notes of bars 13 and 29 are preceded by a grace note A. In bar 21 we see the hold at the high point of the tune for melodic, and not textual, reasons. The tune is Ionian mode.

14. The Irish Sixty-Ninth

This very strong tune is Mixolydian and adds the raised seventh at the cadence points. Like several other songs of Yankee John's, the tonic is not immediately clear. In fact, in this song the tonic is not firmly established until the penultimate bar when the seventh is raised and finally a cadence to the tonic occurs. This is inherent in the tune itself and is not due to any ambiguity in Yankee John's singing.

15. The Irishtown Crew

One of those great, "good-time" songs about getting drunk and going out on a tear. The mode is Ionian.

16. The Jam on Gerrion's Rock

The tune is Mixolydian mode with the seventh raised at the cadence point of lines 1 and 4.

17. James Bird

Two verses were recorded. The singing of bar 2 in the second verse, as shown, has a very different harmonic feel from the first verse. The alternate of measure 7 is just a more ornamented form of what was sung in the first verse. The tune is pure Mixolydian mode.

18. Jamie Judge

The last note of bars 4 and 12 is sung as an ambiguous E-flat—E-natural in the first verse, and as a more definite E-natural in the second. Nevertheless, I believe that the E-flat is correct throughout.

19. Jump Her, Juberju

Transcribed from the singing of Frank Warner as the recording of Yankee John is lost, the scale of this song contains the first five notes of the major scale. The words, "Jump her, Juberju" are apparently a corruption of "A proper due by due" (referring to the wind direction) which appear in a similar English song.

21. The Ballad of Montcalm and Wolfe

This tune is published in Lomax (*FSNA*) from the singing of Frank Warner. Frank made a guess as to Yankee John's intentions at the 5/4 bar and the bar following which are not clear on the recording. Frank changed the last three notes of the 5/4 bar and the first note of the next bar. While the 5/4 bar is reasonably clear on the recording, debate has been heated as to whether the first note of the next bar is C or B-flat. After much discussion and much listening, I am convinced that the C is correct.

22. The Red, White, and Red

Yankee John sang this in a declamatory, proud style, although his family was on the other side. The mode is Ionian.

23. Springfield Mountain

This powerful tune was sung in Yankee John's best dramatic and declamatory style. The tune is pentatonic, mode II.

24. Virginia's Bloody Soil

Transcribed from the singing of Frank Warner, this very powerful song shows Frank's remarkable ability to capture Yankee John's dramatic narrative style. The tune is Aeolian mode.

25. This Day

Frank Warner sang this song in 4/4; Yankee John is clearly singing in 6. The tune is Ionian mode.

26. Down in a Coal Mine

This is one of many songs in the collection that Frank Warner learned and unconsciously changed, often improving the song in the process. Frank rarely sang this song, but the few readers who have heard him may find the chorus disappointing. Nevertheless, this is how Yankee John sang it.

27. In the Pit from Sin Set Free

The words to this song were given to the Warners by someone who came up after one of Frank's concerts. This tune was sent to the Warners by Sam Bayard as one that would fit the rather unusual metrical structure. While we have no way of knowing, it is quite likely that the original tune was stylistically similar to this typical religious revival sort of tune. The mode is Ionian.

28. Longshoreman's Strike

The tune is hexatonic—major, no seventh. The two 9/8 bars are clearly intentional.

29. Nothing's Too Good for the Irish

Taken from the singing of Frank Warner, a certain amount of guesswork has been done here. Yankee John's singing must have been fairly indistinct, as Frank is clearly not sure how to fit the words to a tune in some places and resorts to a kind of spoken narration. The reader will find that the second verse requires some thought in order to make it fit.

30. An Old Indian

One sees here very strongly Yankee John's habit of holding back the time on the second quarter note of some of the 3/4 measures. The penultimate measure in common time is absolutely consistent and unquestionably intentional.

31. Once More A-Lumbering Go

This song was sung to the Warners by Yankee John, but the recording is lost. The song was apparently well known in the Adirondacks, and we have transcribed the tune from the wonderful Adirondack singer Lawrence Older (who played guitar with it). The mode is Ionian.

32. Paddle the Road with Me

This lyrical tune has a very Irish trait of mixing the Ionian and Mixolydian modes in a particular way: the second and third strains end on the flat seventh while the cadences of strains one and four show the raised seventh leading tone.

33. Shanty Boy, Farmer Boy

Again we have ambiguity of mode. The first and fourth strains are Ionian (raised seventh); the second and third strains are Mixolydian (flat seventh).

34. The Shanty Man

Here again is an apparent ambiguity at the third; however, unlike "The Waxford Girl,"

Yankee John's intentions here are clear. He raises the third leading up to the cadence point every time. The mode has the general feel of Dorian, but gets wrenched into the Mixolydian by the raised third at the cadence.

35. A Trip on the Erie
Yankee John is not clear on the tune in measures 9 and 10 and sings them differently each time. I have picked the one that seems to best fit the rest of the tune.

36. The Twenty-Third
Bar 7 is so suggestive of a "five-of-five" cadence that I suspect that the last note was originally F-sharp in bar 7. Yankee John sings it clearly as F-natural. The mode is Ionian.

STEVE WADSWORTH

37. The Farmer's Boy
The song is here sung with the same tune as "Peter Emberly" in the version from Marie Hare (New Brunswick). In the second verse the third note is sung as A rather than C. The tune is basically Mixolydian with raised leading tone at the cadences of the first and fourth strains.

38. Cole Younger
A remarkably complete version of this native American story. Again the tune is basically Mixolydian mode with raised leading tone at the cadences.

39. Curly Head of Hair
Steve Wadsworth was apparently very cosmopolitan in his traditions. "Cole Younger" is 100 percent American, "The Farmer's Boy" is an English song done to a Canadian tune. This song seems to me very Irish in flavor. Pure Mixolydian mode.

LENA BOURNE FISH

Mrs. Fish was a transcriber's dream. I have never heard a traditional source singer who was so clear and definite about her material. In a couple of places on the recordings she stops to correct herself when she has misplaced a syllable in the tune. She knew her material very well indeed. But at the same time, this very definiteness made her singing among the least interesting in the collection stylistically. She tended to sing everything rather fast, as if she were afraid she wouldn't get it all in before the Warners would get bored and decide to leave. Similarly she tended to sing rather metronomically, with little fluctuation or variation. This often obscured the fact that her material was as great as it has turned out to be. The tunes had to be slowed down and sung with some phrasing in order for the quality to be revealed. She seemed to enjoy "announcing" her songs before starting in to sing. She would say "'Lord Bateman' . . ." or "An old pre-Revolutionary War song . . ." and then start to sing. She had a very low voice, and generally the songs have been transposed up at least a perfect fourth, occasionally as much as a full octave from where she sang them.

40. Barbara Allen

How many hundreds of versions of this have been collected? And yet each new version seems to be a gem. The Warners collected several extraordinary tunes to this most durable of ballads, and this is one. It is also remarkable that Mrs. Fish could go, with hardly gasping for breath, from a popular march tune of the period to this, perhaps ancient, pentatonic tune. The 5 meter is absolutely clear and unquestionably intentional.

41. The Castle by the Sea

Here again we have a tune that sounds quite old; the tonic is not firmly established until the last two bars. The tune except for the single C-sharp is pentatonic, mode IV. With the C-sharp it is hexatonic, but (somewhat unusual) the third of the scale is missing, leaving the major or minor character of the tune ambiguous.

42. Gypsy Davy

If the first and last note (C) is taken as tonic, the mode is Mixolydian. But the structure of the tune makes a strong case for a tonic of F (Ionian mode). Anyone harmonizing this tune would probably take F as tonic.

43. Lord Bateman

What a remarkable tune is this. It is ambiguous with regard to mode and even with regard to tonic. I hasten to add that Grammy Fish's singing was not in the least ambiguous; the tune shown is her definite intention. The most likely tonic is the final, C. If this be accepted, then the mode fluctuates in quite dramatic fashion between the Ionian and the Lydian. Knowing of no other tune to this song with this dramatic modal structure, I am led to speculate that Grammy may have corrupted a more "normal" tune. If that were so, I would assume F-natural throughout; this would force B-flat because of the linear tritone in measure 6. If one sings this tune with F-natural and B-flat throughout, one obtains an entirely stylistic and traditional-sounding tune. It is rather like working out a puzzle in "musica ficta" in a piece of medieval music, with the difference that we are not dealing with a definite written source but with the (perhaps faulty) memory of a rural singer. But I again emphasize that Grammy was quite definite about what she was hearing in her head.

44. The Old Wether's Skin

Unlike almost all of the other songs recorded on disks (pre-1950), this song was recorded complete (and it's not a short song). At the ending of the first and last verses she sings, "Dew flies over the green valley," while in all other verses she sings, "Dew flies over the mulberry tree." This may have been accidental, but the symmetry suggests to me that it was deliberate. The tune is hexatonic—minor, no sixth.

457

45. The Ship Carpenter

Grammy was not quite clear on the meter of this song. The first verse began in triple meter (first G a quarter note, first A an eighth note—sounding like 3/8 meter), before settling down into common time. The mode is Ionian.

46. The Battle with the Ladle

This seems an unlikely song to be in the old pentatonic scale. It is pentatonic, mode III if A is taken as tonic. If the final C-sharp is taken as tonic, one gets the very rare pentatonic, mode V.

47. Bill the Weaver

To me this is a classic example of how beautiful an extremely simple tune can be. The mode is Aeolian.

48. Cabin Boy

Grammy has a tendency to push Mixolydian tunes toward the Ionian (standard major scale) by raising the seventh at any opportunity. I feel she has done that here. Two verses were recorded. The G-natural of bar 4 is sung as G-sharp in the first verse. In the second verse the note is ambiguous, tending toward G-sharp. The G-sharp is sung both times in measures 1, 5, and 13, yet I feel that these may well have been originally G-natural. This would give a pure Mixolydian tune except for the raised seventh at the two cadences (last notes of bars 7 and 15).

49. Captain John

Two verses were recorded. The C-sharp in bar 9 is a bit ambiguous in the second. It is quite possible that the second and third strains of the tune were originally identical, in which case this note should be a D. In the first verse she sings the last two bars as F (half note) - D - C# - D. I am convinced that this is a memory lapse. The mode is basically Dorian with Aeolian influence (the two B-flats).

50. Felix the Soldier

This tune sounds as if it should cadence into G-major. The actual cadence to E-minor (bars 7 and 15) is surprising.

51. Gilgarrah Mountain

The Irish popular tune, sung with the rhythms all squared off and made rather metronomic.

52. Hi Rinky Dum

This is another case where the tonic is not firmly established until the final note. Mrs. Fish was somewhat ambiguous about the third quarter note of bar 7. I believe the B-flat to be correct; A was the other possibility.

53. I'll Sit Down and Write a Song

Grammy has a strong tendency to raise notes that feel to her like a leading tone to a cadence point. I believe that may be involved in the striking character of "Lord Bateman." Here in one of the recorded verses she sings the second note of bar 4 as G-sharp for that same reason. I am convinced that that is purely an idiosyncracy.

54. Johnny Sands

Mrs. Fish sang the first four bars in 6/8 meter (quarter, eighth, quarter, eighth, etc.), then settled into the duple meter as shown. The second verse is entirely in the duple meter. The mode is pentatonic, mode III.

55. Only a Soldier

In the second verse the second quarter note of bar 7 is sung as G rather than F. The mode is hexatonic, no seventh (taking F as tonic).

56. The Ploughboy of the Lowlands

This version, unlike most, tells why the father had it in for young Edmund. A fine, English-sounding tune in Dorian mode.

57. The Press Gang Sailor

The only place where the third of the scale occurs in this tune is the last note of bar 2. This note will determine whether the mode is Dorian (F-natural) or Mixolydian (F-sharp). Mrs. Fish's intentions are not completely clear at this spot. I believe that the F-natural is correct and she is drawn toward F-sharp by the scale rising toward G. The reader should be aware that considerable discussion took place with the Warners as to whether she might not have intended F-sharp.

58. Pretty Sylvia

The "mode" of this extraordinary tune cannot be simply stated. This is one of those rare cases in oral tradition where accidentals are inserted not to alter the modal feeling but in fact to change the tonic. The tune has the feeling of modulating through three different keys (in the span of 8 bars!). Beginning in D-minor, the F is sharped to give a leading tone to cadence in G. This in turn serves as a leading tone to C, which appears first as Mixolydian (B-flat), and then a final cadence to C, Ionian when the B-natural leading tone appears. The only other tune in oral tradition of the English-speaking world that I know of that does this sort of modulation is the "Three Knights" (or "The Cruel Brother") collected by Baring-Gould in the West Country of England.

59. The Rambler from Claire

The holds shown in bars 6 and 10 are quite definite and consistent. It is interesting that the hold is used very much as Yankee John liked to use it, that is at the middle quarter note of a 3/4 bar.

60. Young but Daily Growing

This is a version of one of the great classic ballads. The haunting quality of this tune comes, at least in part, from the ambiguity of the tonic. The first two and the last two measures seem to establish G as the tonic (thus Dorian mode) while the whole middle of the tune feels as if D were tonic (Aeolian).

61. The Young Prince of Spain

A four-square sixteen-bar tune in Ionian mode.

62. Imaginary Trouble

The hold at the end of bar 4 is in both recorded verses. In the second verse, the second note of bar 7 is sung as E.

63. Joe Bowers

The basic tune here is clearly Mixolydian mode (C-natural) the two C-sharps are put in almost as decorations on a rising scale to the tonic where the singer feels irresistibly drawn to the raised leading tone.

64. Richmond on the James

This song was sung twice to the Warners, with a substantial time between. The unusual meter is identical in both recordings and unquestionably intentional. In the first recording the first note of bars 6 and 10 is sung as B-natural. In the second recording we find B-flat throughout. The mode is Dorian.

65. On Springfield Mountain

The interest here is in the alternation between 3/4 meter and common time. Again Grammy is quite definite, and one cannot doubt that this is her intention.

66. William the Sailor

The basic tune is pentatonic mode I (taking D as tonic). In verse one she fills in one gap with the C-natural. I believe the alternate shown for verse two is the basic tune.

67. The Bonny Bay of Biscay-O

The singer's intentions on the penultimate note are not quite clear—she may have intended C rather than D. The tune is Ionian mode.

68. The Bull Frog

This little patter song has only three notes in the tune. Mode is anything you like (as long as it has a major third)!

69. The Captain with His Whiskers

The mode is hexatonic major (no seventh); however, the modern, marchlike character of the tune would demand that anyone harmonizing this tune use the major and not the minor seventh. The form is the somewhat unusual A-A-B-A, rather than the more common A-B-B-A (or in a dance tune, which this might well have been, A-A-B-B).

70. Ho Boys Ho

One can't help wondering if the verse wasn't once longer. The mode is Ionian.

71. The Jolly Roving Tar

As far as I know, there is no other source for this very British sounding tune, which is surprising. In the first verse she sings B for the last quarter note of the first measure.

72. The Jolly Tinker

It will be hard to believe for the reader that this was sung as the notation indicates: at the refrain not only does the meter change but also the tempo (that is, the pulse) in such a way as to keep the note-value constant in duration! I know of no other case quite like this, at least in American tradition. Mrs. Fish seems to be quite definite and deliberate in this; the tempo change is not in the least vague.

73. Old Tippecanoe

A campaign song obviously to the tune of "The Bear Went Over the Mountain." The recording skipped during the chorus at the words: "We've not one dollar now where we had twenty," thus I have had to guess at how to fit this excessive number of syllables.

74. The Prop of the Nation

Sung in a proud, marchlike style. The mode is Ionian.

75. The Telegraph Wire

This is almost like a children's street rhyme. The three lines of music are virtually identical to each other except for the last cadence. The mode is Ionian.

76. Touch Not the Cup

Another four-square hymn type of tune, that one could easily imagine played by the Salvation Army Brass (it probably was).

BEECH MOUNTAIN, NORTH CAROLINA

These songs from the Hickses, Presnells, and Homer Cornett of the North Carolina mountains contain some of the finest specimens of the collection, in my opinion, as well as some exceptionally fine traditional singers, particularly Linzy Hicks and Lee Monroe Presnell. They sing in the real old mountain style, highly ornamented and with great intensity.

79. Sweet Willie

This wonderful ballad was also taken from the singing of Frank Warner, who could not remember where he had learned it, even though Anne knew exactly when he learned it and roughly where he was. The tune certainly is characteristic of what might be found in the North Carolina mountains, and we have speculated that Frank may have learned it from Frank C. Brown, whom Frank Warner visited that summer. There is a version in Brown that is extremely close to this. The tune is hexatonic—minor, no sixth.

ROBY MONROE HICKS

80. Way Up in Sofield

As shown in the tune variant, Robie is not the least embarrassed to alter the tune when he needs to to fit extra syllables in, even to the point of adding a full bar. The tune is pentatonic, mode III.

81. Young Johnnie

Here again, it took Robie a couple of verses to settle into a secure tune; in several places he did not quite know how to match the words to the tune and sort of put the words in with a shoe horn. Thus the printed tune is a bit of a compromise among variants. The tune is hexatonic —minor, no sixth.

BUNA VISTA (PRESNELL) HICKS and HATTIE HICKS PRESNELL

82. Drunkard's Doom

This tune is very similar to "A Rude and Rambling Boy" except this one rises at the end to establish F as tonic. The scale is thus pentatonic, mode III.

84. Fathers, Now Our Meeting Is Over

This is transcribed from a cassette Buna sent to the Warners on which she is singing alone. She also leads this song with a group on the Folk-Legacy recording where she does not sing the D-sharp ornament note in the upbeats to the first two phrases. On the solo tape the D-sharp is unmistakable. The tune is pentatonic, mode IV (ignoring the ornamental D-sharps).

85. River of Life
87. Voice from the Tombs
89. The Devil and the Farmer's Wife
90. Pretty Crowin' Chickens

These songs, all sung by Hattie and Rosie Presnell sometimes with their mother, Buna Hicks, were very difficult to transcribe, particularly the words were unclear. The two girls often did not agree, particularly on the words; occasionally one would correct the other, or would be corrected by Buna, so that it would seem like there was an extra note or an odd beat to the bar. On the two pieces in harmony, they seemed to have set family parts which had been sung more or less that way for a long time. "River of Life" has a pentatonic tune (mode III), but the harmony part fills in the gaps to make the normal major (Ionian) scale. The structure of this song was not completely clear. The part I have labeled "chorus" was sung twice, once after the first verse and again at the end. For both structural and melodic reasons I believe that they simply forgot it after the second verse and that it is really a chorus.

"Voice from the Tombs" is a pentatonic tune (mode III) and the harmony part (the upper part) is also almost pure pentatonic—a couple of G's (the fourth) are added at cadence points.

"The Devil and the Farmer's Wife" is sung in unison, but there were many places in which the words were obscure on the tape, I believe because the girls were not sure of them. The tune is hexatonic—major, no fourth. "Pretty Crowin' Chickens" is also sung in unison, I believe with Buna in the lead; the tune is pentatonic, mode III (tonic C).

86. A Rude and Rambling Boy

Though basically very similar to "Drunkard's Doom," here one must take C as tonic and thus find pentatonic, mode I. The fourth quarter note of the first full bar is sung as A in verse one.

88. Where the Sun Don't Never Go Down

This is also recorded, with Buna leading the singing, on Folk-Legacy Records. On the record the first note of bar 12 is C with a grace note A before. The tune is pentatonic, mode III.

91. Talking with the Social Union

The shift from triple to duple meter seems unmistakable here. Mode is mostly pentatonic, mode III, with the gaps briefly filled in (bar 2 alternate and the last bar). The first 4/2 bar is missing from the second verse.

LINZY HICKS

92. Palms of Victory

The tune shown is basically that of the second and third verses—there were several minor differences in the first verse: last quarter note of bar 1 sung as D; first two notes of bar 7 sung as F-sharp; last quarter note of bar 9 sung as D. I felt that he was more secure after the first verse and that these later verses were more likely correct.

93. A Poor Wayfaring Pilgrim

Linzy has a number of varying openings for different verses. The first three notes are sung as: D-A-A, as D-F-sharp-G, and even D-G-G-sharp. The basic tune is pentatonic, mode II, with a couple of chromatic decorations.

94. When Sorrows Encompass Me 'Round

The second verse has two upbeat notes (G-B-flat quarter notes). The middle of the first verse has a very irregular rhythm, almost going into 3/4 at one point. The tune is pentatonic, mode II.

95. Wild Stormy Deep

This tune has a very strong chordal feel to it. It is probably a fairly modern tune, written with the intention of a chordal accompaniment. The tune is pentatonic, mode III.

96. George Collins

Some have speculated that the consistent voice breaks shown here were due to Mr. Presnell's age—that perhaps he hadn't the breath to carry the line. I am convinced that that is not the case, and that the voice breaks are stylistic and entirely deliberate. The tune is pentatonic, mode IV.

97. Red Rosy Bush

An unusually lyrical song for "Uncle Monroe," this tune is very English in character. The mode is Ionian.

98. The Two Sisters That Loved One Man

Here, although there is a kind of choppy, unlyrical style, he clearly has sufficient breath to go a long time. The tune is pentatonic, mode III.

99. Farewell to Old Bedford

This is a very fine tune, again very English in style. In the last verse he repeats the first half of the tune to accommodate the words. It is pentatonic mode II (except for ornament notes in the initial upbeat and in bar 5).

100. My Grandmother's Chair

I believe this song has its origin in the English music halls. "Uncle Monroe" certainly seemed to enjoy singing it.

101. The Rambling Boy

Again the short phrases with breaths between. The tune is Ionian mode.

FRANK PROFFITT

Frank was probably the most difficult singer in the collection from the transcriber's point of view. The majority of the material was recorded on disks in 1939–41. Most have guitar accompaniment. In many cases it is clear that the guitar chords have distorted the tune. In later years Frank, at the urging of the Warners, began again to play the banjo which he had learned from his father. When some of the songs were transferred to the banjo, the old tunes reappeared. He sang a large number of songs to the Warners over the twenty-five years of their friendship; some of these he clearly was not very sure of, and thus either the pitches or the rhythm (or both) varied from verse to verse in a somewhat erratic way. If it seemed that Frank was unsure of the song, we have chosen one of two courses. If the song was well known and collected from other singers, we have generally not included it; if on the other hand the song seemed of unusual interest, we have exercised some judgment as to what the underlying tune was.

There was also a tremendous change in Frank's singing style over the twenty-five-year span. The early material is sung in a young man's baritone voice with a very straightforward rhythm and phrasing, corresponding to the rather basic guitar style. The material recorded in the late 1950s or early 1960s, liberated from the pounding guitar, is sung with much more subtlety of timing and phrasing, and in a voice about a fifth lower with much more character. When Frank was doing a song he really knew well, and playing his wonderful fretless banjo, he was a superb traditional artist. His voice and style were absolutely haunting when he was at his best.

A substantial portion of Frank's material was clearly black in origin—the Proffitts apparently had black neighbors on Beech Mountain—and he absorbed the black vocal style quite well. I have attempted to capture some of that with the notation of the quarter-tones (see Music Editor's Preface).

102. Bolamkin

There is just one line of tune here (repeated); it was very easy to imagine that there may have been more. I have recently found in Brewster, *Songs & Ballads of Indiana* an almost identical tune, but with a different line of tune for the third line of a four-line verse. The Proffitt tune is essentially the first, second, and fourth line of the Indiana tune, which thus has an A-A-B-A structure. I am convinced that the Proffitt tune is a corruption of such a more substantial tune. In the first verse Frank lengthens the second note to a dotted quarter, thus producing a 4/4 bar. The mode is pentatonic, mode III.

103. Dan Doo

The 2/4 bar of rest is, I suspect, just an artifact of the guitar. The tune has a normal twelve-bar symmetry if this measure is eliminated. Except for the penultimate note, the entire tune is on the notes of the G-major chord.

104. Lowland Low

While similar to other traditional American tunes to this ballad, this tune seems repetitive and constricted in range. I suspect that Frank's memory of this tune was not too clear. The tune is pentatonic, mode I.

105. Hang Man

This tune was originally pieced together with some guesswork, as the singing was clearly being affected by the guitar. Frank was playing the chords of D-major in a way clearly inappropriate to this tune. We have recently found an unaccompanied performance of the song, recorded during an interview with Frank conducted by Douglas Kennedy at Pinewoods Camp in 1961. The original guesswork turned out to be quite accurate. The tune is pentatonic, mode IV, which has no third. I have put F-sharp in the key signature, since Frank seems to have thought of the song as "major." The singer who wishes to accompany this song should beware, however. The song requires a modal accompaniment, and is definitely *not* in D-major.

106. James Campbell

A fine pentatonic tune, clearly of considerable ancestry, played on the banjo. The mode is pentatonic, mode I (C is tonic).

107. Lord Randall

Frank accompanied this on the banjo but in a very uncharacteristic style. He simply strums a chord, as if he did not quite know how to accompany the song. The scale is hexatonic, no sixth. But with a major third and raised seventh there is only one realistic choice for the sixth; thus, the mode is essentially Ionian.

109. A Song of a Lost Hunter

The modal character of this hauntingly beautiful tune is of interest. The basic tune is pentatonic, mode IV (no third, no sixth) with a single instance of the third (major) at the last note of bar 3. Given that the third is major, one might conclude that the tune is essentially in E-major and would be harmonized as such (Frank sang it unaccompanied). This is a case where musical instinct must dominate over theoretical rules. I have noted the key signature as E-minor rather than E-major, since I believe that the "feel" of the tune is overwhelmingly minor and not major, the G-sharp at the end of bar 3 serving not as a major third in the basic scale but as a leading tone to the A of the next bar. I believe that anyone choosing to put chords to this would be well served by choosing the key as E-minor.

110. Rose Connally

The song is in concert E-major, but he is playing in C shapes (referring to his left-hand chord position), presumably capoed 4 frets. The repeat of the second half of the tune seems most unusual for a tune of this type and may well be a mistake.

111. Court House

Sung unaccompanied. In the second verse the first note of bar 7 is B, not D.

112. Don Kelly's Girl

The guitar does not constrain him too much here, and the nice syncopated vocal rhythm is readily apparent.

113. Hillsville Virginia (Sidney Allen)

I once heard a friend, who was from the area where the events described in this song took place, sing this song (with fretless banjo) to an old sounding modal tune that could not have been much more different from Frank Proffitt's tune. Frank's tune, being of a rollicking, "good-time" sort of character, seems at variance with the content of the song, although of course when a song arises from some dramatic local event, local songwriters may grab any well-known tune and put new words to it. It is also possible that several different tunes spontaneously arose at the time to describe the events. In any case, I cannot help speculating that Frank knew of the song but did not really remember the tune and put this tune to the words. Or perhaps he remembered the general shape of the tune and was pushed into this tune by the major guitar chords; there are other examples of this in the collection.

114. Lawson Family Murder

Frank played this on the guitar in E. The tune is typical of a certain genre of recent American songs usually narrating a particular tragedy.

115. The Pretty Fair Widow

There were many minor variations in the tune as Frank sang the different verses. The tune shown is a consensus, with the two most frequent alternates shown. The tune is pentatonic, mode III.

116. The Ballad of Naomi Wise

In the first verse the third beat of bar 2 is sung as D rather than E, otherwise pretty much the standard tune.

117. Poor Man

This song is done in a very free-form style over a drone type of banjo. The tune shown has been put into a regular measure length rather with a shoe horn. The singer who wishes to do this song can feel quite free with the timing.

118. Tom Dooley

This most famous of Frank Proffitt's songs was also recorded many times: first in 1940 on the guitar (in G), in 1959 on the banjo (in B-flat!), and again for Folk-Legacy Records (banjo) in 1961. There are differences of both tune and words among these versions. The printed tune is closest to the 1961 recording. All three recordings agree on the tune of bars 3 and 4; these in turn are quite different from the way Frank Warner learned the song. It was Frank Warner's tune that made its way into popular culture and went around the world. Interestingly, the song is now being sung by Frank Proffitt, Jr., who is sure that he learned it from his father; young Frank's tune, however, is as sung by Frank Warner, not his father.

119. Beaver Dam Road

One of many Proffitt songs that are heavily influenced by black singing, if not taken directly from black sources. The quarter tone at the third of the scale, as shown in the key signature, is quite clear and consistent.

120. Cluck Old Hen

This tune is well known to many white mountain musicians, yet it seems to carry the stamp of black origin, or at least heavy black influence. This is certainly true the way Frank performs it. We have, exactly like "Reuben's Train," the quarter tone at the third consistently and the gapped scale anchored to the tonic triad. In this case the scale is a bit fuller than "Reuben's Train," containing also the flat seventh. The early blues players, particularly Charley Patton, would often use a scale that consisted of basically five notes, and was *not* one of the "white" pentatonic modes. The blues scales were always centered on the tonic triad, one-three-five, with the third ambiguous as to its major or minor character. When additional tones are added, they are typically the fourth, and a note which will be either the raised six or flat seven.

121. Goin' 'Cross the Mountain

This is recorded three times: in 1959, 1960, and (for Folk-Legacy Records) 1961. All three versions are slightly different. The printed version is primarily from the 1961 version. The tune is pentatonic, mode III (tonic is D).

122. Gonna Keep My Skillet Greasy

The grace note G-sharp in bars 7 and 8 is my notation for a kind of vocal scoop up from below. The singer wishing to reproduce this decoration should not worry about being too precise on the pitch of the grace note. The tune is again pentatonic, mode III (ignoring the grace notes).

123. Groundhog

This was done verse, instrumental, verse, instrumental with Frank on guitar and another relative on dulcimer. The "advanced" downbeat (last note of bar 2) is from the dulcimer playing. The vocal starts this phrase on the downbeat of bar 3, probably because of the guitar strum.

124. I'm Goin' Back to North Carolina

Played on the banjo, this beautiful song is pentatonic, mode III.

125. I'm Goin' to Pick My Banjo

Played (logically enough) on the banjo, this is another "good-time" time. The mode is pentatonic, mode III.

126. I Wish I Was a Single Girl Again

Again clear evidence of black influence in the quarter tones at the third.

127. When I Was Single

This was apparently a popular song at one time; even my aunt knew it and said she learned it as a teenager. Frank sang it unaccompanied.

128. Single Girl, Married Girl

The alternation between 3/4 bars and common time bars seems to be the intention. Whether that is in fact the correct tune is less clear to me.

129. Johnson Boys

Played on guitar in C, capoed two frets. The alternates shown for bars 2 and 8 are, in my opinion, more likely correct; they were probably changed to the notes shown for the first verse since the latter better fit the guitar chords. Again pentatonic, mode III.

130. Marching On

A free rendering of the "Battle Hymn of the Republic," played on the banjo.

131. Moonshine

At the end of each phrase (after the third beat of bar 2 or bar 4, for example), Frank would sometimes throw in two extra beats of guitar strum. This would seem to happen in a random way, unrelated to any particular narrative intention. I believe that the base tune does not have these pauses.

132. Poor Soldier

As irregular as this tune seems on paper it is not nearly so irregular as Frank Proffitt sang it. He clearly had neither a definite meter nor a fixed sequence of pitches in his head for this song. He had a scale (pentatonic, mode I) and a general shape of the tune. The reader should feel quite free in singing this tune with a timing that seems comfortable and fits the words. I have put down on paper an approximation of the singing of the first verse; the other verses differ at times in pitch and differ constantly in rhythm. The whole is sung in a chantlike manner, very free form.

133. Reuben's Train

Played on the banjo in a highly syncopated style, this song is clearly of black origin. Not only the quarter tone at the third but the scale itself testify to that. The scale contains just four notes and is anchored to the tonic triad (1-3-5). This is often found in early blues material (see, for example, my notes to the recording: *Charley Patton—Founder of the Delta Blues* (Yazoo Records, L-1020).

134. Shulls Mills

Clearly of black origin, judging from the tune. The vocal rhythm was done very freely over a rhythmic guitar. The flat third (A-flat) over the IV chord in bar 5, is *not* a mode change. It is simply the use of IV_7 as sub-dominant in place of the simple IV; this device is typical of black blues-type material.

135. This World Is Not My Home

There are many small variants here in the second recorded verse: the last note of bar 5 is sung as F-sharp, the first note of bar 7 sung as F-sharp, the last note of bar 13 sung as F-sharp. The tune is pentatonic, mode III.

136. Trifling Woman

This was played with banjo; nevertheless I have included chords because the banjo was played in a chordal fashion (and the chords make some sense).

137. 'Way Down in Columbus, Georgia

The original is in B-flat, played on guitar in A shapes and capoed one fret. Again the grace notes in bars 21 and 22 are my representation of a vocal scoop from below.

138. W. P. and A.

Six verses were recorded, all of them different. The first two seem simply unsure; by the third he seems to have settled into a clear tune which is printed here. Verses 4, 5, and 6 are as 3 except that the opening is all on the note A until the last quarter note of bar 1.

139. Wild Bill Jones

This falls in the same category as "Reuben's Train" and "Cluck Old Hen." It is clearly of black origin, or heavily black influenced. Even though the scale is a full seven notes (and more), we have the quarter tone at the third and the scale (tune) strongly anchored around the tonic triad.

CHARLES K. (TINK), ELEAZAR, AND DICK TILLETT AND CAPTAIN ALBERT AND MARTHA ETHERIDGE

There is a great similarity in the style of the singers from the North Carolina Outer Banks, a style that is clearly characteristic of this narrow region, since it contrasts strongly with the singing found in the North Carolina mountain singers. These singers of the coastal region are closer in sound to English rural singers than are any other regional singers I know of. They are closer in repertoire and style to English rural singers than they are to the rural singers of their own state a few hundred miles to the west. The singing of the Outer Banks has a simplicity and a lyrical quality; it has a natural speaking quality that is very winning. Part of the reason that the singing sounds so different from that of the mountains is because the speech seems so different; the older generation do not sound to me like any other speech pattern I know of in the American South; again, they sound to me most like English country people.

140. Lord Thomas

The elder Tilletts apparently had a very complete version of this song, but the recording was lost. Dick Tillett, the son, made a cassette of an elderly neighbor who knew the song. The tune is extremely close to a tune to "Lord Thomas" sung by Rebecca King Jones. I am convinced they are the same version with minor variations. The printed tune is from Ivy Evans, the Tilletts' neighbor, except for the very end. Evans returns to the F for the last note. I have chosen Jones' note C at the end because tunes of this song from that area often have that ending and because the structure of this tune implies so strongly the pentatonic, mode I. I believe Ivy Evans went up to the F to provide a "more normal" sounding major key. The version from Proffitt is also quite similar and finishes with the lower note.

Because of its exceptional quality we are printing the Proffitt tune as well. Frank Proffitt was audibly unclear on how this tune should go. There are wide differences between verses. The published tune is our collective wisdom of what the underlying tune is. The tune is hexatonic, no third (if C is tonic).

141. The Banks of Newfoundland

The last note of bar 3 is not recorded as the disk skipped. I have filled in the note from the English tune, to which this tune is very close. The mode is Dorian.

142. Barbaree

Many readers will be familiar with this song from the singing of Frank Warner or of Jeff and Gerret Warner. Frank changed the tune substantially in the second verse line so that it finished on the fifth (F) instead of the third (D). Thus Frank started the second refrain line on the fifth instead of the tonic. Many songs where Frank changed the tune he improved; I am not sure if he did here or not—the tune is wonderful both ways! The tune is hexatonic (no seventh— B-flat is tonic).

143. Bony on the Isle of St. Helena

I had never heard another version of this song in oral tradition until very recently. An Irish version is being sung now by some English revival singers. "Tink" Tillett's version is more complete, and the verses seem to make more sense. The tune is pentatonic, mode III.

144. The Fisherman's Girl

There are two singers on this song. The second singer sings G for the second quarter note of bar 3, and sings D for the second and fourth quarter notes of bar 12. The mode is Dorian.

145. The Golden Glove

The third quarter note of bar 3 is sung twice as C and twice as B. This is a fine tune; all four lines seem similar, but no two are the same. The mode is Ionian.

146. The Jolly Thresher

The singer seems to have a different opening of the tune in mind when she starts; after a couple of verses she gradually settles into the opening shown. The first verse actually begins most interestingly:

The tune is Mixolydian mode.

147. John Reilly

A tune very much in the same style as "Seventy-Two Today": 3/4 meter, lyrical in style, and pentatonic, mode III.

148. My Parents Raised Me Tenderly

Again a very closely related tune to "Seventy-Two Today" and "John Reilly": lyrical tune in 3/4 meter, pentatonic, mode III (with tonic F).

149. Indeed Pretty Polly

Here we see the striking use of the hold on the second beat of a 3/4 bar, a device so much used by Yankee John Galusha. The tune is Ionian mode.

150. The Prince Boys

This tune is similar to many others to the same song, particularly tunes of English origin (the usual title is "The Bold *Princess Royal*"). Again pentatonic, mode III.

151. Scarborough Sand

It was not completely clear how to notate the variations of meter in this song. Most of it is clearly 3/4; the third bar from the end was clearly 4/4. The two bars with the holds were questionable. The structure shown should give the reader a pretty good idea of how it was sung. If the reader should prefer, the holds in bars 2 and 12 can be ignored.

152. The Sheffield 'Prentice

The alternation between lower and raised seventh (C-natural and C-sharp) is quite clear and definitely intentional. The mode is basically Mixolydian with the seventh raised at cadence points.

153. Paul Jones

Unlike many of the Tilletts' other songs, this is sung in a declamatory rather than lyrical style with dramatic use of the hold on the second beat of the bar, perhaps because the song is rather clearly *not* of English origin.

154. A Poor Little Sailor Boy

This tune is clearly derived from the Irish "Star of the County Down," only the meter has been changed from waltz time to common meter, and the first and third strains end on the tonic rather than the expected seventh (D). I would even guess that this may be a lapse of memory, and the tune the singer first heard actually had the seventh at these two places (first note of bars 4 and 12). The scale is hexatonic—minor, no sixth.

155. A Sailor's Grave

The refrain line (after the repeat) is essentially the second strain of the tune repeated. Thus the tune has the form A-B-A-B-B. The scale is hexatonic—major, no seventh.

156. The Southern Girl's Reply

So many of the Outer Banks tunes seem quite old, at least coming from a period where oral tradition was not conscious of "chords." This tune is such a contrast to that, having a rather Victorian character, which clearly dates it from the latter half of the nineteenth century.

157. Her Bright Smile Haunts Me Still

This tune has a very modern ring to it; Mrs. Tillett sang it with much tenderness and purity. The tune is hexatonic—major, no fourth.

158. Seventy-Two Today

This tune is typical of the easy, lyrical style that one finds in the coastal songs. The tune is pentatonic, mode III.

159. Old Rosin the Beau

The tune is identical to the very well-known one except for the second phrase, which here starts low instead of high and finishes on five of the scale instead of the usual six. I strongly suspect that Dick Tillett from whom the Warners got this tune, corrupted it due to lack of memory as to how the second phrase should go. Again, pentatonic, mode III.

170. Somebody is Waiting for Me

"Tink" Tillett played this as an accordian tune; words were later provided by his son to the Warners. I am certain that the 3/2 bars are just an artifact of the accordian. They all occur at the end of the phrase where "Tink" is not quite sure how to mark time before starting the next phrase. If this had been sung, each of the starting notes of the 3/2 bars would have been lengthened by one pulse (i.e., one half-note).

161. The Snow Is on the Ground

The modal interest is in the tension between the flat and the raised seventh (Mixolydian or Ionian). Actually the dominant feel of the tune is Mixolydian with raised leading tones at cadences in bars 7, 15, and 31.

CURT MANN

162. Lonesome Valley

While this may seem like a transcription for the tabernacle choir, this is in fact how it was sung on the tape. There were three singers (one of whom may have been Frank Warner); the two men sang the verse and the woman joined for the chorus.

MARTHA ANN MIDGETTE

163. Tommy

The last note of bar 2 is often sung as B rather than F-sharp. Ionian mode.

164. Wallabug

The recording skipped a few notes in the third to the last measure. The published tune has a bit of guesswork at this spot. One hears the old modes even in a "silly" song like this, pentatonic, mode III. This mode is extremely popular in the songs from this area.

165. Old Grey Beard

Another "silly" song, but this one is Ionian mode.

CAPTAIN JOHN AND ALWILDA CULPEPER

166. Show Me the Man Who Never Done Wrong

Why is it that there are a lot of lullabys in tradition where the mother is lamenting to the baby that the father is down at the boozers. In this song the situation is reversed. A lovely, rather modern-sounding tune in Ionian mode.

KACK AND SASS HATHAWAY

167. Careless Love

This is one of a number that had to be transcribed from the singing of Frank Warner. As syncopated as the tune appears on paper, it was far more so when Frank sang it, with great variations of timing on the different verses.

SUE THOMAS AND J. B. SUTTON

Frank Warner was known as a consummate interpreter of black traditional material among white singers, with a tremendous ability for syncopation and the highly complex rhythmic variations characteristic of black rural material. It was thus surprising to hear how simple and straightforward was the material from Sue Thomas and J. B. Sutton. The glissando notation for these singers does *not* indicate the break into falsetto, but simply a slide either to a definite upper note, where shown, or to an indistinct trail off.

168. He's Got the Whole World in His Hand
170. Let Me Ride

These two songs were taken from the singing of Frank Warner. The rhythm of "He's Got the Whole World in His Hand" is different from what is usually heard. I have no way of knowing how close this is to the rhythm that Sue Thomas sang.

169. Hold My Hand, Lord Jesus

I heard Frank Warner sing this many, many times. He sang it in a more intense and rhythmically complex style than did Sue Thomas. Her singing seems very—*immediate* seems to be the best word I can find.

171. Nobody Knows

The E-natural in bar 5 is quite distinct from the quarter tone at the third that occurs elsewhere in the tune. It is probably felt as a leading tone to the F of the next bar.

172. You Can't Hurry God

Again here a great directness and simplicity; the quarter tones, of course, are central in much black traditional material.

173. Mail Day

Sung in the slow, heavy style one expects from a prison work song. One hears the very strong pulse, even where the voice has a rest on the beat, that seems to mark where the prison hammer might strike rock. The tune is in the typical black, four-note scale: the tonic triad (with quarter tone at the third) plus one extra note at either the major sixth or minor seventh (major sixth in this case).

174. Thirty Days in Jail

Unlike "O Bud," this tune has a solid blues base; one can "hear" the chord progression underneath.

175. O Bud

The third here does not seem to be the usual quarter tone but a fairly definite minor. Perhaps because the tune is *not* of the blues type (built on the tonic triad with quarter tone third). Instead it is typical of an older kind of black rural tune, that is, almost like a chant on the tonic with occasional brief excursions to the minor third above or below.

ANNIE _____

176. Wictory

Sung to me directly by Anne Warner, the timings were a bit more variable and the meter a bit less clear than I have made it. Note the consistent use of the quarter tone at the *fifth* (and at the third of the dominant chord), again seeming to indicate to me black origin.

WARREN PAYNE

178. Lather and Shave

This song must have been quite popular sometime around the turn of the century, as it has been collected a number of times, particularly from American-Irish sources. It always seems to have the same structure and the same jig-time meter. Captain Payne's tune seems like a simplified version of the usual tune, being tied almost entirely to the tonic triad, except for bars 3 and 4.

TOM SMITH

179. The Wreck on the C & O
There seems to be an extra line of text in the first verse, so the second half of the verse is repeated, as shown (first verse only).

180. Git Along Josie
Tom announces this as "Uncle Fred's banjo tune." The scale is unusual: the first five notes of the major scale—no sixth, no seventh.

181. Lynchburg Town
Unlike the other songs from Tom Smith, this has a very syncopated, rhythmic style. I would guess possibly black origin for it.

182. The Old Geezer
The tune is clearly a variant of "The Red-Haired Boy" (or "The Jolly Beggarman") (without the B part). The first phrase of that tune usually finishes on the flat seventh (Mixolydian) which here would be E-flat. Tom is apparently not comfortable with that and thus ends the first phrase on the tonic. Without that seventh the scale is hexatonic.

JOSEPH HENRY JOHNSON

Joseph Henry Johnson was so close to death when the Warners reached him that he was not really able to sing. He speaks the words clearly on the recording but there are no really intelligible tunes. On one song ("All Seeing Eye"), it might have been possible to hazard a guess at a tune. We felt that the result would have been more our guesswork than it would have been "Uncle Joe"; thus no tunes are given.

ANONYMOUS

186. Raccoon
Taken from the singing (and inimitable banjo playing) of Frank Warner, I do not believe the source from which Frank got this is known. It seems clearly of black origin. For the first

four bars, Frank played a single chord on the first note of the bar and the holds shown in bars 2 and 4 were just silence. The tempo picked up, the banjo strum became continuous—the train really seemed to get moving—in the last four bars of sung tune. As the voice ended Frank would often give a "holler" while going into the instrumental break.

REBECCA KING JONES

187. Barbara Allen

Mrs. Jones's prodigious abilities as a traditional stylist really shine forth in these two wonderful tunes of this great ballad. The two tunes are similar in structure and in meter, but it is clear that they are distinct tunes. Tune I is Mixolydian mode but in the fifth (complete) bar the raised seventh is clearly and consistently used (*not* as a leading tone) in the ornament note. The rising glissando notation indicates the voice break into falsetto, often thought of as a personal characteristic of Almeda Riddle. The second tune is pure pentatonic scale, mode III.

188. Wake, O Wake, You Drowsy Sleeper

The tune is pentatonic (mode III) except for the third quarter note of bar 10. This note is somewhat ambiguous as to whether it is C or C-sharp. I considered notating this as a quarter tone, but felt that a quarter tone at the seventh would be a stylistic aberration both for Mrs. Jones and for her region and her material. I feel that the flat seventh is closest to her intention.

189. Chimbley Sweeper

Several notes are sung differently in the second verse: The first note is sung as F, the last note of bar 3 as G, the second note of bar 7 as C. The tune is hexatonic—major, no seventh.

190. Rocky by Baby, By-O

The tune shown is the singing of the first verse. Later verses differ in many small details. The mode is Ionian.

PRISCILLA DYER ALLEN

191. Bold Dickie and Bold Archie

This was transcribed very early, in 1977. The tune of the fourth verse was taken down at that time, apparently because the tune of the first was unclear on the recording. I have had to use a bit of judgment as to how the syllables of the first line fit in.

477

ROY WALWORTH

192. Doodle Dandy
Again, the reader may be familiar with this from the singing of Frank Warner. Frank changed it (and probably improved it).

CLEM STRUDWICK
LLOYD BOWMAN

193. The Song of the Rebel Soldier
194. An Old Unreconstructed
These two songs apparently have the same tune. No original recording seems to exist; thus, the transcription is from the singing of Frank Warner. The tune is pentatonic, mode III.

DEAC MARTIN

195. Away, Idaho
The source played guitar on the recording and was clearly not averse to some fancy chords (e.g., the C-sharp seventh in the last line).

Selected Bibliography

Abell, Dr. Charles T. Collection of Broadsides, Harvard University Library. Cambridge.

Abrahams, Roger. *A Singer and Her Songs* (Almeda Riddle). Baton Rouge: Louisiana State University Press, 1970.

Adams, Samuel Hopkins. *Canal Town.* Cleveland and New York: World Publishing Co., 1945.

_____. *Grandfather Stories.* New York: Random House, 1955.

Allan, Francis D. *Allan's Lone Star Ballads: A Collection of Southern Patriotic Songs, made during Confederate Times* (Galveston, TX: J. D. Sawyer, 1874).

Appalachian Journal. Boone, NC: Appalachian State University.

Arnold, Byron. *Folksongs of Alabama.* University, AL: University of Alabama Press, 1950.

Arnold, W. H. *Billy's Request Songster.* New York: Popular Publishing Co., 1880.

Ashton, John. *Real Sailor Songs.* London: Leadenhall Press, 1891.

Baring-Gould, S., and H. Fleetwood Sheppard. *Songs and Ballads of the West.* 2 vols. London: Methuen, 1895.

Barry, Phillips. *The Maine Woods Songster.* Cambridge: Powell Printing Co., 1939.

_____, Fannie Hardy Eckstorm, and Mary Winslow Smyth. *British Ballads from Maine.* New Haven: Yale University Press, 1929. (Cited as Barry-Eckstorm.)

Barry-Eckstorm. See Barry, Phillips, Fannie Hardy Eckstorm, and Mary Winslow Smith. *British Ballads from Maine.*

Bayard, Samuel P. *Hill Country Tunes.* Memoir 39. Philadelphia: American Folklore Society, 1944.

Beck, E. C. *Lore of the Lumber Camps.* Ann Arbor: University of Michigan Press, 1948.

_____. *Songs of the Michigan Lumberjacks.* Ann Arbor: University of Michigan Press, 1941.

Beck, Horace P. *The Folklore of Maine.* Philadelphia and New York: J. B. Lippincott Co., 1957.

Belden, H. M. *Ballads and Songs Collected by the Missouri Folklore Society.* Columbia: University of Missouri, 1940. 2d ed., 1955.

Benét, William Rose. *The Reader's Encyclopedia.* New York: Thomas Y. Crowell Co., 1965.

Beston, Henry. *Northern Farm.* New York: Holt, Rinehart & Winston, 1948. Reprinted, New York: Ballantine Books, 1971.

_____. *Outermost House.* New York: Rinehart & Co., 1928.

Boatner, Edward. *Spirituals Triumphant, Old and New.* Nashville: Sunday School Publishing Board, National Baptist Convention, U.S.A., 1927.

Botkin, Benjamin A., with Alvin F. Harlow. *A Treasury of American Folklore.* New York: Crown, 1944.

———. *A Treasury of Railroad Folklore.* New York: Crown, 1953.

Bronson, Bertrand. *The Traditional Tunes of the Child Ballads.* Vols. 1–4. Princeton: Princeton University Press, 1959–72.

Brown, Frank C. *Folk Ballads from North Carolina* and *Folk Songs from North Carolina.* Edited by Henry M. Belden and Arthur Palmer Hudson. Durham: Duke University Press, 1952. (Vols. 2 and 3 of the 1–7 vols. of the *Frank C. Brown Collection of North Carolina Folklore.*)

Brumley, Albert E. *Old Time Camp Meetin' Songs.* Camdenton, MO. 1971.

Buchanan, Annabel Morris. *Folk Hymns of America.* New York: J. Fisher and Bro., 1938.

Bulletin. See *Bulletin of the Folk-Song Society of the Northeast.*

Bulletin of the Folk-Song Society of the Northeast. Nos. 1–12. Cambridge, MA, 1930–37. (Cited as *Bulletin.*)

Burton, Thomas G., *Some Ballad Folk* (with cassette of singers). Johnson City, TN: East Tennessee State University, 1978.

———, and Ambrose N. Manning. *Folksongs II.* Johnson City, TN: Research Advisory Council, E. Tennessee State University, 1969.

Carmer, Carl. *The Hudson.* New York: Farrar and Rinehart, 1939.

———. *Stars Fell on Alabama.* New York: Farrar and Rinehart, 1934.

Cazden, Norman. *The Abelard Folk Song Book.* New York: Abelard-Schuman, 1958. (Cited as Cazden I.)

———, Herbert Haufrecht, and Norman Studer. *Folk Songs of the Catskills.* Albany: State University of New York Press, 1982. (Cited as Cazden II.)

Chambers, E. K. *The Medieval Stage.* 2 vols. Oxford: Clarendon Press, 1903.

Chappell, Louis W. *Folksongs of Roanoke and the Albemarle.* Morgantown, WV; The Ballad Press, 1939.

Chappell, William. *Popular Music of The Olden Time.* 2 vols. New York: Dover Publications, 1965. (First published, London: Chappell & Co., 1859.)

Chapple, Joe Mitchell. *Heart Songs Dear to the American People.* Chapple Publishing Co., 1909. Reprinted, Cleveland: World Publishing Co., 1950.

Chase, Richard. *American Folk Tales and Songs.* New York: Signet Key Paperback, 1956.

———. *Grandfather Tales.* Boston: Houghton Mifflin, 1948.

———. *The Jack Tales.* Boston: Houghton Mifflin, 1943.

Child, Francis James. *The English and Scottish Popular Ballads.* 5 vols. Boston: Houghton Mifflin Press, 1882–89.

Christie, W. *Traditional Ballad Airs.* 2 vols. Edinburgh: Edmonston and Douglas, 1876–81.

Churchill, Winston. *The Crisis.* New York: Grosset and Dunlap, 1901.

Coffin, Mark Tristram. *American Narrative Obituary Verse and Native American Balladry.* Norwood, PA: Norwood Editions, 1975.

Coffin, Tristram P. *The British Traditional Ballad in North America.* American Folklore Society, 1950. (See Coffin and Renwick.)

———, and Roger deV. Renwick. *The British Traditional Ballad in North America.* Enlarged and revised edition, with Supplement by Roger deV. Renwick. Austin and London: University of Texas Press, 1977.

Cohen, Norm. *Long Steel Rail, The Railroad in American Folksong.* Urbana; University of Illinois Press, 1981.

Colcord, Joanna. *Songs of American Sailormen.* New York: W. W. Norton, 1938.

Combs, Josiah H. *Folk-Songs du Midi des États-Unis.* Paris: Les Presses Universitaires de France, 1925.

Copper, Bob. *Early To Rise: A Sussex Boyhood.* London: William Heinemann, Ltd., 1976.

_____. *A Song for Every Season.* London: William Heinemann, Ltd., 1971.

Cox, John Harrington. *Folk Songs of the South.* Cambridge: Harvard University Press, 1925.

Creighton, Helen. *Maritime Folk Songs.* East Lansing: Michigan State University Press, 1962.

_____. *Songs and Ballads from Nova Scotia.* Toronto: Dent and Sons, 1933. Reprinted, New York: Dover Publications, 1966.

_____, with Doreen Senior. *Traditional Songs of Nova Scotia.* Toronto: The Ryerson Press, 1950.

Damon, S. Foster. "Series of Old American Songs." Harris Collection, Brown University. Providence: Brown University Press, 1936.

Davis, Arthur Kyle, Jr. *Folk-Songs of Virginia: A Descriptive Index and Classification.* Durham: Duke University Press, 1949.

_____. *More Traditional Ballads of Virginia.* Chapel Hill: University of North Carolina Press, 1960.

_____. *Traditional Ballads of Virginia.* Cambridge Harvard University Press, 1929.

Dean, Michael C. *The Flying Cloud and 150 Other Old Time Songs and Ballads of Outdoor Men, Sailors, Lumberjacks, Men of the Great Lakes, etc.* Virginia, MN: The Quickprint, (n.d.).

Denson, O. W. *Original Sacred Harp.* Cullman, Ala. 1960.

Doerflinger, William Main. *Shanty Men and Shanty Boys.* New York: Macmillan, 1951. Later edition: *Songs of the Sailor and Lumberman.* New York: Macmillan, 1972.

Eckstorm, Fannie, and Mary Winslow Smyth. *Minstrelsy of Maine.* Boston: Houghton Mifflin, 1927.

Eddy, Mary O. *Ballads and Songs from Ohio.* New York: J. J Augustin, 1939.

Emrich, Duncan. *American Folk Poetry.* Boston: Little Brown, 1974.

_____. *Folklore on the American Land.* Boston: Little Brown, 1972.

Ewing, George W. *The Well-Tempered Lyre: Songs and Verse of the Temperance Movement.* Dallas: Southern Methodist University Press, 1977.

Fife, Austin E., and Francesca Redden. "The Indian Song." *Journal of American Folklore* 67 (October–December 1954): 379–94.

Finger, Charles J. *Frontier Ballads.* New York: Doubleday, Page and Co., 1927.

Flanders, Helen Hartness. *Ancient Ballads Traditionally Sung in New England.* Vols. 1–4. Philadelphia: University of Pennsylvania Press, 1965.

_____, Elizabeth Flanders Ballard, George Brown, and Phillips Barry. *The New Green Mountain Songster: Traditional Folksongs of Vermont.* New Haven: Yale University Press, 1939. (Cited as Flanders-Barry, *NGMS.*)

_____, and George Brown. *Vermont Folksongs and Ballads.* Brattleboro, VT: Stephen Daye Press, 1931. (Cited as Flanders, *VFSB.*)

_____, and Marguerite Olney. *Ballads Migrant in New England.* New York: Farrar, Straus, and Young, 1953.

Ford, Robert. *Auld Scots Ballants.* London: Alexander Gardner, 1889.

_____. *Vagabond Songs and Ballads of Scotland*. First and second series. Paisley, Scotland, and London: Alexander Gardner, 1899, 1901.

Ford, Worthington C. *Traditional Music of America*. The Isaiah Thomas Collection of Ballads. Worcester, MA; The American Antiquarian Society, 1924.

The Forget Me Not Songster, Philadelphia and New York: Turner & Fisher, c. 1850. Earlier editions: Nafis and Cornish, [n.d.]; and Philadelphia and Baltimore, Fisher and Bros., [n.d.].

Fowke, Edith. *Folk Songs of Canada*. Waterloo: Waterloo Music Co., 1954.

_____. *Lumbering Songs from the Northern Woods*. American Folklore Society. Austin and London: University of Texas Press, 1970.

_____. *Penguin Book of Canadian Folksongs*. Middlesex, England: Penguin Books, 1978.

_____, and Joe Glazer. *Songs of Work and Protest*. Reprinted, New York: Dover Publications, 1973.

Fuson, Harvey H. *Ballads of the Kentucky Highlands*. (Words only). London: The Mitre Press, 1931.

Gardner, Emelyn E., and Geraldine J. Chickering. *Ballads and Songs of Southern Michigan*. Ann Arbor: University of Michigan Press, 1939.

Gerould, Gordon Hall. *The Ballad of Tradition*. New York: Oxford Press, 1932.

Gordon, Robert W. *Folk Songs of America*. New York: National Service Bureau, 1938.

Green, Archie. *Only a Miner: Studies in Recorded Coal Mining Songs*. Urbana: University of Illinois Press, 1972.

Greenleaf, Elizabeth, and Grace Mansfield. *Ballads and Sea Songs from Newfoundland*. Cambridge: Harvard University Press. 1933.

Greenway, John. *American Folk Songs of Protest*. Philadelphia: University of Pennsylvania, 1953.

Greig, Gavin. *Folk-Song of the North-East*. 2 vols. Peterhead: "Buchan Observer" Works. 1909–14.

_____, and Alexander Keith. *Last Leaves of Traditional Ballads and Ballad Airs*. Aberdeen: The Buchan Club. 1925.

Grover, Carrie B. *A Heritage of Songs*. ed. Anne L. Griggs. Privately printed, Bethel, ME: Gould Academy, [n.d.]. Reprinted, Norwood, PA: Norwood Editions, 1975.

Herd, David. *Ancient and Modern Scottish Songs, Heroic Ballads, etc.* 2 vols. Reprinted from the ed. of 1776. Glasgow: 1869.

Harris, Joel Chandler. *Nights With Uncle Remus*. Boston and New York: Houghton Mifflin, 1911.

_____. *Uncle Remus, His Songs and Sayings*. New York: D. Appleton & Co., 1883. Reprinted, New York: Grosset & Dunlap, 1921.

Hartley, Dorothy. *Lost Country Life*. New York: Pantheon Books, 1980.

Harvard Catalogue. See Welsh, Charles, *Catalogue of English and American Chapbooks*.

Hayward, Charles. *A Bibliography of North American Folklore and Folk Song*. 2 vols. New York: Dover Publications, 1961.

Henry, Mellinger E. *Folksongs from the Southern Highlands*. New York: J. J. Augustin, 1938.

_____. *Songs Sung in Southern Appalachia*. London: The Mitre Press, 1934.

_____, and Maurice Matteson. *Beech Mountain Ballads and Folksongs*. New York: Schirmer & Co., 1937.

Hochschild, Harold K. *Lumberjacks and Rivermen in the Central Adirondacks: 1850–1950*. Blue Mountain Lake, NY: Adirondack Museum, 1962.

_____. *Life and Leisure in the Adirondack Backwoods*. Blue Mountain Lake, NY: Adirondack Museum, 1962.

Howard, John Tasker. *Stephen Foster: America's Troubadour.* New York: Thomas Y. Crowell Co., c. 1934.

Hubbard, Lester A. *Ballads and Songs from Utah.* Salt Lake City: University of Utah Press, 1961.

Hudson, Arthur Palmer. *Folksongs of Mississippi.* Chapel Hill: University of North Carolina Press, 1936.

Hugill, Stan. *Shanties from the Seven Seas.* London: Routledge & Kegan Paul; New York: E. P. Dutton & Co., 1966.

Huntington, Gale. *Songs the Whalemen Sang.* Barre, MA: Barre Publishers, 1964.

Ives, Burl. *The Burl Ives Song Book.* New York: Ballantine Books, 1953.

Jackson, George Pullen. *Another Sheaf of White Spirituals.* Gainesville: University of Florida Press, 1952.

_____. *Down East Spirituals.* New York: J. J. Augustin, Da Capo Press, 1943–75.

_____. *Spiritual Folksongs of Early America.* New York: J. J. Augustin, 1937.

_____. *White Spirituals in the Southern Uplands.* Chapel Hill: University of North Carolina Press, 1933.

JAF(L). See *Journal of American Folklore.*

JEFDSS. See *Journal of the English Folk Dance and Song Society.*

JFSS. See *Journal of the Folk-Song Society.*

Johnson, James Weldon. *The Book of American Negro Spirituals.* New York: Viking Press, 1925.

Johnson, J. Rosamund. *Rolling Along in Song.* New York: Viking Press, 1937.

Journal of American Folklore. American Folklore Society, 1888–. (Cited as *JAF.*)

Journal of the English Folk Dance and Song Society. English Folk Dance and Song Society, London 1932–. (Cited as *JEFDSS.*)

Journal of the Folk-Song Society. The Folk-Song Society, London, 1899–1931. (Cited as *JFSS.*)

Joyce, Patrick Weston. *Old Irish Folk Music and Song.* New York: Longmans, Green and Co., 1909.

Kennedy, Peter. *Folk Songs of Britain and Ireland.* London: Cassell, 1975.

Kephart, Horace. *Our Southern Highlanders.* New York: Macmillan Co., 1913, 1922. Also new and enlarged ed., 1936.

Kidson, Frank. *Traditional Tunes.* Oxford: Charles Taphouse & Son., 1891.

Kolb, Sylvia, and J. Kolb. *A Treasury of American Folk Song.* New York: Bantam Books, 1948.

Korson, George. *Coal Dust on the Fiddle.* Philadelphia: University of Pennsylvania Press, 1943. Reprinted, Hatboro, PA: Folklore Associates, 1965.

_____. *Minstrels of the Mine Patch.* 1938. Reprinted, Hatboro, PA: Folklore Associates, 1964.

_____. *Pennsylvania Songs and Legends.* Philadelphia: University of Pennsylvania Press, 1949.

Langstaff, John. *Hi! Ho! The Rattlin' Bog.* New York: Harcourt, Brace and World, 1969.

Laws, G. Malcolm, Jr. *American Balladry from British Broadsides.* Philadelphia: American Folklore Society, 1957. (Cited as Laws, *ABBB.*)

_____. *Native American Balladry.* Philadelphia: American Folklore Society, 1950. (Cited as Laws, *NAB.*)

Levy, David Owen. *All the Years of American Popular Music.* Englewood Cliffs, NJ: Prentice-Hall, 1977.

Library of Congress. *Check list of Recorded Songs in the English Language in the American Folk Life Archive to July 1940.* 2 vols. Mimeographed. Brochure of published recordings available through same office.

Lingenfelter, Richard E., Richard H. Dwyer, and David Cohen *Songs of the American West.* Berkeley: University of California Press, 1968.

Linscott, Eloise Hubbard. *Folksongs of Old New England.* New York: Macmillan Co., 1939.

Lomax, Alan. *The Folk Songs of North America.* New York: Doubleday, 1960. (Cited as Lomax, *FSNA.*)

Lomax, John A., and Alan Lomax. *American Ballads and Folk Songs.* New York; Macmillan Co., 1934. (Cited as Lomax, *ABF.*)

_____. *Cowboy Songs.* 2d edition. New York: Macmillan Co., 1938.

_____. *Folk Song U.S.A.* New York: Duell, Sloan and Pearce, 1947. (Cited as Lomax, *FSUSA.*)

_____. *Our Singing Country.* New York: Macmillan Co., 1941.

McCaskey, J. P. *Favorite Songs and Hymns for School and Home.* New York: American Book Co., c. 1899.

McCurry, John G. See *The Social Harp.*

Mackenzie, W. Roy. *Ballads and Sea Songs from Nova Scotia.* Cambridge: Harvard University Press, 1928.

Martin, Deac. Deac Martin's Musical Americana. Englewood Cliffs, NJ: Prentice-Hall, 1970.

Moore, Frank. *Personal and Political Ballads.* New York: George P. Putnam, 1864.

_____. *Songs and Ballads of the American Revolution.* Reprinted, New York: Arno Press, 1969.

_____. *Songs and Ballads of the Southern People, 1861–1865.* New York: D. Appleton & Co., 1886.

Morris, Alton C. *Folksongs of Florida.* Gainesville: University of Florida Press, 1950.

Motherwell, William. *Minstrelsy, Ancient and Modern.* Boston: William D. Ticknor & Co., 1846.

Neeser, Robert W. *American Naval Songs and Ballads.* New Haven: Yale University Press, 1938.

New Comic Songster. Boston: Ditson Co., 1870.

New Lost City Ramblers' Song Book. New York: Oak Publications, 1964; *Old Time String Band Song Book* (new title), 1976.

New York Folklore, Binghamton, NY: New York Folklore Society, 1977– .

New York Folklore Quarterly, Cooperstown, NY: New York Folklore Society, 1948–76.

Older, Lawrence. "Once More A-Lumbering Go," *New York Folklore Quarterly* 22, no. 2 (June 1966): 96–103.

O'Lochlainn, Colm. *Irish Street Ballads.* Corinth Books, Inc., 1960; distributed, New York: Citadel Press.

Ord, John. *Bothy Songs and Ballads.* Paisley, Scotland: Alexander Gardner, 1930.

Original Sacred Harp: Denson Revision: 1971 Edition. Bremen, GA: Sacred Harp Publishing.

Parrish, Lydia. *Slave Songs of the Georgia Sea Islands.* New York: Creative Age Press, 1942.

Pastor, Tony. *Comic and Eccentric Songster.* New York. 1862.

Patterson, Daniel W. *Songs from The Social Harp Performed by Traditional Singers.* Rounder Record No. 0094.

Peacock, Kenneth. *Songs of the Newfoundland Outports.* 3 vols. National Museum of Canada. Bulletin #197, Anthropological Series #65. Ottawa: Queens Printer, 1965.

People's Song Bulletin. New York: People's Songs, Inc., 1945– .

PMLA. Periodical published quarterly by the Modern Language Association. New York.

Pound, Louise. *American Ballads and Songs.* New York: Charles Scribner's Sons, 1922.

Pyrnelle, Mrs. Louise-Clarke. *Diddie, Dumps, and Tot.* New York: Harper & Bros., 1882.

Rabson, Carolyn. *Songbook of the American Revolution.* Peaks Island, ME: Neo Press, 1974.

Randolph, Vance. *Ozark Folk Songs.* 4 vols. Columbia, MO: State Historical Society, 1946–47. Reprinted, Columbia and London: University of Missouri Press, 1980.

Reeves, James. *The Idiom of the People.* New York: Macmillan, 1958.

Richardson, Ethel Park, and Sigmund Spaeth. *American Mountain Songs.* New York: Greenberg, 1927.

Richmond, W. Edson, and William Tillson. See Wolford, Leah Jackson, *The Play-Party in Indiana.*

Rickaby, Franz. *Ballads and Songs of the Shanty Boy.* Cambridge: Harvard University Press, 1926.

Ritchie, Jean. *Folksongs of the Southern Appalachians as Sung by Jean Ritchie.* New York: Oak Publications, 1965.

_____. *Singing Family of the Cumberlands.* New York: Oxford University Press, 1955.

The Sacred Harp. B. F. White and E. A. King. Facsimile of 3rd edition (1859). Nashville: Broadman Press, 1968.

Sandburg, Carl. *The American Songbag.* New York: Harcourt Brace & Co., 1927.

_____. *Remembrance Rock.* New York: Harcourt Brace & Co., 1948.

Sargent, Helen Child, and George Lyman Kittredge. *English and Scottish Popular Ballads.* Cambridge: Houghton, Mifflin Co., 1904. (One volume ed. of the Child Ballads.)

Scarborough, Dorothy. *A Songcatcher in the Southern Mountains.* New York: Columbia University Press, 1937.

Scott, John Anthony. *The Ballad of America.* New York: Bantam Books, 1966. New edition: Carbondale: Southern Illinois University Press, 1983.

Scott, Sir Walter. *Minstrelsy of the Scottish Border.* 4 vols. Edinburgh: Ballantyne, [n.d.]. Reprinted, New York: Thomas Y. Crowell, 1931.

Sears, Minnie Earl. *The Song Index and Its Supplement;* H. W. Wilson & Co. New York. 1926. Supplement, 1934.

SFQ. See *Southern Folklore Quarterly.*

Sharp, Cecil J. *English Folksongs of the Southern Appalachian.* 2 vols. Ed. Maud Karpeles. New York and London: Oxford University Press, 1932.

_____. *Folk-Songs of England.* 5 vols. London: Novello, 1908–12.

_____. *One Hundred English Folk Songs.* Boston: Oliver Ditson Co., 1916.

_____, and Charles Marson. *Folk-Songs from Somerset.* Five Series. London: Simpkin and Co., 1910–1919.

Shoemaker, Henry. *Mountain Minstrelsy of Pennsylvania.* Philadelphia: Newman F. McGirr, 1931.

Silber, Irwin. *Songs America Voted By.* Harrisburg, PA: Stackpole Books, 1971.

_____. *Songs of the Civil War.* New York: Columbia University Press, 1960.

_____. *Songs of Independence.* Harrisburg, PA; Stackpole, 1973.

_____, and Earl Robinson. *Songs of the Great American West.* New York: Macmillan Co., 1967.

SING OUT! Magazine, Inc. New York, 1958– ; Easton, PA, 1983– .

The Social Harp. John G. McCurry. Philadelphia: T. K. Collins, Jr., 1855. Reprinted in facsimile. Daniel W. Patterson and John F. Garst, eds. Athens: University of Georgia Press, 1973.

Southern Exposure. Chapel Hill, NC: The Institute for Southern Studies.

Southern Folklore Quarterly. Gainesville: University of Florida Press in cooperation with the Southeastern Folklore Society, 1937– . (Cited as *SFQ.*)

Spaeth, Sigmund. *Read 'Em and Weep: The Songs You Forgot to Remember.* New York: Doubleday, Page and Co., 1927.

_____. *Weep Some More My Lady.* New York: Doubleday, Page & Co., 1927.

Stick, David. *Graveyard of the Atlantic.* Chapel Hill: University of North Carolina Press, 1952.

_____. *The Outer Banks of North Carolina.* Chapel Hill: University of North Carolina Press, 1958.

Sturgis, Edith B., and Robert Hughes. *Songs from the Hills of Vermont*. New York: G. Schirmer, Inc., 1919.

Swing, Raymond Gram. *How War Came*. New York: W. W. Norton & Co., 1939.

Talley, Thomas. *Negro Folk Rhymes*. New York: Macmillan Co., 1922.

Thomas, Isaiah. Collection of early American Broadsides purchased from a printer and seller in Boston, 1813. Now in the American Antiquarian Society, Worcester, MA. (Cited as Thos. Coll.)

Thomas, Jean. *Ballad Makin' in the Mountains of Kentucky*. New York: Henry Holt & Co., 1939.

_____. *Devil's Ditties*. Chicago: W. W. Hatfield Co., 1931.

Thompson, Harold W. *Body, Boots, & Britches*. Philadelphia: J. B. Lippincott, 1940. Reprinted, Syracuse, NY: Syracuse University Press, 1979.

_____, and Edith Cutting. *A Pioneer Songster*. Ithaca, NY: Cornell University Press, 1958.

Thos. Coll. See Thomas, Isaiah.

Vaughan Williams, Ursula, and Imogen Holst. *A Yacre of Land*. London: Oxford University Press, 1961.

Vaughan Williams, R. and A. L. Lloyd. *The Penguin Book of English Folk Songs*. Baltimore, MD: Penguin Books, 1959.

Walker, William. *Southern Harmony*. 1854. Compiled by William Walker, Spartanburg, SC, printed in New Haven, CT, 1835.

Warren, C. J. *The Temperance Harp: Original and Selected Music for All Temperance Occasions*. Newark, NJ: Aaron Guest, 1843.

Wellman, Manly Wade. *Giant in Gray: A Biography of Wade Hampton*. New York: Charles Scribner's Sons, 1949.

Wells, Evelyn K. *The Ballad Tree*. New York: The Ronald Press, 1950.

Welsh, Charles, et al. *Catalogue of English and American Chapbooks and Broadside Ballads in Harvard College Library*. (*Bibliographical Contributions* No. 56) Cambridge: Library of Harvard University 1905. (Cited as Harvard Catalogue.)

West, John. *The Ballad of Tom Dula*. Durham, NC: Moore Publishing Co., 1970.

White, E. B. *Essays*. New York: Harper & Row, 1977.

White, Newman Ivey. *American Negro Folk Songs*. Cambridge: Harvard University Press, 1928.

White, William Chapman. *Adirondack Country*. New York: Duell, Sloan, and Pearce; and Boston: Little Brown & Co., 1954.

Wier, Albert E. *Love Songs the Whole World Sings*. New York and London: Appleton & Co., 1916.

Wigginton, Eliot. *Foxfire 3*. Garden City, NY: Anchor Press/Doubleday, 1975.

Wilgus, D. K. *Anglo-American Folksong Scholarship Since 1898*. New Brunswick, NJ: Rutgers University Press, 1959.

Wolford, Leah Jackson. *The Play-Party in Indiana*. Ed. and rev. W. Edson Richmond and William Tillson. *Publications* 20, no. 2. Indianapolis: Indiana Historical Society, 1959.

Work, John W. *American Negro Songs and Spirituals*. New York: Crown Publishing Co., 1940.

Wright, Joseph. *The English Dialect Grammar*. 1905. Reprinted, Oxford: Oxford University Press, 1968.

Wright, Robert L. *Irish Immigrant Ballads and Songs*. Broadsides published by H. De Marsan, New York [n.d.]. Reprinted, Bowling Green, OH: Bowling Green University Press, 1975.

Index

489

Index of Titles and First Lines

TRADITIONAL AMERICAN FOLK SONGS

was composed in 10-point Digital Compugraphic Sabon and leaded 2 points by Metricomp,
with display type in Roman Shaded Elongated by J. M. Bundscho, Inc.;
printed by sheet-fed offset on 80-pound, acid-free Warren Lustro Offset Enamel Dull Cream,
Smythe-sewn and bound over binder's boards in Joanna Arrestox B,
also adhesive bound with paper covers by Maple-Vail Book Manufacturing Group, Inc.;
and published by

SYRACUSE UNIVERSITY PRESS

SYRACUSE, NEW YORK 13210